Academic Literacy and the Nature of Expertise:

Reading, Writing, and Knowing in Academic Philosophy

Academic Literacy and the Nature of Expertise:

Reading, Writing, and Knowing in Academic Philosophy

Cheryl Geisler
Rensselaer Polytechnic Institute

GOVERNORS STATE UNIVERSITY
UNIVERSITY PARK
IL 60466

LEA LAWRENCE ERLBAUM ASSOCIATES, PUBLISHERS
1994   Hillsdale, New Jersey   Hove, UK

Lawrence Erlbaum Associates, Inc., Publishers
365 Broadway
Hillsdale, New Jersey, 07642

Cover design by Mairav Salomon-Dekel

Library of Congress Cataloging-in-Publication Data

Geisler, Cheryl.
    Academic literacy and the nature of expertise :
reading, writing, and knowing in academic philosophy / Cheryl
Geisler.
        p.   cm.
    Includes bibliographical references and indexes.
    ISBN-0-8058-1067-6 (alk. paper). — ISBN 0-8058-1068-4 (pbk. :
alk. paper).
        1. English language—Rhetoric—Study and teaching—Research.
    2. Learning and scholarship—Authorship—Philosophy.   3. Higher
    education—Philosophy.   4. Knowledge, Theory of.   5. Reading—
    Philosophy.   I. Title
    PE1404.G38   1994
    808'.042—dc20   93-42080
                                                                      CIP

Books published by Lawrence Erlbaum Associates are printed on acid-free
paper, and their bindings are chosen for strength and durability.

Printed in the United States of America
10 9 8 7 6 5 4 3 2 1

This book is dedicated to the memory of
Mattie Elizabeth Anderson Geisler,
my mother.

CONTENTS

PART IV   REFLECTION AND REFORM

PREFACE

The concept of *expertise* is a difficult one. In American culture, the figure of the "expert" invokes strong and ambivalent reactions as we, on the one hand, look to experts for guidance in everything from toothpaste to national fiscal policy, and, on the other, excoriate these same people for running roughshod over average citizens and using lucrative professional monopolies to give advice we no longer trust. Although common perceptions ordinarily have little to do with the course of research, this ambivalence of feeling actually captures quite well the current divisions in research on expertise and, furthermore, points to a dilemma researchers face in investigating the relevance of this concept to *literacy*.

The concept of literacy, on the other hand, has a more egalitarian ring. Not being an expert in our society is seen as the default value, something of which no one is ashamed and some are even proud. Being illiterate is a different matter. We regularly espouse the ideal, if not the practice, of teaching everyone to read, and recent educational reforms have attempted to add writing to this agenda. As a result, reading and writing are considered almost a birthright. Literacy is expected to be, in terms I introduce in an upcoming chapter, a competency, not an expertise.

For these reasons, some readers may question my bringing them together in a study of academic literacy and the nature of expertise. Yet a growing body of research on literacy practices, both in the academic professions in which expert knowledge is constructed and in the schools in which this knowledge is routinely transmitted, repeatedly points to the complex ways in which reading and writing have been transformed in the academy. Texts, like other objects of expert knowledge, appear to afford and sustain both expert and naive representations: the expert representation available to insiders to the academic professions and the naive representation available to those outside. As a result, reading and writing, which on the surface look like practices that are open and easily available to all, may actually have become arcane practices restricted to just a few.

ASSUMPTIONS

In this book, I attempt to develop a model of academic literacy as a cultural practice bound to expertise by the cultural movement of professionalization. Through a series of investigations at a specific site of academic literacy, philosophical ethics, I describe this practice, analyze its consequences, and suggest, insofar as possible, directions for reform.

Theoretically, I have approached expertise in the academy as a phenomenon with cognitive, sociological, and cultural manifestations. I have worked from the assumption that academic literacy is a cultural practice with effects that can be recognized in a multitude of places: (a) in *genre*, how texts are written and interpreted rhetorically; (b) in *cognition*, how individuals organize and manage the doing and thinking of reading and writing texts; (c) in *schooling*, how teachers and students working together transmit or fail to transmit expertise; and (d) in *institutions*, how groups are organized to create and receive expert advice. Methodologically, this assumption has led me to combine a number of analytic traditions: rhetorical analysis of genre, protocol analysis and interview analysis of individuals, conversation analysis of individuals interacting, and critical analysis of the role of these practices in the organization of society.

The road by which I reached my conclusions was not a straight one and I anticipate that the readers who will be interested in my conclusions—rhetoricians, language researchers, cognitive researchers, and social critics—will also not find the way particularly easygoing either. In particular, as just noted, I have drawn on a wide range of methods in my investigations, a decision that virtually ensures no one will find all of the discourse easy to understand or accept. Readers interested in the rhetorical analysis of texts, for instance, might be tempted to pay more attention to the rhetorical study of genre; readers interested in cognition might want to restrict their attention to expert–novice differences, the expert–novice study; readers more interested in schooling might want to focus on the study of classroom interaction; and readers interested in cultural criticism might want to go directly to my arguments on reforming academic literacy.

Nevertheless, I urge all readers to attend to the arguments and evidence presented in other, less familiar sections for two reasons. First, I do not believe my conclusions about the relationship between academic literacy and the nature of expertise will be clear without the full range of evidence I have presented. Second, I have tried throughout the book to attend not only to my specific topic of academic literacy, but also to the metatheoretical issues involved in investigating practices bound to a particular cultural institution such as the academy. Thus I hope that the variety of approaches I have taken and the results they have produced will help researchers in every area of literacy and expertise to develop a better paradigm for scholarly investigation, one more resonant with the nonfoundational epistemology that many of us have in theory already adopted. This metatheoretic point cannot be clear—and certainly cannot be persuasive—without consideration of the whole.

THE ARGUMENT

My main argument in the pages that follow is that the cultural movement of professionalization has used the technology of literacy to sustain claims to professional privilege, creating a *great divide* between expert and layperson. Academic literacy has had this effect, I suggest, via a *dual problem space framework* that bifurcated expertise into two distinct components, domain content and rhetorical process. This bifurcated practice, in turn, shapes the distinct activities and representations used by academic experts. In particular, it transforms them from indigenous practices into practices more appropriate for the formal culture of the academy, thereby obscuring the ways in which expertise nevertheless makes use of the resources of indigenous culture.

On the other side of the great divide, I argue that professionalization has created the general public. In schools, the general public are given access to the domain content of expertise as decontextualized facts divorced from rhetorical processes. In doing so, American schooling places them halfway between their indigenous culture and the culture of the academy, producing a crippled cultural practice capable of the knowledge consumption required for marketing professional services, but a practice incapable of cultural production on its own.

As a technology, academic texts are aimed at the construction of a virtual experience of consensus to induce future communal action. But, in many ways, this experience is more apparent than real because a common perspective between author and readers is presumed rather than created. Current discourse conventions, that is, do not acknowledge a multiplicity of perspectives. In fact, disciplinary communities are organized to eliminate this multiplicity. Consensus is created not by persuasion but by disciplinary indoctrination. As a result, the only individuals with sufficient access to a discipline's domain content to make arguments are those who have already pledged their allegiance to the discipline's assumptions. The academy has thus sidestepped the rhetorical burden of expertise, the burden of persuading others to believe and to act.

For all these reasons, I believe that academic practitioners need to engage in reflection on and reform of their practices. Much is made today of school reform, but in most cases, academic practitioners make these calls for the reform of others and never of themselves. The argument made here, however, is that some of the persistent inequities in American schooling began with the academy's alliance with the agenda of the professionalization movement. So long as this alliance persists unquestioned, so long as the university functions primarily as a credentialing wing for the professions, I believe we will continue to construct and reconstruct the great divide in every act of our daily reading, writing, and knowing.

THE ORGANIZATION

The two central organizing concepts for this study of academic literacy and the nature of expertise are literacy and expertise. Because researchers concerned with one are unlikely to be familiar with the other, I review the literature on both in some detail in the chapters making up part I. Chapters 1 and 2 contrast the literacy practices of experts and novices in the academy. Chapters 3 and 4 look at the cognitive and sociological aspects of expertise. In chapter 5, I pull all of this together with a dual problem space framework that suggests how academic literacy practices have created a great divide between expert and layperson. This framework then sets the agenda for the investigations of academic philosophy that make up the rest of the book.

In part II, I address the methodological issues involved in studying the relationship between academic literacy and the nature of expertise. Chapter 6, in particular, reexamines the case for using a special kind of data, think-aloud protocols. Reconceptualized within a more modular theory of mind, this kind of data can provide researchers of literacy and expertise with important information about what practitioners do and think. In chapter 7, I then go on to consider how best to model this data: not as cognitive process as has been traditional, but rather using the concept of cultural activity. Overall, these two chapters make the case that researchers of academic literacy should pay equal attention to both the temporal activities by which participants act and the spatial representations with which they think.

Part III reports the specific studies of academic philosophy undertaken in this project. In chapter 8, I describe the initial design for the data-gathering effort as well as the analytic framework adopted in subsequent analysis. In general, these studies have been investigations at a single site of academic literacy, and my specific questions have concerned the relationship between literacy practices at this site and more indigenous cultural practices—conversation, narrative, and apprenticeship. The remaining chapters of part III report the results of these analyses.

Chapter 9 looks at the genre of the philosophic essay. Using the discourse of contemporary philosopher Richard Bernstein and the historically important philosopher William James, I introduce the concept of literacy as a technology for creating virtual experience, and analyze the particular virtual experience created by the philosophic essay. The comparisons of Bernstein and James help us to see this academic genre as located at a particular moment in the history of professionalization.

Chapters 10 and 11 look at the composing practices of two experts and two novices writing a philosophic essay about the ethical issue of paternalism. Chapter 10 focuses primarily on the activities and representations used by the experts. Chapter 11 looks more carefully at the representations used by the novices. Overall, these two analyses suggest ways in which these participants' uses of reading and writing reflect their separation across the great divide between expert and the general public.

Chapter 12 looks at the dynamics of classroom interaction at the boundaries of expertise. By mapping the changing interaction patterns over the course of a semester and examining their relationship to the private understandings of an expert teacher, we begin to understand how expertise may be transmitted from generation to generation without the need for explicit articulation or reflection.

In part IV, I step back to consider the implications of my analyses. In chapter 13, I give an example of my own experiment with the discourse conventions of the academy, reflecting on the ways that academic texts mask the multiple worlds of actual composing. In chapter 14, I move to issues of reform, considering three directions in which changes should be undertaken in order to disentangle the legitimate claims of expertise from the agenda of the professionalization movement. They are, in increasing order of magnitude: rethinking literacy research, reforming academic practice, and reshaping American schooling.

The appendices include the technical information and data that underlie the research reported earlier. Appendix A includes a chronological bibliography of the cognitive process tradition in writing research. Appendices B through E describe my techniques for data gathering. Appendices F, G, I, and L contain actual data. Appendices H, J, and K describe my procedures for data analysis. I have made an effort to be more comprehensive than usual in reporting this information because, although I build on techniques in a number of fields, I have made significant amendments to all of them. Methodology is the argument too often left covert. I put mine into the public realm for further discussion and refinement.

NOTE TO READERS

Fundamentally, I have written this book as an effort at shared self-reflection. Most of us are practitioners of academic literacy just as much as those who nominally participated in the studies reported in what follows: I because I wrote this book; you because you read it. In making and receiving descriptions of its practices, I believe we should be constructing concepts and models that both ring bells in our own experience—as students, as teachers, as parents, as writers, as citizens—and give us the wherewithal to reflect on those practices.

As a result, I have moved, never easily, through multiple research paradigms, some with numbers, some without; some purely descriptive, others highly speculative; some purely social scientific, others purely humanistic; some in the objective and authoritative voice of the researcher and scholar, others in the personal voice of someone not yet at home in the discourses of the academy. As I have spent the years with my data, I came to believe it was inadequate simply to describe the practices of academic literacy without also going on to reflect upon them, to judge them, and to consider reforming them. I felt this was necessary not only to maintain my own well-being and integrity, but also to serve as a citizen in the public sphere.

For this reason, I intend this book to be useful to four kinds of people: (a) researchers interested in literacy or expertise; (b) educators and policy makers interested in shaping and transmitting literacy or expertise; (c) practitioners who, as a daily fact of life, read and write within the academy; and (d) members of the general public concerned about the role of the academy in society. I have not been able to escape this being an academic book. The technical details are there, cumbersome, inevitably foreign. It is full of more references than anyone would want to know about, more jargon than I have desired. But I have also tried to the best of my ability not to presume my arguments, not to use my own claim to expertise as an excuse for not giving you reasons to be convinced. If you are like me, the topic—academic literacy—is a practice in which you directly engage for more than half of your waking hours. You know it very well.

Because of this direct experience on your part, I have been particularly at pains to make myself clear. I want you to understand my reasons for believing that what we do every day in our reading and writing perpetuates a cultural myth that, in the final analysis, does us no good. I believe it is time for us to change. But because no single practitioner can specify the direction for change, we must remake academic practice together. This is the report of one person's thoughts on why and how.

ACKNOWLEDGMENTS

Nine years of effort leave me with more debts that I can acknowledge. My first debt is to my mentor and now colleague, David S. Kaufer. Without his confidence, I would not have been included in the WARRANT Project under the auspices of which most of the data reported in this book were collected. Without his challenging and far-ranging discussions, I would not have had the tools to pursue the project. And without his honesty and self-reflection, I could not have begun to understand what it means to be an expert.

My debts also extend to the larger research community at Carnegie Mellon University where this research was begun. In later chapters, I have tried to untangle some of my conceptual debts to Richard Young and Linda Flower from the program in rhetoric, and to John Anderson, Herb Simon, Jill Larkin, and Dick Hayes from the program in cognitive psychology. I do not attempt it here again, but only nod in the direction of these, my teachers. A special acknowledgment goes to Christine

M. Neuwirth and Preston K. Covey who, along with Dave Kaufer, guided WARRANT; to Ann Penrose, Alexander Friedlander, and Wendie Wulff who helped collect the data; to Steve Ehrman who, as a program officer at the Fund for the Improvement of PostSecondary Education, gave us our chance; and to the members of the National Academy of Education who, through a fellowship supported by the Spencer Foundation, provided crucial support in bringing this project to fruition.

I must also acknowledge the complicating and enriching influence of my colleagues and students at Rensselaer Polytechnic Institute, where I have brought this project to a close. As voices of conscience for the humanistic tradition, S. Michael Halloran and James P. Zappen lurk in the background of this work, repeatedly reminding me to consider the impact of expertise on the public sphere. I also want to thank Teresa Harrison for an unexpected friendship and for sharing the effort toward a self-reflective enterprise.

I owe more to my students than I can tell. I have particular debts: I want to thank Annika Aren and Barbara Lewis who helped to develop the coding for the data, and Bernadette Longo who provided valuable assistance in bringing this manuscript into final form. But more generally, I need to acknowledge the contributions of the students in my seminar on literacy and those specific students whose work on literacy and professionalization has provided an invaluable counterpoint to mine: Cynthia Haller, Christine Henwood, Martha Levine, and Barbara Lewis.

The influence of my friends is more than writ large in this text though I ask them to take no responsibility. Christina Haas, Ann Penrose, and Gary Schumacher have listened to me and encouraged me more times than I can remember. Hollis Heimbouch, my editor, believed in the project. Mark and Naomi made my leftover waking hours into a life.

Finally, I want to acknowledge the debt I owe my families: the Geislers from the steel mills of the Monongahela, and the Andersons from the high fertile valleys tucked into southwest Virginia. Following in the no-nonsense tradition of the Appalachians, they put into my bones the constant reminder that smarts extend well beyond the academy and much of what is valuable simply escapes words.

Cheryl Geisler

PART

I

CORE CONCEPTS

1

LITERACY AMONG EXPERTS
IN THE ACADEMY:
THE ACADEMIC PROFESSIONS

The ability to read and write are usually regarded as a birthright in this country. The transmission of reading skills to the general public has been part of the agenda for American education since the initiation of the public school movement (Cook-Gumperz, 1986; Graff, 1979; Soltow & Stevens, 1981). What we mean by that right, however, has changed with time and place. As Resnick and Resnick (1977) were the first to point out, expectations for literacy skills have not been constant. When Protestant reformers achieved nearly universal literacy in England and Sweden in the 18th and 19th centuries, for example, they considered the recall of familiar texts without interpretation or writing to be an adequate measure of literacy skills. Educators in the elite technical schools of France, by contrast, demanded the interpretation and application of novel ideas (Resnick & Resnick, 1977).

Despite this historical variation, schooling in the United States has been premised on the idea that there is a single literacy that should be made available to all. And with the UNESCO (United Nations Educational, Scientific, and Cultural Organization) campaigns for literacy, this assumption was extended transnationally into developing nations (UNESCO, 1976). These efforts, as Resnick and Resnick (1977) pointed out, represented the first attempt to apply elite standards to an educational system with more universal coverage. That is, governments began to expect for the first time that all citizens should learn the complex skill of acquiring new information from text.

This demand for universal elite literacy has had consequences for the two sets of people who regularly coexist and interact with each other in the academy: those academic professionals who make a permanent living through research and teaching, and those temporary students who pass through and pay a fee for knowledge and skills. In particular, as we see in chapter 2, treating the first group as the "experts" in the academy and the second group as the "novices" has appeared to simplify the issue of what students should be taught about reading and writing. Indeed, the unspoken assumption has often been that students' literacy mirrors or should mirror the literacy practices of the academic professions.

What are the literacy practices of the academic professions? This chapter attempts a preliminary answer to this question by comparing a cultural ideal, the autonomous text, with the practical realities in the particular case of the sciences. Although this cultural ideal is far from an accurate portrayal of what scientists do when they read and write, as is shown later, it does shape their reading and writing practices in very complicated ways.

THE CULTURAL IDEAL OF THE AUTONOMOUS TEXT

Until recently, most academics, including both the researchers who studied literacy practices and the everyday users of those practices, believed that the academic professions produced and interpreted texts in line with the cultural ideal of the autonomous text—a belief that a text can stand independent of its context of production or interpretation, that a text can mean the same thing to all readers in all ages. A growing body of evidence suggests, however, that this is, at best, a troubled ideal.

The Cultural Ideal

Without a great deal of thought, most people assume that the literacy practices of the academy are based on a mix of three kinds of skill: an advanced facility with words, a strong sense of logic, and a deep understanding of a specialized domain of knowledge. In this model, academics are expected to read and write their way to the construction of knowledge by establishing valid facts using the methods of their fields, putting these facts together to construct an argument according to the general canons of logic, and then clothing the results in a language that would enable readers to understand them clearly. The responsibilities for these skills were neatly divided among three distinct fields: Specialized fields would contribute the content, the field of logic would determine the structure, and the field of rhetoric would determine the form.

Under this division of labor, literacy seems to involve the construction and interpretation of "autonomous texts" (Olson, 1977). That is, under the ideal of the autonomous text, we expect readers to be able to understand texts without reference to the contexts in which they are produced or interpreted. What texts mean is taken to be equivalent to what texts say. Good reading will reflect the logical analysis of the actual meaning of the words explicitly represented on the page. And good texts will mean the same things to all readers in all ages. Such autonomous texts appear to be well suited to the construction of universal principles—the main business of the academy—and thus are often taken to represent a major cultural advance over the simple orality they replaced.

Not surprisingly, scholars believed that this ideal literacy was rooted in the same soil that nourished the Western tradition as a whole: fifth-century Athens. In 1963, Havelock first made this connection by claiming that Plato's perfect Republic was fundamentally a literate creation. Outlawing the poets of an interactive oral culture, according to Havelock, Plato posited a higher reality of visible stable forms. In doing so, the argument ran, Plato was unconsciously moving to replace an oral with a literate culture.

In the same year, Goody and Watt (1963) extended this analysis by comparing preliterate thought, as revealed by a variety of anthropological studies, with the literate thought exhibited by the early Greeks. Of particular interest was the difference in attitude toward history. According to Goody and Watt, preliterate societies, who rely on oral transmission, continually and unconsciously readjust their histories to reflect current social facts. As an example, when the chiefdoms of the state of Gonja in Ghana were reduced from seven to five in the course of a generation, the number of sons attributed to the founder of the state by oral genealogies showed a corresponding reduction from seven to five. Other oral genealogies showed a similar pattern. According to Goody and Watt, this preliterate attitude toward history was fundamentally changed by the advent of widespread literacy. The historian Thucydides, for example, departed from the custom of simply recording oral accounts of events and instead tried to adjudicate among them by detecting inconsistencies. In doing so, he was, like Plato, arguing for the replacement of an oral and changeable tradition with a more stable and autonomous tradition of texts.

In 1977, David Olson attempted to extend this theory of a "great divide" between orality and literacy to describe the changes that occur when individuals learn to read and write. According to Olson, the literate tradition of the Greeks culminated in 17th-century England with the essayist technique articulated by John Locke (1690/1982) and espoused by the newly formed Royal Society of London (Sprat, 1667/1966). In this new essayist tradition, the interpretation of texts was expected to be independent of the contexts in which they were produced. That is, unlike conversation, texts were expected to be understandable without independent knowledge of who was speaking, with what intention, and for what purpose. Instead, meaning was assumed to be represented explicitly and, as Olson first coined the term, *autonomously* in the text itself.

This historical development of literate thought, according to Olson (1988), is repeated each generation as students learn to read and write. According to this developmental hypothesis, students come to school with a preliterate sense of language as contextualized "utterance"; they have made sense of language by relying solely on the conversational context in which words are used. As a consequence, they pay little attention to the actual meaning of words or the syntax that holds them together. Learning to read, then, means acquiring not only decoding skills but also skills of decontextualized interpretation, of finding meaning in the text rather than in the context.

The early work of the linguist Chafe on the differences between spoken and written language added support to this developmental hypothesis. In a series of ingenious studies of people's retelling of the story in a silent movie, Chafe (1980) had found that the basic unit of oral language was not the same as the written sentence. Extending this analysis, Chafe (1982, 1985) later pointed to a host of other features which distinguished spoken and written discourse in terms of relative involvement with either the speaker or the content. Although Chafe later amended his position in ways more fully described later, this early stage of his argument gave credence to the idea that students who move from a predominantly oral conversational context at home to a predominantly written textual context in school are making a transition from contextualized utterance to autonomous text.

Unknown to Western researchers until relatively recently, the work of Soviet psychologist Vygotsky and his student, Luria, also give both empirical and theoretical support to the theory of autonomous text. In his best known work, *Thought and Language*, not published in the West until 1962, Vygotsky suggested that written speech represented the far end on a continuum of explicitness. Vygotsky placed what he called inner speech on the other end of this continuum and oral speech in the middle. Writing presented the greatest challenge to students, according to Vygotsky, because it required the deliberate restructuring of their personal webs of meaning from inner speech along the more explicit lines demanded by written texts.

Attempting to test Vygotsky's (1962) theory by studying the impact of literacy and schooling, A. R. Luria performed a series of experiments on peasants in the early stages of collectivization in the USSR. The results of these studies showed that peasants with just a few weeks of schooling exhibited significantly different reasoning strategies than their preliterate counterparts. For instance, when asked to reason syllogistically, preliterates tended to rely on contextual evidence to draw conclusions. Those newly literate, however, were able to draw the correct conclusions by relying only on the abstract propositions encoded in the premises given to them by the experimenter (Luria, 1976). Thus these peasants seem to have made the transition from contextualized utterance to decontextualized text in just the way Olson (1988) suggested.

Overall, then, research and scholarship published in the decades following the seminal works of Havelock (1963) and Goody and Watt (1963) continued to explore the implications of an ideal of literacy as autonomous text. In educational research, this model was used to develop instructional strategies to help students with difficulties they had in learning to read and write. Rubin (1980), influenced by an early version of Olson's (1988) article, provided a taxonomy of seven dimensions of difference between oral and written language and suggested a program of instruction that would introduce them to readers one at a time in "manageable steps." Perfetti (1987), although acknowledging some similarities between speech and print, nevertheless assumed that learning to read was hard because of the decontextualized nature of print. And in the area of writing, Flower (1979) used the evidence of the great divide to describe the changes needed to move from "writer-based" to "reader-based" prose. Finally Bereiter and Scardamalia (1982) described learning to write as a process of moving "from conversation to composition," and proposed procedural facilitation as a way of supporting this transition.

Troubles with the Ideal

Troubles with the ideal of the autonomous text became evident almost immediately. For one thing, even though this model of academic literacy had become almost commonplace, it flew in the face of an older tradition of rhetoric. According to this classical tradition, the finding of arguments, the organization of arguments, and the wording of arguments were all language-bound activities and all, therefore, within the proper domain of rhetoric. Eventually, this domain was carved up: Invention moved into the empirical sciences. Organization moved into logic. In fact, by the mid 20th century, style was the only concern remaining within the legitimate purview of rhetoric—or composition, its modern counterpart (Halloran, 1983; Howell, 1956, 1971; Kennedy, 1963, 1972, 1980; Ong, 1958/1974; Young, 1980).

This arrangement remained unquestioned until the arrival in the late 1950s of what Perelman and Olbrechts-Tyteca (1958/1969) called "the new rhetoric." These new rhetoricians challenged the assumption that right thinking was the proper domain of formal logic and instead attempted to recover the rhetorical tradition of argumentation and reasoning. Toulmin (1958), in particular, questioned the assumption that a single formal logic could be depended upon to adjudicate truth regardless of context. He suggested instead that the criteria for judging an argument varied from field to field. The reasons that would convince a physicist, for example, would be different than those demanded by an art historian. And what would convince an art historian would fail to move a literary critic. Following up on Toulmin's insight, a number of contemporary scholars have been investigating the arguments of specific fields particularly as represented in written texts (Bazerman & Paradis, 1991).

Perhaps the most significant blow to the ideal of the autonomous text came with the publication of Scribner and Cole's (1981) monumental study of the cognitive effects of literacy. Taking advantage of the co-occurrence in Liberia of three literacies—a Western-style schooled literacy, a nonschooled Qur'anic alphabetic literacy, and nonschooled syllabic Vai literacy—Scribner and Cole set out to examine differences among five groups: the nonliterates, Vai script monoliterates, Arabic monoliterates, Vai-Arabic biliterates, and the English schooled. They used a battery of experimental tasks similar in spirit to those used earlier in the century by Luria: geometric sorting tasks to test abstract reasoning, classification tasks to test taxonomic categorization, recall tasks to test memory, syllogistic reasoning tasks to test logic, and a name interchange task to test for language objectivity. The results of these comparisons were relatively straightforward: Exposure to Western-style schooled literacy consistently predicted performance on higher order skills, but exposure to nonschooled literacies did not. Simply becoming literate, then, appeared to be unrelated to the kinds of reasoning skills assumed by the ideal of the autonomous text. Becoming literate in the specific context of Western schools, however, was highly correlated with these skills.

Scribner and Cole's (1981) results undercut the ideal of the autonomous text by showing that literacy did not necessarily lead to a single set of cognitive effects. Other studies also began to question the exact relationship between literacy and the orality against which it had been compared. Linguists—most notably Chafe himself (Chafe & Danielewicz, 1987) and Tannen (1985, 1987)—quickly realized that they had been comparing a particular form of orality, conversational interaction among peers, with a particular form of literacy, academic prose. Once the range of discourse forms was broadened, the results were less clear.

Chafe and Danielewicz (1987), for example, found that two oral forms, conversation and lectures, could indeed be distinguished from two literate forms, personal letters and academic papers, on a variety of linguistic features, including the range and level of vocabulary and the length and connection among intonation units. In oral discourse forms, these features appeared to be noticeably reduced as speakers made more limited and colloquial word choices in shorter intonation units typically connected by nothing more complex than coordinating conjunctions. These features, Chafe and Danielewicz suggested, might well arise from the need to construct oral language on the fly. Other features more closely related to the ideal of the autonomous text, however, showed different results. In terms of the relative involvement or detachment of the speaker, oral conversation was more closely matched with written letters in showing high involvement, whereas the two discourses of the academy, lectures and papers, tended to exhibit more autonomy from context.

Symmetrically, a set of even earlier studies of traditional societies indicated the presence in oral forms of autonomous features previously attributed exclusively to written texts. In an analysis provided by Akinnaso (1982), for example, a diviner's chant was shown to have relied for its power on decontextualized meanings that transcended the immediate situation in which the divination was requested. According to Akinnaso, the chanter's discourse adopted a detached interaction style that invited no participation by the client. The chanter produced a highly integrated structure and used a specialized vocabulary that could be reproduced in form, content, and style in a wide range of circumstances.

And, as Akinnaso pointed out, these are all autonomous features thought previously to be the exclusive domain of literate discourse.

Other studies of the discourse of traditional societies indicate that autonomous linguistic codes often exist side by side with more contextualized codes, both in oral form. Comaroff (1975), for example, found that Tshidi orators provided political commentary using a more formal linguistic code of well-known formulas and implicit reference when they were stating eternally shared values; they resorted to a more explicit and personal linguistic code to discuss the actual and controversial actions taken by the king. Similarly, Salmond (1975) found that the Maori tradition of oratory combined a formal discourse, used to establish relative prestige among competing groups, with a more informal discourse, used to wield real political influence. Among the Malagasy in Madagascar, Keenan (1975) found that an elaborate ceremonial speech was used in the initial stages of marriage negotiations to establish prestige whereas a less elaborate speech was reserved for actually bringing the wedding to pass. Finally, Hobart (1975) observed that orators in Balinese villages used a ritualistic code to conduct business in formal village assemblies, whereas political patrons used everyday speech to exercise factional power in private "backroom" conversations.

Two observations on the parallels between Western discourse practices and these traditional practices are relevant here. First, it is important to note that in all these traditional societies, the use of the more autonomous code was both socially relevant to the exercise of political power and cognitively relatively difficult to master. As a consequence, the more formal discourse effectively served a gatekeeping function even in forums where participation was nominally open to all. Second, although this formal code was useful to speakers in establishing relative prestige and power over those not able to master the code, it was less adequate for their actual conduct of business once power had been assured. That is, in every case, these traditional orators moved from formal to more informal codes when they wanted to carry out the business of the moment such as making political commentary (the Tshidi), establishing political consensus (the Maori), bringing a marriage to conclusion (the Malagasy), or brokering factional interests (the Balinese). The formal and more autonomous code, then, was a prerequisite for access to power, but not the actual code in which such power was exercised. As we see later, such a differentiation of discourse codes appears to be at work within the academy as well.

Taken together, the results of these studies tend to undercut the ideal of the autonomous text, at least as it applies developmentally to individuals within a single society. To begin with, the results of the Chafe and Danielewicz (1987) studies show that people in Western literate societies have access to a range of discourse types, in both oral and written forms, which vary in their autonomy from context. In addition, studies of oratory in traditional societies indicate that this range of autonomy is also available to participants in primarily oral cultures. Combined with the pattern found by Scribner and Cole (1981), this evidence suggests that the argument for attributing an improved ability to reason to the acquisition of literacy can no longer be sustained. Instead, textual autonomy and the reasoning skills that accompany it appear to be specific to Western-style schools. It is in the academy, then, that the ideal of the autonomous text appears to play itself out. In the rest of this chapter, we take the case of the sciences as a way of understanding this relationship between literacy and the academy.

DISCOURSE AND KNOWLEDGE IN THE SCIENCES

The sciences are probably the most heavily studied professions in the academy. Although the new rhetoricians did not have just the sciences in mind when they claimed that knowledge making was a rhetorical affair, this generalization clearly does apply to every aspect of scientific inquiry. Beginning with discovery in the laboratory and ending with the codification of scientific facts in textbooks and review articles, each stage in the production and consumption of scientific texts brings in contextual factors that appear to make them poor candidates for the status of autonomous texts. Nevertheless, as we see in what follows, the entire rhetoric of science is premised on the belief that such autonomy is, in theory, possible.

Context and Discovery in the Sciences

The overarching aim of the rhetoric of scientific inquiry is the discovery of patterns in nature (Prelli, 1989). To achieve this end, scientists must discriminate in the laboratory between observations that are truly indicative of the state of nature and those that arise from confounding factors specific to the laboratory context. Thus every scientific discovery must make a transition from simply being a part of the context-bound data stream recorded in a laboratory in such and such place at such and such time on such and such date to being a scientific object—something out there, in nature, always.

Garfinkel, Lynch, and Livingston (1981) provided us with a rare glimpse of the transition from context-dependent data to context-independent object by publishing a tape recording made at Steward Observatory of the University of Arizona during the night in 1969 when the optically discovered pulsar was first observed. Although it is clear from this transcript that the scientists in the observatory realized from the first that their incoming data stream might be the pulsar, the "it" they talked about at first was just a local pattern here on the screen: "it's growing" (p. 149); "it's moved over" (p. 151); "it's still right in the middle of the screen" (p. 151). With these phrases, the scientists were clearly referring to the actions of the pattern on the screen, not an object out there.

In the course of a few minutes of laboratory work, however, the discourse shifted. Once the scientists convinced themselves that the pulse was not an artifact of the instrumentation, they began talking about an "it" that was an object out there with enduring characteristics that could be understood without reference to the laboratory context: "how many photons coming in per second to this pulse" (p. 156); "the luminosity of this object" (p. 156); "the color" (p. 156). With this new discourse, they were granting existence and attributes to an object out there that their previous discourse had withheld. And when these scientists finally reported their observations of the pulsar in *Nature*, they dropped all evidence of the "it" of their local laboratory context in favor of an "it" of the object out there: "We wish to report the discovery on January 16, 1969, 03 30 UT, of strong optical pulses from the pulsating radio source NP 0532 in the Crab Nebula" (p. 143).

The language transformations that occurred in this one example of scientific discovery illustrate what appears to be a common pattern in scientific discourse. As the scientists moved from the early stages of observation, when the "discovery" was not yet certain, to the later stage, when they believed they had something, they gradually reduced the amount of language related to the specific context in which the observation was originally made—the screen—and they increased their reliance on a simple description of the natural phenomenon as they believed it to be independent of human observation—a pulsar with a specific luminosity and color.

Metadiscourse, Readership, and Knowledge in the Sciences

When scientists move to print, the amount of certainty they are willing to grant an observation is most often signaled linguistically by the amount of metadiscourse they include in the text. Metadiscourse, as the name suggests, is discourse about discourse. It is discourse that calls attention either to the relationship between the author and the claims in the text or to the relationship between the author and the text's readers. In her monograph on metadiscourse, Crismore (1989), adapting Vande Kopple's (1985) system, noted that instances of metadiscourse typically have one of three interpersonal functions: (a) to assess the certainty of a statement ("undoubtedly"), (b) to mark attitude ("it's obvious that"), or (c) to draw readers into a dialogue with the author ("My dear reader").

The exact pattern of metadiscourse found in any scientific text appears to be something of a personal thing. Crismore and Farnsworth (1990), for example, found that two sections of the same article written by different authors used remarkably different rates of metadiscourse. Gould, the first author of one of the articles analyzed by Crismore and Farnsworth, used a rate of about 3.87 instances of metadiscourse per 100 words of text in his section. Woodruff, the second author, used an average of only 2.96 instances of metadiscourse per 100 words in his section.

Within an author's style, however, variations in the amount of metadiscourse appear to be tied to the nature of the readership the author expects. When Gould wrote about the same material for a lay audience, for instance, his rate of metadiscourse dropped from the rate just mentioned, 3.87 instances per 100 words of text, to a rate of only 2.58 instances (Crismore & Farnsworth, 1990). In other words, the number of interpersonal appeals Gould made to his readership was greater when he wrote for specialists than when he wrote for a lay audience.

Such metadiscourse variation by readership is consistent with the results of several years of observation by sociologist Latour at the Salk Institute for Biological Studies (Latour & Woolgar, 1979). In his research at this lab, Latour found that the Institute's publications were intended to convey distinct types of knowledge to distinct categories of readers. Texts in the first two of the following categories, for example, were expected to contain new information that would contribute to scientific knowledge. The remaining two were written to disseminate information well known within the speciality to those outside. These text categories included: (a) texts written for a select band of insiders (55% of publications), (b) texts written to the membership of the speciality as a whole (13% of publications), (c) texts written for specialists in other fields (27% of publications), and (d) texts written for lay audiences, including those generally interested in popular accounts of scientific research and practitioners looking for useful information (5% of publications).

Latour and Woolgar (1979) found that one of the main differences between these categories of text was the amount of metadiscourse they contained. In general, according to these researchers, statements in the Salk Institute publications clustered along the following metadiscourse continuum:

1. Type 1 statements were speculations or conjectures, usually found at the end of an article or in private discussions.
2. Type 2 statements were claims that called attention to the circumstances affecting their status, usually found in research papers.
3. Type 3 statements were statements with attribution or modality that linked the basic claim to the source of the claim, often found in review articles.
4. Type 4 statements were claims about things in the universal present tense, usually found in textbooks.
5. Type 5 statements were the taken-for-granted facts that rarely got mentioned except to outsiders.

Texts written to disseminate knowledge generally clustered around Types 4 and 5 without much metadiscourse. Texts written to construct new scientific knowledge, by contrast, usually clustered around Types 1, 2, and 3, heavily laden with metadiscourse. According to Latour and Woolgar, scientists at the Salk Institute hoped to transform their statements, which always began life in a Type 1 form close to the contingencies of laboratory experience, into Type 4 statements that could stand alone as a representation of a pattern in nature.

This transformation of statement types, it is important to note, removed metadiscourse from these scientists' texts, thereby removing the textual signals intended to evoke context. Stripped of metadiscourse, Type 4 statements do not do the things Crismore (1989) said metadiscourse does: remind readers of their uncertainty ("Undoubtedly X is . . ."); invoke author's attitudes and beliefs ("It is interesting to note that X is . . ."); or invite readers to play a role in interpretation ("Readers may want to consider the effect of X is . . ."). Instead, Type 4 statements function solely as descriptions of the objects of scientific inquiry in simple declarative present tense ("X is . . ."). Thus, just as at the Stewart Observatory, the scientists at the Salk Institute appear to have sought to reduce their acknowledgment of context as they disseminated their knowledge claims to readers more and more removed from the laboratory context.

Latour and Woolgar (1979) were suggesting that statements without metadiscourse are more common in texts written for lay audiences than in texts written for scientists themselves. Other evidence exists to support this contention. Fahnestock (1986), for example, found metadiscourse differences between pairs of articles on the same topic published in two journals of the American Association for the Advancement of Science intended for different readerships. In one pair, for example, the original text, written for a scholarly readership (*Science*), was filled with metadiscourse hedges:

> The bees masticate and consume flesh at the feeding site. They do not carry pieces of flesh to the nest, but *appear* to hydrolyze it with a secretion produced by either mandibular or salivary glands, which gives the feeding site a wet appearance. Individual bees captured while feeding, then forced to expel the contents of their crop were carrying a slurry of flesh, measuring between 37 and 65 percent dissolved solids by volume.[17] Bees tagged while foraging in the morning continued to depart and arrive at a carcass throughout the day, *suggesting* that animal food is passed by trophallaxis to other workers in the nest. Nest mates *may* then convert flesh into glandular substances. (emphasis added by Fahnestock, 1986, p. 283)

With metadiscourse, italicized in this version, the authors of this *Science* text acknowledge their role as scientific observers in making inferences from specific local observations, and they hedge the certainty of those inferences. In this way, they couple their attempts to reveal a pattern in nature with an acknowledgement of the local context of their observations. In the corresponding text written for a lay readership (*Science83*), however, this metadiscourse was dropped: "[1] The bees chew flesh [2] after coating it with an enzyme that breaks it down. [3] They partially digest it, then fly back to the nest, [4] where the substance is regurgitated to fellow worker bees" (Fahnestock, 1986, p. 283; numbers added for purposes of the following discussion).

It is precisely this metadiscourse, however, that enables readers to determine the appropriate level of certainty to grant the claims the text contains. Specifically, it is only the metadiscourse in the original *Science* text that allows us to see the level of certainty we should attribute to the claims made in the *Science83* text. For instance, we know that statement (1) in the *Science83* text ("The bees chew flesh") is pretty certainly true because the *Science* text suggests it was directly observed by the author ("The bees masticate and consume flesh at the feeding site"). From the *Science* version, we can also tell that statement (2) in the *Science83* version ("after coating it with an enzyme that breaks it down") was not directly observed by the scientists, but is a probable inference based on the presence of wetness at the feeding site (they "*appear* to hydrolyze it with a secretion produced by either mandibular or salivary glands, which gives the feeding site a wet appearance"). We also know from the *Science* version that statement (3) in the *Science83* version ("They partially digest it, then fly back to the nest") is based on data analysis back in the lab rather than direct observation ("Individual bees captured while feeding, then forced to expel the contents of their crop were carrying a slurry of flesh, measuring between 37 and 65 percent dissolved solids by volume."). And finally, from the *Science* version we know that statement (4) in the *Science83* version ("where the substance is regurgitated to fellow worker bees") is a more remote inference based on the fact that the same bees keep coming back to feed even when, we assume, they should be full ("Bees tagged while foraging in the morning continued to depart and arrive at a carcass throughout the day, *suggesting* that animal food is passed by trophallaxis to other workers in the nest. Nest mates *may* then convert flesh into glandular substances.").

In the text written for scientists, then, metadiscourse allows readers to discriminate among levels of inference and certainty attached to the claims made in the text. It thereby provides readers with the opening tools they would need to extend, question, or even overturn those claims. Readers might offer an alternative explanation for wetness at the feeding site, for example, or they might try to observe bees pass food to workers back at the nest. The lay version does not afford opportunities for such judgment making and extension, however. Without metadiscourse, all claims look equally plausible and equally true to readers who have no additional knowledge beyond the text.

Perhaps for this reason, such lay texts make up a small proportion of scientists' total output (32% at the Salk Institute) and are generally considered by the scientists to be less valuable than texts written for professional scientists. Nonetheless, according to Latour and Woolgar (1979), texts for lay readers serve an important function in assuring scientists continued access to public research funds (see also Myers, 1985). In particular, they show how scientists' research not only makes a contribution to the knowledge of their specialized communities but also is beneficial—or at least interesting—to society as a whole.

WRITING IN THE SCIENCES

Texts written by scientists for other scientists within their own speciality make up the lion's share of scientific discourse and this is discourse that contains, as we have just seen, repeated acknowledgments of context through the use of metadiscourse. Researchers studying the actual dynamics of writing in the sciences have pointed to two important contextualized tasks that scientists have to accomplish when they write: codifying the context of production through a review of the literature, and codifying the context of interpretation by developing a role for an implied reader.

Writers Codifying the Context of Production

One of the major tasks scientists as writers face when they write within their speciality is codifying a context for their work, the previous literature into which they see their work fitting. To be successful, scientists need to characterize the previous literature in such a way that their own results appear to be a natural extension of the field's current state of knowledge. In other words, scientists must construct a narrative of their field that shows their own work to be the appropriate next event.

The "create-a-research-space" model proposed by Swales and Najjar (1987) attempts to capture the basic moves scientists use to accomplish this task. In research article introductions, according to these authors, the first move authors make is to establish the significance of their topic. Here, for example, is how Swales and Najjar made Move 1 in the introduction to their own research article: "Introductions to research articles or papers have become in the last few years an important proving ground for our current capacity to understand the process and product of specialized academic writing" (p. 175). The next move is to summarize selectively from previous research: "The extensive case studies of Latour and Woolgar (1979), Knorr-Certina (1981), and Gilbert and Mulkay (1984) provide solid evidence for the complexity of the compositional process at the introduction stage" (p. 175). "We have thus reached a position where it would seem reasonable to assume that a research article introduction typically closes with a promissory statement . . ." (p. 179). The third move is to indicate a gap in this previous work: "However, it is much less clear whether the close will also contain a summary announcement of the principle findings [APFs] . . ." (p. 179). And finally, the fourth move is to indicate the potential of the current research to fill that gap: "The present article reports on a localized case study of the APF aspect of article introductions in two contrasting fields . . . and over time . . ." (p. 180).

The intent of this series of linguistic moves is to present the current research as a natural extension of the current state of knowledge in the field. Such naturalness, however, masks a rhetorical achievement that cannot be taken for granted. According to Bazerman (1988), for example, researchers in the hard sciences have achieved a greater degree of codification than have colleagues in the social sciences. That is, scientists appear to have achieved more agreement on the "story" of their fields than have scholars in the other academic professions. Watson and Crick, for example, inserted their research on DNA into the previous literature in a story of just three short paragraphs. Merton, a sociologist who could not assume a similarly shared narrative, took several pages to accomplish the same task.

The process of research codification also took time to develop according to Bazerman (1991). In his 1767 treatise on the *History and Present State of Electricity*, for example, Joseph Priestley appeared to have developed what Bazerman called the "literary technology" for attributing codified meaning to previous research. In the same work, however, Priestley failed to show how his own investigations addressed a gap in that research. In terms of the Swales and Najjar (1987) model, then, Priestley developed Moves 2 and 3 without Move 4.

Nowhere in modern scientific practices is the task of relating one's own research to knowledge in the field more important than in writing research proposals. As Myers (1985) showed, in order to get funding, research biologists must achieve a balance between asserting the novelty of their work and asserting its continuity with prior research. Techniques for establishing this balance, however, vary depending on the researcher's prior relationship with the field and chosen direction for future research. For example, one researcher observed by Myers was entering a field new to him, using foreign methods and a different interpretive framework. In revisions of his proposal, he chose to downplay his theoretical interests, which diverged from the community's, and highlight his data, which might be of shared interest. A second researcher observed by Myers followed an opposite course. Because he had been involved in his field for a long time and did not have novel data, he chose in his revisions to highlight the way his theoretical commitments could advance the field. Despite differences in strategy, both of these researchers were trying to achieve the same end of responding to and developing a consensus in their respective fields.

Research proposals appear to differ from scientific articles in the degree to which the role of the individual researcher is acknowledged. In the research proposal, as Myers (1985) showed, the individual researcher must highlight the significance of his own contribution or risk losing funding. Once research is funded and completed, however, the agency of the researcher fades into the background and, instead, nature as agent becomes foregrounded. Gilbert and

Mulkay (1984) have called the language by which this is accomplished—language that tends to downplay the role of self, avoid discussion of the role of prior theoretical commitments, and eliminate accidental features—the "empiricist's repertoire." As the excerpt from the research report cited earlier indicates, this language works hard to eliminate contextual factors and present an unmediated vision of an external reality. Nature appears to speak for herself.

The empiricist repertoire is not the only language available to, or even necessary for, the scientific enterprise. Gilbert and Mulkay (1984) suggested that the scientists they studied made regular use of two distinct repertoires of language when discussing their work. The first, the empiricist repertoire, is, as we have seen, the language of the published scientific report. It presents the research result as the inevitable outcome of properly controlled laboratory observation. But just as authorities in traditional societies resorted to a more informal discourse to conduct their business, so too do scientists appear to use a more informal discourse to "do science" in their laboratories. Gilbert and Mulkay called this second discourse the "contingent repertoire": It is the language of scientists' informal talk and, with it, they present the results of their research as the outcome of a host of contingent factors such as local laboratory craft knowledge, prior theoretical commitments, and social relationships.

Significantly, research scientists seem to use these two repertoires in different circumstances. When accounting for their own work in which they believe, scientists rely upon the empiricist repertoire, portraying their results as a true representation of nature. When they talk about competing research results, however, they use the contingent repertoire as a way of explaining how other scientists may have come to conclusions different than their own. Thus, language about contextually-dependent variables is almost always used to attribute error to others whereas language without reference to context is generally used to attribute scientific validity to the work one accepts.

The procedure of accounting for other scientists' errors using the contingent repertoire does not always lead to a coherent representation of scientists' actions in the world. That is, in trying to explain why other scientists may have come to the wrong conclusions, a writer need not produce a single narrative of the scientist's actions that makes sense. Yearly (1981) showed, for example, that Kirwan's review of the work of Sir James Hall, published in 1802 in the *Transactions of the Royal Society of Edinburgh*, portrayed Hall's results as arising out of incompetent laboratory techniques when they were at odds with Kirwan's own position and as a significant contribution when they were supportive. No attempt was made in the review to explain how Hall's work could be, at the same time, incompetent and significant. In fact, as Yearly suggested, these two accounts, one from the empiricist repertoire and one from the contingent repertoire, appear in different sections of the review article and would not normally be compared by the "average" reader.

Writers Codifying the Context of Interpretation

Implicit in the discussion so far is the idea that scientific texts project a role for an "average" or implied reader. Research article introductions, like those described by Swales and Najjar (1987), invite this reader to share a common view of a codified past, to detect gaps in that past, and to view the current research as a response to that gap. Research proposals, like those described by Myers (1985), go even further in requesting this reader's financial support for gap filling. Research reviews like that of Kirwan (Yearly, 1981) expect this reader to follow the line of argument in the text as presented and thus not notice inconsistent accounts presented at widely spaced intervals. And, as Myers (1991) suggested elsewhere, review articles attempt to enlist this reader in an ongoing project by constructing a shared view of the past and future. Thus, in the course of codifying the context in which they have produced their texts, scientists appear also to codify the context in which they expect their text to be interpreted.

The decision to use scientific texts to create and develop a role for an implied reader appears to be a modern development. One of its earliest users, according to Bazerman (1988), was Sir Isaac Newton, who developed the technique in response to difficulties he had publishing his optics work in the *Transactions of the Royal Society*. Originally, Newton had published an expository narrative that essentially recounted a reconstructed history of his personal experience with the physical phenomena and then presented the theoretical "doctrine" he had built upon these observations. In telling his own story, Newton made no attempt to direct his readers' interactions with the optical phenomena beyond inviting them to repeat his experiments and see the results for themselves.

Such a rhetorical strategy, which had apparently worked well for him when he presented his work in lectures to his students at Cambridge, failed with his fellow members of the Royal Society. As real readers, they did not repeat his experiments or, if they did, they did not get the results he said they would. The process of answering their criticisms, according to Bazerman (1988), led Newton to construct more carefully a "virtual" experience for readers. That is, he walked them through a series of claims, each supported by results from a carefully described experimental procedure. According to Bazerman, Newton had learned the hard way that he could not depend on real readers to interpret experience as he wanted them to. Instead, he had to lead them as implied readers through his line of reasoning and experience step by step.

Writers can construct roles for their implied readers differently even when they appear to be in similar situations. Gragson and Selzer (1990), for example, compared the different roles created by two articles in biology written for the same readership at the same time. One, by Maynard Smith, constructed a role for the implied reader as disciplinary student, needing guidance toward the knowledge held by a more accomplished professor. The other, by Gould and Leowontin, created a role for the implied reader as coequal critic of the status quo, equally conversant with a broad range of cultural knowledge. Although Gragson and Selzer described the differences between these two texts as the results of scientists' "considerable freedom to exercise choices" (p. 25), it seems likely that the authors' decisions were significantly narrowed by their choice of claims and their prior histories as authors. Gould and Leowontin, in particular, may have constructed a role for their reader as rebel because they themselves were arguing for a rebellious position. And readers may have been more willing to see Gould adopt a nontraditional discourse because of his previous reputation for such "rhetoric." Thus, just as Myers' (1985) biologists were constrained by their own beliefs and history of interaction in the field, so too Smith and Gould and Leowotin may have been constrained by their own beliefs and prior history even though they appear to have been responding to the same readership.

Once texts begin to focus on creating a virtual experience for implied readers, a split can arise between the experience by which a scientist discovers ideas and the experience by which readers are invited to share those ideas. One way to look at this is that the necessarily crooked path of rhetorical invention becomes straighted for the purposes of presentation and persuasion. In the earlier days of the Royal Society, as we have seen, research reports seldom presented experimental method in any detail, assuming that "the phenomena of nature were robust, uniform, and self-evident" (Bazerman, 1988, p. 72). In addition, as Bazerman noted, the experience itself was often literally shared as experiments were repeated before the assembled members of the Royal Society. Under these circumstances of public presentation, the experience of the scientist and the experience of the reader could not easily diverge

As we have seen in the case of Newton, a greater attempt was made to specify experimental procedure in the face of controversies over results. It became increasingly evident that nature was not as easily revealed as the early members of the Royal Society had assumed. By creating a virtual experience, then, the methods section of research reports developed to assure readers that the phenomena being discussed were indeed real even though they had not done the experiment themselves.

But, for several reasons, these methods sections could not achieve this goal by simply narrating actual laboratory practice. To begin with, scientists do not report all their false turns and failed experiments (Knorr-Certina, 1981). As well, the order in which the experiments were performed may not match the order in which they are presented, as apparently was the case with Newton's optics experiments (Bazerman, 1988). In addition, scientists who want to conform to their readers' expectations about scientific method may downplay the role of theory in guiding their observations, as Darwin apparently did (Campbell, 1987).

One of the most important reasons that scientists' texts do not exactly match their laboratory experiences has to do with the nature of their knowledge. Knowledge of laboratory procedure is a kind of tacit knowledge that cannot be fully articulated. As Polanyi (1958) pointed out, much of scientific knowledge, especially about instrumentation, is in subsidiary awareness, known in the fingertips—as in knowing how to grasp a hammer. It is not in focal awareness that can be articulated. Collins' (1985) study of the replication of the TEA-laser, a simple piece of laboratory instrumentation, indicates just how complicated this tacit knowledge can be. It took H, the scientist followed by Collins, 5 months and several interactions with a successful laboratory to build a working TEA-laser for his own lab. Many other labs tried and failed. According to Collins' analysis, the tacit knowledge involved had two striking characteristics: First, it could only be gained by firsthand and extended contact with already accomplished practitioners. And, second, its passage from one practitioner to another was "invisible"; one could only determine whether one had the knowledge by trying to build the equipment for oneself and seeing if it would work.

Because of this large component of tacit knowledge in laboratory practice, scientists routinely acknowledge that methods sections do not provide enough information for readers to successfully carry out the experiments they describe. At best their directions serve as linguistics tags (Howard, 1982) for standard procedures in the field. For all these reasons, scientific reports concentrate on creating a virtual experience for implied readers that will convince them that proper experimental procedures were carried out rather than providing them with a full and accurate history of those procedures.

READING IN THE SCIENCES

Even though scientists as writers apparently expend considerable energy in creating an appropriate role for implied readers, the question of what real readers do remains. Although comparatively little work has been done on scientists reading, several studies do suggest that when they turn from writing their own reports to reading the reports of others, scientists actively resist the codification efforts that writers have made. Instead they try to reconstruct the contextual factors they consider indispensable for evaluating the merits of a scientific claim.

Readers Resisting the Codification of Interpretation

As we have seen, scientists as writers attempt to codify the context in which their texts will be interpreted by creating a step-by-step virtual experience for implied readers to "live through" while reading. Two studies suggest, however, that scientists as readers seldom allow a text to control their reading in quite this way.

When Bazerman (1988) observed seven physicists reading articles in their field in the library, he found they seldom read an article completely. They viewed a full reading as an apparently costly interaction that they undertook, if at all, only at a very late stage in interactions with a text. Instead, they began by reading the table of contents, and occasionally the abstract, to determine whether the article was relevant—on a relevant topic, using a relevant methodology, written by a relevant authority, or representing work by a relevant laboratory. If the text passed this test, they next scanned the article for new information: Theoreticians looked for new results; experimentalists looked for new methods. If this scanning generated confusions, they then weighed the costs of a more careful reading against the expected gains for their own work. But, even once they had undertaken the task of careful reading, it was seldom straight through, but instead was undertaken in layers of increasing difficulty. Few articles, then, ever got read in any detail, even fewer got read in their entirety, and almost none got read in the carefully constructed sequence projected for the implied reader.

A second study by Charney (1993) reveals in more detail the kinds of resistance that scientists may offer when they read texts by their colleagues. Charney asked seven evolutionists to read and react to the same article by Gould and Lewontin that Gragson and Selzer (1990) analyzed in the study reviewed earlier. Two were masters students, two were PhD candidates, one was a postdoctoral fellow, and two were tenured faculty. Charney made the point that the Gould and Lewontin text, "The Spandrels of San Marco," is unusual rhetorically: It makes literary allusions and uses nonbiological examples to make a point about evolution. And the circumstances under which Charney asked her readers to read was also unusual: They were reading the article more than 10 years after it had been published and it had already altered the course of their own disciplines. They were also asked to think aloud as they read.

Nevertheless, the mature professionals in this study acted very much like the physicists Bazerman (1988) observed. For one thing, both tenured faculty members declined to read the article straight through and described this decision as their normal procedure. The scientist, AN, was particularly explicit about his resistance: "I think if you go right into an article, and you read it word for word from the beginning, what happens is that you'll be pulled along by the author and you're not going to be critical. . . . As opposed to, if you have an overview, then you can keep your critical facility alive." Furthermore, all three of Charney's (1993) faculty members spent significantly more time than did the graduate students going beyond simply comprehending the text to evaluate its claims and characterize its structure and genre. As Charney pointed out, then, "the more professionally advanced readers were *more* prone to treat the text rhetorically," thereby resisting the role that Gould and Lewontin had so carefully crafted for them.

Readers Resisting the Codification of Production

Scientists as writers, as we have seen, appear to want the scientific claims they have constructed out of a context-bound data stream to be gradually freed from metadiscourse as they are transformed from the Type 1, 2, and 3 statements

Latour and Woolgar (1979) found typical of specialists' texts into the Type 4 statements enshrined in textbooks. When scientists read other scientists' texts critically, however, they appear to want to reverse this process. That is, when reading the work of their colleagues, they resist this codification of the contexts of production and work, instead, to recover just those details of context that scientists as writers had been hoping to strip away.

A number of studies have noticed the critical edge with which academic professionals approach the task of reading texts by their colleagues. Bazerman (1988), for instance, characterized this as the "wary communal endeavor" (p. 246) of integrating another's work into one's own. Bazerman's results, furthermore, suggest that this wariness becomes more intense the closer the text is to one's own speciality. When the physicists he observed read outside of their area of specialization, for example, they tended to take the claims the texts contained as reliable, something that might be built upon. But in their own area, they were inclined to be intensely and often negatively critical.

Charney (1993) found a similar pattern in her study of evolutionists reading Gould and Lewontin. Faculty were significantly more likely than graduate students in the same field to assess the text's claims. Furthermore, even when the graduate students did engage in assessment, they ended up agreeing with the authors most of the time (84% agreements). Faculty, however, were more inclined to disagree (63% agreements). The more active researchers, then, were also the more actively critical.

A related study by Wyatt et al. (1991) suggests that this pattern of responding negatively to texts in one's area may not be limited to the hard sciences. Wyatt and his colleagues observed 15 university faculty in the social and behavioral sciences reading journal articles they selected as part of staying current in their fields. A preliminary analysis of this voluminous data showed that only 1 of these 15 faculty read their selected text straight through without jumping forward or backward across sections in the text. And 12 of them, or fully 80%, negatively evaluated these self-selected texts while reading.

When scientists resist the role of implied reader and negatively assess their colleagues' texts, they seem to be operating with interests that do not match the interests of their colleagues. But what, we might ask, are they interested in? According to Bazerman (1988), the scientists he observed were particularly attentive to methodological details. They were highly critical when writers appeared not to follow procedures or consider factors that they knew from firsthand experience to be important determinants of good experimental results. And they were highly gratified when writers provided small details about their laboratory procedures that, though not sufficient to tell the uninformed how to replicate the work, did strongly indicate that the researcher had attended to the kinds of details that make a difference. By noticing the inclusion of such methodological tidbits—or the failure to include them—these scientists seemed to have deconstructed the apparently smooth virtual experience that the text laid out for them and attempted to construct in its place what they considered to be a more accurate representation of the writer's actual laboratory procedure.

Haas (1994; Haas & Flower, 1988) termed this process of attempting to reconstruct the context in which a text was produced "rhetorical reading." In the earlier study with Flower, Haas had found that experienced graduate students read academic texts with an extra set of these "rhetorical reading" strategies that college freshmen did not use. In fact, college freshmen spent only 1% of their time paying attention to such details as who wrote this text, what was their motive, and what was going on at the time it was published. The graduate students, however, noticed these things more than 10 times as frequently (13%). Haas (1994) later described how one of these rhetorical readers, an engineering graduate student, read the psychology textbook preface she used in this study:

> During his reading, he assigned the author both a gender ("this guy") and a profession ("he's some kind of scientist"). The reader also tried to account for the author's motives: "This guy is crying out for" a new kind of science. Later, the reader hypothesized a source for the text, at one point speculating that it came from a scholarly psychology journal and noting that the article "wouldn't work for the man-in-the-street." (p. 49)

Textbooks, as we have seen, are atypical texts for scientists to be reading. And graduate students, as we have also seen, are less likely to be critical readers than are researchers already occupying faculty lines. Nevertheless, this graduate student does appear to be trying to resist the codification of production and reconstruct the context in which the knowledge claims in the textbook were produced. In this sense, then, he seems to be operating very much like the physicists observed by Bazerman (1988). By attending to such information as the author's name and affiliation and place and date of publication, readers inside the academic professions try to reconstruct contextual information that the text itself does not directly discuss.

The two final studies we look at in this chapter are helpful for indicating how the features readers attend to in texts can be radically altered as they are socialized into the scientific community. In both studies, students in the second half of their undergraduate education—the 2 years following their declaration of majors in the sciences—read in significantly different, and more professionalized, ways than students in their first 2 years or majors in other fields.

First, a study by Penrose and Fennell (1992) found that junior and senior science majors in undergraduate school were already beginning to read texts differently than were either their counterparts in the humanities or students just beginning their undergraduate careers. In this study, Penrose and Fennell asked four groups of readers to read 10 sentences taken from scientific journal articles that described a link from data to conclusion. In each case, the verb was left out, and the readers were asked to fill in the blanks in sentences such as in the following: "These data _____ that the minimal response rate of interest should be .15" (Figure 1). The first set of readers, 17 scientists from across the university, provided the norms against which the other readers' responses were compared. Nonconventional responses usually inappropriately attributed agency to the data ("data *claim* that"). The conventional responses by scientists, on the other hand, either inserted simple verbs that did not imply agency ("data *suggest* that") or more complicated rhetorical predicates containing actual or implied agents ("data *lead us to conclude* that").

The results showed that, in general, all juniors and seniors did better than the freshmen in producing conventional responses that matched the simple verbs used by the scientists. The junior and senior science majors, however, were more likely to produce the complex rhetorical predicates that the scientists had used (10.5%) than were the junior and senior English majors (5.5%). Furthermore, science majors were more likely than the English majors to posit relatively weak links between data and conclusion using the verb *suggest* (59% of science majors vs. 25% of English majors). Conversely, English majors were more likely to use the uncommonly strong verb of *prove* (62%) than were the science majors (41%) or the scientists themselves (24%). Thus science majors were more likely than either freshman or English majors to recognize the human agency involved in linking data to conclusion and more likely to see these links as contingent. Penrose and Fennell (1992) concluded:

> Our data *suggest* that as students enter and move through the university they develop a basic understanding of the role of human agents in the construction of knowledge as well as a basic familiarity with the linguistic conventions for expressing those relationships. But it appears that it's only as students enter the more specialized sub-community of science that they begin to recognize that scientific knowledge, too, is interpretive, subjective, and attributable. (p. 10, emphasis in the original)

This process of linguistic socialization was also documented in a second study, a longitudinal case study by Haas (1994) of one woman's changing reading strategies as she moved through the 4 years of her undergraduate career into a graduate program in biology. In over 20 hours of open-ended interviews made over these 4 years, Eliza showed herself to be significantly more attentive to the contexts in which texts were produced in her junior and senior years than she had been in her freshman and sophomore years. She was more likely to use texts and their authors in the subject position in her sentences. She was more likely to see these texts and authors "doing" things rather than simply "being" or "saying" things. And she was more likely to include the names of authors among the human agents she mentioned. Overall, then, Eliza appears to have changed her reading strategies in exactly the way Penrose and Fennell (1992) predicted as she moved into her scientific profession.

THE COMPETING INTERESTS OF WRITERS AND READERS IN THE SCIENCES

To return to the theme with which we began, the picture of the sciences we have painted in this chapter suggests that the relationship between the ideal of the autonomous text and the reality of scientific practice is a complex one. Most obviously, we have found that scientists do not ignore contextual factors when they read and write texts within their speciality, but instead fight for control over those contexts in a struggle that often pits readers' interests against writers' interests. Specifically, scientists, as writers of text, appear to want to use language that can function independently of its contexts of production. This propensity is evident at both ends of the scientific process as we have observed it: In the laboratory, as the study by Garfinkel et al. (1981) indicates, scientists move quickly from language about local objects to language about universal objects in the face of discovery. And in texts written for lay readers, such as those studied by Fahnestock (1986), observations about the natural world are often presented without the accompanying information about the contexts of observation. Thus, it appears, as Latour and Woolgar (1979) originally claimed, that scientists as writers do aim to produce autonomous texts, or, as Prelli (1989) put it, to reveal the natural world unencumbered by the vagaries of human perception.

Between these two contexts, however, scientists as readers appear to demand that texts account for and to a local context. As the work of Myers (1985) shows eloquently, readers of grant proposals expect a very careful balance between researchers' claims for the novelty of their research and researchers' claims for continuity with previous research. Thus, fundable research is not simply research that promises to reveal patterns in nature, but also research that responds to the local conditions of the observer's community. In addition, publishable research is not simply research that presents a series of claims about objects out there. Instead, it is research that constructs a virtual experience for a reader in order to supply assurance that the observer has employed the requisite controls (Bazerman, 1988).

Both the expectation for codification of prior research and the expectation of an implied reader role suggest a local accounting to the contexts of interpretation. That is, scientists as writers expect to speak forward to the projected context in which their work will be read and interpreted. For this reason, we find scientific texts unusually laden with metadiscourse that directs implied readers in their interactions with the texts' claims: directions for assessing the validity of those claims (hedges) and directions for interacting with the text itself (commentary).

Scientists as readers appear to be particularly leery about following these directions however. As Bazerman's (1988) study of physicists reading physics and Charney's (1993) study of evolutionists reading Gould and Lewontin indicate, scientists do not follow the neat sequential path that texts lay out for them, but instead try to extract just what is of interest in as little time as possible. And what is of interest, interestingly enough, appears not to be the claims directly made by the texts, but rather any information that can be gleaned about the contexts of production: Who are these authors? Where are they from? Who trained them? Who are they friends with? What are their theoretical commitments? What procedures did they use? Have they been careful?

Answers to these questions can be partially constructed from information directly presented in the text, but are very likely to be supplemented by interpersonal contacts through what Crane (1972) called the the "invisible colleges" holding together researchers within subspecialities. Using the contingent repertoire (Gilbert & Mulkay, 1984), scientists swap a great deal of information about each other's work that never makes its way into print but that is, nonetheless, indispensable for interpreting and using what does get printed.

In the face of this discrepancy between the ideal of the autonomous text and the reality of scientific practice, we might be tempted to dismiss the autonomous ideal as simply a "myth" in the sense Cazden (1989) originally suggested: as an inaccurate portrayal of the literacy practices of scientists. But such dismissal would be premature for, as we have also noted, the ideal of the autonomous text is mythic in an additional and significant sense: It is a driving myth, the paradigmatic accomplishment toward which scientists strive. In fact, if we were to "get rid of" the ideal of the autonomous text, it is not clear what scientists would take to be the goal of their work.

What we have in this academic profession, then, appears to be a set of competing interests mediated by a cultural myth: writers who want to drop all reference to the local context in order to extract statements about objects out there and readers who go out of their way to reconstruct the local context of these statements in order to decide how to interpret and use them. What makes this competition so interesting, however, is that in the sciences—as in most academic professions—the writers and readers are exactly the same people: writers of their own texts, readers of other people's texts. In other words, readers and writers are fighting against themselves.

Several mechanisms appear to be in place to make this self-competition less obvious. For one thing, as Gilbert and Mulkay (1984) suggested, scientists use a bifurcated discourse practice, reserving a formal discourse repertoire for the discussion of their own work and resorting to a second more informal repertoire to dismiss the work of their rivals. In addition, as this review has suggested, this self-competition is sustained through a cycle of text-based activity that reserves one language for the contexts of producing texts (writing) and one for the contexts of interpreting them (reading). In this way, both social space (us vs. them) and cognitive time (read now; write later) serve to isolate potentially jarring discourse practices and mask the discord of competing self-interests.

Socially and cognitively, then, the literacy practices of scientists are very complicated indeed. For what purpose is such complexity sustained? In whose interests has this bifurcated practice been developed? To answer these questions, we must look to other constituencies outside the academic professions themselves. In the next chapter, then, we begin this examination by looking at the literacy practices of the other set of people who join the academic professionals in the academy—the students.

2

LITERACY AMONG NOVICES IN THE ACADEMY: STUDENTS IN SCHOOL

We usually use the term *school* as I have done in the title of this chapter: to conjure up images of students lined in rows upon rows of desks, books open, pencils sharp. Only when we are trying to be quaint do we use the term *academy* instead. But it is really only with the term *academy* that we can easily discern the common *academic* interests that join together the academic professionals we looked at in the previous chapter with the academic novices, the students, with whom we are concerned in this chapter. Deep down, both of these groups organize their lives around the reading and writing of academic texts.

The schools are so closely connected with literacy in our culture that until a decade ago it was possible, as we saw in chapter 1, for scholars to confuse the effects of one for the effects of the other—to think that reading and writing per se brought about the intellectual changes that we now know are a specific product of Western-style schooling (Applebee, 1984b; Scribner & Cole, 1981). But we are still left with the question of what it is about Western-style schools, our schools, that gives the reading and writing within them their peculiar flavor?

Consider, for a minute, schools without texts.

It is hard. Literate activities are part and parcel of what we intend when we send our children to school. They were what we had in mind when we founded our public schools (Cook-Gumperz, 1986) and they largely determine students' overall success in the school curriculum (Wells, 1986). And, as we see in this chapter, in the everyday tasks of instruction, texts play a central role in the exchange of factual information, the main business of current school practice. It is here in the schools, then, that the ideal of the autonomous text takes on a more veridical quality, not serving simply as a seldom-attained goal driving the construction of knowledge—as in the academic professions—but actually regulating the practices of students and teachers in their efforts to figure out what is required and what is allowed in the getting and using of knowledge in school.

DISCOURSE AND KNOWLEDGE IN THE SCHOOLS

In the sciences, as we have noted, local context is a key resource in the tasks of knowledge production. Personal experience in the laboratory is the foundation of scientific knowing. In the schools, however, the situation is remarkably different. Schools ask students to leave their personal knowledge at the classroom door and move instead into a world of decontextualized facts. Academic knowing and contextualized understanding are taken to be at odds.

As first studied by Mehan (1979), the standard interaction pattern of classroom lessons is organized around the exchange of factual information: The teacher elicits information, usually with a question. The student replies. And the teacher provides feedback about this reply. This pattern of conversation, dubbed the IRF structure for its sequencing of initiation, response, and feedback, has been documented in a variety of school contexts (Cazden, 1979; Edwards & Mercer, 1987), and, as Heritage (1984) pointed out, it is the way we know we are "in school." That is, if someone asks us a question to which she already knows the answer and then evaluates our response for its correspondence with this predetermined answer, we know we are being treated like students—no matter what our age or physical surroundings.

One of the main functions of these IRF structures is to control what counts as relevant academic knowledge. To begin with, the information required in IRF sequences in schools is usually factual in nature. Of the 480 teacher initiations upon which Mehan (1979) based his analysis, for example, 279 or fully 58% were requests for factual replies. Indeed, these fact elicitations were more than three times more frequent than any other kind of teacher elicitation.

In addition, teachers use these IRF sequences to signal the kind of factual information they have in mind. Through selective feedback, they give positive rewards to appropriate student responses and negative rewards for responses that go out of bounds. According to Edwards and Mercer (1987), "IRF structures . . . function in defining and controlling what . . . knowledge and understanding will be. They are part of a set of communicative devices whereby the teacher acts as a kind of filter or gateway through which all knowledge must pass in order to be included in the lesson as a valid or useful contribution" (p. 132).

Here, for example, is how selective feedback worked in an extended IRF sequence taken from a study by Edwards and Furlong (1978) in a resource-based classroom in England. This student was having trouble answering a question presented in a booklet about map reading: "Which side of the island . . . has most trees? Why?" To help, the teacher constructed a series of IRF structures to indicate which areas of the student's knowledge were relevant to the task. The student tried to cooperate by volunteering possible answers (moisture, sun, growth), but was unable to come up with the answer the teacher had in mind. Finally, the teacher provided the correct answer himself (wind conditions) and then asked another couple of questions to see if the student could follow his line of reasoning:

	P:	Sir, I don't understand. I've done the answer to that one, but then it says, "Why?"
	T:	Right, why's are always difficult, the difficult ones.
I		Which side of the island, east or west, has most trees?
R	P:	The east.
I	T:	Well, what sort of things would decide where things grow?
R	P:	Well, there's moisture and good soil.
F	T:	Moisture, good soil.
I		What else?
R	P:	A bit of rain, sun.
F	T:	Well, rain would be part of moisture. Sun.
R	P:	Sun.
F	T:	There's one important thing you've left out.
R	P:	Growth.
F	T:	That's connected with the things you've just mentioned.
I		But there's one important thing that you've left out.
R	P:	((Silence.))
I	T:	One important thing you've left out. ((He makes a movement with his hand to indicate a tree blowing in the wind.))
R	P:	((Silence.)) Sir, I don't know. ((Silence again.)) Sir, whether it's been planted.
F	T:	Yeah, but you talked about that.
R		It's really the sort of—um, it it's sheltered, if it's windy.
I		Now wind conditions are going to affect that, aren't they? How?
R	P:	'Cos if it is a strong hurricane it might blow it up, blow it down.
I	T:	And if it is a cold wind, what might it do?
R	P:	Freeze it and, um, it will die.
F	T:	So it won't grow so well, will it? (pp. 114–115, IRF coding added)

Even in the community-based schooling studied by Edwards and Furlong (1978) from which this excerpt is drawn, it was often personal knowledge that teachers and students assumed must be set aside in order to acquire academic knowledge. Here, for example, is a conversation from the same classroom in which a student appears ignorant about the very community center he had been attending every day for the past several months:

I	T:	Well, Abraham Moses is a community centre, isn't it? Now why do people come here?
R	P:	To work.
I	T:	What else? Not only—I mean, you come to work, yeah, but there are other things as well.
R	P:	Help.
F	T:	To get help, yes. OK.
I		What else?
R	P:	((Silence.))
I	T:	Name some other parts of the Centre.
R	P:	((Mumbles.))
I	T:	Pardon?
R	P:	The gym. (Edwards & Furlong, 1978, p. 104)

As Edwards and Furlong pointed out, this boy certainly knew why some people came to the community center and certainly he was familiar with its various parts. But what he did not know was what the teacher wanted him to say—what of his personal knowledge could be allowed into the domain of academically relevant knowledge. By mumbling through his parts in this IRF sequence, he deferred to the teacher's judgment about what counted, waiting to get more information about what the teacher had in mind—which he eventually did later in this conversation.

By repeated participation in these kinds of conversational interchanges in school, most students learn that academically relevant knowledge is different from the knowledge they bring from home. By the time they graduate, they are well trained at picking out this kind of information and ignoring the rest. Consider, for instance, the following story given by Edwards and Mercer (1987):

Suppose you are the conductor of a bus. The bus leaves the depot on its way towards the town centre. At the first stop it picks up 12 people. At the next stop another 11 get on. At the third stop 7 get off and 15 get on. At the fourth stop 21 people get off and 14 get on. The bus continues to the next stop where 7 people get off and a drunk climbs aboard. The conductor takes his fare, but the drunk is disruptive, and at the next stop 13 people complain to the conductor and get off the bus. The conductor tells the drunk to get off. The drunk does so reluctantly, after first asking the conductor's name.

Try to answer these questions before reading any further:

1 How many passengers are still on the bus?
2 What is the conductor's name? (pp. 54–55)

The problem with this second question, according to Edwards and Mercer, is that it goes out of the bounds of academic knowledge. It asks us as readers to remember a piece of information—look at the first sentence—that our schooled experience long ago taught us to forget: our personal role in the construction of knowledge.

READING IN THE SCHOOLS

Texts play a major role in the transmission of academic knowledge in schools. On the one hand, as texts to be read, they function as the source and authority for the knowledge to be acquired. On the other hand, as texts to be written, they serve as the demonstration that this acquisition has taken place. As we see in what follows, it is a set of reading and writing practices quite distinct from those used in the academic professions that grants texts this kind of authority. It is through these schooled literacy practices, then, that the ideal of the autonomous text comes alive.

We look at reading first.

What Students Read in School

The most frequent kind of text that students read in school is the textbook. According to one estimate, students from kindergarten through 12th grade spend an average of 75% of classroom time and 90% of homework time working with textbooks (Goldstein, 1978, cited in Apple, 1989). As Olson (1981) pointed out, these textbooks are expected to serve an archival purpose in our society, "preserving important cultural information" (p. 107).

These "textual archives" are often the embodiment of autonomous texts in Olson's (1981) terms. Linguistically, they emphasize the definition of terms, use complete unmarked grammatical forms, and provide explicit logical structure. In terms of interpersonal relations, they have the authority of presenting "the authorized version of society's valid knowledge" (p. 108). They require students to assume the "responsibility . . . primarily . . . of mastery of this knowledge" (p. 108). And they separate text from writer, thus "put[ting] the words 'above criticism.' " (p. 109). "When a child reads a text or when a teacher teaches what a text says," Olson continued, "the language appears to originate in a transcendental source just as does ritualized speech—it is not ordinary speech and so it seems above criticism" (p. 109).

These linguistic features do not make textbooks very easy to read. When texts originally written for adults are adapted to meet publishers' readability guidelines, for example, they eliminate much of the contextualizing information for the claims they contain (Davison & Kantor, 1982, cited in Pearson, 1984). And, as Armbruster (1984) pointed out, these texts are "inconsiderate" to readers according to what researchers now know about reading: They fail to signal global structure. They fail to include information about the motivation and goals of the people being described. They fail to make the relationships among ideas explicit. And they fail to give proper emphasis to the main ideas. Not surprisingly, in a study by Reder and Anderson (1980), students given summaries of textbook chapters were better able to learn main ideas and make links to new information than those who read the textbook chapters themselves.

Despite their apparent autonomy from context, the content of contemporary textbooks is determined through a complicated interaction of commercial, public, and scholarly interests. At the university level, for example, textbooks are usually authored by academic professionals, but many of these projects start with solicitations from acquisition editors who perceive a market in a specific area. These editors, then, play a major role in deciding what of all academic knowledge should be archived in Olson's (1981) sense.

At the level of K–12, academic, commercial, and public interests come into even more complicated interplay. To be sure, academic professionals are usually involved in textbook production as named authors. But the actual writing is often left to a committee of authors retained by the commercial publishing company. These committees do not operate autonomously in deciding what to include in writing however. Their decisions are often driven by the statewide textbook adoption policies that have been instituted by nearly half of the states (Arons, 1989). Nevertheless, even though state legislatures sometimes try to mandate specific content decisions, publishers usually prefer to steer clear of controversial issues (Apple, 1989). Thus what gets put into textbooks in the elementary and secondary years is often the intersection of scholarly knowledge and public belief—that which all groups can agree on. All in all, then, it is only in this complicated sense that textbooks can be said to "archive" cultural knowledge.

How Students Read in School

Although a great deal is now known about the kinds of texts students read in schools, much less is known about how these texts are incorporated into routine school activities. Nevertheless, some intriguing work has been done on the role of texts in lessons on learning to read. Two studies in particular suggest that one of the major lessons students learn when they are taught to read is to treat texts as the fully explicit source for academic knowledge—to treat them as autonomous texts.

In an analysis of one teacher's reading lessons, for example, Heap (1985) found that the basic IRF sequence we looked at earlier was expanded by the teacher to require "text-consulting" as the source of information for correct responses. Even in questions that might appear to call for personal opinion, Heap found that the teacher had a predetermined response in mind, one that could only be found by consulting the text, as in the following segment:

> T: O.K. ah—why—why do you think that the *bird*, when—when Jimmy found
>   it on the dock ( ) why do you think the bird didn't fly away?
> ?:   It couldn't. ( )
> T: Or tried to get away.
> ?:   Mn mmnh
> T: He couldn't fly because his wing was hurt but why didn't he try to get away
>   from Jimmy.
> ?:   He tried?
> T: No he didn't try to
> ?:   didn't try
> T: get away. But why not? ( )
> ?:   Oh
> T: Katina?
> Ka: Jimmy feeds it every day ( ) when it passes by
> T: Right so he knows Jimmy, doesn't he. Good for you (Heap, 1985, p. 262)

Here we see that the teacher began by asking for an apparently personal opinion: "Why do you think" the bird in the story did not fly away when Jimmy, the main character, found it? The unidentified student (?) suggested one very plausible explanation, that the bird was too injured to fly. But this was not the reason the teacher had in mind. The same student next suggested that the bird did try to fly away, but the teacher rejected that possibility even though nothing in the story contradicted it. Finally, the teacher praised Katina for an answer that was based on information provided earlier in the text—that the bird did not fly away because Jimmy had fed it every day.

Through this interaction, the teacher provided students with two significant cultural lessons about the function of texts in school. First, the teacher let the unidentified student know that the text was to be treated as a maximally explicit source of information: Thus, if the text did not say the bird tried to get away, then the bird did not try to get away. Second, the teacher let the students know that text was to be treated as a direct representation of a maximally coherent reality: Thus she praised an explanation that tied together information in two segments of text (the bird did not fly away because he was used to being fed by Jimmy) and she ignored an explanation that simply used personal knowledge to extrapolate from information given in a single segment (the bird did not try to fly away because he was hurt). In this interchange, then, students were being taught how to interpret texts based only on information given on the page without recourse to their external contextualized understandings.

By requiring students to consult texts for correct responses in IRF sequences, teachers reinforce not only the autonomy of texts but their own authority as well. In the previous segment, for example, the students presumed that the teacher knew why the bird did not fly away and that their job was to use the techniques of reading to come to the same conclusion. But, as Baker and Freebody (1989) suggested in connection with a second study of reading lessons, often no extant reading technique will guarantee that students "get" the teacher's answer in advance of the feedback provided in the IRF sequence. In the following interaction with nonreaders for example, the students had no way other than guessing to figure out the answer the teacher clearly had in mind:

I	t:	What sort of train is that?
R	p:	Big?
R	p:	Little?
R	p:	Steam?
I	t:	How do we know it's steam Jody?
R	p:	'Cause of the smoke.
F	t:	Yes. The smoke here [points to the picture]. (p. 267)

Two points need to be made about this interaction. First, the teacher's preferred answer to her question, "What sort of train is that?" was not the only possible answer. Even if the students had been limited to the text-consulting technique described by Heap (1985), the text and pictures still suggested many more attributes for the train than "steam." Jody just happened upon the attribute and the text feature the teacher had in mind and then received positive feedback that reinforced her guess. The second point is that, despite this actual multiplicity of possible answers, both the teacher and the students in the class acted as if the teacher's preferred answer was the only one possible given correct reading techniques. That is, if Jody suggested "steam" it must be because she used the exact same—and the exactly correct—reading technique employed by her teacher. In this way, students are taught to believe that academic knowledge is always retrievable from autonomous texts when read correctly, even when they themselves cannot produce this autonomous reading. As Baker and Freebody (1989) commented, "Jody is here not only being told that her answer is correct, but that she must have found it correctly. That is, correct answers are retrievable from the text using correct procedures" (p. 268).

Baker and Freebody's (1989) analysis clearly echoes Heap's (1985) findings concerning the way texts are incorporated into the standard IRF sequence of school lessons to reinforce textual autonomy. In addition, their evidence also supports his contention about the place of personal knowledge in the classroom. In the following interchange apparently calling for students' personal opinion, for example, the teacher studied by Baker and Freebody assumed that there was a "correct" way to develop this personal opinion based solely on information in the text:

t: If you had a chance to be one of the things in our story which, or—someone in the story which would you like to be?

p: hh!
t: Carl?
p: The cricket. I mean the big weta.
t: (the big weta
p: (Oh so would I
t: Why would you like to be the big weta
p: 'Cause he comes last
t: He comes last, but what's what happens to him that's so uh so good do you think
p: 'Cause he, he gets to stay in the bed.
t: He gets to stay in the bed. (p. 277)

Here the teacher rewards a student for providing a personal opinion based on evidence in the text. Clearly, students might actually have many reasons for wanting to be one of the things in the story they have just read—reasons related to their personal experience with the animals in question or with their particular life circumstances. Nonetheless the teacher's final feedback reaffirmed what these students had taken for granted—that the only acceptable reasons are those that make sense exclusively in terms of the information provided by the text.

Overall, then, the teachers in these two studies employed strikingly similar strategies for embedding texts in the typical IRF sequence of classroom lessons. They both favored text-consulting as a tool for constructing a single coherent interpretation. And they both valued inferences based exclusively upon the text at the expense of those that incorporated personal or contextualized understanding. Although we have no direct way to assess how widespread these two strategies may be, some indication has been provided in a review by one of the leading researchers in reading instruction. According to Pearson (1984), most teachers do very little by way of directly teaching comprehension strategies in reading lessons. Instead they simply ask questions to assess the results. Furthermore, teachers often skip teachers' manual suggestions that remind them to connect texts with students' personal experience. Though far from definitive, these tendencies are consistent with the patterns described earlier in which teachers require students to use texts as the explicit source and autonomous authority for academic knowledge in school.

In closing this section on reading, we should note that what students are being taught not to do in interpreting texts may be as significant as what they are being taught to do. In particular, in the two classrooms examined in this section, students were taught not to consider ways in which a text's resources might not be sufficient for interpretation. They were taught not to use rhetorical reading strategies to go beyond the text. These prohibitions both served to maintain and reinforce the ideal of the autonomous text by teaching students to hold themselves accountable as "bad readers" when their interpretations failed rather than encouraging them to question the ideal of the autonomous text itself.

WRITING IN THE SCHOOLS

As we noted in the last chapter, writers and readers are exactly the same people in the academic professions. In particular, scientists as writers write exactly the same kinds of texts that they as readers read. In the schools, however, we find no such symmetry. Students are not the writers of texts they read. Instead, they write most often to demonstrate that they have read and understood texts written by others. As a result, students tend to write with the same kinds of decontextualized strategies with which they were taught to read. That is, they organize their writing practices to produce autonomous texts.

Why Students Write in School

Why do students write in school? Two major studies, one conducted in England in the late 1960s and one conducted in the United States in the late 1970s, suggest that, by and large, students usually write for the purpose of demonstrating knowledge for a teacher as examiner. The first study, carried out by Britton, Burgess, Martin, McLeod, and Rosen (1975), solicited writing samples from students enrolled in a range of British schools in their first, third, fifth, and seventh years in a range of content areas. Over 2,000 texts were finally selected, the work of 500 boys and girls. The second study, carried out by Applebee and his colleagues (Applebee, 1981), surveyed 754 teachers nominated for their teaching excellence in their content areas in a stratified sample of American schools in Grades 9 and 11. These teachers answered a questionnaire about the writing they had assigned to a recent class and supplied sample papers from that class. In both studies, the researchers analyzed the results using similar categories for audience and function, Applebee using a modification of the categories developed earlier by Britton.

The results for both studies point to the limited nature of the writing students are asked to do in school. In both cases, the predominate audience for students' writing was the teacher. The predominate function was informative. By and large, students' texts appeared to function either in a teacher–student dialogue as a means for students to acquire academic knowledge or in a pupil–examiner relationship as a means of demonstrating that knowledge had been acquired. In Britton's (Britton et al., 1975) study, for example, nearly 90% of all students' work was written for the teacher in one of these two roles: In the early years, the teacher usually functioned in a teacher–learner dialogue; by the 7th year, however, the teacher usually functioned as an examiner. Most of this writing was transactional (64%) with nearly 37% given to classification.

Because Applebee's (1981) criteria for what counted as writing was broader than Britton's (Britton et al., 1975), his results allow us to examine the place of this extended writing in the secondary schools he surveyed. His results show that although students were often asked to put words on paper in school, they did not frequently do so to develop their ideas in any extended way. In fact, Applebee found that only 26% of his 9th-grade teachers and 36% of his 11th-grade teachers frequently assigned writing of a paragraph or more. Most reported assigning shorter pieces—multiple-choice, fill-in-the-blank, copying, and short answers—that did not require extensive thinking. Again, as in Britton's study, most of this writing was for informative purposes.

Two follow-up studies by Applebee (1984a) confirm the limited nature of the writing students do in school. In the first study, Applebee surveyed the kinds of writing assigned in the three most popular textbooks used in seven content areas. He found that most of these textbooks recommended writing activities of less than a paragraph with the teacher as examiner in mind as audience. Second, in a case study of 15 students enrolled in a good school in the San Francisco Bay area, Applebee found that even these students in a good school produced most of their writing for teacher-as-examiner for informative purposes.

What Students Write in School

When students write to demonstrate knowledge for the teacher as examiner, they typically produce what is known as the "school essay" (Hounsell, 1984; van Peer, 1989, 1990)—a text that introduces a thesis in its opening paragraph, provides support for this thesis in succeeding paragraphs, and restates and occasionally comments on this thesis in the closing paragraph. In Applebee's (1984a) longitudinal study of 15 students mentioned earlier, for example, fully 66% of students' texts used this essay form, which he called analytic, often to compare alternatives or to analyze cause and effect relationships. Another 22% of the students' texts used a more simple narrative structure, often simply to restate an idea provided by a teacher's question and then provide elaboration with a time-ordered sequence of information. Occasionally, these students' texts exhibited a mixed structure with more easily managed narrative structures embedded in a more global thesis-support analytic framework.

Interestingly, almost all of these student texts are based on other writers' texts. Applebee (1984a) found, for example, that 72% of student writing relied on either the teacher or school texts as its source of information, and only 27% used personal experience. This reliance on texts as sources appears to characterize not only the school essay studied by Applebee, but also a range of more specialized texts that students write in school. Perhaps the least complex of these texts is the summary, but the synthesis and the research paper are also found at more advanced levels as well. In all three of these genres, students appear to use writing to reproduce rather than extend what they have read and, in doing so, often frustrate the expectations of teachers operating under more rhetorical assumptions.

A summary is the simplest text that attempts to represent in some form what another text says. According to Brown and Day (1983), summary strategies span a range from those that simply delete information from the source text, through those that combine information, and finally to those that call for inventing whole new topic sentences. In an early study, Brown, Day, and Jones (1983) found that students as young as 5th grade could use simple deletion strategies to summarize whereas students in the 11th grade and first year of college were more likely to use strategies that combined and reordered information. A later study by Garner, Belcher, Winfield, and Smith (1985) suggests that fifth graders could recognize the benefits of these more complex strategies even when they did not use them. Nevertheless, students seemed to prefer to write summaries by selecting what they consider to be important information from other writers' texts and deleting extraneous information. Few students at any level actually reordered this information and even fewer invented new topic sentences. The 10 undergraduates studied by Sherrard (1986), for example, used the following set of strategies, rank ordered for frequency, for moving information from source to summary text: (a) omitting a sentence from the source text, (b) including a sentence from the source text "as is," (c) combining two consecutive sentences in a source text, (d) combining three consecutive sentences in a source text, and (e) combining four consecutive sentences in a source text. In the taxonomy originally developed by Brown and Day, this represents the lower end of possible summary strategies.

On the face of it, other texts written from sources appear to not allow for such a simple set of reproductive strategies. Synthesis, for example, requires students to combine information from more than one text, a sophisticated skill usually reserved for the later years of undergraduate and graduate school. The results of several studies seem to indicate, however, that even students at these upper levels preferred the same kind of copy and delete strategies we observed for simple summary. In a study comparing college juniors and seniors who were more or less able in reading comprehension, for example, Spivey (1984) found that more able comprehenders invented thematic chunks as a way of organizing information from the source texts. The less able comprehenders, by contrast, organized their texts in a flat structure reminiscent of a simple list of facts with little invented structure. In a later study in which the same level of student was asked to write a comparison of sources, Spivey (1991) found similar results: Students with greater verbal ability as measured by a prescreening reading test were more likely to invent their own macrostructures to organize information from sources. Significantly, however, less than half of these upper division college writers used this inventional strategy. Nevertheless, teachers seem to prefer this more rhetorical strategy: In Spivey's second study, syntheses that contained invented higher level organization were rated more highly than those that did not.

A study by Ackerman (1991) of students in graduate school suggests that students' propensity for engaging in more rhetorical strategies depends on the students' relative status in the text's domain. In a study of 40 graduate students, 20 in psychology and 20 in management, Ackerman found that when students were asked to synthesize information from texts outside of their specialization, they tended to reproduce the text they read: They made few elaborations while reading and included less original information when writing. When they were asked to synthesize information from source texts in their own fields, however, they adopted a more rhetorical stance: They read to construct an image of the rhetorical context in which the texts were written and attempted to respond to those texts by saying something new based on their own personal knowledge.

The research paper, the last genre of "writing from sources" that we examine, shows a similar duality of strategic approaches, one simply reproductive, one more rhetorical. College students surveyed by Schwegler and Shamoon (1982), for example, believed that research papers were supposed to help them learn about a topic and demonstrate that learning to a teacher. Faculty, on the other hand, believed the research paper should be an exploration of the state of an issue at a particular time. Nelson (1990), following 13 students through six different courses at Carnegie Mellon University, also found students' interpretations diverging from faculty expectations: Her students often interpreted teachers assignments as simple requests for the demonstration of course content. The course faculty, however, often had the construction of independent argument in mind.

How Students Write in School

When students write in school, they appear to be using what Bereiter and Scardamalia (1987) called a knowledge-telling strategy: Students begin by retrieving ideas from long-term memories in response to cues in either the assignment topic or the discourse's genre conventions. Once they remember an idea, they test it for appropriateness to the composition. If it passes, they add it to the text. Students continue content generation in this fashion until they can retrieve no more ideas. At this point, composing stops. This knowledge-telling strategy apparently results in a highly cursory writing process for students: As studies have repeatedly shown, students tend to write quickly, attend to low-level details, edit to clean things up, and then turn the essay in to a reader who evaluates it against a mental "template" for what is expected. Both students as writers and teachers as their readers, then, engage in practices regulated by the ideal of the autonomous text.

Emig (1971) first observed students' cursory writing process in the late 1960s with a study of eight high school students—two average and six above-average writers—from Chicago area schools. Despite their writing success, only one of these eight students regularly engaged in any kind of planning in advance of composing. Lynn, for example, spent just 3 minutes planning the essay she wrote in her first session with Emig, and a similar amount of time planning the second essay even though she was told to think about it in advance. According to Emig, the interview comment from one of these students was typical of almost all these students' attitudes toward planning: "I start to write and just wherever I end up, I end up . . .' " (p. 82).

A similar pattern emerged in Pianko's (1979) study of 10 remedial and 7 traditional writers enrolled in a freshman composition course in a community college in the fall of 1976. On five separate occasions, Pianko asked these students to take as much time as they needed to compose a 400-word essay under what she described as "fairly usual classroom conditions" (p. 7). These students remained remarkably disengaged from their writing: Their average prewriting time was 1.26 minutes; the average total writing time was just 38 minutes. Fourteen of these 17 students did no planning on paper and most reported mental planning during rather than before writing.

In two articles published in 1980, Flower and Hayes (1980a, 1980b) reported similar observations on students' cursory planning. Using think-aloud protocols, Flower and Hayes found that the one more experienced writer for whom they gave specific data engaged in far more rhetorical planning than the novice with whom she or he was contrasted (Flower & Hayes, 1980a). They also reported the results of an unpublished study in which they found that student writers generated 60% of their ideas in response to the topic and 30% in response to the rhetorical problem. Experienced writers reversed these proportions, spending 60% of their time thinking about the rhetorical problem and only 30% of their time thinking about the topic.

Unpublished data from Zbrodoff (1984) also suggest that students engage in a highly cursory process. In this study, students in grades 5 and 10 spent less than 10 seconds planning before starting to write a simple assigned story even when given unlimited composing time. Adults spent considerably more time planning—although their time was still generally under 1 minute (Bereiter and Scardamalia, 1987). In their own studies, Bereiter and Scardamalia similarly found that students spent on average less than 1 minute planning before beginning to write.

Although we do not have time to review the extensive literature on student revising (Emig, 1971; Faigley & Witte, 1981; Fitzgerald, 1987; Flower, Hayes, Carey, Schriver, & Stratman, 1986; Hayes, Flower, Schriver, Stratman, & Carey, 1987; Perl, 1979; Selfe, 1984) and teacher response (Brannon & Knoblauch, 1982; Horvath, 1984; Onore, 1989; Siegel, 1982; Sommers, 1982; Sperling & Freedman, 1987; Ziv, 1984), it is important to note that patterns in both of these practices reinforce what we have seen for student planning: Students for the most part believe that revising means editing and seldom make changes to text that affect meaning. And teachers routinely respond to students' texts by evaluating them against a mental template for what they expect to see. Overall, then, students appear to be remarkably unengaged in the process of reproducing their knowledge in autonomous texts.

LITERACY AND LEARNING IN THE SCHOOLS

Reading and writing, as we have seen, are ubiquitous in schools. Texts to be read serve as an important source for the knowledge students are expected to learn and texts to be written serve as an important demonstration that this learning has taken place. But what exactly is the effect on the students themselves of all this reading and writing? The most obvious effect that might be expected from all this knowledge getting and knowledge telling is the acquisition of culturally important information. But, as we see in this section, the results of research on the relationship between literacy and learning pose a puzzling challenge to any educator interested in justifying the dominance of school literacy practices on the grounds of its benefits to students' learning.

The Impact of Reading on Learning

As we noted previously, textbooks' impact on student learning appears to be somewhat hampered by linguistic features that make them inconsiderate to readers (Armbruster, 1984). The interesting series of studies that we look at in this section also suggest that the effects of students' prior knowledge may be significant to learning. In particular, two additional factors seem to be critical to determining what students learn: first, whether students hold beliefs that are incompatible with what the textbook says and, second, whether the textbook directly addresses and refutes these incompatible beliefs.

Lipson first documented the failure of textbooks to change students' prior knowledge in dissertation research published in *The Journal of Reading Behavior* in 1982. Lipson asked 14 pairs of third graders, one an average reader and one below average, to read eight textbook passages. In the first session, prior to reading, Lipson assessed the students' knowledge about the topics of the texts they were to read by asking them to choose which of two statements was true: a correct statement about the topic or a comparable but incorrect statement. If the students were unsure, they were asked to pass on the question. In the second session a week later, students were asked to read the eight passages one at a time and then choose among the same pairs of statements.

To analyze this data, Lipson (1982) calculated the probability that students would select the true statement on the postreading test given their answers on the pre-reading test. For both average and poor readers, the results were striking. Not unexpectedly, if students selected the true statement before they read, they still chose it afterward (86% of the time for average readers; 85% of the time for poor readers). If they passed on the question before reading, they were still fairly likely to select the true statement after reading (80% of the time for good readers; 71% of the time for poor readers). But if they selected the incorrect statement prior to reading, they were significantly less likely to select the true statement after reading (69% of the time for good readers; 62% of the time for poor readers). Thus the only information that these students appeared to acquire from texts was that which matched or did not contradict their prior knowledge.

Alvermann, Smith, and Readence (1985) observed a similar pattern in a modified replication study with 56 sixth graders from the Atlanta metropolitan area. In a carefully crafted design, students were asked to serve as consultants to the researchers who were interested in writing textbooklike passages for sixth-grade students. One passage contained information that was fairly consistent with students' prior beliefs. The other passage contained information that was more counterintuitive. In the actual experiment, students began by completing a multiple-choice test to assess their prior knowledge on the topic. A month later, half of them were asked to activate their prior knowledge by writing down everything they knew on these topics. Finally, all students then read the passages on the topics and took several tests to assess their knowledge after reading.

Three results from this experiment are worth noting. First, those students who activated prior knowledge on the counterintuitive topic before reading recalled less of the passage than those who did not activate their prior knowledge. Second, if the specific prior knowledge these students activated before reading was incorrect, they were very likely to continue in the same incorrect belief even after reading. And third, many of these students had some awareness of the incompatibilities between their prior knowledge and the passages they had read. In fact, 14 of these 28 students indicated that they had further questions about the counterintuitive topic and 10 of these specifically asked questions about the counterintuitive information the text had contained.

The results of these two studies strongly suggest, then, that standard textbook discourse does not easily communicate counterintuitive concepts to students. Some research suggests, however, that changes to textbooks can be made to increase the likelihood that students will pay attention to the information they contain. In particular, if the texts are altered to contain explicit refutations of students' misconceptions, they appear to be more able to change students' minds. A study by Hynd and Alvermann (1986), for example, found that 38 undergraduates corrected about 50% of their misconceptions about Newtonian mechanics when given refutation text, significantly more than those given a parallel standard text. In a related study, Dole and Niederhauser (1990) found that refutation texts were more likely to change sixth-grade students' minds than either the original passages taken from a science textbook or ones rewritten to be more considerate in Armbruster's (1984) sense. In this study, however, even altered texts did not make a significant dent in students' misconceptions: 85% of the misconceptions students held before reading remained after reading.

Overall, then, it appears that students asked to read textbook materials reliably learn the information they contain when it is compatible with their prior knowledge. If texts go against the grain of their prior beliefs, they tend to ignore them. Furthermore, although these results can be somewhat mitigated if texts explicitly address and refute students' misconceptions, this pattern cannot be eliminated entirely. As we see in the next section, a similar, though perhaps more complicated, story can be told for the limited impact of writing on learning.

The Impact of Writing on Learning

As we have already seen, students do not actually do very much extended writing in the schools and the writing they do is for the purpose of demonstrating knowledge to the teacher as examiner. The underlying assumption of much recent writing research has been, however, that writing can do something more. In particular, writing has often been assumed to lead to a deeper level of processing and therefore to better learning. Much effort has been expended trying to test this hypotheses since it was first articulated by Emig in 1977, but, as two recent reviews suggested, the results have been both contradictory and confusing (Penrose, 1992; Schumacher & Nash, 1991). In what follows, however, we see that these results can be understood once we distinguish between the literacy practices required in schools and those used in the academic professions.

Early studies seem to confirm the hypothesized benefits for writing on learning. In 1985, for example, Copeland reported the results of a study in which she asked 120 sixth-grade students in central Texas to read passages about an unfamiliar game, engage in postreading activities, and then take two kinds of comprehension tests, one on applying the information to another task and the other on simple factual recall. The results showed that students did significantly better on both tests after writing than after answering multiple-choice questions or doing directed rereading. Follow-up analyses indicated, furthermore, that both the nature of the writing and the nature of the test were important to producing these positive results. Students who wrote texts that attempted to explain the game to a friend as required by the directions did better on the application test than did those who wrote simply to describe. They also did better if they included ideas related to the ones on the later test. Only the inclusion of test-related ideas seemed to make a difference on the comprehension test for factual recall however. Whether or not the students had undertaken the task of explaining the game to a friend did not affect their ability to remember what they had read.

At roughly the same time but a half continent away, Langer and Applebee were undertaking a line of research that initially yielded similar positive results for writing on learning (Langer, 1986; Langer & Applebee, 1987). Langer asked six high school students to read two passages from an American history textbook, thinking aloud as they worked. Sometimes students were asked to take notes in their usual manner; sometimes they were asked to answer study questions; sometimes they were asked to write an analytic essay. The results showed that students took about twice as long to complete their task when writing than when taking notes or answering study questions. Furthermore, they apparently used this extra processing to engage in activities that were relatively rare in the other two conditions: hypothesizing, making metacomments, using evidence and validation, and evaluating. Finally, this extra processing seemed to pay off: Langer found that students improved the quantity and organization of their broad topic knowledge to a greater extent when writing than in the other two conditions.

In 1987, one of Applebee and Langer's graduate students, Durst, completed the final study usually taken to suggest positive effects for writing on learning. In this study, rather than comparing essay writing to other kinds of postreading activities, Durst compared the effects of analytic essay writing with summary essay writing. He asked 20 high school juniors from the San Francisco Bay area to read passages taken from American history textbooks.

Like Langer (1986; Langer & Applebee, 1987), his prompt for the analytic essay asked students to develop a personal opinion about the material from this reading. The prompt for the summary essay simply asked, "In your own words, summarize the events discussed in the reading passage." Also like Langer, Durst asked these students to compose aloud as they worked. To measure the effects of writing, Durst analyzed the essays the students wrote as well as the cognitive activities in which they engaged. Like Langer (1986; Langer & Applebee, 1987), Durst (1987) found that students writing the analytic essay took the longest time to complete their work. And, like Langer, he found that students who wrote analytic essays spent proportionately more of their time in higher order thinking than did the writers of summary. Thus Durst's analysis appears to bear out Langer's finding that analytic essays produce a distinct pattern of higher level cognitive operations. Students' cognitive activities while writing analytic essays do appear to be more complex than when they take notes, answer study questions, or write simple summaries.

Presumably, then, the results of these two studies, when combined with Copeland's (1985) earlier results, seem to offer support to teachers who want to change current school practices by assigning more extended analytic writing in their courses as a way of helping students to learn. Such a conclusion, however, would be premature. In fact, a second set of studies that actually measured the effects of writing on students' learning of passage-specific knowledge suggest that writing, particularly analytic writing, may be a poor way to acquire school knowledge.

The first of these studies was published in 1984 by another of Applebee and Langer's graduate students, Newell. Newell asked eight high school juniors from the San Francisco Bay area, all recommended by their teachers as good readers and writers, to read and write about passages taken from social science and science textbooks. The writing tasks were the same as those used by Langer—study questions, note taking, and analytic writing—but this time, the students did all three tasks twice, once on passages about which they had poorly organized knowledge and once on passages about which they had highly organized knowledge. Before reading and writing, students were told they were going to be tested on the passages, and afterward, they were tested for the depth and organization of their broad topic knowledge related to the passage as well as for their recall of passage-specific information.

The results of this comparison confirm, first of all, that analytic essay writing does take a long time. Newell's (1984) students took an average of twice as long to finish the analytic essay as they did to take notes or answer study questions. This increase in processing time apparently benefited the students who had poorly organized topic knowledge to begin with: They gained an average of 1.42 more on their knowledge score measuring the depth and organization of their topic knowledge after writing. Study questions also brought about significant increases however: Students with poor topic knowledge gained an average of .83 on their knowledge score after answering study questions. For students with highly organized knowledge, the results were not dramatic or significant. High-knowledge students gained an average increase of only .54 on their knowledge score after writing and a gain of only .25 after answering study questions.

In measuring changes in the depth and organization of students' topic knowledge, Newell (1984) was duplicating Langer's (1986; Langer & Applebee, 1987) design. In measuring recall, he was going beyond it to ask, How well did the writing tasks affect students' ability to learn specific pieces of information present in the passage? His study, then, was the first to look for specific learning effects for analytic writing comparable to those Copeland (1985) had found for writing an explanation to a friend. Here the results showed no benefit for analytic writing. That is, students recalled just about as much when they took notes and answered study questions as they did when they wrote analytic essays. This result, clearly not what Newell expected, suggested that even though students spent twice as long on the task of writing analytic essays, they did not improve their memory for specific pieces of information in the original text. In fact, Newell's students turned out to have the best memory for text-specific information when they were allowed to take notes in their normal fashion.

A study by Penrose (1992) also suggests that students may be the best judge of how to study texts when the goal is to acquire specific knowledge for tests. Penrose asked 40 college freshmen to read one of two texts on which they had low topic knowledge. One of these texts was a popular science article on hurricanes originally published in the *Smithsonian* magazine. The other was a more analytic discussion of the nature of paternalism written by an academic for his students. After reading, half the students were asked to "study for a test"; the other half were asked to "write a report." The overall results showed, in Penrose's words, that "students were more likely to remember individual facts from their reading if they had directly studied the text than if they had written an essay about it" (p. 476). That is, the nature of the study task had a significant effect on students' ability to take the comprehension test. Specifically, students who studied in their normal fashion did significantly better in answering the questions requiring simple recall and application.

A third study using a comprehension test similar to that used by Penrose (1992), this one reported by Langer and Applebee (1987), showed similar negative results for writing. After reading passages selected from high school social studies texts, 208 students, half from 9th-grade English classes in the San Francisco Bay area, the other half from the 11th grade, engaged in one of four study conditions: normal studying, note taking, answering study questions, and analytic writing. Four weeks later, students took a 20-item multiple-choice comprehension test as well as a recall test similar to that used earlier by Newell (1984). These results also showed a significant negative effect for analytic writing. At both the 9th and 11th grades, students asked to write analytically after reading did worse on both the comprehension test and the recall test than they did in the other three conditions.

As Schumacher and Nash (1991) noted in a recent review of this literature, the results of these studies suggest that analytic writing is not a good way for students to acquire the kinds of information routinely tested in school. A final study conducted by Langer and Applebee (1987) suggests why: When the students in this study wrote analytic essays, they focused on a narrow range of information relevant to the thesis they were developing. That is, if they were trying to identify "the two or three most important reasons for industrial growth in the late nineteenth and twentieth centuries"—the typical prompt used by Langer and Applebee in all of their studies—they simply reviewed the text to pick out their "two or three most important reasons" and ignored the reasons they judged less important. On just this subset of content to which they paid attention, they did seem to have an advantage over those who answered study questions or wrote simple summaries. But when content was looked at more broadly, their performance suffered compared to those who had used other postreading activities.

In general, then, students and teachers in school appear to be justified in not assigning very much extended analytic writing. In fact, this kind of writing seems to distract students from learning the broad range of content required by the tests they take. The more common types of school writing, note taking and answering study questions, appear to be better suited to preparing students for kinds of knowledge displays routinely required in school. When students are asked to do something other than read standard textbook prose or demonstrate factual content on tests, the story changes dramatically however. To begin with, if students are required to make significant selections and transformations of knowledge, extended writing may be of benefit. Copeland (1985), for instance, had asked students to read about a game, write to explain it to a friend, and take a test predicting the next move. These are all very different tasks from those normally encountered in school, and in this situation, writing did seem to offer students an advantage. In fact, it directed them to exactly the kinds of information that formed the basis of the test and helped them to process it in a way the test required.

Durst (1987), likewise, had departed from the standard school tasks in significant ways. Both he and Langer (1986; Langer & Applebee, 1987) had asked students to develop a position on an issue using evidence from the textbook reading. Unlike Langer, however, Durst did not specify the content upon which the students were to focus, only the general area of concern, economic lessons. Furthermore, Durst's students had a much bigger job to accomplish in developing their theses. Whereas Langer's students simply had to make a selection among points already made in the analysis provided in the source text, Durst's students had to construct their own points out of source texts deliberately chosen to be narratives rather than analyses. Durst had thus forced students to create a text structure different than the one they had read. To do so, they appear to have engaged in higher level cognitive activities than normal. Both Durst and Copeland's positive effects for writing on thinking occurred, then, in the contexts of tasks that made significant departures from the standard knowledge-transmission purposes of the schools.

The kind of text assigned seems to make a difference to learning as well. When Penrose (1992) asked her students to read the popular science article on hurricanes, she found the differences between studying and "writing a report" to be significant though complex: Those who wrote a report used more complex thinking strategies; those who studied reread the source text more and did better on the application questions; and those who studied by writing generative notes took longer but did better than those who simply copied down factual information. On the paternalism passage, however, all these effects disappeared. It did not seem to matter much how the students approached this text: After both studying and writing, students could apply concepts equally well; they took the same amount of time to read and did about the same on the comprehension passage; and they engaged in the same level of cognitive activity. In fact, students appear to have used more constructive effort to process the paternalism text than did those students who read about hurricanes, even though they actually spent less time with the text and, in the end, scored lower on its content when tested. Overall, then, the paternalism text itself seemed to have determined the way it would be processed whereas the hurricane text afforded two distinct patterns of processing.

Penrose (1992) notes several differences between the hurricane text and the paternalism text that may account for these differences. First, they were at different levels of difficulty: The hurricane text measured at a 12th-grade reading level; the paternalism text at 17+. Second, they were from different disciplines: The hurricane text was scientific; the paternalism text was from the humanities. And third, they had different organizational structures: The hurricane text was a narrative of scientific change; the paternalism text was an analysis of paternalistic practices.

From the perspective of this review of literacy practices, we can note one additional difference between these texts: The hurricane text more closely resembled the kind of textbook prose that students are accustomed to reading in schools; the paternalism text was more closely related to texts written by academic professionals. In particular, the two texts used different styles of metadiscourse to invite readers to enter into different kinds of relationships with the knowledge they presented. The hurricane text, for instance, referred to the reader exactly twice, both in the same sentence, as part of a "we" who now know a great deal about hurricanes thanks to the efforts of scientists: "Today *we* know a great deal about these storms, but we knew very little only a century and a half ago" (p. 493, italics added). The text that preceded and followed this statement was a mixture of statements about events leading to scientific discoveries made by other people in the past ("early weather observers were puzzled by what appeared to be sudden shifts in wind direction") and statements about what hurricanes actually do now in an eternal present ("Around the fringes of the enormous whirlwind, gale-force winds spin out like sparks from a pinwheel."). Thus, at no time in the text, was knowledge about hurricanes presented as something that readers could construct as agents. In this sense, then, it was closely related to standard decontextualized textbook prose.

The paternalism passage, by contrast, referred to its readers on 10 separate occasions, and the metadiscourse did not keep the readers outside of the construction of knowledge about its topic. Instead, it invited readers to join the author in offering a critique of mistaken beliefs held by historians and sociologists: "Historians and sociologists have described such relationships as 'paternalistic.'... Too often, however, the term misleads. Describing such systems as paternalistic causes *us* to overlook important characteristics of these relationships" (Penrose, 1992, p. 495). The text then went on to provide a timeless description of the parent–child relationship ("Parents are caring protectors") and an analysis of that description as a critique of the commonplace beliefs ("We now need to ask what features of the original parent/child relationship transfer to the notion of social or economic paternalism."). In sum, then, this text was an academic argument with all the typical moves identified by Swales and Najjar (1987) for establishing the significance of a topic, summarizing the previous knowledge on that topic, and moving to fill a gap in that knowledge.

Once we see the two texts in Penrose's (1992) study as typifying the two distinct groups that make up the academy, we can better understand her complex results. When students were asked to study the kind of material they were used to reading in school (the hurricane text), they spent some time on the task and did well on the comprehension task, but they did not seem to become overly engaged in the process. When they were asked to write about this same text, however, they spent more time and became more engaged, but with a consequent decline in their test performance. These results, then, echo the earlier findings of Newell (1984) and Langer and Applebee (1987).

On the academic argument, however, it did not seem to matter whether students were asked to study or write. In neither case did they spend much time on the text, perhaps because they could not find the kinds of factual information they were accustomed to looking for, and they did not do well on the comprehension tests afterward. But they did seem to engage in some higher level processing, perhaps in the effort to make sense of the unfamiliar genre of academic argument. These results seem to echo the results of Durst's (1987) earlier study when students were asked to create original analyses.

Researchers of writing have been particularly reticent about drawing out the negative impact of writing on learning described previously. After finding negative effects for writing on comprehension, for example, Newell (1984) concluded that "essay writing may aid the learning of concepts found in prose passages excerpted from science and social science textbooks" (p. 281) even though his own results did not support this conclusion. In their book-length monograph, Langer and Applebee (1987) similarly concluded that writing helps learning, although they acknowledged that different kinds of writing seem to produce different kinds of learning. And, in a comprehensive review of this literature published in the *Handbook of Reading Research* in 1990, Tierney and Shanahan concluded that "the previous research studies provide consistent support for viewing writing as a powerful tool for the enhancement of thinking and learning" (p. 272).

Reviews, however, have begun to acknowledge more openly the inappropriateness of using extended writing for the kind of learning typically required in the schools. As we have seen, Schumacher and Nash (1991) suggested there is a mismatch between writing and the goal of acquiring knowledge. Furthermore, Penrose (1992) was fairly plain that her results "remind us . . . that students can 'engage in' writing without much thought, without the active involvement or critical reflection we associate with participating or generating knowledge in a discipline" (p. 491). And even in 1985 Copeland warned of the limitations of using writing to learn: "[I]n using writing to help students to learn, one should structure writing activities so that they help students incorporate in their writing those particular ideas they are expected to learn. If students write about a topic but are not asked to do so in a way that helps them to focus upon the targeted information, writing may not help students achieve the learning goals set forth" (p. 25).

LITERACY AND LEARNING AT CROSSED PURPOSES IN THE SCHOOLS

As we have seen on several occasions in this chapter, members of the academic professions, both researchers and teachers, are often surprised and dismayed by what students do with reading and writing in school. Taking for granted that acts of literacy serve a naturally epistemic function (Emig, 1977; McGinley & Tierney, 1989; Scott, 1967), they assume that students' literacy practices will or should mirror their own rhetorical practices. As we have seen throughout this chapter, however, the right to do something with knowledge, particularly the knowledge encountered in books, is not a right routinely extended to students in school. At no part in the cycle of school literacy do either teachers or students routinely expect to see knowledge transforming in students' texts. Indeed, regulated by the ideal of the autonomous text, students early on are asked to stay as close to source texts as possible and are graded for their compliance with this expectation. Given this message, then, it is hardly surprising—or even as accidental as Bereiter and Scardamalia suggested in their 1987 monograph—that knowledge getting and knowledge telling are the most common models followed by students in school.

As our look at the relationship between literacy and learning has shown, however, these school practices can hardly be characterized as effective. To be sure, under those conditions when the content of textbook prose matches or extends students' preconceived ideas—when, in other words, academic knowledge extends or reinforces everyday beliefs—reading appears to work just fine as a way to learn. Writing, however, appears to be not only superfluous to students' learning, but actually detrimental to the process. In other words, on the simple tasks of knowledge getting, writing is at best a crippled practice.

Furthermore, when the textbook prose contains counterintuitive concepts—which, as we see in the next chapter, make up the heart of expertise—even reading becomes crippled. With just reading, students do not do a particularly good job of learning concepts that go against their everyday beliefs. At best, they simply add them to a storehouse of decontextualized and irrelevant academic knowledge. At worse, they reject them outright.

Can we improve this situation by changing students' literacy practices? Although no research has yet been done to answer this question for writing (Schumacher & Nash, 1991), the research just reviewed for reading does seem to suggest that benefits might be gained by asking students to read something other than standard textbook prose. Dole and Niederhauser (1990), for example, brought about significantly more conceptual change with textbook prose modified to include metadiscourse in such sentences as: "Some people think that food is used only in people's stomachs, but this is not true" (p. 306). These kinds of changes, however, are exactly the kinds most textbook writers are not likely to make. Specifically, when a textbook selection is revised to make it "refutation text" in Dole and Niederhauser's sense, it not only draws readers into the text by addressing their beliefs, but it also calls attention to the arena of human belief and action underlying its claims about the world. As a result, such revisions anchor a text's claims to an interpretive context rather than making them appear to originate from a transcendental source. The result is that the text appears to be less autonomous in Olson's (1981) sense. Revisions like those suggested by Dole and Niederhauser, then, move in the opposite direction of the general attempt of the academic professions to see their claims accepted as true independent of context. That is, in the taxonomy developed by Latour and Woolgar (1979), such revisions would take what are essentially Type 4 statements and recontextualize them as Type 3 statements that acknowledge the source of their credibility.

Although at first blush it may appear ironic that the form of claim toward which the academic professions aim is exactly the form that is ineffective in changing readers' minds, this irony may be exactly the point. As we have seen in chapter 1, the metadiscourse in scientific texts is a sign of a complex set of relationships—between writers and readers, between writers and their knowledge, and between writers and the larger society. We thus cannot change the metadiscourse in texts—or the crippled literacy practices of students in school—without also altering the relationships out of which these texts arise. And, as we see in the next two chapters, these relationships have been shaped by the nature of expertise.

3

EXPERTISE AS COGNITIVE ABSTRACTION

At the heart of every expertise is a claim to the command of an arcane knowledge that goes beyond everyday understanding. That is, expertise is usually taken to be something more than mere competence in a domain. In linguistics, for example, "competence" refers to the normal command of one's native language. Barring neurological difficulties or extreme social deprivation, everyone is expected to become a competent speaker. Expert knowledge, on the other hand, is assumed to be arcane knowledge that can only be acquired through specialized training and practice. Not everyone will get it, even among those who try. For this reason, few of us would quarrel with the characterization of expertise given by Freidson in a 1984 collection on *The Authority of Experts*:

> There are some tasks that almost everyone in a given society at a given point of history can perform merely by virtue of being an adult who possesses such conventional skills of everyday life as being able to dial a telephone or drive an automobile, and there are others which can be performed after only brief training or instruction. There are still other tasks which require either extensive training or experience or both, and in this case, the performers are true specialists with skill and knowledge—that is, with expertise—which is distinctly theirs and not part of the normal competence of adults in general. (p. 14)

Readers interested in the topic of expertise will find a curious schizophrenia in the existing research. On the one hand, an extensive body of work has been done on what might be called the cognitive aspects of expertise. By comparing experts with novices in specific knowledge domains, these researchers have made significant discoveries concerning the abstractions with which experts think. A second group of scholars, on the other hand, has been more concerned with the sociological aspects of expertise. By looking at the interaction between experts and the larger society, these scholars have also made significant contributions, this time in understanding how the professionals have used expertise to establish and maintain their status in society.

For the most part, these two groups have not interacted with one another despite their common topic. We might be tempted to account for this lack of interaction on the basis of fundamental differences. In particular, whereas one group seems to want to disseminate expertise further, the other seems to want to see expertise reoriented if not eliminated entirely. In most expert–novice studies, for example, expertise has been valorized as a cognitive achievement to be investigated. In most sociological investigations, by contrast, expertise has been critiqued as the source of many of the major ills in Western society.

Although it is possible to polarize the literature on expertise in this way, this is not the approach I take in this book. Instead, I suggest that underlying these apparently divergent goals is the potential for a powerful synthesis that can lead us to a far more comprehensive, and thus far more empowering, understanding of expertise. In particular, I suggest ways in which these two seemingly opposing positions need to consider what the other has to offer in order to understand expertise. That is, in the final analysis, I argue that a cognitive account of expertise can make no sense without an understanding of the social dynamics underlying experts' relations with each other and with the larger society. And a social critique rings hollow without a description of the cognitive activities and representations that together constitute expert and novice practice.

The payoff for this synthesis is particularly important for an aspect of expertise that, by and large, has been ignored in research and scholarship on this topic: the transmission of expertise in the academy. Traditional cognitive work has assumed that the transmission of expert knowledge, once properly characterized, is unproblematic. Traditional sociological work, more concerned with the restriction of expertise, has by and large ignored the fact that expert knowledge does indeed get passed on to somebody some time. By overlooking the dynamics by which expertise is or is not transmitted from one generation to another, I believe that both positions remain in the dark about the focal process by which expertise constitutes and reconstitutes itself anew for each generation.

And by and large, in this society and in this time, this process of transmission happens in the academy and happens in interactions over text. In other words, the patterns of literacy practices we have begun to discern in the course of the last two chapters are not just the outcome of expertise but are indeed its very lifeblood. By looking at the literacy practices of the academy within a broad framework provided by synthesizing cognitive and sociological perspectives on expertise, then, we will have not just a better understanding of academic literacy, but a better understanding of the nature of expertise itself. Such, anyway, is the conviction that has motivated the work to be reported in this book. In this chapter, then, we take the next step in this argument by examining the evidence researchers have accumulated concerning the nature of expertise as cognitive abstraction.

THE LEGACY OF GENERAL PROBLEM SOLVING

The cognitive aspects of expertise have been most heavily investigated by cognitive scientists interested originally in problem-solving skills. This early approach is well represented by the work of Newell and Simon which began in the late 1950s in a collaboration with Shaw on the General Problem Solver and culminated in 1972 with the publication of *Human Problem Solving* (Newell & Simon, 1972). As Gardner (1985) pointed out in his history of cognitive science, Newell, Simon, and Shaw originally believed that expertise in a domain was basically a matter of powerful general thinking processes coupled with domain-specific knowledge. That is, they believed it was possible to account for sophisticated thinking in specialized domains simply as the transposition of general problem-solving strategies from one knowledge domain to another. Their efforts, however, eventually led them to conclude that expertise was more highly dependent on domain specific knowledge than on the domain general strategies they had originally been hoping to identify.

Newell and Simon (1972) defined problem-solving behavior as the effort to bridge the gap between a current state of affairs (the problem) and the desired state of affairs (the goal). According to the theory they developed and embodied in a series of computer programs known collectively as the General Problem Solver (GPS), humans solve these problems symbolically, representing what they know about the task—the task environment—as a set of symbolic objects. And each object has associated with it a set of possible operations. This set of symbolic objects along with the possible operations formed what Newell and Simon eventually called a "problem space" (see also Newell, 1980).

When a person solves a problem, according to Newell and Simon (1972), they engage in a "search" of a problem space, attempting to find a path between the initial problem representation and the desired goal state. Each point in a problem space, then, can be envisioned as a state of symbolic knowledge. A person moves from point to point in this space by selecting and applying operations appropriate to the current knowledge state. For instance, the path a person might take through a problem space for making a cake is shown in Fig. 3.1.

Newell and Simon (1972) originally developed the GPS to model human problem-solving as a set of general problem solving heuristics. By the time they finished *Human Problem Solving*, however, they had essentially abandoned this generalist position. In fact, after studying three distinct areas of human problem solving, they concluded that very few features of human problem solving were invariant across problem domains. These features—the structure of memory,

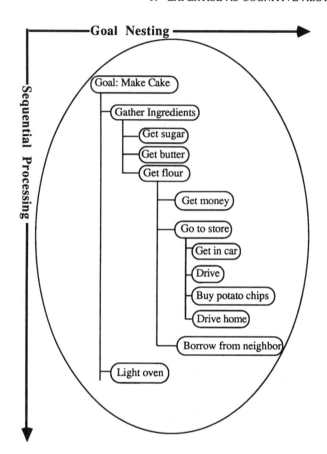

FIG. 3.1.   A possible path through the problem space for making a cake.

serial processing, and goal orientation—were sufficient, they believed, to determine that humans will represent any problem in a problem space and will solve that problem by applying operations to move across this space serially from problem to solution. But, they concluded, the actual structure of this problem space was not determined by the nature of human cognition and instead could vary from domain to domain.

In terms of Fig. 3.1, we can understand Newell and Simon's (1972) conclusions as suggesting that even the admittedly simple activity of making a cake shares certain features with other human problem-solving activities. First, making a cake can be represented as a set of states organized serially over time, that is as a series of states that occur one after the other going down the vertical axis in Fig. 3.1. Second, making a cake can be represented as well as a set of states organized hierarchically by goals, that is as a set of tasks and subtasks that nest within one another along the horizontal axis in Fig. 3.1. Finally, making a cake can be represented as constrained by the limitations of human memory in such things as how many ingredients a person can remember at one time, how a person uses external memory aids like cookbooks and shopping lists, and how a person accesses long-term memory for ideas such as good birthday cakes to make. In Fig. 3.1, for example, a memory failure seems to have resulted in the cook's decision to buy potato chips at the store rather than the flour needed for the cake. This memory failure led, in turn, to a subsequent decision to borrow the flour from a neighbor.

According to Newell and Simon (1972), then, a full accounting of the relationships among the actions in Fig. 3.1 cannot be made without these three fundamentals: serial processing, goal nesting, and memory limitations. Together, these commonalties allow any problem-solving activity to be represented as a path through a problem space. Despite these similarities, however, Newell and Simon ultimately concluded that problem-solving activities had less in common with one another than they had originally believed. In particular, different problem-solving activities appeared to employ distinct symbolic objects and distinct operations on those objects. And distinct problem-solving activities would show distinct patterns of organization. Baking a cake, for instance, often involves manipulating such objects as cake batter and oven temperature in a pattern strongly organized by the linear structure of a cookbook recipe. Joint problem solving to build a bridge, by contrast, often involves manipulating an entirely different set of symbolic objects in a pattern that is more likely to be heavily influenced by the spatial representation of a blueprint.

In addition, Newell and Simon (1972) discovered that even the same problem-solving activity could be represented in radically different problem spaces by different people and even by the same person at different times. Thus, one person could represent the problem of getting a birthday cake as a matter of purchasing one and therefore investigate ways to carry out operations associated with making a purchase—getting money, securing transportation, and so on. Another person, however, could represent the problem as a matter of making a cake and therefore look into an entirely different set of operations— gathering ingredients, turning on the stove, and so forth. And even the same person could change problem spaces as the result of adversity, insight, or even memory failure. Once the flour had been forgotten, for example, the cook in Fig. 3.1 might abandon the plan of making a cake and instead begin to work on a plan to buy one at a bakery.

PROBLEM SOLVING WITH PHYSICS WORD PROBLEMS

In coming to their conclusions about the extreme variety in the symbolic representations underlying human problem-solving activity, Newell and Simon (1972) were joining an emerging consensus in artificial intelligence about the importance of knowledge rather than process in defining expertise (Gardner,

1985; see also Glaser, 1984). Originally, computer scientists had come to this conclusion on pragmatic grounds. They simply found that computer programs that employed a rich representation of specialized domain knowledge performed better than those that employed general-purpose heuristics such as Newell and Simon had formulated. Later, as researchers began investigating the kinds of knowledge used in various complex or "knowledge-rich" domains, more and more evidence began to accumulate about the extreme variety of symbolic representations that people could use to solve problems in these domains.

Nevertheless, it also appeared that experts as a group might be operating with representations that differed in some characteristic ways from those used by novices without the expertise. One domain in which these differences have been most clearly documented is physics word problems. In a series of studies initiated in the early 1980s, researchers found that, on the one hand, undergraduates in physics solved word problems from standard textbooks with concepts fairly close to everyday understandings. Experts, on the other hand, perceived and manipulated more abstract discipline-specific objects. These researchers characterized the representations these novices used as "naive" or "literal" representations whereas those of the advanced graduate students and professors were described as "physical"—using concepts from physics (Chi, Feltovich & Glaser, 1981; Clement, 1983; Larkin, 1981, 1983; Larkin, McDermott, Simon & Simon, 1980; McCloskey, 1983; Wiser & Carey, 1983).

We can get a sense of the differences between these representations by looking at a word problem Larkin (1983) used with University of California, Berkeley, undergraduates who were 8 weeks into their first university-level physics course. Larkin had also asked professors and advanced graduate students in the Department of Physics to solve the same word problem given in Fig. 3.2.

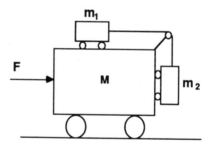

What constant horizontal force F must be applied to the large cart in Fig. 5.3 (of mass M) so that the smaller carts (masses m_1 and m_2) do not move relative to the large cart? Neglect friction.

FIG. 3.2. A physics word problem used by Larkin (1983, pp. 80–81). Reprinted by permission.

The following is an excerpt from a protocol characterized by Larkin (1983) as arising from a typical naive representation in physics: "Well, I'm right now trying to reason why it isn't going to move. I mean I can see, if you accelerated it at a certain speed, the wind would push on m_1 so m_2 wouldn't fall" (p. 81). This pattern of thinking, according to Larkin, exhibited three characteristics associated with naive representations. First, the novice mentions objects that are "familiar" entities fairly close to everyday experience. For example, m_1, though not identified beyond being an "it," is still clearly something that could "fall" and "move." Second, the novice assumes the attributes of these objects are the results of diffuse contextual factors. Thus, if m_2 does not fall, it must be because of forces beyond those specified in the problem, in this case, the force of the wind. Finally, the novice constructs inferences by simulating changes over time. Thus, this novice first imagines accelerating M; this acceleration then causes wind; this wind then keeps the cart from falling.

The representation used by the expert in physics was quite different: "Well, with a uniformly accelerating reference frame, right? So that there is a pseudo-force on m_1 to the left. That is just equivalent—Just necessary to balance out the weight of m_2" (Larkin, 1983, p. 81). Here, an abstract "physical" representation is being used. First, the expert mentions objects—reference frames and pseudoforces—taken directly from disciplinary knowledge. Second, the expert considers attributes localized to the objects themselves rather than diffusely distributed in the environment. Forces, for example, are in the masses rather than the result of environmental forces like wind. And finally, the expert makes inferences using a spatial rather than temporal framework. The forces, for example, can be represented using spatial vectors at a specific point in time without considering how the carts got there or what might happen to them 3 minutes later.

In general, research on expertise in knowledge-rich domains suggests that the use of either expert or novice representations affects every phase of the problem-solving process, not just the final outcome. In a set of studies by Chi et al. (1981), for example, experts appeared to categorize physics problems very rapidly on the basis of their perceptions of abstract features. They then took considerably longer to construct a full representation of the problem based on these initial perceptions. Finally, they solved the problem quickly once these full representation had been constructed. Novices, on the other hand, were quick to represent a problem based on literal features but then took longer in the problem solution phase. Overall, then, experts' representations appeared to contain not simply information about the features of the physical entities but also information concerning the appropriate operations to apply to those entities to reach a solution quickly (see also Lesgold et. al., 1988).

The novices' representations, by contrast, provided them with no clues about appropriate solution methods. Students asked to solve words problems instead often resorted to a general problem-solving strategy, a means–ends analysis

(Newell & Simon, 1972), to work backward from known attributes to the desired solution. Knowing, for example, that a word problem asked for a solution in terms of acceleration, students began by searching a just-read chapter to find an algebraic formula containing acceleration as a term. Next, the students employed means–ends analysis to substitute values from the rest of the word problem for the other terms in the formula. Finally, the equation was solved to produce a value for the original unknown term. The overall result of this process was that students might success-fully solve a word problem without employing the kinds of abstract objects about which experts would be thinking in the same circumstances (see also Larkin et al., 1980).

Larkin and others (Larkin, 1981; Larkin et al., 1980; see also Anderson, 1983) suggested that actual practice in solving word problems, rather than explicit information given in standard textbooks or lectures, may be the basis upon which novices eventually develop the abstract representations characteristic of expertise. Larkin (1981) suggested, for example, that solving thousands of word problems enables students to directly and unconsciously index solution methods by features of word problems in the same way that experts do. Once this "proceduralization" is accomplished, students are able to forego working backward with means–ends analysis and instead work forward "intuitively" from problem to solution in the same confident manner that experts do.

PROBLEM SOLVING IN MORE ILL-DEFINED DOMAINS

The contrast between experts and novices in this one admittedly limited domain of solving physics word problems suggests two possible features that might charac-terize expertise more generally. The first is a representational difference: The development of expertise in physics word problems seems to involve a shift from a representation fairly close to the everyday literal perceptions of laypersons toward a more abstract representation of disciplinary specialists (Bundy & Byrd, 1983; Clement, 1983; deKleer, 1983; diSessa, 1983; Forbus, 1983; Gentner & Gentner, 1983; Greeno, 1983; McCloskey, 1983; Williams, Hollan, & Stevens, 1983; Wiser & Carey, 1983; Young, 1983; see also review by Glaser, 1984). The second is a procedural difference: The development of expertise in solving physics word problems also seems to involve the exchange of laborious domain-general strate-gies like means–ends analysis for more intuitive domain-specific procedures. In physics word problems, that is, becoming an expert seems to mean not only exchanging one set of symbolic objects and operations for another. It also requires that the actual relations between objects and operations be restructured so that the content of the representation (its objects) becomes interknit with its processes (or operations) through a process of proceduralization. For novices in comparable situations, the choice of content and process remain distinct.

When cognitive researchers began to study the more ill-defined problems we might normally associate with expertise, they found evidence for the first of these differences, the exchange of literal for abstract representations. But the evidence for proceduralization was less clear-cut. In fact, the problem-solving process in ill-defined domains appeared to be complicated by what might be best described as their rhetorical nature. A closer look at a handful of these studies illustrates this difference.

Physics word problems differ from the problems faced by real-world experts in one obvious way. Most experts are asked to deal with situations that do not have answers in the back of the book. That is, most domains of expertise involve some component of judgment as to what counts as a satisfactory outcome. As a result, those equally expert in a given area are likely to disagree about what constitutes an appropriate solution. Simon (1973) called these kinds of problems "ill-defined" to distinguish them from the "well-defined" problems with which he and Newell had originally worked.

One study that has been conducted on ill-defined problems was completed by Voss and his colleagues at the Learning Research and Development Center in Pittsburgh in 1983 (Voss, Greene, Post, & Penner, 1983). These researchers chose to look at complex problem solving in the social sciences, certainly a domain in which little agreement exists concerning what constitutes an appropriate solution. In particular, participants in these studies were asked to take the perspective of the USSR Ministry of Agriculture and develop a plan to deal with poor agricultural productivity in the Soviet Union, a continuing, complex, and ill-defined problem.

One set of participants represented the usual range of expertise within a single specialization: 10 novices were enrolled in an introductory course on Soviet domestic policy. Three intermediate experts were completing their first or second year of graduate work in political science with a special interest in the Soviet Union. Five fully expert faculty taught at the University of Pittsburgh with a specialization in the Soviet Union. And one PhD student was finishing his dissertation in the same specialization before taking a position at Ohio State University.

In addition to this usual range of expertise, a second set of participants was also selected to represent a range of specializations: Four advanced graduate students were studying Latin and/or South America. Three social science faculty were specialists in Latin America or American Government and Policy. Four faculty were from a field, chemistry, outside of the social sciences. Finally, one scholar was from Eastern Europe, and one nonacademic expert was a foreign service officer who had served in South America. All of these participants were asked to think aloud as they worked on the Soviet agricultural problem and the researchers analyzed the resulting protocols.

The results of this analysis supported the general contention that expertise in an area involves a switch to more abstract representations. The novices in the introductory course on Soviet domestic policy, for instance, tended to develop very concrete solutions to the Soviet agricultural problem, thinking in terms of such things as "tractors." The intermediate experts, those completing 1 or 2 years of graduate work, proposed sets of slightly more abstract solutions such as "better machinery," "better transportation," and "more money for agricultural development." Finally the experts in or about to assume faculty positions offered single abstract solutions such as "infrastructure development." Comparing across specializations, the solutions proposed by experts in related social science fields shared some of the Soviet experts' abstractness, but the solutions proposed by chemists more closely resembled the concrete proposals made by novices. Although the results of this study thus provided further evidence of the abstract nature of expert knowledge, they did not suggest that having access to these abstractions automatically provided experts with an appropriate way to solve the problem. In particular, the Soviet experts in this study did not seem to have developed the kind of efficient forward-search strategies characteristic of their physics counterparts. Instead, they used what Voss et al. (1983) called chains of reasoning to explore the implications of possible solutions before they actually developed the highly integrated and abstract solution with which they finally concluded. In other words, their expertise seemed to extend rather than reduce the amount of processing required to link problem with solution.

Studies of problem solving in other ill-defined domains also showed experts using similar extended chains of reasoning to link abstract problem representations to appropriate solutions. Reasoning, for example, was important to expertise in the ill-defined domain of medical diagnoses as modeled by Clancey (1988). Clancey had begun work with a program for medical diagnosis, MYCIN, which did not include any information about its reasoning procedures. Instead, specific features of medical problems were indexed to specific diagnoses in the kind of highly proceduralized knowledge structure that Larkin and others had attributed to physics experts. Clancey found, however, that this structure was unsatisfactory for the two expert activities he had in mind: He wanted an expert system that could consult with doctors, and he wanted a system that could train medical students. For either of these purposes, Clancey claimed, a distinct representation of diagnostic reasoning procedures was crucial: Without them, doctors would not believe the "expert" consultant. Without them, students would not learn their diagnostic skills.

Research in another scientific domain also suggested the importance of extended reasoning for expertise in ill-defined domains. In a series of studies, Lesgold et al. (1988) compared the diagnostic skills of radiologists at three levels of expertise: first- and second-year residents in radiology, third- and fourth-year residents, and radiologists with 10 or more years of experience who were recognized as outstanding practitioners by their colleagues. In line with the other research we have been examining, they found that the experts' representations of the X-ray films were more abstract than those of the novices. In addition, the experts appeared to engage in more elaborate reasoning to develop links between these abstract representations and diagnoses of the patients' conditions. In their protocols, for example, the experts' chains of reasoning linking findings concerning patients' anatomies with a possible diagnoses were both longer and more frequent than those of the novices.

Another feature that also seems to characterize expertise in ill-defined domains is the ability to adapt domain abstractions to specific case data. In the radiology study just described, for example, the expert radiologists built specific abstract models of each patient's anatomy that took into account context-specific features of the patient and radiological setting. The residents, by contrast, tended to match the features of X-ray films to general models of patient anatomy without considering case-specific data. For example, when shown an X-ray in which the shadow cast by the heart was slightly larger than normal, the residents tended to diagnose the heart as enlarged. The experts, on the other hand, considered contextual conditions that may have affected the film: the position of the patient's chin, the rotation of the chest, and the effect of the patient's prior condition (Lesgold et al., 1988). These case-specific considerations eventually led the experts to adapt their general models of patient anatomy to the specific case and thereby produce an entirely different and more accurate diagnosis.

The study of expertise in social sciences already discussed (Voss et al., 1983) can also be interpreted as showing evidence for experts' attention to case-specific data. One reason that Soviet experts' reasoning path was more elaborate than those of novices, for example, seems to have been their knowledge of and attention to features specific to the situation in the Soviet Union. The experts, in particular, elaborated upon such recommendations as "develop the infrastructure" to consider features of the Soviet system such as ideology, bureaucracy, and even peasants' preference for farming their private plots of land. The experts in the related social sciences specialization of Latin and South America also seemed to rely on case specific data although they did so by constructing analogies to the features of the countries with which they were familiar. Neither the novices nor the chemists used comparable case-specific information.

Another study that suggests the importance of case-specific adaptations involved observations of decision-making in the Australian criminal courts (Lawrence, 1988). In her studies, Lawrence found that two experienced magistrates looked for specific features of each legal case in order to deal with the defendants as individuals. Correspondingly, their sentences were case-specific and aimed at preventing the defendants from committing the same crime again. The one novice in this study did not seem to make these kinds of adaptations to the specific cases. An aspiring magistrate who had completed his legal training and was working as a clerk and chamber magistrate in the same city court, the novice examined the cases for features that would place them within abstract categories just as the experienced magistrates had. But then, rather than adapting his abstractions to deal with the individual defendants, he seemed more concerned with developing sentences that would be in line with the general sentencing precedents of the courts.

The final evidence for the importance of case-specific data comes from two studies by Johnson (1988), one of physicians' skill at ranking medical students for residencies at teaching hospitals, the other of security analysts' skill at predicting changes in security prices. In both situations, Johnson found that the experts were not very good at attending to what Kahneman and Tversky (1973) called base-rate data: data concerning how factors covary over a large number of instances. But the experts were very good at attending to case specific data such as the nature of medical education at specific schools or particular incidents in the companies that issued the securities. In fact, although experts' predictions were not, in general, very good, those instances where they excelled appeared to be exactly the places where they made use of case-specific information.

COGNITIVE ASPECTS OF EXPERTISE

Solving a physics word problem or thinking aloud for an hour about Soviet agricultural problems is a far cry from the complex practices engaged in by academic professionals such as the scientists we described in chapter 1. Yet this review of cognitive investigations into expertise does suggest at least three characteristics that merit further consideration in our explorations of expertise in the academy.

To begin with, the greater abstraction of experts' representations is a consistent finding of studies of expertise across a wide range of both well- and ill-defined domains. As we have seen, experts in physics think about "force" and "mass" whereas novices think about "carts" and "springs." Experts in the social sciences think about "infrastructure development" whereas novices think about "tractors." Experts in radiology think about "patient anatomy" whereas novices look at "shadows" on X-ray films. The presence of abstractions in these domains speaks directly to and fleshes out experts' claim to an arcane knowledge that goes beyond everyday understanding. For experts appear not only to know a great deal more in their area of specializations, but they also appear to represent the world—or the part of it that lies within their expertise—in a way more abstract and less literal than laypersons without their expertise.

A second characteristic of expertise, at least in ill-defined domains where problems have no agreed-upon solutions, is use of elaborate reasoning procedures to link these abstract representations with appropriate solutions. We have noted the presence of these elaborate reasoning strategies in ill-defined domains such as the social sciences, medical diagnoses, and radiology. What these areas seem to have in common is a requirement that the link between features of the problem and the proposed solution be made explicit and supported by reasons.

According to Voss et al. (1983), this reasoning is important in the social sciences because it compensates for the lack of agreement over what would constitute an appropriate solution. That is, social science experts may embed complex reasoning structures within standard problem-solving activities because they anticipate that whatever solution they propose will not simply be accepted without argument. But Voss and his colleagues also made the point that this lack of common agreement is more the norm than the exception in the problems with which experts routinely deal. Even in physics, for example, real experts do not spend their days solving word problems whose answers are available in the back of the book. Instead they engage in research in which honest disagreements over the nature of phenomena and appropriate methodology are the rule rather than the exception (see, e.g., Galison, 1987). Under these conditions, it may be that even physicists engage in the extended reasoning that seems to distinguish experts in the social sciences and medicine.

Fundamentally, this need to construct reasoned arguments appears to be related to the need for experts to convince others—often nonexperts—to accept and act upon their expert judgments. Social scientists, as Voss and his colleagues (1983) acknowledged, do not have the power to carry out their proposed solutions; they must construct arguments to persuade others in the required joint activity. Diagnostic consultants, as Clancey (1988) noted, cannot simply expect doctors and medical students to accept their diagnoses without question; they must offer reasons that link symptoms with those diagnoses. And, although Lesgold and his colleagues (1988) did not discuss the argumentative burden in radiology, it is likely that radiologists cannot expect to have their diagnoses accepted by the doctors and patients with whom they consult unless they can offer good reasons in their support.

A third feature that may characterize expertise in ill-defined domains generally involves case-specific adaptation. In a range of domains—social science, radiology, law, medical admissions, and securities forecasting—we have seen that experts attended to case-specific considerations that novices, even those more advanced, ignored. That is, in these domains, experts did not simply map their abstract representations directly onto the evidence at hand but instead adapted them to construct specific representations—of a specific country (Voss et al., 1983), a specific patient (Lesgold et al., 1988), a specific defendant (Lawrence, 1988), a specific medical school applicant (Johnson, 1988), or a specific company (Johnson, 1988).

This third feature may be a rather late development in the acquisition of expertise. As we have seen in radiology, for example, third- and fourth-year residents, though working with the same abstractions as the 10-year veterans, appear to have overgeneralized at the expense of case-specific features. As a result, they force fit their perceptions to the generalized abstractions and, in some cases noted by Voss and his colleagues (1983), actually did worse than the first- and second-year residents who were working without abstractions.

The same story may have been true in the criminal courts of Australia studied by Lawrence (1988). There the experienced magistrates adapted judicial precedents to the circumstances of the individual defendants whereas the trained but less experienced chamber magistrate produced sentences in line with the general sentencing patterns of the courts. Although many factors may have led to these apparently disparate judicial philosophies, it also seems possible that the aspiring magistrate had not yet developed the ability to construct case-specific representations in addition to the generalized abstractions with which he apparently worked.

In suggesting that elaborate reasoning and case-specific adaptations are important features of problem solving in ill-defined domains, cognitive studies may be pointing to—although not naming—aspects of expertise that are distinctively rhetorical. To begin with, the suggestion that expertise in ill-defined domains requires the use of specific reasoning strategies aimed at the construction of arguments in support of appropriate solutions echoes the basic point made by the new rhetoricians and discussed in chapter 1. As you may recall, these new rhetoricians had suggested that expert practitioners in a domain employed field-specific reasoning in support of assertions about what to do and what to believe (Perelman & Olbrechts-Tyteca, 1958/1969; Toulmin, 1958). And, as we have seen in the case of the sciences, such arguments also appear to be necessary in the academic professions as a way of codifying the context of interpretation—creating plausible narratives that readers and authors can jointly inhabit and from which they can move together into shared futures. Thus it seems possible that the elaborate reasoning structure noticed by cognitive researchers in ill-defined domains may be evidence of the same kind of rhetorical effort to control the context of interpretation.

In addition, the ability of experts in ill-defined domains to make case-specific adaptations also has a rhetorical flavor. When the experts in these studies adapted their abstract frameworks to make judgments in specific cases, they allowed aspects of the context in which they were working to shape their judgment. As we have already seen in chapter 1, scientists also used contextual features of the laboratory context to produce their knowledge claims. Thus, in both cases, an attempt was being made to speak to features of the context of knowledge production. Such contextualization of abstract knowledge has been proclaimed by new rhetoricians, especially Perelman (1980; Perelman & Olbrechts-Tyteca, 1958/1969), as characteristic of any successful human endeavor.

In these cognitive studies of expertise, then, we have further evidence that the new rhetoricians were right: Expert knowledge, perhaps precisely because it is arcane, appears to be highly rhetorical. Because experts' knowledge is abstracted from everyday understandings, experts must make an effort to mediate between their disciplinary representations and two specific contexts in which they work: the context of knowledge production, the specific cases about which knowledge claims are to be made, and the context of interpretation, the specific audiences to whom such knowledge claims must be made meaningful and useful.

4

EXPERTISE AS PROFESSIONALIZED KNOWLEDGE

Logically, the claim to expert knowledge—an arcane knowledge that goes beyond everyday understanding—might be made by anyone who had developed an abstract representation of a particular domain. With just cognitive criteria in mind, for example, we could claim to be an expert in typing as easily as in law or physics (Rumelhart & Norman, 1982). We might even make the case that energetic devotees of romance novels should be considered experts in their chosen field because of their highly developed critical sense (Radway, 1984). Perhaps even the solitary enthusiast who collects all manner of opossums should be called an expert when his knowledge of North America's only marsupial surpasses ordinary understanding.

The typist, the romance reader, and the opossum enthusiast do not, however, ordinarily merit the appellation of expert—and for reasons that have little to do with cognitive abstraction. The typist, for example, is often excluded on grounds that the skill is a manual achievement too widely available to be distinctive. Romance reading—certainly not a manual skill—is excluded on the grounds that it is a leisure-time activity of little social value. And the opossum collector appears to be ruled out not only in terms of social value, but also because it is simply too uncommon.

Such commonplace reasoning, though not airtight or even consistent, signals the widespread identification of the cognitive achievement of expertise with the more sociological phenomenon of the professions. In fact, in industrial—and postindustrial—economies, it has become almost impossible to understand expertise independently of the unique social position garnered by the modern professions. To develop a comprehensive framework for understanding the nature of expertise, then, we must move in this chapter to consider how the nature of expertise has been shaped by the professions.

THE RISE OF THE MODERN PROFESSIONS

The modern professions occupy what Freidson (1984) has characterized as the upper tier of the primary labor market. Unlike blue-collar workers or even lower tier white-collar workers, members of these occupations have relatively stable work careers that they enter after acquiring the appropriate credentials (Collins, 1979; Freidson, 1984; Larson, 1977). Once on the job, they are often left unsupervised or, if supervised, are under the watch of a member of the same profession (Freidson, 1986). To secure better work conditions, they may move from job to job (Collins, 1979; Freidson, 1984). Because professional status is an achievement sought by many occupational groups, the line between professional and nonprofessional is a shifting one. In addition to containing the traditional Anglo-Saxon professions of divinity, law, and medicine, the modern professions also include such occupations as dentists, engineers, architects, librarians, accountants, nurses, and academics. Less obvious but nonetheless usually included are social workers, technical writers, and public school teachers. With the rise of the professional manager, even members of the business community, traditionally excluded from professional status, are sometimes included.

The modern professions are a relatively recent phenomenon that arose with the reorganization and consolidation of professional activity that took place during the second half of the 19th century. Before this period, the term profession was almost exclusively reserved for the three classic professions inherited from the Anglo-Saxon tradition and largely restricted to members of the upper class: law, medicine, and the clergy (Larson, 1977). By the end of the century, however, a wide array of professional organizations had been founded, giving expression to the aspirations of an expanding middle class and replacing what had been an upper-class solidarity based on social ties with a solidarity based on ties of occupation (Collins, 1979; Freidson, 1984, 1986; Haskell, 1977; Larson, 1977).

During this time, the pace of professionalization was almost frenetic. Of the occupational professions, dentists were the first to organize in 1840. The American Medical Association followed suit in 1847. Civil engineers tried to organize in 1852 and later succeeded in 1867. Other occupational groups followed in rapid order: pharmacists in 1854, teachers and architects in 1857, veterinarians in 1863, social workers in 1874, librarians in 1876, lawyers in 1878, accountants in 1887, nurses in 1896, and opticians in 1897 (Larson, 1977).

The academic professions were also organized during roughly this same period. The Association of American Geologists, founded in 1840, blossomed into the American Association for the Advancement of Science in 1847 (Haskell, 1977).

Chemists organized the American Chemical Society in 1876; mathematicians founded the American Mathematical Society in 1894; physicists started the American Physical Society in 1899 (Kevles, 1979). In the social sciences, the American Social Science Association was founded in 1865 and subsequently gave rise to the American Historical Association in 1884 and the American Economic Association in 1885 (Haskell, 1977). In the humanities, the American Philological Association was founded early in 1869, the Modern Language Association in 1883, and the American Philosophical Association relatively late in 1901 (Veysey, 1979).

This spectacular increase in professional activity entailed costs to society that the United States was able to afford for the first time only after the Civil War. As a result of industrialization, a surplus national wealth was now available that enabled society to direct resources away from the production of material goods and into other activities (Collins, 1979; Larson, 1977; Oleson & Voss, 1979). Such resources could have gone into an increase in the overall amount of leisure available to the public, but, as Collins pointed out, this did not happen at the rate we might have expected.

Instead, increased professional activities served as an important factor in bringing the new market forces of industrialization into equilibrium. On one side of the equation, the professions formed the backbone for an expanded consumer market for the fruits of increased industrial productivity. In most cases, the professionals received greater economic rewards for the exercise of their expertise than the nonprofessionals they had replaced. When midwives, for example, were replaced by obstetricians, the rewards of expertise in the birthing process grew. The expansion of the professions into the middle class, then, created a pool of disposable income that had not existed earlier in the century, thereby providing new markets for increased production (Collins, 1979).

On the other side of the equation, professional activity also reduced the overall level of industrial production. Most obviously, it allowed individuals to remove themselves from the labor force while earning the credentials that attested to their expertise (Collins, 1979). Less obviously, professionalization reduced industrial productivity by increasing the overall level of political work in the society. Political work, according to sociologist Collins, is work that controls the conditions of production rather than resulting in production itself.

The professions used political work in two important ways. First, to ensure the conditions for their own professional autonomy, members of the professions engaged in political work that ran the gamut from national movements for professional certification to the daily intrigue necessary to maintain favorable work conditions (Freidson, 1986). In addition, and perhaps more important, members of the professions engaged in political work by adopting service ideals aimed at ensuring the productivity of others rather than being productive themselves (Larson, 1977). For example, one of the most important professionalization efforts, the civil service reform movement, arose from the desire to centralize and rationalize delivery of the social services necessary to keep the work force healthy and productive (Haskell, 1977). Most other professionalization movements also aimed to provide some kind of support services (Haskell, 1984; Veysey, 1965).

Overall, then, professional activities had the effect of increasing the level of consumer consumption while at the same time reducing the level of industrial production. In economic terms, these were effects that the United States could first afford only under the conditions of an economic expansion. But economic surplus was only half the story. The other half of the story involved the question of why, for the first time, the society needed an expanded professional corps: "What is it about modern society that causes men [sic] to rely increasingly on professional advice? Under what circumstances do men [sic] come to believe that their own judgment, based on common sense and the customary knowledge of the community, is not adequate?" (Haskell, 1977, p. 28). The answer to this question, phrased here by historian Haskell, lay in a significant increase in social complexity. Overall, according to Haskell, we can understand the modern professions as a reaction to the widespread failure of the classic professions to provide satisfactory advice to a society in the grip of increasing complexity. In essence, the local lawyer, doctor, and priest could no longer provide citizens with enough control of their daily existence to maintain traditional authority, and the new professions stepped in to fill the gap.

This new complexity resulted from three related factors. First, communication and transportation networks had been drastically improved in the early decades of the century. Information, for example, that took 10 days to travel 200 miles in the 1790s was able to travel nearly four times as far in the same time period by the 1840s (Haskell, 1977). Second, the population was expanding and becoming increasingly urban. Manhattan, for instance, grew from a city of just over 33,000 in 1790 to the home of more than 800,000 in 1860. Philadelphia grew from 42,000 to well over 500,000 in the same period. Boston grew from 18,000 to nearly 180,000 at the same time (Bender, 1984). Finally, what had been a basically Anglo-Protestant culture was undergoing intense diversification as a result of immigration. The Protestant, English-speaking, and northern European stock that made up 85% of the population in 1790 found itself constituting a bare majority by 1900 (Collins, 1979).

Revulsion at the negative effects of these changes motivated intellectuals during this period to develop arguments supporting professionalization (Haskell, 1984). In the terms of the day, these intellectuals saw most men as doomed to competition in a free market where the only currency was wealth. To check the worst offenses of this unregulated competition, they began what Larson (1977) has called, following Polanyi, an antimarket countermovement. They wanted to create special market shelters for collections of individuals who would carry out their work not simply in response to the dictates of the marketplace, but also in accordance with internally set standards for serving the common good. As labor activist R. H. Tawney saw it in 1921:

> The difference between industry as it exists today and a profession is, then, simple and unmistakable. The essence of the former is that its only criterion is the financial return which it offers to its shareholders. The essence of the latter, is that, though men enter it for the sake of livelihood, the measure of their success is the service which they perform, not the gains which they amass. They may, as in the case of a successful doctor, grow rich; but the meaning of their profession, both for themselves and for the public, is not that they make money but that they make health, or safety, or knowledge, or good government or good law (R. H. Tawney, *The Acquisitive Society*, quoted by Haskell, 1984, pp. 189–190).

What men like Tawney in England, Durkheim in France, and Peirce in the United States saw as the guarantor of professionals' service for social good, according to Haskell (1984), was their intense collegiality. Durkheim, for one, appears to have believed that moral behavior naturally arose in the kinds of small stable social environments that professions provide. Peirce, as Haskell pointed out, was less utopian and probably more honest about the mechanisms for consensus: He expected true knowledge to win out in an intense competition of ideas motivated by the desire for glory and prestige. But, in any case, these and other thinkers were in agreement that only a "community of the competent," sheltered from the brutality of the market, could provide an antidote to the excesses that had arisen with industrialization (Haskell, 1977, 1984; see also Larson, 1977).

Many professionalization movements followed through on these theoreticians' commitments to relieving the misery caused by industrialization. The public health movement, for example, united lawyers, engineers, architects, public figures and physicians in the struggle to improve sanitation in the cities (Larson, 1977). The American Social Science Association grew out of the attempts of state charity boards to coordinate social services related to health, penology, mental disease, and poverty (Haskell, 1977).

The modern professions did not automatically win the right to serve society, however. The typical Jacksonian democrat of this era, holding a strong belief in laissez-faire capitalism, was in little mood to grant the professions' requests for the special protections they felt they needed to carry out their work: "[T]he professions were confronted in the 1830's with what seemed to be a howling mob bent upon the destruction of every stronghold of aristocratic privilege. In state after state popular legislatures pulled down the barriers to professional practice, disestablished the professions, and let it be known in no uncertain terms that the boundary between authentic wisdom and charlatanism had evaporated" (Haskell, 1977, p. 80). In this climate, the newly emerging middle-class professions could no longer count on the mechanisms that had secured the older, more upper-class professionals their livelihood. Instead, they needed to develop strong arguments to secure broad-based public confidence (Freidson, 1986; Larson, 1977).

THE ACADEMIC GUARANTEE OF EXPERTISE

Cognitive expertise, guaranteed by the academy, was at the heart of the professions' attempt to secure this public confidence. In the traditional view, it was this expertise that was assumed to enable professionals to deliver a service beyond what could be achieved either by the layperson acting on her own or by the charlatan purporting to act on her behalf. "Whatever else they are," Freidson concluded in his 1984 survey of existing definitions of the professions, "professionals are experts" (p. 14; see also Collins, 1979; Freidson, 1986; Larson, 1977). Upon this cognitive bedrock, all other characteristics of the professions were built.

Expertise, to begin with, was taken to be the driving rationale for professionals' right to autonomy (see especially Freidson, 1984, 1986). Because professionals were assumed to have expert knowledge that others could not understand, they were usually allowed to maintain direct control over their own affairs. For example, they usually controlled entry into professions by controlling professional schools and licensing boards, and they were often granted the sole right to regulate the performance of their members via peer review mechanisms. In the workplace, they were granted unusual freedom in defining the tasks they undertook, the methods they adopted, and the timetable for their accomplishments.

Second, expertise was used to justify the high social status associated with being a member of the professions (Freidson, 1984, 1986). Because expertise was cognitively complex, it was assumed to take a long time to develop. Without high pay and prestige, many feared that individuals would be loath to shoulder the costs of a professional education or delay entry into the work force for the required period. Thus, it was taken to be in society's best interests to guarantee professionals a social status that would induce them to bring their expert knowledge to bear on social problems.

Finally, expertise was seen to necessitate the high normative standards taken to be the hallmark of professional conduct. Because expert knowledge could not be directly evaluated by outsiders, the professions were expected to have developed internal codes of ethics guaranteeing their members' commitment to society's best interests (see especially Larson, 1977). Members of the clergy, for example, were expected to serve the spiritual needs of their parishioners without regard to their social status. Lawyers were expected to serve the public good, even dedicating part of their time to *pro bono* work that brought no financial rewards. Doctors were expected to make medical judgments on the basis of patients' best interests without regard to expected financial returns. Scientists worked for the progress of mankind. Teachers strove for the success of their students.

Overall, then, the professional privileges of autonomy and high social status, constrained by a normative commitment to service, were all built upon a foundation of cognitive expertise. It should not be surprising, then, that the rise of the American university, guarantor of this expertise, almost exactly paralleled the rise of the professions in general. Following an initial decline in the aftermath of the Jacksonian era, academics—like other professionals—emerged by the end of the century as far more numerous and far more middle class than they had been in earlier decades. In fact, midcentury had found colleges in the midst of a 30-year period of stagnation resulting from the same Jacksonian distrust of privilege that had plagued the professions generally (Veysey, 1965). Of the 1,000 colleges founded before the Civil War, for example, over 700 failed (Collins, 1979). By 1870, however, university reformers had turned the tide, and undergraduate enrollments more than quadrupled from 52,000 in 1870 to almost 240,000 in 1900. Graduate enrollment increased more than a hundredfold in the same time period, going from 50 to 6,000 (Oleson & Voss, 1979).

The changing fortunes of the academic professions were closely tied to changes in the credentialing requirements of the professions generally. At the opening of the century, the only professional career that had required a college degree was the clergy. Physicians were usually trained by apprenticeship. Lawyers might attend college, but usually learned their job skills through apprenticeship as well (Hall, 1984). Over the course of a few decades, this pattern was to be altered significantly as universities took on the central task of certifying professional expertise through the awarding of credentials (Freidson, 1986).

Some form of credentialism became pervasive throughout the professions (Freidson, 1986; see also Collins, 1979). In some cases, credentials given by the state granted a profession an exclusive right to practice the designated expertise—physicians, for example. Less commonly, state credentials granted a profession the exclusive right to use a particular title—as the title "psychologist" has been restricted in New York State, for instance (Freidson, 1986). Many more credentials are granted by private associations—the Academy of Certified Social Workers, for example. In every case, however, university course work became the key requirement.

This credentialing system, in turn, both guaranteed academic professionals some lifetime jobs in universities and colleges and mandated course work in their areas of specialization. In an effort to "guarantee the guarantee," universities and their programs set up their own credentialing associations like the North Central Association of Colleges and Universities and the Accreditation Board for Engineering and Technology (Freidson, 1986). To win accreditation, universities were usually required to provide for a significant number of tenure-track careers for holders of PhD's and protect these specialists against direct competition for students by offering, and sometimes requiring, a specified selection of courses. In this way, the need of the professions for the legitimizing force of expertise supported the expansion of the academic professions themselves (Freidson, 1986).

THE PROFESSIONALIZATION OF EXPERTISE

By locating the source of their professional competence in the academy, the professions had enduring effects on our modern understanding of expertise. The separation of knowledge production from knowledge use led to an internal stratification of the professions into academic and practitioner wings (Freidson, 1986). Once this stratification took place, relations between the two groups, far from even or simple, shaped the nature of expertise.

One of the first consequences of this stratification was a definition of expertise as knowledge that was different from and subsequent to liberal studies. Such a definition was the result of a standoff between the advocates of university reform who were moving into an existing collegiate system and the defendants of liberal culture who already lived there. As Lawrence Veysey's (1965) analysis showed, a very vocal group of academics, with close connections to the older and more exclusive collegiate tradition of the classic professions, strongly resisted the academic reformers' move to embrace the more modern commitments to social service and expertise (see also Veysey, 1979). Instead, they hearkened back to the values of liberal culture, arguing for the need for the well-rounded individual and warning against the dangers of specialization. These advocates of liberal culture, rather than staying the course of professionalization, settled instead for controlling a protected enclave in the first 2 years of undergraduate school (Higham, 1979). In this way, they established the gateway to professional expertise as different from and in opposition to the professional goals that most often brought students to the university in the first place.

A second consequence of professional stratification was the transformation of expertise into a formal culture at odds with everyday or indigenous culture. Formal culture, as Collins (1979) defined it, is culture produced by specialized culture-producing organizations. It is distinct from indigenous culture or culture produced through the experience of everyday interaction. Because the professions needed to justify their professional privilege on grounds that would not offend democratic sensibilities, they found the apparent neutrality of formal culture appealing. Expertise appeared to be unaffected by special interests of race, class, or gender, and, indeed, freely available to all who would struggle for it (Larson, 1977). In addition, according to Collins, formal culture also provided the professions with other benefits: "Formal culture is more widely useful than indigenous culture; it can relatively quickly negotiate ties among individuals who otherwise have little in common to exchange. Thus formal culture has been the basis for impersonal bureaucratic organizations, for generating political loyalties to an overarching state, for mobilizing mass occupational groups and large-scale social movements" (p. 61). By being transformed into formal culture, then, expertise became useful to the professions for more than its cognitive benefits. It provided a new kind of impersonal solidarity that could replace the ties of indigenous or home culture.

Nevertheless, the relationship that developed between expertise and indigenous culture was more complex than simple difference. Early leaders of the professionalization movement wanted to use the university to preserve the intellectual authority of the indigenous culture of the upper-class eastern elites into which they had been born (Haskell, 1977). They saw this authority being dangerously eroded by modern developments (Bender, 1984; Haskell, 1977; Higham, 1979). Joseph Henry, early president of the Smithsonian Institute, for instance, believed that: "We are over-run in this country with charlatanism. Our newspapers are filled with puffs of Quackery and every man who can burn phosphorous in oxygen and exhibit a few experiments to a class of young ladies is called a man of science" (Quoted in Haskell, 1977, p. 66). In a similar manner, Charles Eliot Norton wanted to make Harvard a refuge from "the crowd": "The principle of equality is extended into regions where it has no proper validity. Our public life, our literature, our journals, our churches, our amusements, our politics, all exhibit a condescension to the crowd. . . . There is a lack of independence and of leading; a lack of superior excellence in nobler fields of effort and expression" (Quoted in Bender, 1984, p. 88)

Looking to the university, then, these men did not seek to create expertise *ex nihlo*, but instead to rationalize and systematize the indigenous cultural practices they took for granted. Indeed, they wanted to make these practices a more potent force in their struggle against other indigenous cultures whom they feared were gaining power. Civil service reform, for example, was championed by the American Social Science Association in order to remove certain areas of public decision making from the public sphere where they had become subject to ward politics (Haskell, 1977). The American Bar Association movement likewise aimed to restrict the activities of the ethnic lawyers who often protected the political machines of the cities (Collins, 1979). By repackaging Anglo-Protestant elitist culture as neutral expertise, these men hoped to retain their traditional intellectual authority.

For rank-and-file practitioners, however, the formal culture of the university became appealing exactly because it represented a break with their indigenous home culture. They were, by and large, the sons of men who had made their fortunes through business rather than inheritance (Veysey, 1965). Having just gained entry to the professional class, however, they were not eager to lose the legacy of authority to which they believed they—or rather their sons—were newly entitled. For this reason, they supported—and were perhaps even more attached to—a definition of expertise as something distinct from indigenous culture.

The third significant consequence of the stratification of the professions was to define expertise as formally excluding civic action. Originally, leaders of the professionalization movement had anticipated that expertise would remain linked to the civic authority of the eastern elites even after it had moved into the formal culture of the university. In fact, in the vision of early social reformers, formal culture was to be integrated with civic culture. For example, Henry P. Tappan, who later went on to assume the presidency at the University of Michigan, proposed a national university for New York City that would serve as a center for the city's cultural institutions. He proposed, furthermore, that professors be required to give public lectures on popular topics in addition to teaching in their areas of specialization (Bender, 1984).

Even Daniel Coit Gilman, first president at Johns Hopkins, seemed for a while to have believed that academic expertise was compatible with civic action (Haskell, 1977). Although Johns Hopkins is usually taken to be one of the first research-oriented universities (Shils, 1979), for several years Gilman entertained a proposal made by Benjamin Peirce for the merger of the university with the American Social Science Association, a group made up largely of nonacademic social reformers (Haskell, 1977). Eventually, however, Gilman rejected Peirce's proposal, and, according to Haskell, two issues may have been on his mind. On the practical side, Gilman may have feared that the social activism of the American Social Science Association would alienate some of his major contributors. Like other entrepreneurial university presidents of his time, Gilman was heavily dependent on the contributions of industrialists to fund his expanding university. In general, without industrial support, the university system could not have taken its modern shape. In 1899, for example, nearly 70% of the 34 largest gifts to public causes, for a total of $55 million, was given to institutions for higher learning (Oleson & Voss, 1979).

Gilman may have had more theoretical reservations as well. Standing behind Peirce's proposed merger was a belief that academic expertise and civic action were closely linked. Many of the early founders of the American Social Science Association believed that once the facts of social conditions had become known through expert inquiry, the choice of appropriate civic action would be obvious and immediate (Haskell, 1977). Gilman, however, appears to have concluded that such a link was inappropriate. According to Haskell:

> The point of Gilman's distinction between investigation and agitation was not to condemn agitation, but simply to observe its inherently controversial nature and declare it unfit for professionalization. . . . Gilman recognized that abstract inquiry into the essential nature of man and society was sufficiently removed from the fray that it might yield a professional consensus; however, practical agitation was not

so removed. If authority in the field of man and society was to be established at all, the friends of authority would have to settle for half a loaf—they would have to form rigorous communities devoted to investigation and interpretation, leaving agitation to fend for itself. (p. 163)

The commitment to consensus as the mechanism by which the professions could deliver expertise thus led academics to remove civic action from its formal slate of justifiable concerns. This isolation from civic action was made practicable for academics, in part, by the conditions of their work. Especially in the early period, university professors carried out their research in what they considered the "spare" time left over from their teaching duties (Shils, 1979). Thus public issues did not generally affect academic professionals in the same way that they affected their nonacademic counterparts.

Civic action, of course, did not so much disappear from the professional arena as devolve to agents other than the academics. This led to the fourth and final major consequence of the stratification of the professions for expertise: its informal relationship with civic action. Despite the efforts that academics made to keep expertise neutral, practicing professionals did need to make decisions and take action in their daily work. In some cases, as Freidson (1986) has pointed out, practitioners felt they made these decisions without regard to their expertise:

The practical contingencies of day-to-day work so vary from the ideal or hypothetical circumstances assumed or demanded by academics in professional schools that novices are said to suffer reality shock or burnout on entering practice. Those who survive adapt their expectations and actions to the practical exigencies of work by using compromised situational judgements informed but not always dominated by the standards they were taught in school. As survivors they cannot fail to develop a certain skepticism, if not hostility, toward the assertion of cognitive authority by professors and researchers who create standards under considerably more protected circumstances and with more abstract goals than that of coping with daily work. (p. 212)

More often than Freidson's analysis would indicate, however, expertise came to be connected with civic action in a variety of informal ways.

First of all, an informal relationship between expertise and civic action often led academics to concentrate their attention in areas with midrange complexity. In work settings, as Collins (1979) has pointed out, power comes to those who control tasks that are neither so complex as to elude prediction nor so simple as to be absolutely predictable. When, for example, success is seen to be utterly unpredictable, it is not taken to be the outcome of expertise, but rather of talent that occurs by some chance combination of genetics and historical circumstance. When success is seen to be entirely predictable, on the other hand, it is taken to be routinized work better left for nonprofessional workers. For this reason, creative writing, often taken to be an unpredictable talent, has resisted professionalization, whereas theme writing, seen as an utterly routine skill, has been left to adjuncts and graduate students. Once writing was defined as rhetorical skill with somewhat predictable outcomes (Young, 1980), however, arguments for the professionalization of composition teachers could be made (Hairston, 1982).

Furthermore, expertise was often linked informally with civic action as the platform upon which professionals argued for specific positions on civic matters. Sometimes these individuals spoke on their own behalf (Freidson, 1986), but even more often they lent their expertise to employing institutions through a variety of complex arrangements (Larson, 1977). In some situations, the employing institution uses the professional's expertise to justify actions inconsistent with the dictates of professional judgment. Teachers, for example, may know what it takes to educate all of their students, but may be denied the time or the materials to carry out this task (Freidson, 1986). In other cases, institutions appear to allow expert judgment to carry the day, but actually preselect the expert judgment they pay for (Etzioni-Halevy, 1985; Larson, 1984). When expert witnesses are sought in legal cases, for example, lawyers check in advance to make sure the expert will support the client's position. If not, another expert is sought. In each of these cases, the institution is using the professional's expertise as grounds for taking civic action.

THE IMPACT ON AMERICAN SCHOOLING

The shaping of expertise by the stratified interests of the professions might have been a local affair had it not been for the way universities set out to eliminate their rivals as they emerged in the late 19th century. Originally, as Collins (1979) pointed out, neither secondary nor professional schools saw themselves as part of a sequence leading to or from the baccalaureate degree. In fact, secondary schools originally competed with universities and colleges for students and covered much of the same curriculum. Professional schools likewise began as rivals by offering an alternative degree to the standard Bachelor of Arts.

Using their power as accredited and accrediting institutions, leading universities quickly moved to eliminate the rivalry of these two alternative institutions. First, leading universities, through the newly founded American Association of Universities, pushed to make 12 years of schooling the standard admission requirement for students attending member schools (Collins, 1979). Other schools, in an effort to meet accreditation standards, went along. As a result, secondary schools that had originally competed with undergraduate colleges for students now served instead as feeder schools.

At roughly the same time, leading professional schools moved to eliminate their rivals by raising admission standards, requiring first 2 and eventually 4 years of undergraduate work (Collins, 1979, Chapter 6). Rival professional schools who had less stringent requirements began to lose credibility and either changed their requirements or went out of business. In addition, undergraduate schools that granted degrees in less than 4 years saw the value of their degree eroding and made adjustments as well. Overall market forces thus shaped educational institutions into a sequence that, theoretically, could lead students from a universal primary schooling through to professional certification. By the end of the century, then, the components of what had been once a diverse and highly competitive academic system had been yoked together into the seamless sequence we now know as the modern American system of schooling.

By sequencing educational credentials in this way, American schooling assumed two functions with respect to professionalization: First, as we have already noted, the academy took on the task of certifying the cognitive expertise of a limited number of individuals who would eventually make up the core of the modern professions. This task required academic institutions not only to transmit expertise, but also to develop expert knowledge in such a way that it would provide professionals with a market advantage. As we noted in the last section, this interaction shaped the nature of expertise in decisive ways.

Second, the academy took on the task of educating the general public who would not finish the entire credentialing sequence. In many systems, this second task would have been undertaken by a different set of educational institutions. In France, for example, students who will enter the professions branch quite early in their schooling from those who will not, and the content of their education is tailored accordingly (Collins, 1979). In the United States, however, these two sets of students were educated simultaneously. That is, at the same time and in the same classrooms, students who would eventually become experts in the domain content of the curriculum sat side by side with those who would become consumers of that expertise.

By performing these two tasks simultaneously, American education appeared to make expertise universally accessible. The prospect of upward mobility was held out to all students. Each level of educational credentials could serve as the potential next step toward social improvement, and at no point in the system were students categorically denied the right to go on. In addition, the great proliferation of areas of specialization often meant that students who failed to succeed in one area might find a home in another. Social status was thus allocated by a mechanism that put the burden on an individual's motivation and cognitive resources rather than inherited advantage. Career decisions were delayed and seldom considered irreversible (Bowles & Gintis, 1976). As a result, the potential ethnic and class conflicts that might have arisen by any more overt attempt by the professions to monopolize expertise were muted (Collins, 1979). As Higham (1979) noted, "the best strategy for American specialists was to play down vertical relationships, expand horizontally, and thereby erect a great decentralized democracy of specialists. The conflict between a Jacksonian distrust of privileged elites and the advance of specialization was resolved by widening immensely the opportunity to specialize and restricting the opportunity to dominate" (p. 10).

For the professions, the benefits of educational sequencing went beyond simply quieting democratic concerns about their professional privileges. As Larson (1979) pointed out, the modern professions not only had to arrange the conditions for their own market advantage through a credentialing system, they also had to create the market for their professional services. That is, the general public had to be educated concerning those areas of activity that had best be left to experts.

General education was made to accomplish this task. As Bourdieu and Passeron (1977) noted, the education of the general public did not so much have to transmit the formal content of expertise as inculcate a belief in its superiority. That is, the system needed to produce what Bowles and Gintis (1976) called a stratified consciousness by which one side of the market understood and exercised expertise whereas the other side of the market did not understand this same expertise but did respect it. The professions' desire to serve humanity thus developed into a "pastoral power" (Foucault, 1983, p. 215), and educators became what Bauman (1987) characterized as the "gardeners" of the general public. That is, they became responsible for eradicating indigenous or "wild" culture that students brought to school and replacing it with a more cultivated or formal culture (Bauman, 1987).

Market forces thus created expert power—or what Foucault (1980) called disciplinary power—not by the direct oppression of the general public, but by denying legitimacy to their everyday knowledge and putting forth formal knowledge in its place (see also Fisher, 1987; Killingsworth & Steffens, 1989; Lieberman, 1970). Thus, through the sequencing of American schooling, the professions reached out and transformed our entire understanding of the nature of expertise.

5

LITERACY AND THE NATURE OF EXPERTISE

Expertise has one obvious connection with the literacy practices of the academy as we have observed them over the last few chapters: It forms the basis of the striking difference between the practices of the experts, at least as exemplified by the scientific professions, and the practices of novices, as exemplified by students in school. This difference, as we have seen, has been surprising to both researchers and teachers who, for the most part, have expected to find academic literacy practices arrayed along a developmental continuum with professional practices at one end and student practices spread out across the other. The evidence we have encountered so far, however, suggests that these two sets of practices are substantially different in character. In particular, the literacy practices of experts in the academy are organized around the creation and transformation of academic knowledge; the literacy practices of novices, on the other hand, are organized around the getting and displaying of that knowledge.

Despite this difference, these two sets of literacy practices do exhibit similarly puzzling elements of discord. In fact, across both groups in the academy, rationales for reading and writing break apart at unexpected places. Among experts, in particular, discord arises from conflicting writer–reader roles: Scientists, as writers, appear to strive to produce a virtual experience that they, as readers, strive to resist. Indeed, it is only by reserving one language for writing texts about their own work and using another language for reading texts about the work of others that practitioners manage this conflict. Thus it seems to be a cycle of text-based activity that allows experts in the academy to be productive in the face of the discord between the highly rhetorical nature of their literacy practices and their avowed ideal of producing autonomous texts.

In the literacy practices of novices in the academy, by contrast, discord does not appear to arise from a discrepancy between practice and ideal. Indeed, the entire school system seems to be regulated by the ideal of the autonomous text. Discord does arise, however, from a mismatch between the avowed goal of these practices and the actual outcome for students. As we have seen, school reading is a surprisingly poor way to learn knowledge that departs from everyday concepts. And school writing turns out to be a surprisingly poor vehicle for the transformation of ideas. All in all, the literacy practices of the schools, then, appear to be crippled in just those places where education might edge students closer to expertise.

Such puzzling discords only begin to make sense once we turn to examining the literacy practices of the academy within a broader framework of expertise— the task we finally undertake in this chapter. By looking at the literacy practices of the academy within a broad framework provided by synthesizing cognitive and sociological perspectives on expertise, we develop not only a better understanding of academic literacy, but also a better understanding of the nature of expertise itself. In particular, as we see in this chapter, these literacy practices can be best understood not just as the outcome of expertise but indeed as its very lifeblood.

THE DUAL PROBLEM SPACE FRAMEWORK

The need of the professions to establish their legitimacy in the face of early 19th-century American distrust of privilege led them to transform the academy into a seamless credentialing sequence with general education at its start and highly specialized professional training at its completion. Under this organizational structure, the academy undertook two contradictory tasks with respect to expertise. On the one hand, it was charged with the task of producing experts—producing the expert knowledge upon which professionals would act and passing that knowledge on through certified educational programs. On the other hand, it was charged with the task of producing the consumers for expertise. As we have seen, this required inculcating a respect for expertise and delimiting its proper areas of operation—all without actually transmitting the expertise itself.

It is my argument, and the argument of the rest of this book, that the academy dealt with these contradictory tasks by using the technology of literacy to separate expertise into two distinct dimensions of knowledge. As shown in Fig. 5.1, the first of these is the dimension of domain content; the second, the dimension of rhetorical process.

This separation has transformed not only social institutions, but, as I outline later, the shape of expert thinking itself. In particular, I am suggesting that the institutional forces of professionalism have shaped and are shaped by a cultural practice of expertise that plays itself out, cognitively, in the two distinct problem

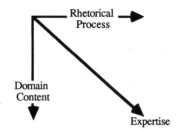

FIG. 5.1. The two dimensions of expertise.

spaces shown in Fig. 5.2: a problem space in which experts explore the domain content of a particular field, and a problem space in which they consider a field's rhetorical dimensions.

For the most part, cognitive science has not seriously addressed the possibility that expertise might involve more than one problem space. The work of Bereiter and Scardamalia represents one notable exception however. In their 1987 monograph, these authors were the first to suggest that writers negotiate between the two different problem spaces of domain content and rhetorical process.

Although Bereiter and Scardamalia (1987) did not provide a full analysis of how these problem spaces might interact, a simple example can be imagined. The content problem space of a third grader trying to write an essay on her favorite topic, for instance, might consist of domain content concepts such as "dog," "collie," and "dalmatian." Within this problem space, the writer might explore her domain content knowledge through such operations as class inclusion ("How many kinds of dogs can I think of?"), use ("What are dogs used for?"), and life cycle ("How long do dogs live?"). The rhetorical problem space, on the other hand, would be shaped by the writer's relationship to the intended audience. Its objects might include potential readers who are examined in such terms as recent experience ("What have my readers heard about recently?") and general beliefs ("How do my readers feel about this?"). According to Bereiter and Scardamalia, successful writers must shift between these two separate problem

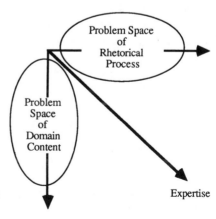

FIG. 5.2. The dual problem spaces of expertise.

spaces, allowing the results of exploration in one space ("We've all just seen
101 Dalmatians.") to guide exploration in the other ("What are dalmatians used
for?") and vice versa ("I know a lot about collies. Why would my readers be
interested in collies?"). By doing so, writers engage in knowledge transformation
rather than simple knowledge telling.

Characterizing expertise as made up of dual problem spaces helps make sense
of the complex pattern of expert problem solving in ill-defined domains we
reviewed in chapter 3. There, as we saw, the most obvious characteristic of the
problem solving of experts studied by cognitive psychologists was the abstractness
of their domain content representations. This abstraction, furthermore, seemed to
emerge early in experts' training. Nearly all of the students in these studies, for
instance, appeared to use some kind of abstraction by early graduate school.

Such abstraction did not appear to constitute the whole of their expertise,
however. Further training and experience were required before these students
would develop the second characteristic of expertise we noted earlier: the capacity
to adapt abstractions to case specific data. Without such adaptation, however,
domain content abstractions seemed crippled. On the basis of the abstract
sentencing precedents of the Australian courts, for instance, the aspiring
magistrate studied by Lawrence (1988) produced sentences that ignored the issue
of how to best prevent specific defendants from committing the same crime
again. Based solely on their abstract models of patient anatomy, the resident
radiologists studied by Lesgold and his colleagues (1988) produced misdiagnoses
that ignored patient history and the radiological setting. With just social scientific
abstractions to go on, the experts in Latin and South America studied by Voss
et al. (1983) developed an analysis of the Soviet agriculture problem that failed
to consider aspects of Soviet culture.

These results suggest that the ability to adapt to case-specific data is distinct
from and subsequent in development to the domain content abstractions on which
they are based. This difference and sequencing can be accounted for, I am
suggesting, by modeling expertise as the interaction of a relatively early developing
problem space of domain content and a later developing problem space of rhetorical
process. In the domain content problem space, experts develop the abstractions that
enable them to go beyond everyday understanding. But it is through the rhetorical
problem space that they develop the reasoning structures that enable them to bring
those abstractions to bear upon the contexts in which they work.

THE DIFFERENTIAL DEVELOPMENT OF DUAL PROBLEM
SPACES IN THE ACADEMY

By describing the achievement of expertise as the interaction of two distinct
problem spaces, we can provide a better account for the basic pattern of development in our schools. As shown in Fig. 5.3, both the domain content problem space

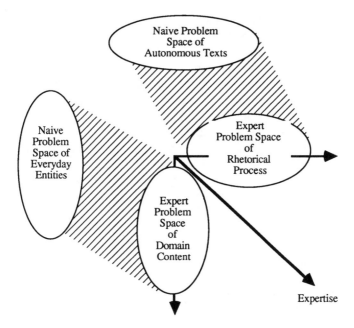

FIG. 5.3.   The relationship between naive and expert representations.

and the rhetorical process problem space are susceptible to either a naive representation fairly close to everyday understanding or a more abstract representation
characteristic of expertise. We have already seen how, for instance, in the problem
space of domain content, expertise reconfigures naive and everyday objects into
more abstract entities with different features and different relationships.

In the second, or rhetorical, problem space of expertise, as the voluminous
research in the first two chapters suggests, we find the same pattern. In writing
from sources, for example, most students use reproductive strategies that stay
close to the content of the source text. In doing so, they operate with a more
everyday understanding of texts as autonomous repositories of knowledge,
completely explicit in their content but utterly opaque in their rhetorical
construction. Experts, by contrast, take these same textual objects and manipulate
them in more abstract ways, attending, for example, to the metadiscourse features
the students ignore and ignoring the virtual read-through experience to which
students attend.

The development of these two problem spaces does not take place in two neat
developmental sequences, as suggested by Fig. 5.1, but rather seems to overlap
in three distinct periods. During the period of general education, roughly
kindergarten through early undergraduate school, students appear to operate with
naive representations in both problem spaces. As the research on physics problem
solving suggests, students by and large approach the domain content of the

curriculum by assimilating information into their everyday understandings or by maintaining distinct representations, one for the formal knowledge of the classroom and one for their everyday life. Participation in the IRF structures of schools teaches children that academic knowledge is different from and superior to the indigenous knowledge they bring from their home cultures. The problem space of formal concepts thus may become more extensive as more and more concepts are added, but it remains basically naive.

During this same period, as suggested in Fig. 5.4, the rhetorical problem space is severely underdeveloped. Students are encouraged to view texts as the totally explicit source of formal knowledge—as autonomous texts. In the first few years of elementary school, some attention is paid to learning the reading procedures by which this knowledge can be read out. But from then on, relatively little attention is paid to text. Writing during this period is comparatively rare, but when it does occur it serves simply to reverse reading procedures: That is, the text to be written is made isomorphic with the structure of the domain content as the writer understands it, using Bereiter and Scardamalia's (1987) knowledge-telling procedures. Under this naive representation, rhetorical process is almost entirely collapsed onto the problem space of domain content. Texts are taken to be equivalent to what they say.

Sometime during the early years of undergraduate school, some students begin to work with more abstract representations in the problem space of domain content as shown in Fig. 5.5. Such development does not appear to be the result of any direct teaching but rather the result of hours of individual effort at hands-on problem solving. That is, students who acquire the abstract representations necessary to do expert work appear to do so tacitly. Their textbooks and classroom lectures seldom acknowledge the existence of these abstract representations or give directions in how to use them (Clement, 1983; Larkin, 1981; McCloskey, 1983). Nevertheless, some students do begin on their own to think about the domain content in these more abstract terms.

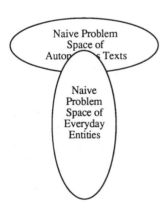

FIG. 5.4. The collapsing of problem spaces in K–14

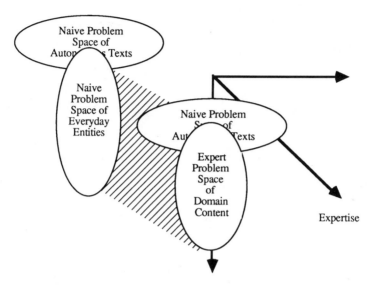

FIG. 5.5. The emergence of the expert representation of domain content in undergraduate school.

During this intermediate stage, the rhetorical problem space remains basically naive however. Textbooks, still the mainstay of the curriculum, are interpreted as containing the domain content upon which students will be tested. Writing, on the rare occasions it is used, serves to duplicate the knowledge structure of these texts. Students know intuitively that to do more would jeopardize the mastery of content knowledge they will be required to demonstrate on tests. It is only the occasional academic researcher, wandering into the school, who is surprised by what they do. Knowledge still has no rhetorical dimension.

Beginning in late undergraduate school for some, graduate school for others, this naive representation of the rhetorical problem space undergoes a major reorganization and abstraction. As shown in Fig. 5.6, the rhetorical dimension of expertise suddenly emerges as something distinct from the domain content. Texts are now seen to have authors, to make claims, to be acts that can be understood only within a temporal and interpersonal framework. Some issues are hot, some issues irrelevant, some issues settled. Some authors are credible; some discredited; some irrelevant. People write texts not simply to say things, but to do things: to persuade, to argue, to excuse.

This emergence of an expert representation of the rhetorical problem space is the final stage in the acquisition of expertise. For it is only when both the domain content and the rhetorical processes of a field are represented in abstract terms that they can, together, engage in the dynamic interplay that produces expertise. Teachers, who once remained remote lecturers on issues long dead to their fields, now come alive as mentors in cutting-edge research. The oral discourse and

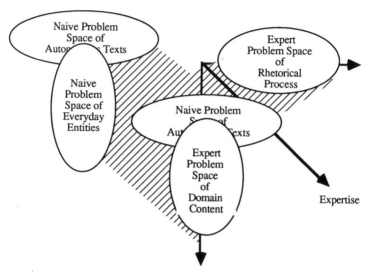

FIG. 5.6. The emergence of the expert representation of rhetorical process in graduate school.

accompanying hands-on activity of knowledge construction start to restructure the basically one-dimensional formal domain content abstractions learned earlier. Rhetorical knowledge and domain content knowledge, as Bereiter and Scardamalia (1987) first suggested, come into dynamic transformative interplay. Expertise, then, is recovered whole, becomes a knowing that linked to a knowing how.

LITERACY AND THE GREAT DIVIDE

The cognitive tradition—the source of the concept of "problem space" used in the previous discussion—can rightly be understood as part of the movement to open up expertise, to make it explicit and more available to those who are not born to it in apprenticeship training. Consistent with this goal, nearly all investigations of cognitive expertise have accounted for expertise as a complex skill that, if better understood, could be made more freely available to more students earlier in their careers. Bereiter and Scardamalia (1987), for example, clearly hoped to encourage students to abandon their simplistic knowledge-telling model of writing and instead adopt a more reflective dual problem space model.

But in order to actually meet the goal of opening up expertise, we cannot afford to remain blind to the sociological dynamics by which cognition has been used to support accounts of school failure. Dual problem spaces, for example, could be understood simply as the way experts handle the complex tasks of expertise. Simon (1973) has noted in connection with ill-defined problems in general, for example, that experts tend to decompose a problem into subproblems each of which can, to some extent, be solved independently. This decomposition, he further suggested, follows the naturally occurring weak boundaries among entities in a system. Thus, a good decomposition is supposed to keep entities with strong bonds together and separate those with relatively weak bonds.

Using this explanation, we might assume that experts operate in the dual problem spaces of domain content and rhetorical process because of naturally occurring bonds and boundaries among concepts. That is, by operating in the problem space of domain content, experts could be simply keeping domain concepts with domain concepts; by operating in the problem space of rhetorical process, they could be simply keeping rhetorical concerns with rhetorical concerns. This interpretation of the dual problem space framework would be a dangerous one, however, for it accepts as "natural" what is actually the outcome of social arrangements and cultural power. In particular, it might suggest that academic expertise is so cognitively complex that we can reasonably expect only some students to master it.

We must avoid this interpretation. Some kind of decomposition may be inevitable given the limitations of human information processing, but no particular decomposition is itself inevitable when the entities involved are cultural objects. Instead, we must consider the ways in which culture can influence not only the deployment of material resources and the development of institutional structures, but also the structure of thinking itself. The development of the dual problem spaces of expertise simply dovetails too well with the institutional requirements of professionalization to be accepted as simply the outcome of processing limitations. Thus, in building a dual problem space framework, we need to ask: Why these bonds? Why these boundaries?

The answer to these questions appears to be that the separation of expertise into the distinct problem spaces of domain content and rhetorical process is an important mechanism by which our society delivers expertise to some but withholds it from others. Expertise, which was restricted in the late 19th-century to the indigenous culture of the upper-class eastern elites, appears to have been taken over by the middle-class professionalization movement and divided into two distinct components: a formally explicit knowledge of domain content that became the mainstay of a universal education aimed at producing laypersons, and the more informal and tacit knowledge of rhetorical process that remained the more or less hidden component of advanced training aimed at producing a new class of professional experts.

As a result, our current educational sequence provides all students with a naive understanding of the more formal component of expertise but withholds an understanding of this tacit rhetorical dimension. In this way, as suggested in Fig. 5.7, a great divide has been created—not a great divide between orality and literacy as literacy scholars originally suggested, but rather a great divide with

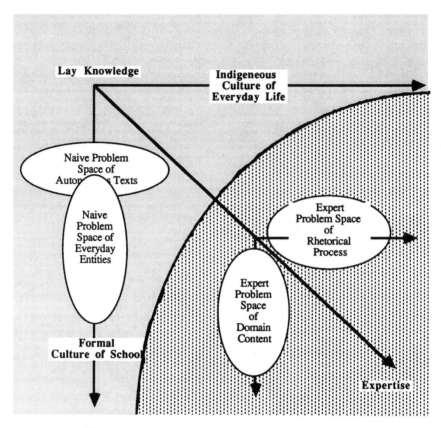

FIG. 5.7.   The great divide between expert and lay knowledge.

experts on one side with a complete if disjoint practice of expertise, and laypersons on the other side facing what seems like a choice between buying into the formal culture of the schools or remaining loyal to their indigenous home cultures.

This great divide has been maintained for the most part through the literacy practices of the academy. Literacy in the early years, as we have seen, is predominantly concerned with building a naive representation of the domain content problem space. Stripped of metadiscourse, texts neglect the rhetorical dimension of expertise, making the problem space of rhetorical process absolutely indistinguishable from the problem space of domain content. As a result, students may be able to use textbooks to perceive that their everyday understandings are inconsistent with formal knowledge. But they do not seem to be able to use them to gain insight into the context-bound processes by which such formal knowledge can be integrated with personal knowledge brought from their indigenous home cultures.

At this level, then, the literacy practices of the schools help to create a layperson attitude. In textbooks, knowledge is packaged in exactly the way that it will be most likely to be ignored or misunderstood by students. When these students grow up to be laypersons, they will be well educated in what Halloran (personal communication, 1992) has called *professional incompetence.* That is, they will already know that domains of knowledge exist that they do not and cannot understand, and they will thus be willing to look to professionals in these domains and thus guarantee them their livelihood.

Persistence beyond this level of the system is the key to the acquisition of expertise, and the literacy practices of the schools are the key to that persistence. Taken at their face value, school texts appear to be lifeless artifacts that, by their very autonomy, invite little by way of further interaction. Interaction, indeed, seems to be beside the point. Rather than engaging students on grounds where their personal experience and beliefs might be relevant, reading and writing in the schools seem to require an abandonment of indigenous home culture, a trading of everyday concepts in favor of the formal culture of books. Students unwilling to make this trade will not pass over the great divide.

As an ideology of privilege, professionalization does seem to induce some individuals to make this trade, however. As we have noted earlier, one group of students who seemed eager to make this trade in the late 19th century were those motivated by the prospects of upward mobility. In the early decades of the professionalization movement, educational credentials did appear to be effective in creating a fairly sizable redistribution of income from the upper class to the newly emerging middle class (Collins, 1979). Once the surplus wealth of industrialization had been redistributed and absorbed by this emerging professional class, however, upward mobility no longer seemed assured (Collins, 1979). Groups might cling to the professional ideal as a prospect but it was often at variance with the reality of a stratified society in which only some professions attained the full complement of professional privileges and, within the same profession, only some individuals reaped unusual economic advantages (Freidson, 1986; Larson, 1977). At this point, then, professionalism was transformed into more of an ideology shaping individual aspirations than an actual reflection of reality. It is still, however, an ideology that can motivate some students to persist in school.

By and large, however, most students who persist with literacy in the schools are relying on what Bourdieu and Passeron (1977) have called the "cultural capital" they bring from home (see also Collins, 1979; Gouldner, 1979). As Heath's (1983) research indicated, students from middle-class Anglo-Protestant homes bring to school a whole host of interaction patterns with texts that are not common in the other indigenous cultures. These early literacy events appear to be a powerful determinant of students' later success in school (Wells, 1986). Such interactions, Scollon and Scollon (1981) suggested, enable children to recast themselves as textual agents, thus rehumanizing autonomous texts and understanding them as a part of their everyday lives. Such an advantage, in effect, initiates students' development of a problem space of rhetorical process years ahead of those who do not bring comparable cultural capital from home.

If, for whatever reasons, students persist in school, they will move on to undergraduate school where they will be exposed for the first time to the problem-solving contexts in which abstractions about domain concepts are valuable. This is the boundary with expert practice and, not coincidentally, it is here that differences are the greatest between what experts do and what laypersons do. For, as we have seen, laypersons solving the well-defined problems of textbooks struggle with laborious means–ends analyses to come up with the right answer. Experts in the same situations, by contrast, call on highly routinized forward-search procedures in which the solutions are built into the very way they represent the problems. At this boundary with expertise, knowledge is in so little dispute that everyone has agreed to archive it in textbooks; solutions are so pat they can be made available at the back of the book. Articulate problem solving in the rhetorical problem space is thus unnecessary, and knowledge takes the highly tacit form most difficult for experts to articulate and therefore most difficult for students to learn.

Only after students declare their majors, select professional schools, or apply to graduate school will they be allowed to move on and reap the rewards of professional expertise. By this time, students will have demonstrated a decided aptitude in their chosen area of specialization, almost single-handedly developing the more abstract representations characteristic of the expert problem space of domain content. In addition, they will have passed through 2 years of general education aimed at inculcating the virtues of an upper-class liberal culture. Only with these declarations of cognitive and sociological affiliation in place will they be invited to cross the great divide.

Once at the cutting edge—where knowledge is most contingent and problems are by definition ill defined—students find the reasoning procedures experts use to explore the problem space of rhetorical process more explicit and accessible. Experts do not simply see the solution to more ill-defined problems but explore extensive chains of reasoning aimed at being informative and persuasive. Texts, reconceived, are central to this activity. Now metadiscourse, instead of appearing to be a bothersome or irrelevant aspect of the text, becomes the source of important clues: How certain is this author's claim? Did this researcher do the right thing in the lab? Does this guy know what he's talking about? Texts that used to be read straight through are now taken apart for clues.

A process of rhetorical recovery is initiated. And what is recovered, strangely, are the temporal and human aspects of indigenous culture that students once thought they had to leave behind. It is the details of lived experience, in the lab, in the conference room, in the funding agencies, that must be recovered. But it is a reconfigured indigenous culture, one more abstract in which the "career" of a professional serving humanity, uncovering truth, and contributing to progress takes on a public significance. Professional identity becomes part of personal identity (Larson, 1977). The abstract temporal dimensions of cultural progress, the getting and using of knowledge, become the temporal rhythms of the professional's daily life.

THE PROBLEM OF REFLECTION: ISSUES FOR THIS BOOK

Within a broader framework of expertise, we can now understand the notion of the autonomous text as mythic in a sense far beyond that originally intended by critics of the textbook tradition (Cazden, 1989; Heath, 1987; Scollon & Scollon, 1981; Street, 1984; Walters, Daniell, & Trachsel, 1987). First, as an inaccurate portrayal of the literacy practices of academic experts, it is a false myth, debilitating the general public and their potential for civic action. Second, as the paradigmatic accomplishment toward which these academic experts strive, it is a driving myth, representing the goal behind the development of all expert knowledge. And finally, insofar as it accurately describes the ways in which students are encouraged to read and write, it is a regulating myth helping students and teachers alike to figure out what is required and what is allowed in school. It is the cultural myth of the autonomous text, then, that sustains the dual problem spaces of expertise, enabling the formal domain content of the academy to appear separated from the indigenous rhetorical processes that give it life.

For what purpose has such complexity been sustained? In whose interests has this bifurcated practice been developed? Any complete answer to these questions must admit that expertise is not simply a developmental phenomenon. It is simply not the case, for example, that students in the general curriculum are taught to read in a way that must only be further developed when they go on to the university. After 14 years of being taught that the text has all the answers, is it any surprise that some students find it hard to understand that they must read rhetorically, that they must ask about the author's purpose and context in order to use knowledge productively? Even those who operate as experts in one domain resort to relatively naive strategies in other domains and take texts at face value (Ackerman, 1991; Bazerman, 1988). In each area of specialization, then, students must actually be untaught the distrust of personal opinion and contextualized understandings that has been drummed into them through the period of general education.

We might argue, of course, that this lack of rhetorical interpretation arises out of these laypersons' absolute lack of knowledge. That is, perhaps students can only draw on background knowledge if they have such knowledge. Although such a statement looks eminently reasonable, we must recognize that it can only be made once we have already discounted all knowledge outside the academic framework. After all, experts are not the only ones who can make connections between specialized content and experience. They are simply the only ones whose experience counts.

The contrast between the neat developmental sequence suggested by Fig. 5.1 and the complex transitions diagrammed in Fig. 5.6 is a telling one: The development of the two problem spaces of expertise does not take place along two independent and straightforward continua as Fig. 5.1 suggests. Instead, obscured by the myth of the autonomous text, the rhetorical problem space is only allowed to emerge, as shown in Fig. 5.6, within the context of an already abstracted representation of domain content. In this way, the processes of cognitive development have become heavily intertwined with the sociological dynamics legitimizing professional privilege. That is, the circuitous development of rhetorical process practically guarantees that experts will be the only ones able to use a field's texts in any kind of sophisticated manner, will be the only ones who can sustain serious interaction or invite serious response on specialized content.

Such exclusionary practices cry out for reform—or at least reconsideration. Some attempts have been made in this direction: Fisher (1987), for example, suggested that we revitalize public discourse by returning to a narrative rationality within the reach of common citizens as opposed to the technical rationality of experts. Others have called for a more "conversational" mode of expert discourse (Bernstein, 1983; Brodkey, 1987b; Frentz, 1985; MacIntrye, 1981; McCloskey, 1985; Rorty, 1979; Turner, 1980; White, 1980). In these arguments, both narrative and conversation have been praised as being better suited to constructing public knowledge, dealing with moral issues, and, more generally, reflecting the historical situatedness of all human knowing.

But, for the most part, such calls for reform have not been situated within any deep-seated understanding of how expertise is played out not simply in the words inscribed in textual artifacts, but in the daily practices by which people like ourselves read, write, and know. We simply cannot make real sense out of the literacy practices of the academy unless we understand how the institutional forces of professionalization are played out in the minute practices of individual practitioners as they read and write.

And, in one way or another, we are those individual practitioners. Simply by virtue of being at home in these texts, reading and writing these texts, we are involved. Even those of us in the academy who do not see ourselves as implicated must come to terms with the way academic literacy practices have been shaped by the professionalization project. It is all too easy to view expertise as the outcome of monolithic institutional forces over which we, as victims or innocent bystanders, have little control. But as long as research on expertise is written as the account of what other people do, the account will be a false account. Real reform can only be accomplished through an attempt to understand how our own practices of reading, writing, and knowing operate within the dual problem spaces of domain content and rhetorical process, thereby creating and re-creating the great divide. Only by engaging with this problem of reflection, seeking explanations that ring bells with our own experience, with what we ourselves do, will we be getting closer to the truth—and getting closer to change.

The stakes for such change are high. As long as students think that they have to abandon the resources of their indigenous cultures in order to succeed in school and in the professions, a significant portion who refuse to take the move will be forced to drop out. A significant portion who do take the move will be crippled.

And how many among us can say with confidence, "I am not crippled" or "I have not dropped out"?

The studies that follow attempt to engage with this problem of reflection through a systematic investigation of a single site of academic literacy, the study of ethical issues within the discipline of academic philosophy. This area and the area of the humanities in general—at least outside of literature (Fahenstock & Secor, 1991; MacDonald, 1990)—have received much less attention from researchers and scholars. But for the purpose of understanding the relationship between academic literacy and the nature of expertise, such an examination is important. Unlike the sciences that made up the backbone of the professionalization movement in the 19th century, the humanities formed a traditional stronghold against professionalization, seeing themselves as the last bastion of liberal culture (Veysey, 1965).

Furthermore, as we noted in chapter 4, philosophy was almost the last of the academic disciplines to organize professionally. In fact, the American Philosophical Association was not founded until 1901, 32 years after the first professional organization in the humanities, and 61 years after the first professional organization in the sciences. Thus, it becomes particularly interesting to ask, How have readers and writers in this stronghold of antiprofessionalism developed their literacy practices? Do we find evidence that they too engage in the kind of bifurcated practice typical of the sciences or are there significant distinctions to be drawn?

The study of this single site of literacy obviously cannot provide a definitive answer to this question, but it is an important step in understanding the full impact of professionalization upon academic literacy and the nature of expertise. Developing this understanding will necessarily involve us in looking at the detailed activities and representations of readers and writers with texts. As we see in the next few chapters, however, building an appropriate methodology to look at people's activities as well as their representations is not a trivial task.

II

STUDYING SPACE AND TIME

CHAPTER

6

OBSERVING WRITERS WITH PROTOCOL DATA

Think-aloud protocols would appear to be a perfect source of information concerning the relationship between academic literacy and the nature of expertise: They seem to tell us how participants actually go about completing their work—their rhetorical processes—as well as how they go about representing their ideas—the domain content. Yet any researcher who wants to take advantage of these apparent strengths must seriously consider the arguments that have been made both about the ecological validity of protocol data and about their theoretical status. Indeed, the use of think-aloud protocols has been regularly criticized both in cognitive psychology where it originated (Nisbett & Wilson, 1977) and in writing research where it has never become a mainstream method (see Appendix A).

The purpose of this chapter is to address these concerns. In the first half, we look at the evidence that protocols are, as a practical matter, a distinctive and somewhat routine product of participants' literacy activities. In the second half, we look at attempts to establish the theoretical status of this distinctive form of data. In general, the evidence suggests that, when properly taken, protocols provide useful, albeit indirect, evidence concerning what participants do and think—at least insofar as this doing and thinking involves language—although such evidence may be far from a running record of participants' cognitive processes as has often been assumed.

PROTOCOL DATA AS A PRACTICAL MATTER

On their face, protocols appear to preserve detailed information concerning what writers do and think. In particular, they appear to show the interweaving of three basic literacy phenomena:

1. Writing Phenomenon: What did the participants write?
2. Reading Phenomenon: What did the participants read, either from texts given or from the developing text so far?
3. Thinking Phenomenon: What did the participants think that appeared in neither the texts being read nor written?

For example, in the following protocol excerpt taken from Flower and Hayes (1981c), we first see how the reading of a given text, the task directions, was interwoven with the participant's thinking:

> *My job for a young—*

Oh I'm to describe

> *my job for a young thirteen to fourteen year-old teenage female audience— Magazine—Seventeen -*

a- My immediate reaction is that it's utterly impossible. I did read Seventeen though—I guess I wouldn't say I read it—a- I looked at it, especially the ads, so the idea would be to describe what I do to someone like myself when I read—well not like myself, but adjusted for—well twenty years later. -a- Now what I think of doing really is that—until the coffee comes I feel I can't begin, so I will shut the door and feel that I have a bit more privacy,

-um- Also the mention of a free-lance writer is something I've—I've no experience in doing and my sense is that it's a—a formula which I'm not sure I know, so I suppose what I have to do is -a- invent what the formula might be, and—and then try to -a- try to include—events or occurrences or attitudes or experiences in my own job that would -a- that could be—that could be conveyed in formula so let's see . . . (p. 235)

Next we see how this thinking became interwoven with the participant's writing:

I suppose one would want to start—by writing something—that would -a- attract the attention of the reader—of that reader and -a- I suppose the most interesting thing about my job would be that it is highly unlikely that it would seem at all interesting to someone that age—so I might start by saying something like

> *Can you imagine yourself spending* a day—

> *many days like this—waking up at 4:30 a.m., making a pot of coffee . . . looking around . . . my— . . .* (p. 235)

And finally, we see how this writing was interwoven with the participant's rereading of the developing text:

"looking around" *your house, letting in your cats* . . . -a- *walking out -*
"out" *with coffee* and a book *and watching the dawn materialize* . . .
I actually do this . . . although 4:30's a bit early, perhaps I should say
   5:30
so it wouldn't seem—although I do get up at 4:30 -a-
   "watching the dawn materialize" *and starting to work -*
   "to work" *by* reading—*reading the manuscript—of a Victorian writer* . . .
   with a "manuscript of a . . . a Victorian writer" . . .
   a person with
   a manuscript of a student—much like yourself—much like—much like -a-
   "a student" *or a book* by Aristotle
they've heard of Aristotle or—who could I have it be by—
   Plato probably. (p. 235)

Although it might be possible to recover some of this information using other
methodologies—collecting all of the texts this participant created, for example,
or asking the participant to recall the decisions that underlay those texts—we
would probably not be able to reconstruct as complete a record of these literacy
activities without the kind of information that protocols provide.

Despite this apparent advantage, however, serious concerns have been raised
about the ecological validity of protocol data: Is what we see in protocol
transcripts truly indicative of what real participants do and think while completing
real tasks? Do we, in particular, have any reason to believe that protocols can
tell us something about the interaction of participants' rhetorical processes and
domain content? Can they tell us, in short, anything about the relationship between
academic literacy and the nature of expertise?

Answers to these questions can be sought either through a practical
examination of the character of protocol data or through a theoretical discussion
of the status of protocols in general. In this section, we will take the more practical
approach: Although, as we see later, serious questions remain concerning the
theoretical status of protocols vis-à-vis cognitive processing, in this section we
are more concerned with the practical evidence that protocols represent a
distinctive and somewhat routine phenomenon related to the normal course of
participants' literacy activities.

The Distinctive Form of Protocol Discourse

One of the recurring concerns expressed over the use of protocols in literacy
research has involved the nature of the discourse they represent. What does it
mean, exactly, for participants to "think aloud"? One argument has been that
these verbal data represent nothing more than narratives that participants construct
to explain rather than reflect what they are up to (Cooper & Holzman, 1983).
Another argument has been that such verbal data are simply conversations with

admittedly silent researchers whose presence, nevertheless, creates conversational obligations (Dobrin, 1986).

As a practical matter, such arguments suggest that protocols are not a distinctive kind of discourse. That is, if participants who give protocols are simply constructing narratives of what they are doing or engaging in conversation with researchers, we would expect their protocol discourse to look like these other kinds of discourse rather than to have their own distinctive character. This prediction, however, is not supported by an examination of protocol data. In fact, protocol data appear to be a distinctive form of verbal data that can readily be distinguished from both conversation and narrative.

Characteristically, protocols have a three-part structure in which an action is proposed, executed, and evaluated:

Propose → Execute → Evaluate

In the following randomly chosen excerpt taken from one of the protocols described in Part III of this book, for example, Jeff was just starting his eighth protocol session and, having read through a number of articles defining paternalism, was trying to figure out what he thought. His talk has the characteristic three-part structure of protocol discourse. He began by using himself as subject and an imperative verb—"let me"—to propose for himself a goal to act:

1. Alright so then let me get this all straight again . . .

Then, he followed through on the action he had proposed—"getting this all straight again":

2. *A believes that . . .*
   A's action is for S's good . . .
   A's qualified . . .
   his action is immoral . . .
   is justified . . . independently . . . of S's consent past present or future by a belief that *S believes that he generally knows what is for his own good.*

Next, he made an evaluation, "that fifth one is a little weird":

3. Now that . . . oh that fifth one is a little weird because that does seem to rule out paternalism of of a parent because . . . [long pause] because you might not necessarily believe that your child believes that he that your child generally knows what is for his own good . . . does acting paternalistically require messing with someone's autonomy . . . hmm . . .

Finally, he went on to propose his next goal:

4. Okay let me go through this [pause] . . .

This characteristic three-part structure sets protocol discourse apart from both narrative and conversation. To begin with, if this protocol were a narrative constructed for our benefit, we would expect to see something quite different than the Propose → Execute → Evaluate structure. As many theorists have noted, narratives present the transformation of one situation into another (Black & Bower, 1980; Prince, 1973; Rimon-Keenan, 1983; Tomashevsky, 1965; Trabasso, Secco, & Van Den Broek, 1984). As a result, in their simplest form, they have the following three-part structure:

Setting → Event(s) → Outcome

They begin with a setting that represents some current status quo—a princess is asleep in a castle overgrown with tangled briars. Next, they describe certain events or chains of events that change this status quo—a prince braves all manner of perils to get through the briars and kiss the princess. Finally, they tell of the outcome of these events, which represent a new status quo—the prince and princess are married and the kingdom is restored. Although protocol discourse does involve human actions that could ultimately be narratized by participants after the fact—Jeff could, for example, later describe his own action related previously as "I disagreed with Gert and Culver's fifth condition"—they are not presented as reversals of the status quo during the protocol itself: When Jeff completes the three-part structure described earlier, for example, he just goes on to consider his next action.

In a similar vein, if protocols were conversations held with silent researchers, we would expect to see them share the characteristic three-part turn-taking structure of conversational interaction (Heritage, 1984):

Initiate → Respond → [Repair]

In the first turn of the conversation, a speaker initiates an interaction—Sue makes an invitation for dinner. In the next turn, a second speaker responds—Janet declines because she is busy that evening. And, finally, in an optional third turn, the first speaker repairs any contextual misunderstandings indicated by the second speaker's response—Sue clarifies that she is asking about the following night. Although such conversations can often propose actions in a way similar to the actions proposed in protocol discourse, they need not do so. Participants, for example, can initiate with a greeting that simply needs to be acknowledged. And even when the conversation does involve a proposal for action—Jeff, might, for example, say "Let's get this all straight again" to a collaborator—the appropriate conversational response is an agreement to act—"Okay"—rather than the act itself. In this sense, then, protocol discourse is quite different from the discourse of conversation.

Just as distinctive as what is in protocol discourse is what is left out. In particular, protocols, when properly taken, do not contain the kinds of explanatory material we would expect to find in either narrative or conversation. Missing, specifically, are explanations of actions, references to sources of information, and reasons for attending to information. In the protocol excerpt quoted earlier, for example, Jeff did not explain that he was writing something down in item 2, nor that what he was writing consisted of the five conditions for a definition of paternalism given by an author he had read earlier. He also did not mention that he was numbering these conditions from 1 to 5—although he acted on this knowledge later in talking about "that fifth one" ("S believes that he generally knows. . . ."). Furthermore, he made no mention that he was actually copying these conditions—and not from the original text, but from an earlier page of notes. Neither did he explain the content of what he was thinking: that the issue of whether a parent can be paternalistic was important because another author had brought it up as a counterexample; and that "messing with someone's autonomy" was his way of characterizing the fifth condition. All of this must be inferred by the analyst based on knowledge of what came before and after in Jeff's protocols and on what was in Jeff's dated notes.

It is important to acknowledge, however, that, on occasion, participants' protocol discourse does not take on the characteristic three-part structure described previously, and instead assumes a more conversational form. Usually this occurs for brief periods in the opening and closing sections of protocol sessions as participants make a transition to their work. It is also common in the first 20 minutes or so of participants' first protocol while they become familiar with the think-aloud procedure. One of the most striking examples of this adjustment period occurred when I was working with a philosopher on the paternalism task described later in this book. It was my job to get him started and I showed up at his home on the day he had chosen. After explaining how to do a protocol, giving him some practice, and explaining the paternalism task, I took a chair to sit outside the door of his study, which I kept ajar to make sure he did not fall silent. Instead of giving a protocol, however, he started to give a commentary, using a conversational structure that seemed deliberately aimed at getting me to respond. I agonized through the silences when I knew he was waiting for my responses, saying nothing except "keep talking" when the silence was long enough. This lasted not more than 5 minutes, however. Apparently concluding that I was too far away to understand what he was saying, he finally gave up and switched into what I have called the typical structure of protocol discourse. He continued in this way on his own for the next 15 weeks.

For the most part, participants who have a greater-than-appropriate awareness of the research context show easily detectable signs. For instance, when a writer voices well-formed sentences like, "My immediate reaction is that it's utterly impossible" as in the protocol excerpt given earlier from Flower and Hayes (1981c), they are clearly providing helpful explanations of their reaction for the benefit of the researchers rather than simply reacting. A less explanatory report would have been, "utterly impossible." When such explanatory material occurs at the beginning of a protocol session, as in the aforementioned excerpt, and declines as the participant becomes absorbed in the task, there is little danger to the validity of the data.

In rarer cases, however, participants may persist in their inappropriate conversational cooperation. Such appears to have been the case with at least one of the participants used in Flower and Hayes' (1981c) research. In a response to Cooper and Holzman's criticisms published in 1983, Steinberg, for example, explained that he had not made any comments about lunch or about the noise in the hall when he had given a protocol because he was trying to focus on the task of composing. Such comments are indicative of a level of conversational cooperation that may well have compromised the ecological validity of this participant's protocol.

Nevertheless, such conversational cooperation is usually limited and can be straightforwardly detected in the protocol verbalizations themselves. Furthermore, in many cases, problems can be eliminated simply by reminding participants just to say what is on their minds, not to explain what they are doing. When protocols are given under these more appropriate conditions, they invariably contain very little of the explanatory material more typical of conversation or narrative and, furthermore, show the distinctive three-part structure of protocol discourse.

The Routine Nature of Protocol Data

A second recurring issue concerning the use of protocol data in literacy research has involved their potential for distorting the task being studied. Cooper and Holzman (1983), for example, questioned the validity of any data about writing that looks as focused as the excerpt given earlier from Flower and Hayes (1981c). Do protocol participants, they wonder, ever worry about lunch? Indeed, if protocols represent a distinctive form of discourse as suggested in the last section, the danger of distortion appears to become even more acute: Particularly, if participants articulate and attend to their actions and thoughts in a way they otherwise would not, protocol data may distort participants' normal literacy practices.

Considerable evidence suggests, however, that protocol data collected under appropriate conditions are a somewhat routine product of reading and writing. To begin with, when participants are asked to give protocols, they appear to have little difficulty doing so (Flower & Hayes, 1985), and those who report giving them say that they were not hard (Murray, 1983; Steinberg, 1986). In fact, one of the freshmen in the study described in Part III reported that by the end of her work for us she had become so accustomed to composing aloud that she found herself unconsciously breaking into speech in the library while writing a paper for another course.

In addition, protocols do reveal the kind of shifting attention that we expect to find during routine reading and writing. Despite Steinberg's (1986) assertion that protocol subjects keep their minds strictly focused on task and Smagorinsky's (1989) claim that protocols are representative of writing done under intense exam conditions, think-aloud protocols can be gathered in situations that are more naturalistic in terms of both time frame and setting. When participants work in more normal surroundings over a time frame of weeks rather than minutes, we see ample evidence of wandering attention. For instance, when Berkenkotter kept the tape recorder on Donald Murray as he worked in his study over weeks, he had many of what he later called his "bathroom epiphanies" (Berkenkotter, 1983; Murray, 1983). And in one of the studies to be reported in Part III, Leslie's thoughts wandered to pizza, sing-song ditties, and the noise in the hall. Under similar conditions, Roger also got distracted: the doorbell rang, he had to chase his cat off his notes, and he expressed a serious need for his morning coffee.

The presence of these wanderings of attention seems to indicate that participants can behave in a way we would normally expect while giving a protocol. Particularly when they work in more naturalistic conditions and are given task directions that discourage retrospective explanation and favor concurrent report (Flower et al., 1990, for an example), participants seem to have little difficulty saying what is on their mind. In fact, they have an intuitive feel for it. This fact, as we see in the next section, raises theoretical issues regarding the exact nature of protocol data, but, as a practical matter, protocols do seem to tell us a great deal about what participants do and think as they engage in literacy practices.

PROTOCOL DATA AS A THEORETICAL MATTER

As we have seen in the last section, protocol data appear to be a distinctive and somewhat routine product of participants' literacy practices. With minor modifications in task directions, people working under naturalistic conditions seem readily able to distinguish between conversational explanation and protocol discourse. Furthermore, they encounter little difficulty in producing the latter. But what, exactly, does it mean to "say everything that's on our minds"? Where does such discourse come from? To answer this question, we must move beyond practical matters to discuss the theoretical status of protocol data.

The Standard Theory

The most comprehensive account of the theoretical status of protocol data was provided by Ericsson and Simon in their 1984 monograph on *Protocol Analysis*. Expanding an earlier review (Ericsson & Simon, 1980), Ericsson and Simon developed what has become the standard theory for protocol analysis. In particular, they argued that think-aloud protocols, taken under the appropriate conditions, represented a record of the changing contents of a person's working memory.

Using a fairly common model of human information processing developed by cognitive psychologists in the late 1960s (Atkinson & Shiffrin, 1968), Ericsson and Simon (1984) assumed that people were serial processors of information. This information, they assumed, was channeled through a *working memory* that contained all the information to which a person was actively attending. Unlike long-term memory, working memory had a fixed capacity and rapid decay. That is, a person could attend to only so much information at a time—+ or –7 in George Miller's (1956) original formulation—and, if unattended, the information would rapidly decay and be lost. Ericsson and Simon then used this theoretical account to outline three specific factors that they believed would affect the character of protocol reports in predictable ways.

Time, the first of these factors, would affect the completeness and occasionally the accuracy of a protocol report. In particular, if verbalizations were concurrent with the task being studied, then a protocol could be a fairly accurate report of the contents of working memory. But if the verbalization was delayed (or retrospective), the protocol became a more accurate representation of just the subset of working memory contents that had moved into long-term memory. Furthermore, with delayed verbalization, people were more likely to reconstruct reports to mirror what they believe they have done rather than what they did do as Nisbett and Wilson (1977) claimed.

The nature of the task, the second factor mentioned by Ericsson and Simon (1984), would affect the accuracy and usefulness of the protocol report. Protocols were by definition verbal reports and could accurately represent only those contents of working memory that were already in verbal form. According to Ericsson and Simon, the verbalness of these contents varied with task: A painter might use very little verbal information to paint a picture; a writer, presumably, used a great deal more to produce an essay.

The third factor that could affect the validity of a protocol, according to Ericsson and Simon (1984), was the task instructions or what we might call the rhetorical situation. Briefly, the more participants attempted to explain to someone what they were doing rather than simply saying what was crossing their minds, the less accurately the protocol report could be expected to represent the normally attended-to information in the task. That is, the kinds of information participants were accustomed to providing when explaining how to do a task could be expected to differ in systematic ways from what they normally attended to when working by themselves. In explanation, we elaborate, we make analogies, we give background information and assumptions, and we draw on our own beliefs and common beliefs about how the task is done. All of this additional information could significantly alter the contents of a protocol report and could even affect participants' ability to complete a task. We all know of things we can do until asked to explain them.

Like any good theory, Ericsson and Simon's (1984) framework does a good job of accounting for many of the practical issues involved in using protocol data. In particular, it not only provides a theoretical foundation for the threats to ecological validity we noted earlier, but it also describes the conditions under which these threats need not be serious. First, the standard theory suggests when we might expect protocol discourse to shift to more narrative discourse: If participants delay verbalization in time, Ericsson and Simon suggested, we can expect them to lose information from working memory and instead rely on the incomplete information in long-term memory. Such reliance would probably produce a narrative structure. Second, the standard theory suggests when we might expect protocol discourse to shift to more conversational discourse: If participants work with a strong sense of the rhetorical situation of the research, Ericsson and Simon suggested, we can expect them to modify the normally attended-to information in order to accommodate the researcher's needs. Such modification would probably produce a more conversational structure.

In addition to clarifying issues we noted earlier, Ericsson and Simon's (1984) theory also does a good job of directing our attention to another issue that has not been raised much in the literature on protocol methodology. This concerns the impact of the second factor suggested by the standard theory, the nature of the task. Basically, according to Ericsson and Simon, if a task is verbal by nature, protocols pose a secondary task with few overhead costs to attention. They may slow the main process down a bit, but leave it basically unchanged. If a task involves significant nonverbal information, however, concurrent verbalization can significantly alter a task and make protocol methodology less appropriate for research purposes.

Although it might seem easy to assume that, of all tasks, literacy activities would be "verbal"—compared to chess, for instance—we need to be careful about coming to this conclusion too quickly. Flower and Hayes, for example, did not themselves believe this to be the case. In 1984, they published a multiple representation hypothesis that suggested that writers attend to information in a variety of forms ranging along a continuum from verbal to nonverbal. These forms included such things as images, metaphors, schemata, and abstract concepts as well as prose.

Minimally, the multiple representation hypothesis would suggest that protocols would be, at best, incomplete records of the information attended to during composing. That is, protocols would contain only that information that was present in working memory in verbal form. Anything nonverbal would be taking up working memory's limited resources, but would not normally be verbalized. As a result, participants working on tasks with significant nonverbal components would produce gaps in protocol transcripts. If, however, participants are urged to verbalize following the standard procedure often recommended for protocol studies (Hayes & Flower, 1980a), they may attempt to translate this nonverbal information into verbal form. This effort would probably not only slow down their normal activities but also very likely alter them as well.

All this would tend to suggest that, at least according to the standard theory, questions concerning the ecological validity of protocol data can ultimately be settled only through a complete model of the task being studied. Such a model would specify not only how participants complete the task but also how they produce the verbalizations and gaps in protocol transcripts. Only such a model could provide both rational methods for assessing when participants have been pushed into inappropriate verbalization and theory-based procedures for inferring the relationship between those verbalizations and the cognitive processes of the task being studied. Indeed, Ericsson and Simon (1984), in general, urged that the "processes associated with verbalization should be treated as an integral part of any model of the cognitive processes for a given task" (pp. 106–107). As we see in the next chapter, however, a model with this kind of detail has not yet been proposed for the tasks of reading and writing.

More Recent Theory

More recent theories of cognition suggest, however, that researchers of literacy need not—and, in fact, should not—undertake the burden of articulating a complete model of cognitive processes before taking advantage of protocol methodology. In fact, according to these "modular" theories of mind, protocol data may be, at best, only an an indirect indication of what participants are thinking and doing. From the perspective of cognitive psychology, this indirect evidence may be too remote from the universals of human cognition to be useful, but it would hardly be irrelevant to the study of academic literacy and the nature of expertise.

Of this recent work, the intermediate-level theory of consciousness offered by Jackendoff (1987) may be the most relevant to our study of academic literacy and the nature of expertise. Building on earlier work by Fodor (1983), Jackendoff assumed that people are better modeled as parallel processors who can attend simultaneously to information in a number of distinct forms rather than as serial processors who can attend only to one thing at a time. Thus, in place of a single working memory, this revised theory posits several working memories, each associated with a distinct module of mind: one for language processing, one for visual processing, and, according to Jackendoff, one for musical processing. At any given time, Jackendoff suggested, our consciousness represents only a small part of cognition. In particular, in any given module—linguistic, visual, or musical—we are not aware of either the very lowest levels of representation arising from perception or of the highest level that supports our conceptual thinking. Instead, our awareness rests at an "intermediate" level of representation somewhere between the two.

In the particular case of language processing, Jackendoff (1987) believed this intermediate level of representation is phonological. As a result, we have the phenomenological experience of "hearing" ourselves think, even though these phonological representations are only distantly related to conceptual thinking. Furthermore, the two can occasionally become unhinged: We can think of things that we cannot say, for example—the "tip of the tongue" phenomenon—and we can say things that we are not thinking—as when a song runs through our mind nonsensically.

For our work on academic literacy and the nature of expertise, this intermediate-level theory of consciousness is important because, if correct, it offers an alternative theoretical foundation for protocol data. Instead of being a record of the contents of a single working memory, this revised theory would suggest that protocols represent the contents of only one of several working memories, the one specifically concerned with language processing. And instead of being a fairly complete record of the cognitive processes involved in language processing, this working memory would contain only intermediate linguistic representations as they are kept "in registration" with higher level thoughts. Thus, even though protocols may allow researchers to "overhear" participants thinking, we cannot assume that what we hear is all that is going on. At best, protocols would be distant echoes of conceptual thinking.

Nevertheless, even this indirect evidence can tell us something about what participants do and think—at least insofar as this doing and thinking involves words. With protocols, for example, we might not be able to follow the details of participants' cognitive processes. But we probably could reconstruct a record of their activities in the world and with text—what they read, what they write, and, presumably, what they think if those thoughts are linguistic. With protocols, furthermore, we might not be able to identify the specific representations supporting participants' conceptual understanding. But we probably could identify some of the characteristics of this understanding—how entities like texts and authors are being represented, for example, or what features are attributed to them.

Thus our ultimate answer to the general question of using protocol data to study literacy activities should probably take two parts. To begin with, the guidelines originally provided by Ericsson and Simon (1984) appear to provide sensible advice concerning the conditions necessary to protect the ecological validity of the data. Under the appropriate conditions, concurrent verbalization appears to provide a distinctive kind of data about what writers do and think. Internal evidence from the protocol itself and external evidence about the conditions under which the protocol was taken as well as the texts that were produced can be used to assess whether these conditions have been met. And given the delicate balance necessary for maintaining these conditions, it behooves each researcher who uses protocols to offer evidence that these conditions have been met. This is, in part, what I have tried to do in this chapter.

Second, as this chapter also indicates, even protocol data gathered under appropriate conditions cannot unproblematically be theorized as representing a running record of a serial cognitive processor. More modular theories of mind suggest, in particular, that protocol verbalizations should be considered indirect evidence concerning cognition—perhaps even, as Jackendoff (1987) suggested, just intermediate phonological representations distantly related to full conceptual thinking. From the perspective of cognitive psychology, these representations may be too remote from the universals of human cognition to be useful, but they would hardly be irrelevant to the study of academic literacy and the nature of expertise. Indeed, as we see in the next chapter, protocols may provide us with just the tool we need for investigating how broad cultural phenomena like professionalization shape and are shaped by the literacy practices of individual practitioners.

7

MODELING WRITING
AS ACTIVITY

Compared to the concerns that have been expressed over protocol methodology in the last decade, comparatively little attention has been paid to issues of modeling. Even though the most complete and sophisticated model of writing, proposed more than 10 years ago, drew on the now suspect standard theory of protocol analysis discussed in the last chapter (Hayes & Flower, 1980a), little attention has yet been paid to developing a more appropriate alternative. Particularly if we accept the evidence presented in chapter 6 that protocols are a distinctive and routine product of participants' literacy practices, the question of how best to model these data becomes both legitimate and pressing.

This is the question pursued in this chapter. In particular, we use published protocol data to compare the cognitive process model with a model based on the more cultural concept of *activity* (Wertsch, 1981). In general, we find that this concept does a better job of capturing the temporal aspects of participants' reading and writing, and, for this reason, may be an especially appropriate tool for modeling the interaction between participants' rhetorical processes and their domain content.

THE PUBLISHED DATA

The task of comparing alternative strategies for modeling protocol data has been made easier by Hayes and Flower's (1980a) publication of detailed protocol data in their chapter on "Identifying the Organization of Writing Processes." In this chapter, Hayes and Flower were attempting to test the validity of their cognitive process model through two separate analyses. The first analysis asked whether the major cognitive processes of writing could reliably be distinguished from one another based upon the form of the written material that writers produced. The second analysis asked whether coders could reliably classify protocol segments according to the cognitive process being used. The data presented during the course of these two analyses provide us with rich material for comparing the cognitive process model with a model based on the cultural concept of activity.

One caveat is in order. By presenting these data in what follows, I do not mean to suggest that they should be accepted without reservation. It is important to keep in mind that the data were limited: They were based on 458 clause-length segments taken from one half of one protocol from one person. Nevertheless, as the most complete data set yet published, it represents a starting point by which we can compare the cognitive process model with a model based on the more cultural concept of activity.

The Distinct Episodes of Composing

One of the most striking aspects of the protocol data analyzed by Hayes and Flower (1980a) was its self-consciously episodic nature. In particular, the participant appears to have self-consciously organized his composing as a linear sequence of episodes which, according to Hayes and Flower's analysis, he signaled with the following metacomments:

Episode 1.	Segment 2:	"And now what I'll do is simply jot down random thoughts . . .";
	Segment 5:	"Topics as they occur randomly are . . ." ;
	Segment 48:	"Organizing nothing as yet.";
	Segment 69:	"Other things to think about in this random search are. . . ."
Episode 2.	Segment 117:	"Now I think it's time to go back and read over the material and elaborate on its organization . . ."
	Segment 161:	"Now this isn't an overall organization. This is just the organization of a subpart.";
	Segment 237:	"There's an organization."
Episode 3.	Segment 239:	"Let's try and write something";
	Segment 243:	"Oh, no. We need more organizing";
	Segment 269:	"I can imagine the possibility of an alternate plan";
	Segment 271:	"But let's build on this plan and see what happens with it."

The Distinct Products Produced in Each Episode

Hayes and Flower's (1980a) analysis suggests, furthermore, that these episodes could be distinguished from one another on the basis of the noticeably different texts produced in each one. Those texts produced in Episode 3, for example, tended to have good syntactic form and were often associated with an interrogative. Those produced in Episode 2 tended to have a discernible structure. Those produced in Episode 1 tended to have none of these features.

The Distinct Organization of Each Episode

Finally, Hayes and Flower's (1980a) analysis suggests that each of these episodes was dominated by a distinct core process accompanied by a common set of secondary processes. As shown in Table 7.1, for example, Episode 1 was

TABLE 7.1
The Transition from Process to Process in the Three Episodes
Analyzed in Hayes and Flower (1980a)

Episode 1	*To Generate*	*To Organize*	*To Translate*	*To Edit*	*Total* #	*Total* (%)
From Generate	**50**	2	0	8	60	(82)
From Organize	3	0	0	0	3	(4)
From Translate	0	0	0	0	0	(0)
From Edit	7	1	0	2	10	(14)
Total	60	3	0	10	73	(100)

Episode 2	*To Generate*	*To Organize*	*To Translate*	*To Edit*	*Total* #	*Total* (%)
From Generate	7	3	0	5	15	(18)
From Organize	**5**	**44**	**0**	**5**	**54**	**(66)**
From Translate	0	0	0	0	0	(0)
From Edit	3	7	0	3	13	(16)
Total	15	54	0	13	73	(100)

Episode 3	*To Generate*	*To Organize*	*To Translate*	*To Edit*	*Total* #	*Total* (%)
From Generate	2	0	2	6	10	(9)
From Organize	0	0	0	0	0	(0)
From Translate	**6**	**0**	**46**	**15**	**67**	**(62)**
From Edit	2	0	19	10	31	(29)
Total	10	0	67	31	108	(100)

Note. Frequencies for the core process of each episode are in boldface type. From Hayes and Flower (1980, p. 27, Fig. 1.13). Adapted by permission.

dominated by a process Flower and Hayes called generating, accounting for 82% of the protocol segments. Episode 2 was dominated by episodes they named organizing, accounting for 66% of the protocol segments. And Episode 3 was dominated by the process they named translating, accounting for 62% of the protocol segments. In addition, all three episodes contained small but significant percentages of each of two secondary processes: generating and editing.

Specific data about the transitions from one process to another within each episode are also shown in Table 7.1. For each episode, the table provides the number of times the participant went from one process to another. For example, in Episode 1, a core process of generate was followed by another generate 50 times and by an edit 8 times. Together, these data on transitions suggest several important features of how the participant organized his episodes:

1. Once the participant was in a core process, he tended to stay with that core process (50 times in Episode 1; 44 times in Episode 2; 46 times in Episode 3).

2. Core processes in one episode were unlikely to shift to the core processes of other episodes (in Episode 1, generate → organize: 2 times, generate → translate: 0 times; in Episode 2, organize → translate: 0 times; in Episode 3, translate → organize 0 times).

3. Secondary processes tended not to follow themselves (generate followed by generate: 7 and 2 times in Episodes 2 and 3 respectively; edit followed by edit: 2, 3, and 10 times in Episodes 1, 2, and 3 respectively).

4. The interrelationship between secondary processes changed from episode to episode. Editing, for example, was about twice as likely to occur in Episode 3 (29%) as in Episode 1 (14%) or Episode 2 (16%).

Overall, then, the published protocol data provided by Hayes and Flower (1980a) suggest that this participant self-consciously organized his composing in an episodic structure, associating each episode with distinctive metacomments, distinctive textual products, and a distinctive mix of core and secondary processes. These, then, are the data against which we can compare the cognitive process model and a more activity-based model.

THE COGNITIVE PROCESS MODEL

In their early publications, Flower and Hayes made three separate presentations of their cognitive process model: The first, with Hayes as first author, appeared in the book edited by Gregg and Steinberg (Hayes & Flower, 1980a). The second, again with Hayes as first author, appeared in an invited and little known issue of *Visible Language* (Hayes & Flower, 1980b). The last and most well-known one, with Flower as first author this time, appeared in *College Composition and Communication* (Flower & Hayes, 1981a).

In the first two of these publications, three components of the model were given. The first was the block diagram given in Fig. 7.1, which specified three major cognitive processes, planning, translating, and reviewing, as well as a monitor controlling the transition from one process to another. The second was a set of flow charts for the processes of generating, organizing, translating, and reviewing which were given in separate figures in Hayes and Flower (1980a), but incorporated into the block diagram in Hayes and Flower (1980b). The third, given in Fig. 7.2, was a production system that modeled how the Monitor controlled transitions among processes. This third component, even though it was dropped in the 1981 presentation, makes important predictions relative to the protocol data presented in the last section. In this section, then, we look closely at how both the block diagram component and the production system component account for the published protocol data.

The Block Diagram Component

The Hayes and Flower (1980a) block diagram component, reproduced in Fig. 7.1, models writing as a hierarchy of major processes with embedded subprocesses. The first major process of planning consisted of the subprocesses of generating, goal setting, and organizing. The second major process of reviewing

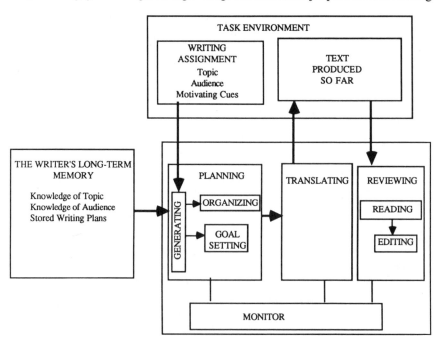

FIG. 7.1. A block diagram showing the organization of the cognitive processes of writing (Hayes & Flower, 1980a). Reprinted by permission.

1. (Generated language in STM   -->   edit)

2. (New information in STM   -->   generate)

3. (New element from translate   -->   (goal = review))

4. (New element from organize   -->   (goal = translate))

5. (New element from generate   -->   (goal = organize))

6. (Not enough material   -->   (goal = generate))

7. ((goal = generate)   -->   generate)

8. ((goal = organize)   -->   organize)

9. ((goal = translate)   -->   translate)

10. ((goal = review)   -->   review)

FIG. 7.2. The production system component of the cognitive process model
(Hayes & Flower, 1980a). Reprinted by permission.

consisted of the subprocesses of reading and editing, although, in later versions, reading was replaced by evaluating and editing was replaced by revising. The final major process of translating appeared without subprocesses. In the original block diagram component, the relationship among these processes was signaled, as in Fig. 7.1, by arrows. Heavy arrows linked the major processes of planning, translating, and reviewing. Lighter arrows linked the subprocesses: In planning, generating was linked either to organizing or to goal setting; in reviewing, reading was linked to editing.

In assessing the fit between this block diagram model and the published data, we may observe generally that it seems to make more distinctions among processes than the data actually warrant. To begin with, the data offer no support for the independent existence of a goal-setting subprocess. As Table 7.1 indicates, Hayes and Flower (1980a) account for their protocol data with just two of their planning categories, generating and organizing, leaving out goal setting altogether. Furthermore, the data do not support grouping generating and organizing under the single process of planning. Indeed, generating and organizing appear to occur in distinct episodes and lead to distinct written products. They thus seem as independent from each other as they are from translating.

The Production System Component

The second component of the Hayes and Flower (1980a) model, the production system shown in Fig. 7.2, describes a sophisticated mechanism by which participants were modeled as moving from process to process. In a formalism common in artificial intelligence, these transitions were modeled through a system of *production rules*. As shown in Fig. 7.2, each of these production rules was made up of a left-hand side that specified the conditions in participants' working memories that would constitute a "match" to the production and a right-hand side that specified the actions participants would take once a match occurred.

Like all production systems, the Hayes and Flower component was based on the standard theory reviewed in chapter 6: It assumed participants were in a single state of working memory at any given time. It also assumed they moved through these states serially: Whenever the state of a participant's working memory changed, the monitor attempted to match the new memory state to the right-hand sides of the productions in the order in which they were listed. The first production to match was executed. This action then changed the state of the agent's working memory and the monitor started over again with another attempt at matching.

We can make this abstract description of the production system more concrete by following a participant operating under the production system given in Fig. 7.2. This system is actually only one of four "configurations" that Hayes and Flower (1980a) proposed, but the other three differ only in minor details. Using it, then, we can outline how one hypothetical participant might move state by state through the writing process:

	State 1	The process begins when the writer realizes she does not have enough material.
	Match	6. (Not enough material $\rightarrow$ [goal = generate])
	Action	This gives the participant the goal to generate material from long-term memory—in other words, to try to think of something to say.
	State 2	This action produces a new state in the participant, a state of having the goal to generate.
	Match	7. ([goal = generate] $\rightarrow$ generate).
Generate	Action	The result is that the participant does, in fact, generate something from long-term memory.
	State 3	This action in turn produces a new state: of having a new element from generate.
	Match	5. (New element from generate $\rightarrow$ [goal = organize])
	Action	As a result, the action is taken to set a goal to organize.
	State 4	Organizing becomes the new goal state.
	Match	8. ([goal = organize] $\rightarrow$ organize)
Organize	Action	Responding to this new state, the participant takes an action to organize.
	State 5	This action produces a new element from organize.
	Match	4. (New element from organize $\rightarrow$ [goal = translate]).

	Action	The participant sets a goal to translate.
	State 6	Translating becomes the new goal state.
	Match	9. ([goal = translate] → translate)
Translate	Action	In response, the participant does, in fact, translate (write) something.
	State 7	This translation produces a new element from translate.
	Match	3. (New element from translate → [goal = review]).
	Action	So the participant sets the goal to review.
	State 8	Reviewing becomes the new goal state.
	Match	10. ([goal = review] → review).
Review	Action	The participant does, in fact, review.
	State 9	Once the participant has reviewed, there is still not enough material for the paper.
	Match	6. (Not enough material → [goal = generate]).
Generate	Action	So the participant generates something else.

This last match returns the writer to State 2, starting the whole sequence over again.

In addition to the standard assumptions common to all production systems, the Hayes and Flower (1980a) system made an additional assumption: that participants operate with a mix of goal oriented and opportunistic actions. Specifically, the production system shown in Fig. 7.2 included goal-orientation as a feature by having productions with left-hand sides that referenced not only conditions in the environment ("not enough material" and "new element from translate") but also conditions in the participants' goals. Production 8, for example, matches on the goal to organize; Production 9 matches on the goal to translate. In fact, the only way participants can take these two actions in this production system is by setting these prior goals.

Not all productions in the Hayes and Flower (1980a) system were goal oriented. Production 1 allowed participants to edit whenever they became aware of editable language. Production 2 allowed them to generate whenever they became aware of new information. Furthermore, because these productions came first in the list, they took precedence over other more goal-oriented actions. In this manner, the production system allowed the actions of editing and generating—unlike those of organizing and translating—to be taken whenever environmental conditions were appropriate regardless of the participant's current goals.

By including both goal-oriented and opportunistic productions in their cognitive process model, Hayes and Flower (1980a) were operating with a hybrid model of cognition, one that was not as exclusively goal oriented as some cognitive psychologists were claiming at the time (Anderson, 1983) nor as opportunistic as others argued (Hayes-Roth & Hayes-Roth, 1975). It was this mixture, furthermore, that enabled them to make one of their major claims: that writing was a recursive activity. For with just goal-oriented productions, the Hayes and Flower production system actually produces only linear sequences of actions like that taken by our hypothetical participant and diagrammed in Part A of Fig. 7.3: Generate is followed by organize is followed by translate is followed by review. With the addition of opportunistic productions, however, the writer can interrupt this linear sequence of goal-oriented actions. As shown in Part B of Fig. 7.3, Production 2 allows her to interrupt a goal-oriented organize to generate a new idea; this generate in turn leads to another and entirely different organize; and from there a new action sequence commences, producing full-scale recursion.

In assessing the fit between this production system component and the published data, we may observe that the data do not seem to warrant the level of complex modeling produced by this mix of goal-oriented and opportunistic productions. They do not, in fact, show evidence of the full-scale recursion diagrammed in Part B of Fig. 7.3: Generating and Editing do indeed appear to interrupt the core processes of all three episodes opportunistically. But, as the data in Table 7.1 suggest, these interruptions do not lead to full-scale embedding. Instead, generating and editing simply interrupt the core process briefly, most often for one or two segments, and then return control to the core process.

AN ALTERNATIVE: MODELING CULTURAL ACTIVITY

Fundamentally, the source of difficulty in trying to fit the published protocol data to the cognitive process model lies in an inappropriate choice regarding the proper level of analysis. As laid out in the first column of Table 7.2, Hayes and Flower (1980a) assumed that skill in writing was made up of a set of cognitive *processes* that could logically occur at any time in composing if the environmental

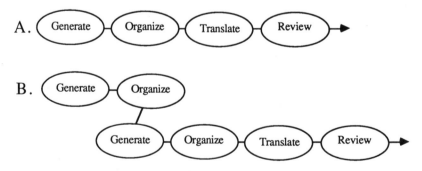

FIG. 7.3. The linearity of a purely goal-oriented production system versus the full recursion possible in a mixed system of goal-oriented and opportunistic productions.

TABLE 7.2
Modeling Writing as Process and Activity: Contrasting Assumptions

Writing as Process	Writing as Activity
Writing processes are not linear.	Writing activities are basically linear.
Processes are hierarchically embedded.	Activities are not decomposable.
People are unaware of their processes.	People are aware of their writing activities.
Processes produce information.	Activities produce textual artifacts.

conditions were appropriate. They further assumed that these processes were organized in complex hierarchical and recursive structures that, for the most part, were beyond ordinary awareness. To handle the resulting complexity, then, they posited a monitor that tied the writer's actions to conditions in the environment through a mix of goal-oriented and opportunistic productions. The outcome of these actions was always assumed to be information which, through working memory, could be shuttled from one process to the next.

Part of the problem with this model seems to lie in the very complexities of what it tried to do. First, the block diagram component made far more distinctions concerning planning than the published data actually warranted, and it grouped generating and organizing hierarchically under planning even though the published data suggested they were relatively independent. Second, the production system component used a mixture of opportunistic and goal-oriented productions to produce the short-lived process interrupts that did occur in the published data, but it also predicted a full-scale recursion that did not occur.

Perhaps even more significant than what the cognitive process model did do, however, was what it failed to do. In particular, it ignored the more obvious temporal features of the participant's episodic structure: As time changed, nearly every aspect of the participant's literacy practices changed with it. To begin with, the participant seemed self-consciously aware of how he changed his action over time, in many cases signaling transitions between episodes with explicit meta-comments:

Episode 1: "And now what I'll do is simply jot down random thoughts. . . .";
Episode 2: "Now I think it's time to go back and read over the material and elaborate on its organization. . . ."
Episode 3: "Let's try and write something."

Second, the participant used these changes over time to produce significantly different textual products: first unorganized notes (Episode 1), later organized lists (Episode 2), and ultimately discursive text (Episode 3). Finally, the participant organized his actions differently with time: In Episode 1, he was engaged mostly in generating ideas, with just a little editing; in Episode 2, he shifted to organizing, with some generating and some editing; and in Episode 3, he became concerned mainly with translating, but with occasional generating and a substantial amount of editing. Thus, temporal features were evident at every turn in the published protocol data.

Nowhere in the cognitive process model, however, are these temporal aspects acknowledged. In fact, by adopting the concept of cognitive process, Hayes and Flower (1980a) actually produced a model that arrayed participants' practices in space rather than in time. This effect was particularly obvious with the block diagram component shown in Fig. 7.1: Despite the presence of arrows, this component was basically an abstract spatial array. In it, a generate was a generate regardless of when it occurred.

The production system component did do a better job of modeling the dynamic quality of participants' actions, but even it did not include any specifically temporal features. Indeed, the only way to get the production system to produce episodic behavior would be to assume that unspecified conditions in the environment or in the participant's goals would somehow cause the participant's actions to be arranged episodically. Such an assumption, however, makes time entirely external to participants' literacy practices and still begs the question of what such external conditions might be.

An alternative set of assumptions could be made if we shift the level of analysis from cognitive process to cultural *activity*. Adapted from Soviet psychology (Wertsch, 1981), the concept of activity represents human actions at the level at which they become self-conscious and culturally meaningful. Activities, in fact, are defined by the cultural objects toward which they are oriented (Wertsch, 1981). Soviet psychologists, unlike Western psychologists, have not assumed that participants' thinking is distinct from the environment, particularly the cultural environment. Indeed, according to Leont'ev (1981), "mental reflection of the object world is not produced directly by external influences . . . but by processes through which the subject enters into practical contact with the object world" (p. 49). The concept of activity names the level at which this practical contact takes place.

The concept of activity grants human action a temporal dimension lacking in the concept of cognitive process. In fact, activities are units of human action that unfold in time at three distinct levels. First, at the level of individual practitioners, activities have an internal temporal structure that corresponds to the episodic structure we have seen in the published protocol data. That is, they represent the minimum level of human action that takes place linearly in time. Second, at the level of social institutions, activities undergo a temporal development by which they are transmitted from generation to generation. Through what Vygotsky characterized as the zone of proximal development, participants internalize activities that were first introduced to them in interaction with others (Wertsch, 1981). And, finally, at the level of culture, activities represent the outcome of the temporal processes of history. In time, in fact, activities come to fossilize the patterns of a society's interaction with the environment and with itself and make these patterns available as a force forming and shaping the behavior of its members (Wertsch, 1981).

Once we shift from conceptualizing writing as processes arrayed in space to conceptualizing it as activities arrayed in time, many of the difficulties we encountered in modeling the published protocol data disappear. No longer do we see writing as made up of a tool kit of cognitive processes that can occur, even without the participant's own awareness, at any time during composing. Instead, as shown in the second column of Table 7.2, we begin to see generating, organizing, and translating as a linear sequence of activities that participants self-consciously organize to produce particular textual artifacts. These textual artifacts, in turn, become the major vehicle by which participants manage to transfer and transform information across activities: The notes of generating become the material for organizing; the outline produced in organizing guides the writing done in translating. Within each activity, of course, some interesting nonlinearity does appear to occur in the form of process interrupts. Nevertheless, activity remains the basic unit of literacy practices—linking participants' actions in time with the textual artifacts of their culture.

RECOVERING THE COGNITIVE TRADITION

The 10 years of research on the cognitive processes of writing have been plagued with controversies over protocol analysis, concerns about coding schemes, and inattention to the full model of the cognitive processes of writing. As I hope my arguments in the last two chapters have indicated, even an insider, adopting the assumptions, techniques, and evidence of the tradition, can find much that is valid in these criticisms. Nevertheless, unlike many, I would not argue for a full-scale abandonment of the cognitive legacy.

Instead, researchers of academic literacy would find it more appropriate to go back and recover the cognitive tradition where it has been strongest: in modeling the spatial representations with which participants think. As chapter 3 suggests, cognitive researchers have found expertise to be more a matter of representation than a matter of process. In the domain of physics problem solving, for example, experts seemed to be different than students not because they used some obviously more effective processes, but because they represented the physical universe in more abstract terms. It is true that these abstract representations did seem to allow experts to use more efficient forward-search procedures, but in more ill-defined problem solving, these processing differences seemed to disappear: In radiology and Soviet domestic policy, for example, experts favored extended reasoning that would allow them to construct the arguments they needed to get outsiders to accept and act on their conclusions.

Because literacy research broke off from cognitive psychology at an early and more process-oriented stage, we have largely remained unaware of this later work on expertise. Nevertheless, this representational perspective turns out not only to be more appropriate for the study of expertise, but also to be more compatible with recent theories of cognition. As we have seen in chapter 6, these theories put participants' cognitive processes out of consciousness and therefore beyond the ken of think-aloud protocols. Any attempt to read fundamental processes out of the record of consciousness would, therefore, be fraught with difficulties, many of which we may have witnessed in this chapter.

Nonetheless, these revised theories do seem to provide exactly the kind of maneuvering room literacy researchers would need to study the interaction of rhetorical process and domain content. By allowing that consciousness is still kept in registration with participants' conceptual thinking, the revised theories suggest the possibility of using verbal data, including protocol data, to track participants' changing representations over the time course of their activities. *Activity* and *representation*, thus, become key analytic concepts. Using them, we can look how participants' rhetorical processes—as projected in time through the structure of their activities—interact with their developing understanding of domain content—as projected in space through the structure of their mental representations. With these analytic tools and the verbal data protocols provide, then, we may come closer to understanding academic literacy and the nature of expertise, the task we undertake in the coming chapters.

STUDIES AT A SINGLE SITE OF ACADEMIC LITERACY: PHILOSOPHICAL ETHICS

CHAPTER

8

DESIGN AND ANALYTIC
FRAMEWORK FOR THESE STUDIES

The studies to be reported in Part III of this book began in January of 1985 under a grant from the Fund for the Improvement of Postsecondary Education to the WARRANT Project at Carnegie Mellon University. For this project, Preston Covey of the Philosophy Department had promised to use case-based reasoning to develop software support for a curriculum in philosophical ethics. From the English Department, David Kaufer brought his perspective on rhetorical theory and argumentation, Christine M. Neuwirth brought her training in computer science and composition, and I brought my interest in reading and writing. In the first half of this chapter, I outline the original design for the data gathering effort we completed in 1985–1986. In the second half, I preview the general framework that guided the subsequent analyses.

I invite you as reader to read this material rhetorically: to view this research as an act taken by someone for some purpose in some situation. At the same time, I also invite you to see this research as the outcome of what might be a set of more universal—or at least less local—principles concerning how research should be done and why. Such principles do not come easily, do not come ahistorically, and do not emerge unrhetorically. Nevertheless, I believe they do emerge. Currently, the academy is struggling toward a more appropriate methodology, one that can straddle the all too common divide between empirical descriptions of what is and philosophical inquiries concerning what ought to be. In the hopes of making a contribution toward this effort, then, I have tried to tease out both the logic and the history underlying the studies that follow.

DESIGN FOR THE DATA-GATHERING EFFORT

The data collection effort began in the spring of 1985 according to the design represented in Fig. 8.1. As this figure indicates, our deliverable to the Fund for the Improvement of Postsecondary Education was a curriculum for teaching philosophy and argumentation. We proposed to shape this curriculum, in part, through empirical observations: First, we expected these observations of "experts" in philosophical argumentation to help us develop strategies for constructing written argument on an issue in ethics. Next, we expected observations of "novices" to tell us what the intended recipients of our curriculum would do on their own. And finally, we expected observations of the dynamics of classroom interaction to tell us how a teacher could mediate between expert strategies and novice conceptions. Thus, overall, the data-gathering approach we developed included three distinct but related foci: experts working on their own, novices working on their own, and a teacher and a class working together.

The Issue

We decided to ask these participants to work on a common issue, the ethical issue of medical paternalism. By the time of our project, this issue had emerged as a central one in medical ethics. In response to growing concerns in the medical community, ethicists were struggling to define the boundaries between doctors' justified and unjustified interference in patients' right to autonomy. The following materials, edited by Kaufer, still serve as a good introduction to this issue at the time:

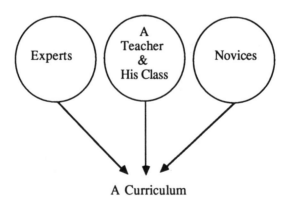

A Curriculum

FIG. 8.1. The original design for the data collection effort of the WARRANT Project funded by the Fund for the Improvement of Postsecondary Education in 1985. Reprinted by permission.

An Introduction to Paternalism #1
Nothing is more necessary to human life, and fortunately nothing more common, than parents' concern for their children. The infant's relatively lengthy period of helplessness requires that others nourish and protect it. And the child's existence as a vital being with an interest in the world, a capacity for eagerness and trust, and a sense of its own worth, all depend upon its receiving loving care, understanding, and attention. With time, the normally developing child relinquishes its almost total dependence; it acquires the capacity to conceive of itself as an agent, to set out on its own, and to live in a world less dominated by its bodily needs and by its parents.

Paternalism as a social phenomenon is prefigured in this elemental and universal situation of solicitous parental conduct that has its roots in our common humanity. But paternalism is of philosophic [ethical] interest, not because of the ways parents legitimately relate to their children—indeed there is an oddity in describing this conduct as "paternalistic"—but rather because something like this practice is introduced into relations among adults. If our responses to adults mirror intrusive and solicitous parental responses to children we behave paternalistically. (Morris, 1981, p. 263)

An Introduction to Paternalism #2
Although the Oxford English Dictionary dates the term "paternalism" from the 1880's, the idea is much older and, indeed, appears very early in human thought. Its meaning, according to the *OED*, is "the principle and practice of paternal administration; government as by a father; the claim or attempt to supply the needs or to regulate the life of a nation or community in the same way a father does those of his children." When the analogy with the father is used to illuminate the role of professionals or the state in health care, it presupposes two features of the paternal role: that the father is benevolent and beneficent, i.e., that he has the interests of his children at heart, and that he makes all or at least some of the decisions relating to his children's welfare rather than letting them make these decisions. Paternalism poses moral questions precisely because it involves the claim that beneficence (doing good or preventing harm) should take precedence over [individual] autonomy (freedom or independence), at least in some cases. (Beauchamp & Childress, 1979, p. 154)

The Issue Over Paternalism
Philosophers and social theorists have long debated the merits of paternalism in society (including, as we will see in most of these readings, health care). To understand the debate, it is useful to consider a passage of J. S. Mill in his *On Liberty*. Mill writes: "[T]he only purpose for which power can be rightfully exercised over any member of a civilized community, against his will, is to prevent harm to others. His own good, either physical or moral, is not a sufficient warrant. . . . The only part of conduct of anyone, for which he is amenable to society, is that which concerns others. In the part which merely concerns himself, his independence is of right, absolute." (Mill, 1909, p. 212)

These statements are now commonly referred to as Mill's harm principle. Roughly put, the harm principle stipulates that the only grounds for imposing upon or restricting the liberty of an individual against his/her will is when the imposition prevents harm to others. You can thus restrict John Smith's freedom if you know that doing so will prevent harm to Tom Jones or Chicago. But can you impose on John Smith for paternalistic reasons? That is, can you impose upon him, against his will, to prevent him from harming himself? This is the question to which Mill emphatically answers no.

Mill believed that paternalism has no place in our culture. The authors in this corpus are hardly advocates of paternalistic practices, but they all see and most try to define—conditions where paternalism may play a useful role. The issues are complicated, however, because paternalism can be defined in a variety of ways and how it is defined matters importantly in how and when people look to justify it. (Kaufer, 1984)

We expected medical paternalism to be a good issue for our studies because it involved a situation with which nearly everyone in our culture had experience: being a patient. At the same time, it also brought in concepts—such as will, autonomy, and rights—that afforded standard philosophical analysis. We anticipated, therefore, that paternalism would raise many of the issues faced by both philosophers and rhetoricians who took on the task of teaching their students to be more critical thinkers.

The Materials

The specific materials we gave to our participants included a number of selections from primary sources. During the fall of 1985, Kaufer did scholarly research on the issue of paternalism in preparation for teaching a class on philosophical argumentation the following semester. Using James Childress' (1982) comprehensive analysis of the issue, *Who Should Decide?: Paternalism in Health Care*, as a starting point, he eventually edited the following corpus of selections that we prepared for distribution to the participants in our studies: Carter (1977), Childress, (1982), Dworkin (1972), Gert and Culver (1976, 1979), and Komrad (1983).

Like any scholarly bibliography, these selections represented a somewhat standard and somewhat idiosyncratic history of the state of the issue at the time. The earliest article, by Gerald Dworkin in 1972, put paternalism on the philosophical map by pointing out that, even though paternalism violated the autonomy of the individual agent, it was often used to justify legal actions. Next, Gert and Culver tried to outline the conditions they thought might justify such paternalistic interference. Carter then proposed an alternative justification. And in 1982, as we have seen, the debate took a decidedly medical slant with the publication of Childress' book. Finally, Komrad, a practicing physician, attempted a response from the doctor's point of view.

Kaufer organized these materials into the three parts shown in the table of contents given in Table 8.1. The first part included the short introduction quoted previously: two excerpts defining paternalism as well as Kaufer's own review of "The Issue over Paternalism." The second included excerpts on the definition of paternalism. The third included excerpts concerned with its justification.

In addition to the primary scholarship, Kaufer included two sets of "cases" of paternalism adapted from Childress (1982). The first set of cases, included in the section on definition, contrasted examples and nonexamples of paternalism such as the following:

1. *Case 2 (example of paternalism):* Mr. N, a member of a religious sect that strictly forbids blood transfusions, is involved in a serious automobile accident and loses a large amount of blood. On arriving at the hospital, he is still conscious and informs the doctor that his religion forbids blood transfusions. Immediately thereafter he faints from loss of blood. The doctor believes that if Mr. N is not given a transfusion he will die. Thereupon, while Mr. N is still unconscious, the doctor arranges for and carries out the blood transfusion.

2. *Case 2a (nonexample of paternalism):* Mr. N, a member of a religious sect that does not believe in blood transfusions, is involved in a serious automobile accident and loses a large amount of blood. On arriving at the hospital, he is unconscious and no one is aware of his religious beliefs. The doctor believes that if Mr. N is not given a transfusion he will die. Thereupon, while Mr. N is still unconscious, the doctor arranges for and carries out the blood transfusion.

3. *Case 2b (nonexample of paternalism):* Mr. N, a member of a religious sect that strictly forbids blood transfusions, is involved in a serious automobile accident and loses a large amount of blood. On arriving at the hospital, he is still conscious and informs the doctor that he would rather die than undergo a blood transfusion. Immediately thereafter he faints from loss of blood. The doctor

believes that if Mr. N is not given a transfusion he will die. After agonizing about what to do, the doctor finally calls in a leader of Mr. N's religious sect to administer final rites to Mr. N before he dies. (Kaufer, 1984, pp. 3–4)

The second set of cases, included in the section on justification, represented more controversial cases of paternalistic interference:

> *Case #3:* One evening five victims of an automobile accident were admitted to the ward of a small rural hospital. The nurse in charge knew the woman who had been driving and her four children who were also injured. Three of the children survived, but the oldest child, a daughter, died shortly after admission. The mother suffered contusions and abrasions, but her major problem was her mental anguish about her children. The nurse asked the doctor, who was busy in the operating theatre, what she should tell the mother about the daughter's death. The doctor told the nurse to reassure the woman at all costs because she was in great distress, and her husband could not be reached until the next morning. All through the night the mother constantly asked the nurse about the children. As the nurse put it, "It went strongly against my conscience to have to look her in the eye and repeat a lie of such magnitude." The doctor told the woman the truth the next day in the presence of her husband. She thanked the doctor for holding back the truth, out of consideration for her condition, but she insisted, "I still wish you had told me last night." (Kaufer, 1984, p. 29)

Altogether, this corpus of material contained 62 pages.

The Task

We asked the experts working through these materials to complete the following task:

> You are writing an article discussing the current state of thinking on medical paternalism.
>
> Your intended audience are readers of a popular magazine such as *The Humanist* or *Harpers*. They are well-educated people who may at some time in their lives have to deal with the issue of paternalism, either personally or professionally; but they are not technically trained in philosophy.
>
> Your article will be a paper in two parts. In the first part you should summarize and evaluate the definitions of medical paternalism given in the first part of the corpus.
>
> In the second part, you should summarize and evaluate the attempts to state the conditions under which paternalism is justified. They can be found in the second part of the corpus.
>
> Please keep all of the things you write in each session and allow us to make copies of them.

The task given to novices was basically the same with a few minor changes: We substituted *Atlantic* for *The Humanist*; we called the paper a "long paper, term-paper length" rather than an article; and we left out the comment about technical training.

For the classroom study, we allowed the teacher to decide for himself how best to design a curriculum that, in the end, would enable students to complete this same task. Further details concerning his curricular plans can be found in chapter 12.

The Participants

The two experts we involved in our study were PhD candidates in the philosophy program at the University of Pittsburgh. Both were men, reflecting the general pattern in the program. Jeff had recently completed his PhD and accepted a position at a prestigious university. Roger was still working on his degree. Preston Covey had solicited their participation through his contacts with the Philosophy Department.

The two novices in our study were second-semester freshmen at Carnegie Mellon University. Both were women and thus somewhat atypical of the undergraduate program. Janet was an engineering student who had received an A in her humanities course the previous semester. Leslie was a design student who had received a B in her writing course the previous semester. Neither had yet taken the required introductory freshman philosophy course. We solicited their participation through an advertisement distributed to all students enrolled in the freshman writing program.

Kaufer served as the teacher for the classroom study. At that time, he was an associate professor of rhetoric in the English Department at Carnegie Mellon University. He had completed his doctoral work in rhetoric at the University of Wisconsin, Madison, and had taken additional training in philosophy, linguistics, and computer science. At the time of this study, he had published extensively on the rhetorical tropes, particularly metaphor, and on argumentation. As coprincipal investigator on the WARRANT project, he was teaching this course for the first time in order to develop a curriculum.

The students for the classroom study came from those enrolled in Kaufer's course. Of the 30 students who took the course, 29 agreed to participate in the study and 24 actually participated. Most of these students were enrolled in programs in the English Department as undergraduate majors in professional writing, technical writing, creative writing, or literature; as master's candidates in professional writing; or as PhD candidates in rhetoric.

In this book, the names of all these participants, with the exception of the teacher, have been changed.

The Data

The experts and novices worked on the paternalism task at their own pace over the course of the spring semester of 1985. For each working session, they produced think-aloud protocols, voicing their thoughts into a tape recorder as they worked, following guidelines adopted from Perkins (1981) and given in Appendix B. The two experts were given tape recorders and asked to turn them on whenever they worked, usually at home or in their offices. The two novices were provided with a private office and worked at regularly scheduled hours during the week.

After each working session and before the next session, these participants were interviewed by members of our research team at a time and place of their convenience. Following the interview schedule given in Appendix C, we asked about what they had accomplished, what they were planning to do, and how they saw their activities fitting into their overall work. We also asked them to bring their notes and texts to refresh their memories and we later collected these texts for analysis. Table 8.2 gives the total amount of data collected for each participant.

The tape recordings of the protocols and interviews were transcribed and ordered chronologically. The protocol transcripts were precoded to identify the basic protocol phenomena discussed in chapter 7: which segments were being read, which were being written, and which were being neither read nor written. The written materials the participants produced were also numbered in the order in which they were produced. In addition, in the margins of the transcripts, we identified the specific segment of text, if any, that was being read or written.

The teacher and his class worked on the issue of paternalism during the same spring semester. For each class session, I worked as a nonparticipant observer (Goetz & LeCompte, 1984) audiotaping the classroom interaction. For all but two classes, I sat at the back or side of the classroom and took notes on what was said, who was talking, and what was written on the blackboard and overhead projector. I also photocopied all material handed out to the students and assignments written by them. The audio recordings were later transcribed and my notes were used to fill in the names of speakers, information written on the board or in overheads, and garbled interactions.

TABLE 8.2
Data Collected for Each of the Participants in the Expert–Novice Studies

Participant	# Protocol Sessions	# Interviews
Jeff	25	22
Roger	12	11
Janet	33	22
Leslie	26	25

Before and after each classroom session, I interviewed the teacher using the interview guide reproduced in Appendix C. My questions covered the teacher's plans for the upcoming class and his characterization and evaluation of events after each class session. Students were also interviewed in random order at the rate of approximately two per week throughout the entire semester. The interview guide for these student interviews, given in Appendix D, included questions about background, expectations, the most recent assignment, and development of the course in general. A few students were interviewed twice, once early in the semester and once later on. Table 8.3 gives the total amount of data collected for the classroom study.

The Rationale

This data-gathering effort amounted to an intense study of a single site of academic literacy. We took an issue at a specific time in the domain of medical ethics and asked participants to react to it in their own way. We were generally motivated by the desire to create a more naturalistic task than had typically been used in expert–novice studies up to that time. That is, we wanted a task that academics might actually take on. But this desire, at the same time, gave the study some unusual characteristics.

To begin with, the choice of a particular issue represented a departure from the cognitive process legacy that had come down to us at Carnegie Mellon. The work of Young and later Flower and Hayes had been rooted in the problem-

TABLE 8.3
Data Collected for the Classroom Study

Week	Class Tapings	Teacher Interviews	Student Interviews
1	1	2	2
2	1	2	2
3	1	2	2
4	2	2	1
5	2	4	1
6	1	3	2
7	2	3	1
8	2	3	2
9	2	4	2
break		1	
10	2	4	2
11	2	1	2
12	2	4	4
13	2	5	2
14	2	3	3
15	1	1	
Total 15	**25**	**44**	**28**

solving framework we examined in chapter 3. That is, it represented a hunch that expertise consisted largely of domain-general strategies that could be used with any particular content. Young, Becker, and Pike (1970) made argumentation appear to cross domains. Flower and Hayes (1981a, 1981b, 1981c) were not concerned with what their writers were reading or writing. In part because of the interdisciplinary nature of our project, however, we could not afford to remain as indifferent to content. As a practical matter, we needed to pick an issue that was relevant to philosophy. Even further, we had begun to believe the growing literature, reviewed in chapter 3, that suggested that content was important to the shape of expertise. Kaufer recalled the decision this way:

> I felt that reading and writing strategies, in essence, were ways of manipulating information through various representations. While the dependence of particular strategies on particular content seemed to me (and still does) an open issue, there was no question that the only way to isolate these strategies was NOT to start top-down (assuming we knew what they were as almost every textbook writer assumed) but bottom-up, to induce strategies from watching people work at the level of particulars (personal communication, 1993).

Several decisions followed almost immediately upon our decision to be issue-specific. The first of these was our decision to study reading as well as writing. Once we had taken the ethics of paternalism as our issue, we could not realistically limit our observations of what people did to their writing alone. Intuitively, we knew that a great deal of the action had to be in the reading. Since that time, of course, many other researchers, much of whose work was reviewed in Chapter 2, have made a similar move to look at reading-writing connections. But at the time, we were just flying by the seat of our pants.

Second, we needed to enlarge the time frame. If we were going to look at how experts and novices developed an argument about paternalism, we were obviously not going to be able to gather data in the hour-long sessions that had typically been used in expert–novice studies. Teachers and students, we knew, took about 15 weeks to do their work. To get comparable data, we decided to give our experts and novices the same.

FRAMEWORK FOR ANALYSIS

Although specific details of how these data were analyzed are provided in the next few chapters, a few opening remarks on the overall analytic framework can be made. Consonant with the theoretical framework introduced in Part I, the general issue I have pursued in analysis has been identifying the relationship between indigenous culture and the formal culture of the academy, particularly as manifested in philosophical ethics.

Traditionally, these two forms of culture were assumed to have nothing to do with each other. Psychologically, as we saw in chapter 3, expert conceptions of a domain content appeared to represent a departure from more indigenous or everyday concepts. Historically, as we saw in chapter 4, educators seemed to demand that the sons of a rising middle class renounce their indigenous culture in favor of the more formal and apparently more universal culture of the academy.

Much evidence exists to suggest, however, that the formal culture of the academy was not as distinct from indigenous culture as this traditional view holds. In fact, academic culture bore an uncanny resemblance to what had once been the indigenous culture of the upper-class eastern elite. As we saw in chapter 4, early leaders of the professionalization movement were quite clear about their desire to use the academy to preserve aspects of the indigenous culture to which they had been born. Furthermore, even in the present day, indigenous culture appears to play a significant role in determining students' success in school. In particular, if the home culture has made literacy activities a part of everyday life, students are much more likely to succeed and persist within the educational system (Bourdieu & Passeron, 1977; Collins, 1979; Heath, 1983; Wells, 1986). Overall, then, the formal culture of the academy seems to represent not an alternative to all indigenous cultures so much as an unacknowledged extension of some of them.

As we noted in chapter 5, philosophy provides a particularly interesting case in regard to its relationship to indigenous culture: It represents a discipline that, for a long period of its history, resisted professionalization. Like most of the humanities, philosophy distrusted the professionalization movement and, in fact, was not fully organized under a professional society until 1901. Amateur philosophizing held the upper hand with the Transcendentalists before the Civil War, and even some of the founding fathers of academic philosophy, including William James, began their work outside of the academy after the war (Kuklick, 1977). In the 1880s and 1890s, however, philosophic inquiry underwent a major reorganization along more academic lines. As in the other disciplines we examined in chapter 4, this professionalization ultimately moved philosophy out of the public arena and into more purely technical concerns. Furthermore, as Kuklick's (1977) extensive analysis of the Golden Age of the Harvard program indicates, this meant moving philosophy away from a concern with ethics. Originally, according to Kuklick, Charles Eliot had revitalized the philosophy department at Harvard to better deal with the ethical issues raised by Darwinism. In response, Josiah Royce and William James, both of whom Eliot had hired, attempted to combine technical excellence with public concerns. But, according to Kuklick (1977), this combination was short-lived:

> For a generation, Royce and James vitalized the view that science and religion were compatible. But the Darwinian controversy was not only a fight between science and religion but also a fight between scientists and ministers as cultural

arbiters. Royce and James simultaneously played both roles, combining fundamental research in basic fields with popular presentation of the practical philosophy. As science vanquished religion, however, philosophers shifted away from the ministerial role, although still working within the speculative framework created during the Golden Age. They ignored the public work of Royce and James and centered their attention on logic and epistemology. The order of the day was technical specialized research published for technically competent audiences in technical journals, with popularization in all areas of speculation frequently relegated to hacks, incompetents, and has-beens. (p. 575)

In this general climate, the study of ethics developed as a minor technical area within philosophy departments with little direct relevance to lay concerns. This began to change, however, in the late 1960s with growing concern over the ethical implications of technological advances in medicine. According to Davis (1990), medical schools came to philosophers seeking advice concerning how to prepare doctors to deal with issues such as paternalism. This dialogue was only the start of what Davis characterized as "the ethics boom"—a resurgence of interest in ethics in a range of professional endeavors. Though these applied ethicists were not considered part of mainstream philosophy by many traditional programs, the issues they brought up—issues such as paternalism—did begin to have an impact on traditional philosophical thinking.

Throughout its history, then, the study of ethics within the discipline of academic philosophy has involved an uneasy relationship with the concerns of indigenous culture. Particularly at the period in which the data for these studies were gathered, this relationship was especially problematic. Applied and more traditional ethicists voiced serious disagreements over how or even whether traditional philosophical concepts should be used outside of the technical domain.

The studies in the following chapters attempt to characterize this uneasy relationship by comparing the activities and representations of practitioners in philosophical ethics with the activities and representations more common in everyday or indigenous practices. In particular, I have made comparisons with three other well-analyzed and often referenced indigenous practices: conversation, narrative, and apprenticeship.

Conversation, the first of these indigenous practices, is the practice that actually creates indigenous culture. According to Collins' (1979) definition, indigenous culture is the culture that normally arises out of the everyday interaction of individuals, interactions, by and large, carried out through conversation. Work by sociologists suggests, furthermore, that these conversations have both a basic structure common to all indigenous cultures and distinctive characteristics specific to particular institutional and cultural settings (Erickson & Mohatt, 1982; Heritage, 1984; Mehan, 1979; Philips, 1972; Sacks, Schegloff, & Jefferson, 1974). In our analysis of academic literacy and the nature of expertise, we draw on this work to ask, in general, how the practices of reading and writing in philosophical ethics are like and unlike everyday conversation.

Narrative, the second of the forms we examine, is usually considered the most indigenous of the extended forms of discourse practice. Story telling seems to occur regularly in all indigenous cultures (Chafe, 1980), and appears to be acquired by children very early (DiPardo, 1990). Although narrative has developed into a form of high art (Chatman, 1978; Genette, 1980), it has also remained one of the constants of everyday interaction (Labov, 1972; Polanyi, 1979, 1982). As a result, narrative has been one of the most heavily analyzed of discourse practices. In our work on philosophical ethics, we draw on this analysis to ask, in general, how the practices of philosophical ethics are like and unlike everyday narratives.

Apprenticeship, the third of the indigenous practices we examine, is the basic interactional pattern by which one generation transmits indigenous culture to the next. In apprenticeship, as distinct from the formal culture of the schools, cultural knowledge and skill are assumed to be handed down from mentor to apprentice in the context of everyday use (Rogoff, 1990). Probably the best known model of apprenticeship was described by Vygotsky (1962) with his zone of proximal development which, in this country, was extended through the ideas of scaffolding (Langer & Applebee, 1987; Wood, Bruner, & Ross, 1976) and, more recently, cognitive apprenticeship (Brown, Collins, & Dugid, 1989). In our analysis of the classroom, we use this model of apprenticeship to ask, in general, how classroom interaction in philosophical ethics is like and unlike indigenous practices of apprenticeship.

Comparisons between the formal culture of the academy and these three indigenous practices are interesting as a way to understand how literacy practices are related to the exercise of expertise in philosophical ethics. These comparisons are made even more interesting, however, because all three of these indigenous practices have often been described as alternatives to traditional academic practices. Conversation, for example, has been praised for being more democratic, historically situated, and suitable for the development of value consensus than is traditional scholarly interaction (Bernstein, 1983; Frentz, 1985; McCloskey, 1985; Rorty, 1979). Narrative has been praised for being more democratic, historically situated, and value oriented than is standard academic prose (Brodkey,1987b; Bruner, 1986; Fisher, 1987; Killingsworth & Steffens, 1989; MacIntyre, 1981; Turner, 1980; White, 1980). And, apprenticeship has recently been offered as a better model for education than traditional classroom lessons (Brown et al., 1989; Rogoff, 1990). Do these calls for a return to one or more of these indigenous practices represent a real alternative to traditional academic practices or are they just another example of the Rousseauian romanticization of the primitive? In order to answer this question—and seriously engage in the task of reflection—we must more carefully understand the relationship between the literacy practices of the academy and the patterns of everyday life. It is with this end in mind that I have undertaken the analyses presented in the next few chapters.

9

THE GENRE OF THE PHILOSOPHIC ESSAY: TRANSFORMING READERS' EXPERIENCE

As the methodological discussion of Part II was meant to indicate, any study of academic literacy and the nature of expertise must begin with an understanding of the cultural objects toward which participants orient their reading and writing. In philosophy, this means understanding philosophic essays. Even though these essays certainly do not represent the whole of philosophers' expertise, they do provide a major driving force for much of their academic life. What, then, do these essays look like?

This chapter aims at a preliminary answer to this question by framing an analysis of the space-time dimensions of the contemporary philosophic essay against two alternative sets of discourse forms: the indigenous forms of conversation and narrative, and the historical forms of early academic writing. For the first of these comparisons, we use the work of contemporary philosopher Richard Bernstein. For the second comparison, we use the work of William James.

Together, these comparisons suggest that a distinctive virtual reading experience is created by the contemporary philosophic essay, an experience that distances it from the patterns of everyday life. The conventions governing this virtual experience, which we conceptualize as a *main path/faulty path* structure, seem to have developed concurrently with the rise of the academic professions at the turn of the century. In particular, they seem to reflect philosophy's historically situated understanding of the relationship between its issues and the everyday life of the general public.

STYLISTIC SHIFTS TO THE CONTEMPORARY
PHILOSOPHIC ESSAY

Like its counterpart in the scientific professions, the philosophic essay traces its roots to the last major stylistic shift leading to modern English, one that occurred during the Restoration period of 17th-century England. During this time, writers associated with the newly formed Royal Society of London—Thomas Sprat and John Locke, the most notable among them—made repeated calls for a complex set of stylistic changes: (a) Anglo-Saxon rather than Latinate vocabulary, (b) simple subject–verb structures rather than complex tropes, (c) description and definition rather than emotional reaction or moral evaluation, (d) third- rather than first-person perspective, and (e) a generally more concise expression.

Members of the Royal Society were generally agreed on the benefits of this shift. With a plainer language and greater consideration for the reader, the readership for scientific discourse would expand from the closed societies of the universities to a broader representation of the public. Early followers of the Society believed that the new scientific techniques of observation and experimentation would open up knowledge making to "Artisans, Countrymen, and Merchants" who often had greater experience with the material world and could take control of learning away from the "Wits, or Scholars" (Sprat, 1966, p. 113). Instead of arcane disputes that caused great confusion and little social benefit (Locke, 1982), the new prose would present things in as plain a fashion as possible, leaving conclusions to the individual's judgment. As a result, society would be less susceptible to manipulation and to the social upheavals associated with the recent civil war.

The 17th-century plain language movement thus constructed the precursor of the contemporary academic essay by locating meaning in the text rather than in the rhetorical situation in which the text had been produced. Locke (1982), in particular, took great care to require knowledgeable authors to provide their own definitions for complex ideas in terms of more simple ideas available to all, and to ask other authors and their readers to accept these definitions and use them in their own discourse. Thus, although acknowledging the conventionality of language and, to some extent, its rootedness in current custom and belief, these authors attempted to widen the readership of the academic essay by removing from its language that which they believed would mislead or distract and putting into it that which would inform.

As many critics have noted, this style was more compatible with the new scientific philosophy, which needed a language to describe the universals of a physical world rather than reflect the peculiar perspectives of individual human beings. Thus this shift moved the proper topics of discourse from the interior mind to an exterior world. In addition, as Adolph (1968) pointed out, this change shifted the burden of interpretive responsibility from readers to authors. No longer were readers expected to follow the twists and turns of authors' thoughts. Instead, authors became responsible for constructing prose that would bring those thoughts clearly to readers' minds. Eventually, as we noted in chapter 1, the stylistic shift toward plain language developed into discourse conventions that favored creating a virtual experience for readers rather than reporting the actual experiences of authors. And, as we see in the next section, this was as true of the contemporary philosophic essay as it is of the contemporary scientific report.

SPACE/TIME DIMENSIONS OF THE PHILOSOPHIC ESSAY

In the genre of the contemporary philosophic essay, the virtual experience created for readers can usefully be conceptualized using the main path/faulty path structure illustrated in Fig. 9.1 (Geisler & Kaufer, 1989; Kaufer, Geisler, & Neuwirth, 1989). Following the conventions of this structure, philosophers present readers with what is, in effect, a "set of directions" for exploring the terrain of an issue mapped by other authors. With these directions, philosophers

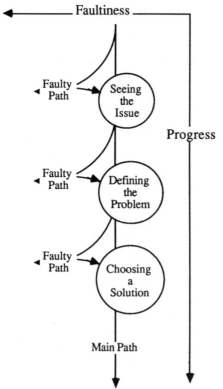

FIG. 9.1. The main path/faulty path structure of the philosophic essay.

aim to move readers from the point at which they can see the issue, to a point where they can define a problem, and finally to a point where they can choose an appropriate solution.

At every point along this main path, philosophers introduce other authors' positions as well as make their own claims. In general, they organize these alternative positions according to a *metric of faultiness*. That is, philosophers highlight the faults in other authors' approaches in order to support aspects of their own position. For instance, they often begin with an approach they consider very faulty. Then, through a critique, they eliminate that approach. Very wrong approaches are dealt with early; more complex and harder to refute approaches are dealt with later. Then, after all the faulty paths are eliminated, the resulting approach—the main path taken by the author—is left as the only remaining alternative.

An example of this main path/faulty path structure can be seen in the skeletal form of the essay written by the philosopher Edward Swain in 1983 to justify wilderness preservation:

¶1 It has not been clear *why* people argue for the preservation of wilderness. The stated reasons have usually taken one of two courses: arguing that wilderness areas and rare species have either *utilitarian* value or *intrinsic* value. . . .

¶2 In his book, *The Arrogance of Humanism*, zoologist David Ehrenfeld makes the perceptive observation that most of the utilitarian arguments are contrived. . . .

¶3 It was not difficult for Ehrenfeld to demonstrate the weakness of these arguments. . . .

¶4 It appears that contrivances to preserve wilderness areas have the potential of causing a public backlash and are therefore probably not the best way for preservationists to succeed. . . .

¶5 Ehrenfeld, convinced that preservation cannot be ensured by contriving and assigning utilitarian, or anthropocentric, values to wilderness areas, goes on to seek a better value system. . . .

¶6 Other preservationists have also reached the conclusion that we need a new value system, often ascribing, as Ehrenfeld does, a religious dimension to nature and to its ecological workings. . . .

¶7 I agree with others who take the contrary stand that an expanded concept of anthropocentrism is actually the *solution* to our environmental problems. We certainly do not need to adopt new value and legal systems. It is reasonable to dismiss the "intrinsic right of existence" value system as unnecessary and unworkable and, instead, to broaden the concept of anthropocentrism to include a human need for a quality environment.

In the first paragraph, Swain both introduces the issue (why preserve wilderness?) and indicates that two approaches have been taken to the issue. In the next three paragraphs, he introduces Ehrenfeld's position and praises it for recognizing the weaknesses in the utilitarian arguments. In paragraphs five and six, he characterizes Ehrenfeld and others as turning to intrinsic arguments. Then, in the final paragraph of this, his introductory section, he claims that a broader utilitarian or anthropocentric position can be defended, thus making intrinsic arguments like Ehrenfeld's unnecessary as well as unworkable. Thus, using the main path/faulty path structure, Swain praised Ehrenfeld's position where it matched his own (in rejecting current utilitarian arguments) and criticized it where it differed (in turning to intrinsic arguments). In doing so, he set the stage for his own main line of argument for a better utilitarian defense of wilderness preservation.

The main path/faulty path structure of the philosophic essay is useful for philosophers because it draws on the two kinds of knowledge making up academic expertise: knowledge of the domain content of the discipline and knowledge of the discipline's rhetorical processes. Swain's (1983) argument, in particular, frames the three domain content claims he dealt with in the context of rhetorical processes by attributing them to other authors: Contrived utilitarian arguments are implicitly attributed to some people ("people argue for"); intrinsic arguments are directly attributed to Ehrenfeld ("Ehrenfeld makes the perceptive observation"); and an expanded anthropocentrism are attributed to the author himself among others ("I agree with others"). Swain, furthermore, achieved a subtle integration of these two kinds of knowledge by arranging these content claims in a descending order of faultiness. Ehrenfeld's critique of contrived utilitarian arguments, for example, is introduced to establish the faultiness of being *contrived* ("the potential of causing a public backlash"), and the author's critique of Ehrenfeld's position is later introduced to establish the faultiness of being *intrinsic* ("unnecessary and unworkable"). By ordering the author attribution of domain content claims, then, Swain gradually prepared the reader to accept a better—not contrived—and utilitarian—not intrinsic—defense of wilderness preservation.

This integration of rhetorical process and domain content is achieved in the philosophic essay through the manipulation of the temporal and spatial dimensions of readers' virtual reading experience. We can understand this best by contrasting readers' actual experience while reading with the virtual experience constructed by the philosophic essay. Most often, readers' actual experience involves passing through time—the time of reading—while remaining fixed at a single point in space—the place of reading. The virtual experience created by the philosophic essay basically reverses these dimensions.

To begin with, the main path/faulty path structure, rather than extending readers' experience over the actual time of reading, reduces the experience to a single point in time. This temporal reduction is achieved largely through the discourse convention of using present tense simple verbs to bring the interaction between author, other authors, and the reader into a timeless dehistoricized present. Thus, in Swain's (1983) argument, Ehrenfeld "*makes*" observations (¶2) and "*goes on* to see a better value system" (¶5) in the same time frame that Swain "*agree[s]* with others who *take* a contrary stand" (¶7). As a result of this discourse convention, the philosophic essay can be seen to "make an argument" for a reader for as long as the text can be read. Indeed, it rings odd to talk of an author's argument in the past tense—to say, for example, that Swain "*made*" rather than "*makes*" his argument—because the past tense verb—although strictly true to the actual historicity of Swain's actions as a person (he might, in fact, now disagree with his earlier position)—is at odds with the virtual experience created during reading.

The main path/faulty path structure also involves a reversal of readers' experience of space. Rather than fixing readers' experience to a single point as is mostly likely true in readers' actual experience, this structure extends readers' experience over multiple points in what Nystrand (1982) called *textual space*. As Fig. 9.1 indicates, this space is two-dimensional: In effect, readers' movement along the author's main path is the summation of two independent movements—a movement of the reader toward the resolution of an issue and a movement of the reader away from faulty understanding (or toward truth). Thus, any other author's position may be closer or farther along the dimension of progress and closer or farther away on the dimension of faultiness.

In essence, the main path/faulty path structure of the philosophic essay represents readers' experience of coming to a true resolution of an issue as predominantly spatial and predominantly timeless. In doing so, it collapses rhetorical phenomena originally experienced in time—authors' interactions with other authors, authors' interactions with readers—and their subsequent expansion over an abstract two-dimensional space. Expertise in philosophy seems, therefore, to have not so much eliminated rhetorical process from the formal culture of the academy as it has transformed it. In particular, rhetorical process has been changed from the predominantly temporal experience of human interaction into the virtual and predominantly spatial experience of moving toward progress and truth. Thus, even experts in academic philosophy—who presumably work with knowledge of both rhetorical processes and domain content—must to some extent keep in mind a distinction between their everyday culture and the formal culture of the academy, at least insofar as they produce texts that conform to the discourse conventions of the philosophic essay.

COMPARISON WITH INDIGENOUS FORMS

What is involved when participants choose to use the discourse conventions of formal academic culture rather than alternative forms more typical of indigenous culture? In particular, what would happen if a contemporary philosopher were to attempt to make an argument using the discourse conventions of narrative or those of conversation? What would be won? What would be lost? To explore answers to these questions, we look in this section at the discourse of the contemporary philosopher Richard Bernstein.

Bernstein's contribution to the development of an alternative discourse for academic inquiry has been widely recognized. In an overview of the projects and prospects for the rhetoric of inquiry, for example, Nelson and Megill (1986) cited him as one of three major skeins of scholarship contributing to a rhetoric of inquiry. A year earlier, Simons (1985) cited him in support of this same movement's nonfoundational assumptions. Bernstein's influence is based in large part on his essay, *Beyond Objectivism and Relativism: Science, Hermeneutics, and Praxis*, published in 1983. In it, he attempted to describe and argue for a common understanding of the conversational nature of human practice and judgment in all disciplinary endeavors, including the sciences, social sciences, and humanities.

In *Beyond Objectivism and Relativism*, Bernstein (1983) struggled against the conventions of the philosophic essay, both calling for a more conversational form of inquiry and employing more narrative interludes. As a result, his text is a particularly good example of the dynamics of the philosophic essay and its trade-offs with more indigenous forms. To examine these trade-offs more closely, we adapt a technique from linguistics that involves contrasting passages from naturally occurring, well-formed texts with alternative, artificially constructed texts. In constructing these texts, we are careful to add no claims beyond those found in Bernstein's original, and are able to observe the effect of different discourse conventions on authors' ability to make academic arguments.

Obviously, the construction of artificial texts requires an exercise in hypothetical thinking and runs the risk of going beyond naturally occurring phenomena. Such thought experiments can be helpful, however, in clarifying the nature of existing discourse conventions and the very real, though seldom articulated, constraints they place upon participants. By and large, contemporary philosophers, including Bernstein (1983), do not write—and in many senses cannot write—their arguments in narratives or in conversations. As a result, sometimes the only way we can recognize a convention is through its deliberate violation.

The Main Line of Richard Bernstein's Argument

In the heart of his argument, Bernstein (1983) relied on the conventions of the philosophic essay we described in the last section. That is, using the main path/faulty path structure, he constructed his argument intertextually by characterizing and critiquing the positions advocated by other philosophers. Particularly in Part IV, "*Praxis*, Practical Discourse, and Judgment," he makes use of an abstract representation of other authors' arguments to lead to his own. Bernstein was even aware of his method:

> In the *Spiel*—the interplay—of contrasting and comparing Gadamer, Habermas, Rorty, and Arendt, I will be employing a notion that runs through all their work. I want to show how they can be read as different voices in a coherent conversation. After bringing out their strengths and weaknesses and showing some of the ways

in which they complement each other, I want to reflect on the common themes that emerge by speaking more directly in my own voice. (p. 181)

Because Bernstein's own argument is that "all three [Gadamer, Habermas, and Rorty] are concerned to show us what is vital to the human project and to give a sense of what dialogue, conversation, questioning, solidarity, and community mean" (p. 206), his rhetoric of conversation echoes his content about the conversational nature of human knowing. It is all the more significant, then, to realize how strongly influenced by the discourse conventions of the philosophic essay—and, thus, how far from conversation and narrative—his actual argument is. For simplicity, we take his treatment of Richard Rorty as a case in point.

Bernstein (1983) used Richard Rorty as the third major author to be discussed in creating the main path of his argument for the conversational nature of practical discourse. This follows his treatments of Gadamer who was the subject of Part II, "From *Hermeneutics* to *Praxis*," and Habermas,who was his first subject in Part IV, "*Praxis*, Practical Discourse, and Judgment." Up to this point in his argument, Bernstein characterized Gadamer and Habermas as "representatives of modernity, at least insofar as they believe that philosophy or some other successor discipline like philosophic hermeneutics or universal pragmatics can still provide the type of support or surrogate for the metaphysical and epistemological comfort that has obsessed philosophers" (p. 201). He introduced Rorty, in contrast, as a " 'postmodern' thinker who seeks to root out the last vestiges of the 'metaphysics of presence' " (p. 201). Thus Bernstein self-consciously began his treatment of Rorty by playing him off against a common position taken by Gadamer/Habermas:

> From Rorty's perspective, the trouble with Gadamer and Habermas is that they are not sufficiently radical in exposing the illusions and pretensions of philosophy (or of some appropriate successor discipline). They still cling to the hope that philosophy or its true successor can be a foundational discipline of culture. Rorty's strong criticisms would no doubt be matched by an equally strong rebuttal. Both Gadamer and Habermas would see Rorty as expressing a new sophisticated version of a very old form of relativism—the type of relativism that they have both sought to defeat. And if they wanted to get really nasty, they might accuse Rorty of failing to perceive the consequences of what he is saying. . . . (p. 200)

Bernstein then backtracked to show that Rorty, in practice, accepts the same values of human dialogue at the heart of Gadamer and Habermas even though, unlike the other two, he does not believe he can mount a foundational defense of them—a defense "with a permanent ahistorical foundation" (p. 206).

Although we do not take the time to continue the analysis of Bernstein's (1983) argument (he went on to characterize and critique the position of Hannah Arendt before laying out his own "in his own voice"), it is important to recognize what Bernstein has done: He has used Rorty to add an additional concept to the approach that he is advocating, to show that knowledge is, at its heart, a historical phenomenon, rooted in the conversation of the day, not an abstract, ahistorical, structure that can be shown to be true for all time. This point is a crucial component of Bernstein's final argument that the *community* necessary to support human activity is an achievement that must be worked at rather than presupposed or taken for granted:

> In the face of the multifaceted critiques of modernity, no one needs to be reminded of how fragile such communities are, how easily they are coopted and perverted. But at a time when the threat of total annihilation no longer seems to be an abstract possibility but the most imminent and real potentiality, it becomes all the more imperative to try again and again to foster and nurture those forms of communal life in which dialogue, conversation, *phronesis*, practical discourse, and judgment are concretely embodied in our everyday practices. This is the *telos* that is common to the visions of Gadamer, Habermas, Rorty, and Arendt. (p. 229)

For our purposes, what is interesting about Bernstein's text (1983) is the way his own argument for the historical, dialogical nature of human knowing is presented in the same abstract ahistorical main path/faulty path structure that characterizes the philosophic essay generally. As we have just seen, Bernstein abstracted Rorty's position to clarify and support his own argument. Linguistically, what happens is that Rorty is represented not as an individual in a historical conversation located in time, but rather as an abstract approach located in a timeless and abstract space through which Bernstein leads his readers toward truth: "From Rorty's perspective, the trouble with Gadamer and Habermas *is* that they *are* not sufficiently radical" rather than "the trouble *was* that they *were* not sufficiently radical"; "Both Gadamer and Habermas *would see* Rorty as expressing a new sophisticated version of a very old form of relativism" rather than "Both Gadamer and Habermas *did see* Rorty as expressing a new sophisticated version."

These linguistic choices—of present rather than past tense, and of conditional rather than indicative mood—are not, as we have already noted, accidental in the philosophic essay. They are indicative of the fundamental structure of Bernstein's (1983) argument not as a historically situated conversation between actual people, but as an abstract, spatially organized, and ahistorical interplay between other possible approaches or paths through an issue on Bernstein's own main path. The time frame of his argument is *now* in the space of interaction between reader and text, in a world in which Rorty, Habermas, and Gadamer are not only in the same room, but are also allowed to speak only at Bernstein's command and then to say what he wants them to say. Of course, there are serious constraints on Bernstein's interpretation of these other authors' positions, but it is important to realize that these constraints are not as absolute as we might often think. Thus, if Rorty does not actually discuss Gadamer in his published works,

Bernstein can characterize what he might have said ("Rorty, if he were to comment on Gadamer, would be no less sharply critical") in order to maintain the virtual reading experience for his readers.

Bernstein's Ancillary Materials

The pragmatic benefits of collapsing time into space through the main path/faulty path structure are easy to see. If philosophers were restricted to reporting what other authors had said to them or to each other in the order in which the conversation had actually occurred, not only would the conversation be more restricted spatially to participants who actually had spoken together, but it would also be restricted temporally to participants who were still alive and active as scholars. Furthermore, not only do philosophers want to represent their conversations with others, but they also want to insert themselves as participants, indeed, the participant with the last (or, at least, most recent) word. The spatial and temporal restrictions of real conversation would certainly lead to an entirely different, if not severely restricted, philosophic discourse.

Nonetheless, the conventions of the philosophic essay can hold sway even when the constraints of time and place are not in force. That is, even when the philosophers have come together in the same room and have made the appropriate interactive responses, the "conversation" will most likely still be abstracted and dehistoricized in the same way when reported in the philosophic essay. This is particularly clear in Bernstein's own work as the following examination of his ancillary materials will show.

Bernstein (1983) began his book with a dedication to the four authors with whom he dealt in the substance of his argument, characterizing them as "four friends." In the preface, he detailed the history of his relationship with them. In particular, he reported that he has been codirector of a conference course on philosophy and social science in Dubrovnik, Yugoslavia, since 1977, an appointment that directly grew out of a 1976 visit by Habermas, the other codirector, to Haverford College, where Bernstein teaches. Thus, he and Habermas have had an ongoing conversation about *praxis* for 7 years before the publication of *Beyond Objectivism and Relativism*.

Bernstein's relationship with Richard Rorty is even longer. They met as undergraduates in the 1940s at the University of Chicago and continued together through graduate school at Yale University. Rorty was a participant in the 1978 Dubrovnik course during which he read and defended *Philosophy and the Mirror of Nature* (1979), the work to which Bernstein (1983) is reacting in *Beyond Objectivism and Relativism*. In fact, it may have been Bernstein's reading of an earlier draft of Rorty's work that induced him to invite Rorty to Dubrovnik in the first place. In any case, as the acknowledgments mention, Bernstein's relationship with Rorty has continued to the extent of Rorty's reading an earlier draft of *Beyond Objectivism and Relativism*.

In the preface, Bernstein (1983) showed himself to be aware of the relationship between the central thesis of the book and the conversational milieu in which he has worked ("I have come to appreciate the meaning and power of friendship and solidarity not only from their writings but also from my own conversations, debates, and dialogues with them," p. xv). Yet, as we have seen, he restricted his reporting of this conversation to the preface and, when he turned to the body of the book, he adopted the ahistorical style of the philosophic essay. But Bernstein, as I have mentioned, did seem more aware than usual of the interplay and tension between historically situated discourse and the ahistorical discourse conventions of his discipline. This can account, I believe, for an anomaly in Part IV on "*Praxis*, Practical Discourse, and Judgement": He began the chapter with what he labeled as a "Historical Interlude" in which he accounted narratively for the development of Rorty's thought. We quote it here in full:

> Richard Rorty, the one native American among these four thinkers, is a contemporary of Habermas. Whereas an explicit interest in understanding *praxis* has been focal for the other three, this has not been true for Rorty. He was a student of philosophy at the University of Chicago and Yale University during the late 1940s and early 1950s, a time when the leading philosophic orthodoxies in America were logical empiricism and so-called ordinary language philosophy. While these movements were spreading and conquering many graduate philosophy departments, both Chicago and Yale were bastions of resistance.
>
> So, even at a later stage of Rorty's development, when he was deeply influenced by the work of Sellars and Quine, Rorty's own early intellectual formation provided something of a critical edge in assessing the various strains in analytic philosophy. His first published article, "Pragmatism, Categories, and Language" (1961), already introduced themes that were to pervade his work: the American pragmatic tradition, and the therapeutic power of the later Wittengenstein. During the 1960s and early 1970s Rorty wrote a number of important papers on the problems that most preoccupied the Anglo-American community of professional philosophers. But a close reading of his papers also reveals that something else was going on. At the same time that Rorty was arguing in a style that had become canonical for analytic philosophers, he also seemed to be raising deeply disturbing questions about some of the unstated presuppositions and unquestioned assumptions of these philosophers. What had at first seemed to be merely hesitations and reservations emerged, in *Philosophy and the Mirror of Nature* in 1979, as a comprehensive critique of not only analytic philosophy but the entire "Cartesian-Lockean-Kantian tradition." And, in marshalling a variety of rhetorical devices and alternative philosophic languages to carry out his therapeutic critique, Rorty exhibited an affinity with the type of deconstructive strategies that have become so fashionable in French poststructuralism. In his most recent work he champions a new form of pragmatism derived from his reading and appropriation of James and Dewey. But throughout Rorty's philosophic development, and despite subtle changes in his thought, one concern runs through all his writing: his fascination with the issues of metaphilosophy, with seeking to unmask the pretensions of various forms of philosophic discourse and

to clarify what role philosophy might yet play in contemporary cultural life. (pp. 179–180)

Although Bernstein (1983) here adopted the conventions of narrative, he still remained influenced by the conventions of the philosophic essay with respect to depersonalization. A reader who had not read the preface might not understand that Bernstein himself was a student at Chicago and Yale and thus was subject as well to the same influences he attributed to Rorty. He might also not realize that Bernstein's "close reading" of Rorty's work was the result not simply of textual interpretation, but also of hours of shared study and conversation. I have suggested previously that many pragmatic considerations might argue against the adoption of more indigenous discourse forms, but it is important to note that with Bernstein's work such conventions are not employed even when the constraints are not present: Bernstein did have these conversations with these people.

Thought Experiments Rewriting Bernstein

As we have seen, Bernstein (1983) did not write conversations and his use of narrative was limited. Nevertheless, spread across his main argument and ancillary materials is enough information for us to construct these alternative texts for him and to think about their relationship to his original text. Suppose, as our first experiment using the linguistic method described earlier, Bernstein had adopted the more indigenous form of conversation and constructed his argument as follows (Here and following I have also used the linguistic convention of placing asterisks before discourse that has been artificially constructed and thus is ill-formed):

*Rorty: The whole history of philosophy has been preoccupied with the desperate [and failed] attempts to discover permanent foundations and basic constraints on the nature of human knowledge.
*Bernstein: Habermas' value for "undistorted communication" is extremely important to the modern world.
*Rorty: You are just going transcendental and engaging in mystification.
*Bernstein: Behind all your dazzling deconstructive critique, you are just an old-fashioned relativist. From the Holocaust, we know the danger of such relativism.
*Rorty: I'm not, of course, interested in condoning the mistakes of the past. But philosophy can offer us little by way of avoiding them in the future.
*Bernstein: Even though you think there is no way you can give an ahistorical and permanent foundation to the value of reciprocal dialogue, you still value that activity in your own life.
*Rorty: As a practical matter, I do espouse these virtues but you are wrong to try to justify them in philosophic terms.

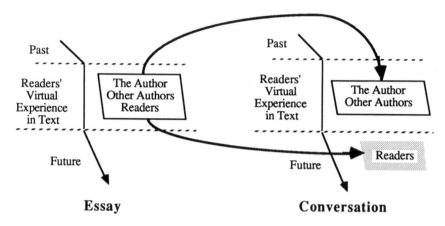

FIG. 9.2.   The change in readers' virtual experience moving from the philosophic essay to conversation.

As diagrammed in Fig. 9.2, this conversation splits Bernstein's interaction with his readers apart from his interaction with other authors, and then leaves the readers out of the discourse altogether. That is, in the virtual experience created by the conversational text, *Bernstein talks to *Rorty but he does not talk to his readers. As a result, readers are free to decide the point of the account: whether *Rorty is right, whether *Bernstein is right, or whether some position constructed between them is correct. In the original, by contrast, we know what Bernstein wanted us to think because he told us. For this reason, we might say that the conversational text has a plurality of perspectives not found in the original.

But to say that the author "tells us" what to think in the philosophic essay is really shorthand for saying that the conventions of the essay make interpretation a public act, subject to discussion, conflict, and resolution. Readers, in other words, are encouraged by the virtual experience of the text to see themselves as members of a common community. Conversation, on the other hand, is private as Condit (1987) pointed out. By moving the author–reader interaction out of the text, the conversational text makes interpretation the private business of individual readers, something taken up outside of and beyond the text itself. As a consequence, the greater pluralism of the conversational form may be purchased at the price of the public nature of knowledge.

What are the consequences of using a more narrative form for argumentation? In our second thought experiment aimed at answering this question, we can use information from the ancillary material to embed Bernstein's original characterization of Rorty's position within a more narrative framework:

*I first met Richard Rorty when we were undergraduates in the late 1940s at the University of Chicago, and we were also together as graduate students at Yale

University. . . . When he sent me a draft of the manuscript of *Philosophy and the Mirror of Nature*, I found myself sympathetic to his critique of foundationalism but was extremely dubious of his conclusions. Thus I invited him to participate in the *Praxis* course in 1978 where we had some of our best conversations.

*There Rorty argued about the nature of philosophy itself. According to Rorty the whole history of philosophy had been preoccupied with the desperate [and failed] attempts to discover permanent foundations and basic constraints on the nature of human knowledge. I argued that Habermas' value for "undistorted communication" was extremely important to the modern world. He told me that I was just going transcendental and engaging in mystification. I told him that behind all his dazzling deconstructive critique he was just an old-fashioned relativist and we know from the Holocaust what such relativism has lead us to in the past.

*Rorty was, of course, not interested in condoning the mistakes of the past, but he claimed that philosophy could offer us little by way of avoiding them in the future. I pointed out to him that even though he thought there was no way he could give an ahistorical and permanent foundation to the value of reciprocal dialogue, he still valued that activity in his own life. He acknowledged that, as a practical matter, he espoused these virtues.

This narrative does what Bernstein's original text failed to do. It situates both *Bernstein's claims and *Rorty's claims in history, thereby providing the reader with some insight into the inventional processes of the author. It might seem, then, that such a revision would increase the solidarity between author and reader. In fact, however, as shown in Fig. 9.3, the effect is the reverse: The constructed text distances the author from the reader, moving him along with the other authors outside of readers' virtual experience and into the past.

In effect, both *Rorty and *Bernstein have become characters in a story that is over and done. As such, our reading of it is shaped by well-established narrative

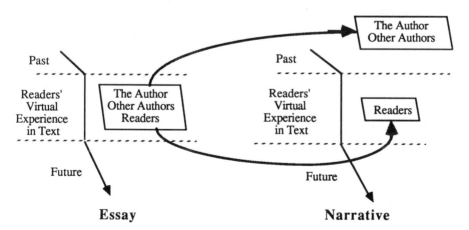

FIG. 9.3. The change in readers' virtual experience moving from the philosophic essay to narrative.

conventions: The "telling" of the narrative—that is, the plane of interaction between author and readers—occupies a present that has, by convention, no duration. That is, the whole story is told to us in an instant. This instant, furthermore, is always set apart from the narrative plane: As Genette (1980) showed, the actions of a narrative approach the action of the telling in time, but never completely overtake it. Author and readers remain apart as Fig. 9.3 suggests. Philosophers who want to make common cause with their readers thus usually avoid narrativizing themselves—as Bernstein avoided doing by writing himself out of his narrative of Rorty's life.

Occasionally, however, philosophers will narrativize themselves within the course of the contemporary philosophic essay, and the results are instructive to consider. As Fig. 9.4 shows, the effect of embedding narrative within the contemporary philosophic essay is to split the author into two, separating a narrativized author, anchored to a historical past, from the current author, acting in a dehistorized present. For instance, if *Bernstein were to make statements about what he argued in 1978 while at a summer conference in Dubrovnik, he would be creating himself as a historical author, and readers of the philosophic essay would still expect a second, dehistoricized, author to emerge to guide their virtual experience. Thus, they would not find it at all surprising for *Bernstein to conclude the constructed first-person narrative related earlier with the following comment relevant to his present position: *Ever since those conversations with Rorty, I have become increasingly aware of how right he was. The real Bernstein, of course, would not wish to recant the positions he had earlier developed in interaction with Rorty and it is perhaps for this reason that he did not include himself as a character in the original narrative of Rorty's life (even though he was clearly there).

In philosophic essays, then, authors rarely integrate narratives of their own rhetorical processes with the claims they wish to make because such narratives have developed into a subtle tagging system to signal readers to place the historical contextualized position on a faulty path. Whenever narratives are

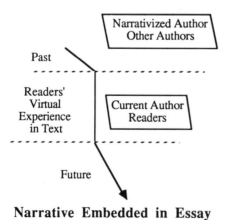

Narrative Embedded in Essay

FIG. 9.4. Readers' virtual experience when narrative is embedded within the philosophic essay.

embedded within the philosophical essay, that is, readers expect authors to act as narrators as well as characters, providing them with the "real" interpretation of the past events, to make a "point" that will help make sense of the present situation that they share (Polanyi, 1979). As a result, contextualization is limited to the plane of interaction in the past. The plane of author–reader interaction still plays itself out in a universalized and timeless present. And in that present, as Fig. 9.4 indicates, readers are still not free to construct their own interpretation, but rather are asked to adopt the interpretation with which the philosophic essay is infused: the author's own (Ruthrof, 1983).

In concluding these comparisons of Bernstein's original and constructed texts, we can see that the adoption of more indigenous forms significantly alters the virtual reading experience created by the philosophic essay. With conversation, as Fig. 9.2 indicates, authors purchase a plurality of interpretation at the expense of the public nature of knowledge. That is, everyone gets the right to their own opinion simply because opinion having becomes a private affair. With narrative, as Fig. 9.3 indicates, they purchase a limited rhetorical context for the past at the expense of the virtual experience of the present. That is, localizing one's beliefs as the outcome of historical events makes authors into narrative characters whose actions, though they may exemplify moral lessons, cannot speak directly to readers about them. Occasionally, these lessons may be articulated through the commentary of current authors, as shown in Fig. 9.4. But such narrative embedding actually leads to a greater distance between the historical past and readers' virtual experience because authors almost always dissociate themselves from beliefs they "used to hold."

For philosophers, the nature of the virtual reading experience created for readers is clearly an important concern. By placing the author, other authors, and readers in common textual space floating in a timeless present, philosophic essays create a common starting point from which readers can be exhorted to action in the future. Without the textual copresence created by the main path/faulty path structure, such exhortations to future action might make little sense. That is, if Bernstein did not exist in the intertextual present with his readers and those he has read, they might be unable to conceive of themselves as joining with him in the common public action he called for at the end of his book:

> There is no guarantee, there is no necessity, no "logic of history" that must inevitably lead to dialogical communities that embrace all of humanity and in which reciprocal judgment, practical discourse, and rational persuasion flourish. If anything, we have or should have learned how much the contemporary world conspires against it and undermines it. And yet it is still a *telos*, a *telos* deeply rooted in our human project. As Marx cautions us, it is not sufficient to try to come up with some new variations of arguments that will show, once and for all, what is wrong with objectivism and relativism, or even to open up a way of thinking that can move us beyond objectivism and relativism; such a movement gains "reality and power" only if we dedicate ourselves to the practical task of furthering the type of solidarity,

participation, and mutual recognition that is founded in dialogical communities. (Bernstein, 1983, p. 231)

In the final analysis, then, Bernstein's own commitment to consensus and joint action with his readers may have undermined his own call for more situated, conversational forms of discourse. The intertextual copresence he created through the virtual experience of his texts has its costs. By bringing himself, other authors, and readers into a single virtual experience, Bernstein has reduced a plurality of interpretive possibilities to a single perspective, his own. In addition, he has removed all traces of the rhetorical context of his claims, thereby creating a universalized, decontextualized representation that neither accurately reflects the nature of academic knowledge nor adequately opens up that knowledge to public scrutiny. As we noted in Part I, these are the same costs extracted by scientific discourse. In other words, although the discourse conventions of the philosophic essay differ in many respects from those of the scientific report, they both create a virtual experience for readers from which joint public action in the future can be launched. Indeed, if writing is a technology (Haas, 1993; Ong, 1982), and texts are artificial agents (Kaufer & Carley, 1993), academic writing may turn out to be a technology for creating and manipulating readers' virtual experience of artificial agency in an intertextual world distant from everyday life.

COMPARISON WITH HISTORICAL FORMS

If the philosophic essay can correctly be described as a technology for creating the virtual experience of artificial agency, it is certainly a technology with a history. That is, academic texts in general, and philosophic essays in particular, have not always constructed readers' virtual experience in the way that the contemporary philosophic essay does. In this section, we attempt to develop a more situated understanding of the contemporary philosophic essay by examining the discourse of one historically important author of academic philosophy, William James.

William James is a particularly appropriate philosopher for this purpose. As the chronology of professional activities in Appendix F indicates, James' career spans almost exactly the period of professionalization described in Chapter 4: He began publishing in 1868 when academic programs in philosophy in the United States were limited to undergraduate instruction in proper morality. When his career ended with his death in 1910, however, almost the entire structure of professional academic philosophy had been put into place.

As Kuklick (1977) pointed out, the development of professional philosophy was due in no small part to the actions of James and his colleagues in the graduate program at Harvard. James' own career was one of the first to follow what is now considered a commonplace tale of professional advancement: Appointed as a lecturer at Harvard in 1873, he gained a full tenure-track appointment as an assistant professor in 1876. A year later, he considered and rejected an offer from Johns Hopkins, which ultimately bettered his position at Harvard. In 1885, he was promoted to full professor, in 1889 to chaired professor, and from then on served as the center point for the Harvard program until he resigned for health reasons in 1907. During this entire time, James was a prolific writer. As the analysis of his publications given in Appendix F indicates, he published 69 texts in 44 years, an average of 1.6 texts per year. Eleven of these were books.

In other ways, James' career exhibits the kind of anomalies we might expect of an institutional practice in its early stages. His career spanned what are now three distinct disciplines, physiology, psychology, and philosophy, apparently without the concern for academic credentials that would be more common today. Though he never practiced medicine, James' only graduate education consisted of an MD earned in 1869. His early appointments at Harvard were in physiological psychology and his early career success was based in this field. By 1880, however, he was becoming increasingly interested in philosophy, and his offer from Johns Hopkins gave him the leverage needed to get assigned graduate courses in philosophy back at Harvard. His appointment was finally moved into the philosophy program in 1880, and almost all of his later publications were in this area. Nevertheless, he remained quite active in psychology, serving as president of the American Associate of Psychologists, the precursor to the American Psychological Association, participating in the public debate relating to the regulation of mental treatment, and maintaining a continuing interest in psychic phenomena.

For all these reasons, the work of William James is a particularly rich area for examining the impact of professionalization on the genre of the philosophic essay. Although a complete analysis of this work is beyond the scope of what we can accomplish in this chapter, a few preliminary observations can be made to indicate the ways in which James seems to have been bound by different discourse conventions than those now operating in the contemporary philosophic essay.

James' Mix of General and Specialist Texts

One of the most striking aspects of James' work is that, unlike contemporary academic philosophers, he wrote consistently for general as well as specialist readers. Indeed, over the course of 44 years, James wrote slightly more general texts than he did specialist texts (32 vs. 30). Figure 9.5 shows how this mix of readership varied with the time of his career.

In the first period of James' career, from 1868–1877, prior to his academic appointment at Harvard, James wrote exclusively for general interest journals, particularly for *The Nation*, but also for *The Atlantic Monthly, The North American Review*, and *The Boston Daily Advertiser*. With the exception of this last one, these were magazines aimed at an elite readership distinguished by

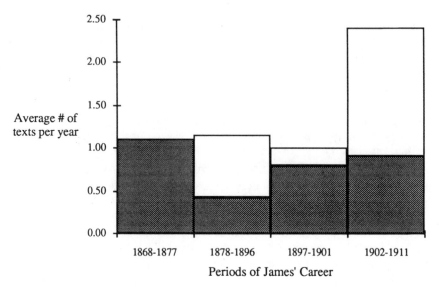

FIG. 9.5. The rate of James' text production over the four periods of his career. Shaded areas represent generalist texts; white areas represent specialist texts.

social class and wealth, and James had firsthand acquaintance with the editor of at least one of them (*The Nation*). During these years, James averaged about one text per year. For the most part, these texts were book reviews with an occasional letter to the editor. In 1875, for example, he wrote in *The Nation* defending vivisection and in 1876 he wrote on the neglect of philosophy.

Shortly after joining the faculty at Harvard, James' publications shifted into the most highly specialized period of his life. In the career-building years from 1878–1896, James maintained his output at roughly one text per year, but specialist texts outnumbered generalist texts almost two to one. Most of these texts were written on psychological topics and his two most common outlets were the St. Louis-based *Journal of Speculative Philosophy* and the British journal *Mind*. Neither of these journals were academic in the strict sense we use today, but both were aimed at readers with highly specialized interests in psychology and philosophy. Toward the end of this period, James presented many of the ideas he had worked out in journal articles in two textbooks aimed at undergraduate psychology courses: *The Principles of Psychology*, published in 1890, and an abridged version, *Psychology: Briefer Course*, published in 1892. These two texts, as well as the body of specialist articles preceding them, secured for James a reputation as one of the leading academic psychologists in the United States.

James' interest in psychology had always had a strong philosophic bent, and philosophic concerns became even more important to him in the second half of his career. Interestingly, his initial reputation in this area was based almost exclusively on texts written for general readers. From 1897 to 1901, his publication rate remained at about one text per year, but the proportion of specialist to generalist texts more than reversed that of his career-building years. *The Will to Believe and Other Essays in Popular Philosophy*, probably the most well known of these general texts, was published in 1897 by Longmans, Green & Co., after they outbid Scribners, Holt, and Houghton Mifflin for the manuscript (Myers, 1992). Many of the essays in this collection were originally given as public lectures to general audiences. The title essay in the volume, for example, was originally written as a talk for the undergraduate philosophy clubs at Yale and Brown. The book sold extremely well in the general market, eventually reaching 12 printings during James' lifetime.

In the last decade of his life, James became determined to develop the ideas he had originally aimed at general readers into a philosophical system that would sustain the rigors of technical inquiry. He accomplished this not by reducing his writing for general readers, but by significantly increasing his writing for specialist readers. As a result, his rate of textual production during the final period of his life, from 1901 to 1911, more than doubled to almost two and a half texts per year. He began this period with the development of the specialist text, *The Varieties of Religious Experience*, as the prestigious Gifford lectures at the University of Edinburgh, and he also published many specialist articles in the new *Journal of Philosophy, Psychology and Scientific Methods*. At the same time, he did not abandon his general readers, although the topics he addressed widened: He took up the Philippine question for the *New England Anti-Imperialist League*, lynching for the *Springfield Republican*, the San Francisco earthquake (which he witnessed) for *Youth's Companion*, the value of a college education for *McClure's*, and psychic research for *The American Magazine*.

James' Representation of Specialist Readers' Virtual Experience

By making a point to address general readers throughout his academic career, James was obviously operating according to different conventions than those guiding contemporary academic philosophers. Even in his writing for specialist readers, however, his work seems to show patterns different than those we encounter in the contemporary philosophic essay. In particular, the nature of the virtual experience James constructed for these specialist readers changed during the middle period of his career from a very early one based on distinctions of social class to a later one based on distinctions of professional affiliation. Figure 9.6 contrasts these two virtual experiences as they were created by two specialist texts James published just 6 years apart during the career-building years just after he joined the Harvard faculty.

In the first of these, an early specialist text, "Remarks on Spencer's Definition of Mind," published in 1878 in the *Journal of Speculative Philosophy*, James created a virtual experience for his readers of reviewing the work of Herbert Spencer in order to detect its obvious flaws. As shown in Fig. 9.6, James portrayed his readers as engaging in debate with Spencer's text unlike readers of the popular press who, being "of a passive turn of mind," more readily accepted Spencer's arguments:

> As a rule it may be said that, at a time when readers are so overwhelmed with work as they are at the present day, all purely critical and destructive writing ought to be reprobated ... But there are cases in which every rule may be broken ... Mr. Spencer's definition of Mind ... may certainly be said to be very far-reaching in its consequences, and, according to certain standards, noxious; whilst probably a large proportion of those hard-headed readers who subscribe to the *Popular Science Monthly* and *Nature*, and whose sole philosopher Mr. Spencer is, are fascinated by it without being in the least aware what its consequences are.
>
> The defects of the formula are so glaring that I am surprised it should not long ago have been critically overhauled. The reader will readily recollect what it is. ...
>
> The picture drawn is so vast and simple, it includes such a multitude of details in its monotonous frame-work, that it is no wonder that readers of a passive turn of mind are, usually, more impressed by it than by any portion of the book. But on the slightest scrutiny its solidity begins to disappear. (James, 1992, pp. 893–894)

In this text, then, James did not take on the task of exhorting his readers to public joint action in the way Bernstein (1983) attempted at the end of *Beyond Objectivism and Relativism*. Indeed, he assumed readers already shared his commitment to rejecting Spencer's ideas. The issue is simply one of giving them good arguments so that they can counterbalance the favorable reception Spencer's views had received in the popular press. This agenda—to better control the public

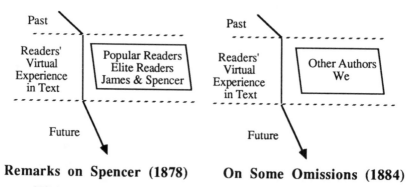

Remarks on Spencer (1878)   On Some Omissions (1884)

FIG. 9.6.   The virtual experiences created by James in a very early text ("Remarks on Spencer's Definition of Mind") and a slightly later text ("On Some Omissions of Introspective Psychology"), both written for specialist readers.

forum—is more clearly tied to the elitism of social class than to the privilege of professionalism.

Sometime during this early period of James' academic career, the virtual experience he created for specialist readers began to take on the more contemporary form. Texts such as "On Some Omissions of Introspective Psychology," which James published in *Mind* in 1884, were clearly professionalized. The issues were defined in technical terms, and, as shown in Fig. 9.6, other authors were, for the first time, brought in through the heavy use of citation; readers were addressed as part of a specialist "we":

> As is well known, contradictory opinions about the value of introspection prevail. Comte and Maudsley, for example, call it worthless; Ueberweg and Brentano come near calling it infallible. Both opinions are extravagances; the first for reasons too obvious to be given, the second because it fails to discriminate between the immediate *feltness* of a mental state and its perception by a subsequent act of reflection. . . . Comte is quite right in laying stress on the fact that a feeling to be named, judged, or perceived, must be already past. . . .
>
> The only sound grounds on which the infallible veracity of the introspective judgment might be maintained, are empirical. If we have reason to think that it has never yet deceived us, we may continue to trust it. This is the ground actually maintained by Herr Mohr in a recent little work. "The illusions of our senses," says this author, ". . . .
>
> But, sound as the reasoning here is, I fear the premises are not correct; and I propose in this article to supplement Mr. Sully's chapter on the Illusion of Introspection, by showing what immense tracts of our inner life are habitually overlooked and falsified by our most approved psychological authorities. (James, 1992, pp. 986–987)

By this time, then, James was using all of the discourse conventions of the contemporary main path/faulty path structure: Other authors were characterized as making arguments in a textual space through which James himself proposed to lead specialist readers closer to the truth.

The changes in James' construction of a virtual reading experience for specialist readers during the early career-building period are both striking and suggestive. Within the space of a few years, he had shifted from characterizing his issues as relevant to the public arena to more clearly locating them as controversies among specialists. In addition, readers who had loomed large as textual agents with distinct agendas in the earlier texts, were now quietly subsumed into a specialist "we." And the agenda for the future changed from regaining control of the public arena to the more contemporary goal of moving a specialist community closer to truth. In a very real sense, then, James' specialist texts showed every sign of adopting emerging discourse conventions for addressing the specialist readers of his developing profession of academic philosophy.

James' Representation of General Readers' Virtual Experience

Even though, as we have just seen, James developed and used the conventions of the contemporary philosophic essay when he addressed specialist readers, he always seemed aware that these conventions were less appropriate for the general readers whom he also made a point of addressing. For example, when James revised "The Sentiment of Rationality," originally published for specialist readers in 1879, in order to include it in *The Will to Believe* 18 years later, he eliminated all footnotes and almost all citations to other authors' work.

Eventually, James went on to develop a distinctive set of discourse conventions to control the virtual experience of his general readers. We can conceptualize this virtual experience as following a dual path structure given in the first column of Fig. 9.7. Unlike the main path/faulty path structure shown next to it, this dual path structure did not force readers to take the same main path through the issues that James himself took. Instead, other perspectives were allowed into the text without necessarily being characterized as faulty. Indeed, James made a point of acknowledging that his general readers have an alternative perspective as valid as his own and took it into account as he moved through the issue.

This pattern of creating dual paths through the virtual experience of reading, one for the author and one for the readers, emerged early in James' work in a talk he gave to the Unitarian Ministers' Institute in 1881. This text was subsequently published in *Unitarian Review* that year, and was later included without revision in *The Will to Believe* in 1897. In the virtual experience of this essay, James (1992) used "I" to mark the path of his own experience in the text

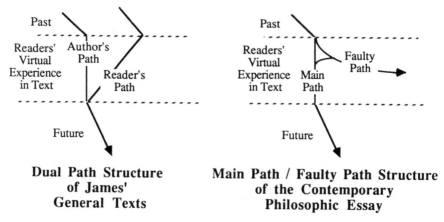

Dual Path Structure of James' General Texts

Main Path / Faulty Path Structure of the Contemporary Philosophic Essay

FIG. 9.7. A comparison of the dual path structure of James' general texts with the main path/faulty path structure of the contemporary philosophic essay.

and "you" to mark the path of the Unitarian ministers, and he repeatedly distinguished between the two paths:

1. "I invite you, then . . ." (p. 542).
2. "If you open, for instance, such a book . . . you will find . . ." (p. 543).
3. "Into this debate . . . I will not pretend to enter. . . . I will only remind you that . . ." (pp. 543–544).
4. "I will presently define exactly what I mean by . . ." (p. 544).
5. "But, first of all, let me ask you to linger a moment longer . . ." (p. 544).
6. "My time is unfortunately too short to stay and give to this truth the development it deserves; but I will assume that you grant it without further parley, and pass to the next step in my argument" (p. 550).
7. "I need not go far to collect examples to illustrate to an audience of theologians what I mean. Nor will you in particular . . . be slow to furnish . . . instances enough . . ." (p. 551).

What James (1992) did here is to create two distinct paths through the virtual experience of reading, one for himself as an expert on physiology and one for his readers as experts in theology. Furthermore, the purpose of his text is to make these paths converge. In particular, halfway through the essay, James makes an explicit appeal to the Unitarian ministers to draw on their own background and experience and join him in the effort to counteract the "mental barbarization" being cause by proponents of positivism:

> . . . when I see their fraternity increasing in numbers, and, what is worse, when I see their negations acquiring almost as much prestige and authority as their affirmations legitimately claim over the minds of the docile public, I feel as if the influences working in the direction of our mental barbarization were beginning to be rather strong, and needed some positive counteraction. And when I ask myself from what quarter the invasion may best be checked, I can find no answer as good as the one suggested by casting my eyes around this room. (p. 556)

And by the end of the essay, when the convergence of the paths is complete, James spoke of his main point as simply something that "[a]ll men know": "This is nothing new. All men know it at those rare moments when the soul sobers herself. . . . The most any theory about it can do is bring us to that" (p. 562).

Unlike contemporary philosophers, then, James did not treat identification with the Unitarian ministers as something to be assumed from the start. Instead, by creating a distinct path for them through the issue, he sought to acknowledge their distinct perspective—even make use of it—and only then engage them with a common purpose. That is, according to the conventions of the dual path structure, consensus was not assumed by the virtual experience of the text but rather was considered something to be attained through it.

James' Beliefs about the Role of the General Public in Academic Philosophy

James probably had many reasons for addressing general readers throughout his career. To begin with, the financial rewards of going through multiple editions of texts intended for general readers could not have been irrelevant. In addition, as we have already seen, James had established a pattern of writing for general readers before joining the faculty at Harvard. It was thus something he knew how to do. We might even speculate that the prohibition against writing popular texts might not have been strong enough in these early years of academic professionalization to offset the fame accrued by writing for magazines like *Youth's Companion* and *McClure's*.

James' concern for general readers ran to more than simply a desire to pursue these extrinsic rewards however. It was intrinsic to his developing understanding of the nature of philosophy itself. In particular, James had come to believe that the general public had an important role to play in the development of philosophic ideas. We can best understand this role in the context of the interactions between the three main groups James saw as having a relationship with philosophic ideas: the lay public, amateur philosophers, and professional philosophers. According to James, each member of the lay public had a philosophy: ". . . the philosophy which is so important in each of us is not a technical matter; it is our more or less dumb sense of what life honestly and deeply means. It is only partly got from books; it is our individual way of just seeing and feeling the total push and pressure of the cosmos" (James, 1987, p. 487). In addition, James believed that a subset of that lay public had earned the right to amateur status through their commitment to philosophic consistency: ". . . some of us are more than mere laymen in philosophy. We are worthy of the name of amateur athletes, and are vexed by too much inconsistency and vacillation in our creed. We cannot preserve a good intellectual conscience so long as we keep mixing incompatibles from opposite sides of the line" (James, 1987, p. 492). And finally, James believed that professional philosophers were distinguished by their original contributions to philosophic thinking: ". . . being an amateur and not an independent originator in philosophy he [the amateur] naturally looks for guidance to the experts and professionals whom he finds already in the field" (James, 1987, p. 492).

James saw the interaction among these three groups as essential to the development of philosophic inquiry. That is, because he believed that philosophy as a discipline addressed issues belonging to the entire lay public—each of whom had a philosophy—and because it attempted to follow consistent reasoning—as demanded by the amateur segment—James believed that only the lay public could be the final judge of professional philosophers' work: "We philosophers have to reckon with such feelings on your part. In the last resort, I repeat, it will be by them that all our philosophies shall ultimately be judged" (James, 1987, p. 503).

James' beliefs about the relationship between philosophy and the general public led him to become increasingly concerned about the impact of professionalization on philosophic inquiry. In the Hibbert Lectures delivered 2 years before his death, for instance, he characterized academic philosophy's growing tendency to make technical concerns paramount and ignore important ethical issues like free will:

> Suppose, for example, that a philosopher believes in what is called free-will. That a common man alongside of him should also share that belief, possessing it by a sort of inborn intuition, does not endear the man to the philosopher at all—he may even be ashamed to be associated with such a man. What interests the philosopher is the particular premises on which the free-will he believes in is established, the sense in which it is taken, the objections it eludes, the difficulties it takes account of, in short the whole form and temper and manner and technical apparatus that goes with the belief in question. A philosopher across the way who should use the same technical apparatus, making the same distinctions, etc., but drawing opposite conclusions and denying free-will entirely, would fascinate the first philosopher far more than would the *naïf* co-believer. Their common technical interests would unite them more than their opposite conclusions separate them. Each would feel an essential consanguinity in the other, would think of him, would write *at* him, care for his good opinion. The simple-minded believer in free-will would be disregarded by either. Neither as ally nor as opponent would his vote be counted. (James, 1987, p. 636)

For James, this situation was highly dangerous; it cut philosophers off from interaction with the general public whose insight and judgment they badly needed:

> In a subject like philosophy it is really fatal to lose connexion with the open air of human nature, and to think in terms of shop-tradition only. In Germany the forms are so professionalized that anybody who has gained a teaching chair and written a book, however distorted and eccentric, has the legal right to figure forever in the history of the subject like a fly in amber. All late comers have the duty of quoting him and measuring their opinions with his opinion. Such are the rules of the professorial game—they think and write from each other and for each other and at each other exclusively. With this exclusion of the open air all true perspective gets lost, extremes and oddities count as much as sanities, and command the same attention; and if by chance any one writes popularly and about results only, with his mind directly focussed on the subject, it is reckoned *oberflächliches zeug* [superficial nonsense] and *ganz unwissenschaftlich* [completely unscientific].... To teach philosophy so that the pupils' interest in technique exceeds that in results is surely a vicious aberration. It is bad form, not good form, in a discipline of such universal human interest. (James, 1987, pp. 637–638)

James' commitment to addressing general readers, then, was an intrinsic part of his view of the philosophic endeavor. Though he valued expertise as the source of original philosophic ideas, this did not keep him from believing that the general public had an important role to play in the development of philosophic ideas.

THE SOCIAL AND HISTORICAL CHARACTER OF THE PHILOSOPHIC ESSAY

Scholars of literature have long recognized that texts have the power to create virtual experiences for their readers, opening up alternative worlds and inviting identification and participation. More recently, those pursuing cultural studies have even begun to consider the ways in which these virtual experiences may support the current social structure by providing readers with enough escape to reduce their desire for real social change (Radway, 1984). Few scholars, however, have considered how academic texts themselves, texts like the philosophic essay, may also create virtual reading experiences.

The analysis pursued in this chapter suggests, however, that the philosophic essay creates a powerful virtual experience for readers by reversing the space-time dimensions of their actual reading experience. Moving experience out of time and extending it over space, the main path/faulty path structure allows readers to imagine themselves traveling with authors through the space of an issue, making progress, moving closer to truth (Fig. 9.1) . Authors' main goal in creating this virtual experience seems to be building a common agenda for the future, a consensus about what should be done.

Our thought experiments with the discourse of Richard Bernstein suggest how fragile this virtual reading experience can be. Shifting Bernstein's argument into more indigenous forms seemed to alter readers' virtual experience in significant ways. Conversation moved readers out of the text and into the future (Fig. 9.2). Narrative left readers in, but instead moved the author out and into the past (Fig. 9.3). In both cases, however, the identification of author and readers was lost and the potential for building a common agenda was destroyed: No single path led both into a common future.

Our analysis of the discourse of William James suggests that the virtual reading experience of the contemporary philosophic essay reflects social and historical facts. By tracking changes in James' writing for specialist readers, we found, for example, that his discourse conventions mirrored the transformation of expertise from a phenomenon of social class to one of professional privilege. In particular, within a few years, James' virtual experience for specialist readers changed from one of an elite battling popular culture over public knowledge to the more contemporary experience of professionals moving closer to truth (Fig. 9.6).

We also found evidence that the virtual reading experience created by philosophic essays reflected the social facts of the situation. In particular, when James wrote for general readers, he did not project the kind of singularity of perspective created by his specialist texts. Instead, his dual path structure (Fig.

9.7) acknowledged differences in perspective and, from that acknowledgment, built a common agenda for the future. This pluralism was accomplished through James' situated understanding of his general readers. In the case of the Unitarian ministers, for example, he drew on substantial knowledge of the tenents of faith that set them apart from the other Protestant sects. In the case of his texts in popular philosophy, he drew on his firsthand acquaintance with members of undergraduate philosophy clubs and the amateur philosophers who packed his public lectures.

Contemporary academic philosophers do not have a comparable social relationship with the general public and their discourse conventions reflect this fact. The relationship with the general public created for contemporary philosophy by the professionalization movement was one of production and consumption. Academics produced academic knowledge; the general public consumed it. Such a transaction did not required a direct interaction between the academic community and the general public and, in fact, allowed the task of popularization to devolve to other more popular writers. James, by contrast, could not pass on this task to others for he believed in the need to listen to the general public, to hear their judgment and to understand their concerns. Different social facts thus created different discourse conventions.

As academics, we often find it all too easy to mistake the apparently powerful virtual experience created by text for the actual experience we have as readers and writers. But, the knowledge making of academic communities consists of more than what is represented in academic texts. Discourse may follow social action. Discourse may even follow along with it. But discourse does not in itself constitute the entirety of academic expertise. As we see in the next few chapters, the move into the academy seems to have transformed not only the texts philosophers write, but also the activities in which they engage and the representations through which they think. Academic expertise seems to involve, in short, a transformation of the entire doing and thinking of everyday life.

ACKNOWLEDGMENT

Quotations from *Pragmatism* are reprinted from William James, *Writings 1902–1910*, a volume in The Library of America series. Copyright 1987 by Literary Classics of the United States, Inc. By permission of The Library of America.

10

COMPOSING THE PHILOSOPHIC ESSAY: TRANSFORMING EVERYDAY CONVERSATION

In the last chapter, we examined evidence that philosophy—like other academic professions—moves readers away from their indigenous home cultures and toward a more formal culture of the academy. In particular, we noted that philosophic essays seem to create a virtual experience that reverses the spatial and temporal dimensions of readers' actual experience in an effort to sustain appeals for joint action in the future. But what has this virtual experience for readers got to do with the actual experience of philosophic composing? Does the writing of philosophic essays require a movement away from indigenous practices comparable to that invited by compliant reading? Or do producers of philosophic knowledge rise above the apparent decontextualization of their texts to integrate their ideas about domain content with their participation in the rhetorical processes of their communities? What, in short, is the relationship between philosophers' literacy practices and the more indigenous practices of everyday life?

The next two chapters attempt an answer to this question through in-depth case studies of the composing practices of the four participants introduced in chapter 8. In this chapter, in particular, we are concerned with how these participants composed their philosophic essays. Adopting a framework developed by Scribner and Cole (1981), we examine three essential components of their literacy practices: their activities, their knowledge representations, and their goals.

The design of this study as a comparison of experts and novices plays a particular role in our analysis in this chapter. Specifically, we assume, for the time being, that the experts were effective practitioners of academic philosophy and that the novices were not. In the next chapter, we attempt a more equitable analysis, dealing with the novices in their own terms, but, for now, we simply use them as a lens through which to examine the composing of experts.

DESIGN

As described in chapter 8, the study reported here examined the practices of four participants asked to read and write about the ethical issue of paternalism. Jeff and Roger were disciplinary insiders: professional philosophers familiar with ethical philosophy. Janet and Leslie were disciplinary outsiders: second-semester freshmen at a private university who had not yet taken an introductory freshman philosophy course. All four read eight articles on the ethical issue of paternalism and wrote an original essay defining paternalistic interference and describing the conditions, if any, under which it could be justified.

As we noted earlier, paternalistic interference is an issue for ethical philosophers because it appears to violate widespread assumptions about individual rights and yet occasionally appears to be justified. John Stuart Mill claimed that the individual had exclusive rights to make decisions regarding his or her own welfare. This "harm principle" has become the starting point for many ethicists' discussions on the nature of rights. Paternalism is a problem in these discussions because it involves the interference by one person in the affairs of another for his or her own good; it thus appears to violate the harm principle. Nevertheless few would argue that it cannot be justified in some cases: parents' paternalism toward children; teachers' paternalism toward students; government paternalism toward the mentally incompetent. In an effort to define the boundaries between justified and unjustified action, ethical philosophers have offered conflicting definitions of paternalistic interference and conflicting specifications of the conditions under which it can be justified.

The two expert philosophers described here were both familiar with Mill's harm principle and with the general discussion of individual rights. Neither, however, was familiar with the issue of paternalism or the particular literature they were given at the start of the project. The two novices were unfamiliar with the technical issues of ethics, but both readily recognized that they had been subject to the paternalism of parents and school.

All participants worked on the task at their own rate for between 30 and 60 hours spread over 10 to 15 weeks during the spring of 1985. As elaborated in chapter 8, data were collected during this time in three ways: First, participants were asked to verbalize their thoughts into a tape recorder whenever they worked on the project, producing think-aloud protocols. Second, participants were asked to keep all of the writing they produced. And third, participants were interviewed between working sessions concerning what they had accomplished and what they were hoping to accomplish on the task.

I analyzed these data for information concerning the three components suggested by Scribner and Cole's (1981) model of literacy practice. That is, my questions concerned the way the participants went about composing: In what activities did they engage? What knowledge representations did they construct and manipulate? And what goals did they have?

THE ACTIVITIES OF COMPOSING

Using a Vygotskian framework (chapter 7), participants' activities were categorized in terms of the cultural products—the texts—they consulted and produced as a result of their actions. Complete definitions for these categories are given in Table 10.1. As this table indicates, the textual product of one activity often became the textual input for another activity: The activity of reading involved participants in consulting the texts on paternalism. The activity of reflecting involved them in going back through these texts to produce notes. The activity of organizing involved taking these notes and producing a linear order of topics. The activity of drafting involved producing continuous text for readers. And the activity of revising involved making changes to that draft.

Once the protocols of each of the four participants were coded using these categories, I then examined the way these activities seemed to structure participants' work. That is, I looked at how the participants varied their use of these activities over their working time. The results of this analysis, shown in Fig. 10.1, suggest that, in general, Jeff and Roger used a more highly differentiated activity structure to organize their work than did either Janet or Leslie. As the graphs in Fig. 10.1 indicate, all four participants used the same set of activities to complete their work: All began by reading, followed with a period of reflecting, moved to organizing, and then finally to drafting interspaced with revising. The only major departure from this sequence occurred with Janet who divided her working time into two halves, the first concerned with the definition of paternalism and the second with its justification. Within each half, however, the sequencing from reading to drafting/revising occurred, albeit in a more abbreviated form the second time around.

TABLE 10.1
Definitions of Categories Used to Segment the Activities of Each Participant

	Materials Consulted	Materials Produced	Sequencing Principle
Reading	readings	own notes	order of words in readings
Reflecting	readings, own notes	own notes	on-the-fly
Organizing	own notes	linear order of topics	on-the-fly
Drafting	own notes, readings, outline	continuous draft intended for readers	outline
Revising	draft	annotations to draft	order of words in draft

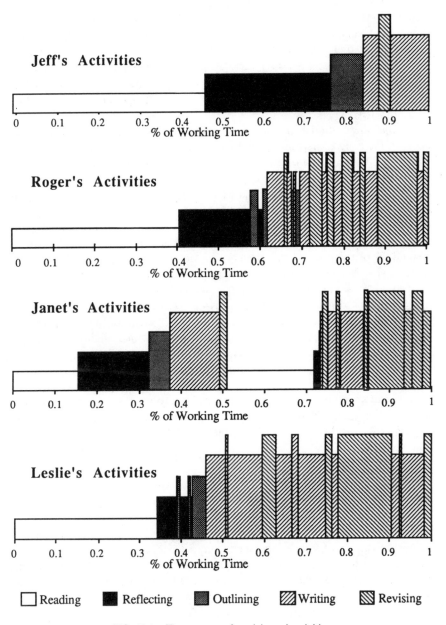

FIG. 10.1.   The structure of participants' activities.

In addition, a comparison of the percentage of working time given by the participants to each of the five activities indicates that all participants gave the greatest percentage of their time to reading (37% average) and the smallest percentage of their time to organizing (5% average). The percentage of time given to reflecting and revising varied with participant. Janet, Leslie, and Jeff spent about the same percentage of time reflecting; Roger spent proportionately more time. Leslie and Jeff revised extensively; Janet and Roger revised proportionately less.

Despite these similarities and individual variations, interesting differences between the experts and novices did emerge in their use of activities. To begin with, even though all participants spent about the same percentage of their time in reading and organizing, both experts took a smaller percentage of their time drafting: 17% and 13% for Jeff and Roger versus 29% and 32% for Janet and Leslie. Because both experts completed the task in less time than both novices, the difference in the actual time spent drafting was even greater. The experts also delayed drafting longer than the novices. The two novices began drafting about 35% of the way through their work. The two experts, by contrast, began drafting at 61% and 76% of the way through their work.

Even more striking was the difference, shown in Fig. 10.2, in how the experts and novices used texts during these activities. Jeff and Roger concentrated on other authors' texts in reading, switched to their own notes with a secondary review of the sources in reflecting, used their own notes in outlining, and worked on their own texts in drafting and revising. The pattern for the novices was not as clear. In particular, both Janet and Leslie consulted other authors' texts throughout their working time, even in drafting and revising—long after the experts had set these texts aside. Both experts, in other words, seemed to have a more clearly defined sense of the texts appropriate to each activity, whereas neither novice showed as decisive a choice of texts over the course of their activities.

THE KNOWLEDGE REPRESENTATIONS

To examine the knowledge representations used by the participants, I analyzed their protocols using a construct developed from the interview data, the construct of *authorship*. Like many academic professionals, we began this study with the assumption that authorship was an important attribute of the texts on paternalism. We had even taken care to choose articles by authors who cross-referenced each other. The interview data caused us to reexamine this assumption however. In particular, the two novices did not talk about the articles as having authors. In fact, Janet regularly referred to the collection of articles as "the book" and, on occasion, described herself as checking what "the book said" about an issue. On the other hand, the experts both regularly spoke in terms of the authors they were reading.

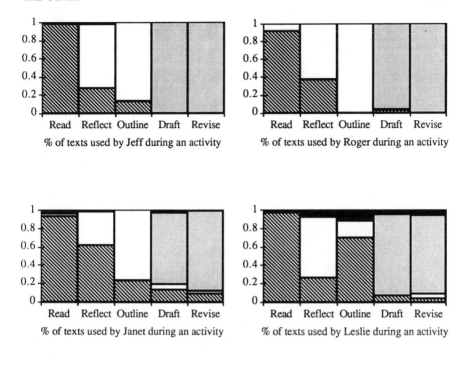

FIG. 10.2.   Participants' use of texts during their activities.

To analyze participants' use of the construct of authorship, I examined the protocol data for the presence of *author mentions*, which were defined to include: (a) names of specific authors (e.g., "Childress"), (b) nominals standing for an aggregate of authors (e.g., "these guys"), (c) nominals standing for roles of authors (e.g., "a moral philosopher"), and (d) pronouns standing in for any of the aforementioned ("she"; "they"). The results of this examination, given in Table 10.2, show that the novices attended to authorship an average 4.9 times in each 1,000 words of think-aloud protocol. The experts, on the other hand, attended to authorship one-and-one-half times as often in the case of Jeff and almost three times as often in the case of Roger.

THE GOALS

To examine what participants saw as the desired goal of their task, I analyzed the final texts they produced (given in Appendix G) using a modified version of Langer's system for the analysis of structure (see Appendix H). Using this

TABLE 10.2
Rate at Which Participants Mentioned Authors per 1,000 Words
of Protocol Transcript

	Rate of Author Mentions[a]
Jeff	7.4
Roger	15.8
Janet	4.6
Leslie	5.2

[a]These rates were calculated using word counts estimated electronically and author mention counts taken from the full set of protocols. Earlier and somewhat lower estimates reported in Geisler (1990) were calculated with manual estimations of words counts and author mention counts using a stratified sample of 10% of the protocols. Thus the figures given here are more accurate.

procedure, I divided the texts into T-units, which were then aggregated into rhetorical sequences linked by one of the following: (a) explicit connecting phrases such as conjunctions, comparatives, demonstratives, enumeratives, or various linking phrases; (b) anaphoric links or any transition from the indefinite to definite article; (c) parallel structure; or (d) a time-ordered narrative sequence. Each of these rhetorical sequences was then diagrammed by attaching each T-unit to one of the preceding T-units with either a subordinate or coordinate link following the procedure described in Appendix H. The product of this analysis was a complex tree diagram in which each T-unit of a participant's text formed a node. In addition to this structural analysis, a cross-check was made of the texts for the presence of author mentions.

The diagrams in Figs. 10.3 and 10.4 show the results of these two analyses, both the top-level structure of participants' texts and the location of the author mentions. On a global level, several generalizations can be made concerning the differences between the expert and novice texts. To begin with, experts' texts are longer (the following statistics are ordered: Janet, Leslie, Jeff, Roger): 1,280, 1,680, 2,930, and 6,010 words, respectively. In addition, they show an advantage in both the number of T-units (70, 93, 121, and 271) and the average length of the T-units (18, 18, 24, and 22 words/T-unit). Finally, they show greater subordination (11, 11, 19, and 16 levels) and contain a greater number of author mentions (0, 12, 44, and 74 author mentions).

A review of the individual texts makes clear the source of these global differences. As shown in Fig. 10.3, the expert texts followed a similar pattern. Major sections presented the terms of definition and justification given by the task. Subordinate to them, secondary units presented cases of paternalism and approaches to these cases. Further, in both expert texts, author mentions were almost exclusively associated with the secondary units presenting approaches. That is, both experts used authorship attribution to define what we call an *approach* that, in turn, was the major structure of their final texts.

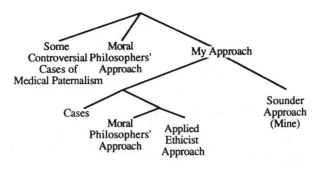

Structure of Jeff's Text

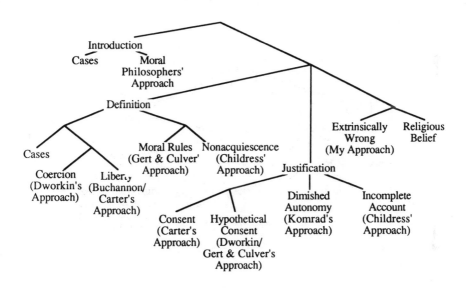

Structure of Roger's Text

FIG. 10.3. The top-level structure of the experts' final texts.

In addition, the experts organized their presentation of approaches similarly. Each began with an approach he considered faulty. Then, through a critique, he eliminated that approach. The order in which the approaches were characterized and eliminated was determined by how faulty the approach was. Very wrong approaches were dealt with early; more complex and harder to refute approaches were dealt with later. Then, after all the elimination was done, the resulting

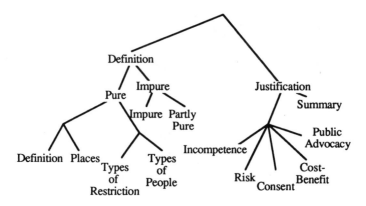

Structure of Janet's Text

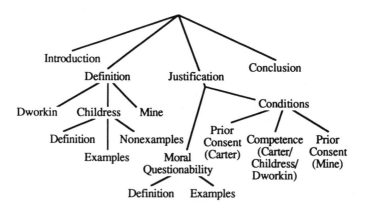

Structure of Leslie's Text

FIG. 10.4.   The top-level structure of the novices' final texts.

approach, the main path taken by the expert himself, was left as the only remaining
alternative. In other words, both experts used the main path/faulty path structure
described in chapter 9.

The following selection from Roger's text can serve as an example of this
main path/faulty path structure. This section, dealing with the approach taken by
Dworkin, is a typical faulty path, containing both a characterization of Dworkin's
approach (52–53) and a critique that eliminates that approach (54–60):

(52) The prominence of such examples as these in the discussion of the moral status of paternalism suggests to Dworkin (source one, above) the following "rough" definition (pg. 7):

(53) D1: "Paternalism is the interference with a person's liberty of action justified by reasons referring exclusively to the welfare, good, happiness, needs, interests, or values of the person being coerced."

(54) The definition D1 is faulty in several respects, and is not made any better by Dworkin's admission that it is "rough". (55) First, as it stands, if the definition is right, there can be no unjustified (i.e. wrong) paternalistic action for D1 says paternalism is justified. (56) Doubtless this is part of the "roughness". (57) Perhaps what Dworkin intends is something more like the following:

(58) D1: "Paternalism is interference with a person's liberty of action of such a sort that if justified at all it is justified exclusively by its positive bearing on the welfare, good, happiness, needs, interests, or values of the persons being coerced."

(59) But this will still not work, as can be seen from Example Three above. (60) In the case of the drug laws, potential buyers who can't buy because the product is not on the market are not coerced at all though they are the ones whose benefit is intended.

The units following this one deal similarly with approaches taken by Buchannon and Carter, by Gert and Culver, and by Childress. The ordering is keyed to how faulty Roger considered the approach. With Dworkin, whom he dealt with first, the approach was highly flawed and the critique was intended to be devastating. With Childress, whose approach he dealt with last, the approach was plausible and this critique was more pro forma:

(94) I will have more to say of this shortly. (95) For now it is enough to point out that plausible definitions satisfying this requirement are in the field. Here, for instance, is Childress' definition (p. 17, source 3):

(97) D5: "Paternalism is nonacquiescence in a person's wishes, choices and actions for that person's own benefit."

"(98) The definition is not without flaw ([99] surely he means "or" not "and", [100] and "nonacquiescence" is even fuzzier than "paternalism") (101) but it illustrates the point.

Although the novices used similar terms of definition and justification to structure the major units of their texts, their secondary units point to significant differences as shown in Fig. 10.4. In her secondary units, Janet, for example, used a typological organization. In the first major section, she enumerated the factors important to defining paternalism; in the second, she enumerated the conditions for justification. Although her protocols suggest she was aware of disagreements between authors, her final text neither included specific authors' names nor indicated any difference in approach among them. Thus, in contrast to the main path/faulty path structure used by the experts, her text seems to represent the issue of paternalism as a single main path with everybody on it.

Leslie organized the secondary units of her text with greater awareness of disagreements. Unlike Janet, she had an abiding and continuing personal disagreement with all the authors she had read. From her protocols and interviews, we know that she had seen her own family disregard her grandfather's wishes not to be placed on a respirator and she was convinced that this had been wrong. Thus, based on a family experience, she was fundamentally opposed to paternalistic interference. In her text, she was careful to state her position by giving her own definition of paternalism and her own approach to justification.

What is interesting to note, however, is that her claims stand in ambiguous relationships to the claims of the authors she was opposing. She did not, for example, make clear how her own definition of paternalism related to other definitions she had reviewed earlier. Is it in agreement? Is it in disagreement? Is it a qualified agreement? She was not clear. Further, even when she was more careful to specify that her claim about justification was in disagreement, she still failed to articulate the grounds for her differences. Instead, she simply characterized the opinion of others and then gave her own as a contrast:

(68) If we accept following the descriptions of incompetence given by Rosemary Carter, Bill is considered competent. (69) There is a group of people who we as society lable as being incompetent, therefore justifying paternalistic acts toward them. (70) These people are discribed and labled as the following: those who are unable to understand or practice satisfactorily the basic requirements of survival, and so whose lives would be at worst in constant peril, and at best grossly unhappy, if not for the intervention of others. (71) Those suffering from mental retardation, below a certain level, and those suffering from certain kinds of insanity are included in this class.

(72) Rosemary Carter's description of competence as a means for justification also speaks for both James Childress and Gerald Dworkin with the following exceptions:
· · ·

(77) Altogether, these people tend to describe the same conditions for justification, but in a different manner with different examples.

(78) While these conditions for justification are accepted by some of today's society, I feel that paternalism can be justified under only one condition, that of prior consent. (79) The conditions of mental retardation, and insanity do not give justification for paternalistic actions. (80) These persons should have the right to incorporate their views and feelings into medical decisions. (81) After all these

people do have the ability to communicate to certain extents. (82) Why should the views of these people be carelessly disposed of.

Structurally, what is lacking here is the critique used so extensively by both experts. Instead of an argument structure that eliminated other authors' approaches on the way to validating her own, Leslie simply presented the two approaches side by side, and distinguished between them on the basis, not of truth, but of authorship: Here is what others believe; here is what I believe.

CONVERSATION AND SOCIALLY CONFIGURED REPRESENTATIONS

The literacy practices of the two experts in this study thus appear to have been aimed at producing positions on the issue of paternalism by characterizing and critiquing approaches taken by other authors. To achieve this goal, both experts read, reflected on what they read, organized their thoughts, and wrote and revised a draft. Throughout their working time, they attended to the authorship of claims and, in their final texts, they used authorship as the defining attribute of the approaches they characterized and critiqued. To what extent can we describe their activities and representations as turns in an "academic conversation"? To what extent, that is, do their interactions with texts seem to be a simple extension of their interactions in everyday life?

One way of answering this question is through a comparison of the data we have just examined with a model of conversation recently proposed by conversation analysts. According to Heritage (1984), conversational participants build, maintain, and shift contexts through the mechanism of three-turn sequences. In the first turn, as shown in the first column of Fig. 10.5, a speaker proposes a given context by using the first part of an adjacency pair such as a greeting, question, or invitation. In the next turn, a second speaker responds with one of the following: the preferred response (an acknowledgment, acceptance, or answer); a dispreferred response plus some account for it ("Oh, that would be

	Everyday Conversation	Expert's Activities
Turn 1:	Proposes context	Writes
		Reads Reflects Organizes
Turn 2:	Responds	Drafts/Revises
Turn 3:	Repairs misunderstandings	

FIG. 10.5. Comparison of experts' activity structure with the structure of everyday conversation.

nice, but I've already made plans"); or a completely unexpected response (staring the speaker in the eye and not returning the greeting). Finally, in an optional third turn, the first speaker can repair any contextual misunderstandings indicated by the second speaker's response.

Applied to the uses of reading and writing in philosophy, this conversational sequence seems to suggest a mechanism by which social context could be sustained through philosophic essays. A philosophic essay could be seen as one philosopher's proposal. The writing of a new essay could be seen as another philosopher's response. Through a series of such written interactions, the context of a philosophical conversation could be built, maintained, or shifted. Developed in this way, this model represents a refinement of the many suggestions that have been made concerning the conversational nature of reading and writing (Bartholomae, 1985; Bazerman, 1980; Bizzell, 1982b; Bruffee, 1984; Latour & Woolgar, 1979; McCloskey, 1985).

This conversational model suggests, furthermore, that the formal culture of academic philosophy may be usefully viewed as an extension of participants' everyday culture. That is, reading and writing appear to build academic knowledge using the same activities employed by conversationalists to build everyday understandings. The results of the analyses presented in this chapter suggest, however, that the relationship between everyday culture and the formal culture of academic philosophy is much more complex. In particular, through their activities, knowledge representations, and goals, Jeff and Roger appeared to be departing in systematic ways from everyday conversation.

Admittedly, Jeff and Roger did attend to authorship with compelling regularity during their activities and used authorship to tag the major approaches they reviewed in their final texts. In this sense, then, their literacy practices were socially configured. And insofar as an awareness of other authors implies interaction with them as interlocutors, we might claim that their reading and writing were somewhat conversational. Other evidence warns us, however, against assuming that these conversations were like those of everyday indigenous culture.

The first piece of this evidence comes from the data on activity structure. As we have already noted, everyday conversation is structured as two-part interchanges with an optional third term for repairs. As shown in the second column of Fig. 10.5, however, Jeff and Roger structured their activities in four-part sequences of reading, reflecting, organizing, and drafting/revising. Assuming that reading is the equivalent of the first speaker's conversational turn and drafting/revising is the equivalent of the second speaker's response, we see that the experts' literacy practices seem to have opened up a reflective space through activities that are simply unavailable in everyday conversation.

The kind of mental work that Jeff and Roger may have been accomplishing in this additional reflective space is further suggested by the knowledge representations they used. In many respects, these representations did not match those of everyday conversation. To begin with, in keeping with the main path/faulty path structure, Jeff and Roger conceived of arguments as made up of approaches that were only indirectly related to other authors' claims. For example, Jeff did not assume a one-to-one relationship between the set of claims he saw being made by Dworkin and the approaches he discussed in his own argument. In fact, once he had characterized and dismissed the definition Dworkin actually gave, he went on to consider what Dworkin might have meant: "Perhaps what Dworkin intends is something more like the following . . . (59) But this will still not work. . . ." If Jeff's goal were simply to respond to previous interlocutors, then discussing what Dworkin might have said makes little sense. But if his intention were to construct a representation made up of a wide range of approaches, then this abstraction is a sensible inventional strategy.

The abstract nature of the experts' representations is also suggested by the way they organized their texts. As noted earlier, both experts arranged their discussions of approaches in descending order of faultiness: More faulty approaches were discussed first; less faulty approaches discussed later. This written practice differs from everyday conversation in two ways. First, conversational interlocutors rarely take on the burden of creating a spontaneous single response to multiple previous speakers' first turns. Instead, they respond to claims locally as they arise, one at a time. Second, on those few occasions when they do address multiple prior claims, the linear ordering is ad hoc. Indeed, if it were meaningful, we would assume that it had arisen from thinking done outside of the current conversation ("I see you've been giving this some thought"). Thus, the experts' responses appear to be consolidated and linearized in ways that are unpredicted and almost inconceivable accomplishments within the constraints of everyday face-to-face interaction.

The final evidence concerning the abstract nature of the experts' representations concerns the conventions by which they treated previous authors. Basically, the authors in these written interactions were treated differently than interlocutors in everyday conversations: Personal attributes and social affiliations were off-limits; actual intentions were irrelevant. For example, Jeff did not argue against Dworkin's approach on the grounds that he was a "Reaganite conservative"—even though his protocol shows that he thought so. Nor did Roger, when attributing an approach jointly to Buchannon and Carter, consider whether these two authors liked each other, or indeed, whether they had ever met. These personal considerations, important in everyday interaction, were inappropriate according to the conventions these experts followed.

Furthermore, philosophers' rights to the third-turn repairs common in everyday conversation are restricted in their written interactions. As mentioned earlier, Heritage (1984) suggested that third-turn repairs are always an option for first-turn speakers who feel they have been misinterpreted. Thus, in everyday conversations, we routinely expect to be able to say, "No, that is not what I meant to say. What I really meant was. . . ." Philosophers, however, are not routinely extended this right. Thus, for example, Dworkin could not reply to Jeff's critique by saying that he did not really mean what he wrote. Miswritings, unlike misspeakings, are not good grounds for repairing intersubjective knowledge. Of course, philosophers have many other ways they can repudiate misinterpretations of their work or repudiate previous positions, but, as Olson (1977) pointed out, these rely on conventions for what words mean rather than on independent evidence of what the philosopher actually intended. In fact, these conventions of interpretation are so widely available that third-turn repairs may be made by someone other than the original author—a freedom less often assumed by third parties in everyday interactions.

ACROSS THE GREAT DIVIDE

Taken together, this evidence suggests that our philosophers were operating with practices that represented a significant transformation of the indigenous cultural practice of conversation. By expanding their activity structure, abstracting approaches, consolidating and linearizing their responses, and accepting restrictions on their right of repair, Jeff and Roger appeared to be working with far more abstract representations of their authorial "interlocutors" than would be used in everyday conversation.

Yet, their practices, though not conversational in the everyday sense, were not strictly unconversational in a more abstract sense. Instead, Jeff and Roger seemed to be working with representations that both departed from some features of everyday practice and yet remained rooted there. Both felt impelled, for example, to accompany their writing with real conversation—in the hallways, on the phone, and at conferences. A representation of authorship like the one described earlier may have been the mechanism by which they were able to integrate their abstract thinking about domain content with their everyday representations of their colleagues. In other words, just as experts in radiology use representations of the body to surpass what can be done with ordinary understanding and yet remain connected to their patients' physical experience, experts in academic philosophy may use abstract representations of the rhetorical processes of authorial interaction to go beyond lay understandings and yet remain connected to everyday culture.

We might thus amend the simple conversational model of literacy presented earlier by hypothesizing an academic practice that both extends and refers back to everyday practices. By opening up the activity structure of everyday conversation, literacy in philosophy seems to provide experts with the reflective space necessary to construct socially configured yet abstract representations. These representations create, in effect, a new plane of intersubjective knowledge for philosophers, a virtual reality of culturally shared abstractions that transforms not only the texts that philosophers write but also the activities and representations through which they work.

As we see even more clearly in the next chapter, however, this is not what Janet and Leslie were trying to do. On the one hand, they did not appear to be operating with an activity structure as remote from everyday conversation. As Fig. 10.1 shows, they made less use of the distinctive reflective space, moving more quickly to drafting/revising after completing their reading. In addition, as Fig. 10.2 indicates, they appeared to be trying to interact with other authors' texts in smaller, more conversational, interchanges throughout their working time rather than restricting their use to the early activities of reading and reflecting as Jeff and Roger had.

In another sense, however, Janet and Leslie seemed far less conversational in their practices than either Jeff or Roger. Unlike the experts, they did not seem to represent their knowledge as a series of approaches distinguished by authorship. What they did instead, however, varied. Janet developed a representation consisting of positions on each of a number of subissues. We know from the protocols that the majority of her reflecting time was spent identifying these subissues and figuring out her position on them. Her final text presented these positions, but it did not explicitly identify them as her own. Nor did it distinguish her positions from positions taken by other authors. Consonant with her goal, she did not attend to the authorship of claims with anywhere near the frequency of either of the experts.

Perhaps driven by her personal experience, Leslie, on the other hand, developed a representation in which authorship played some role. Her final text carefully distinguished between her own position and the position taken by the authors she disagreed with. This structure remained different from that employed by the experts, however, because it did not indicate the relationship between the position she took and the position she was opposing. Indeed, during most of her reflecting time, Leslie tried to construct her own position with little attention given to the positions of the authors she had read. Thus, despite the presence of some author mentions in her final text, she did not attend to authorship in her working time at any greater rate than did Janet.

Thus, in this study, it was the novices, not the experts, who were operating in a world without interlocutors. If we can appropriately describe Jeff and Roger's practices as the transformation of the activities and representations of conversational interaction, we cannot make any such clear statement about what Janet and Leslie were up to. On the one hand, their activities seemed to involve treating texts in a more conversational manner, going back to them for repeated interactions throughout their working time. On the other hand, however, their representations were singularly authorless.

Thus, we seem to have a paradox in what the novices were trying to do: In the temporal dimension of activities, they seemed to be operating with patterns more closely related to indigenous culture. In the spatial dimension of representation, however, they worked with patterns that were neither typical of an indigenous practice like conversation (with its interlocutors) nor typical of the formal practice of academic expertise (with its authors). Instead, Janet and Leslie seemed to be caught in between. Educated to treat texts and the domain content they contain as an arhetorical affair, they were cut off from some of the resources of their indigenous culture, but were not yet privy to the abstractions of formal academic culture. In other words, they remained on the other side of the great divide from Jeff and Roger, laypersons in the realm of academic philosophy. And, as we see in the next chapter, this had important consequences for their understanding of the philosophical issues themselves.

ACKNOWLEDGMENT

Portions of this chapter are from "Toward a Sociocognitive Model of Literacy" edited by C. Bazerman and J. Paradis, 1991, The University of Wisconsin Press. Reprinted by permission.

11

REPRESENTING PHILOSOPHICAL ETHICS: TRANSFORMING EVERYDAY NARRATIVE

Two voices exist inside our heads, according to Jane Tompkins (1988). The first is the logical thinker who wants to get it right, "correct a mistake" (p. 169). The other wants to tell a story about herself, "write about her feelings" (p. 169). According to Tompkins, a literary critic, these two voices are split apart by professional discourse: "The problem is that you can't talk about your private life in the course of doing your professional work" (p. 169).

The split Tompkins (1988) identified is a familiar one to those interested in academic writing. It is the division between expository and narrative writing (DiPardo, 1990), between our personal and public selves (Witherell & Noddings, 1991), between the narrative and the paradigmatic (Bruner, 1986). One discourse is logically and hierarchically organized to describe truth by putting claims clearly before readers for their reasoned judgment (Olson, 1977; see also Locke, 1982; Sprat, 1966). The other is chronologically and causally organized to construct a world view by inviting readers into the events and values of its characters (Bruner, 1986; Fisher, 1987; Polanyi, 1979). Traditionally, as DiPardo indicated, expository prose has been the highly valued member of this discourse pair, the language of power and knowledge making. Narrative, by contrast, has been the poor stepchild, invited in as a kind of preliminary to more serious work, but abandoned as soon as possible afterward in the effort to teach students how to write (Flower, 1979). Its episodic structure and lack of explicit "point" were seen to make it an ineffective tool for knowledge making.

Recent theorists have begun to reconsider this position. Acknowledging the personal aspect of knowledge making, these scholars have noted the importance of covert "stories" in knowledge-making communities. As DiPardo (1990) noted, "The process of understanding experience is informed by more rational, factual kinds of knowledge, and in turn informs such knowledge. Our stories figure prominently in what we chose to care about, think about, write about . . ." (p. 63). Bringing these narratives to the fore, it is often thought, will help open up knowledge making for participation by previously disenfranchised groups. Quoting Hymes, DiPardo pointed out that story-telling rights are routinely extended to comembers of a community as a way of contributing to knowledge, and the failure to extend these rights to outsiders may indicate their lack of social rights rather than cognitive potential. By explicitly valuing narrative, the argument goes, we may open up the floor to those now silenced. Belenkey, Clinchy, Goldberger, and Tarule (1986) suggested, for instance, that a narrativelike connected way of knowing that expects identification rather than analysis is more compatible with many women's ways of knowing. And Fisher (1987) argued that a narrative rationality would put nonexpert on equal footing with expert in the public arena.

What is common to both those who espouse the more traditional essay form and those who favor a narrative alternative is the belief that these two discourse types do indeed involve different ways of knowing (Bruner, 1986). This study, however, began with a slightly different perspective. Continuing my investigation into the nature of expertise in academic philosophy, I wanted to know what expert philosophers did to construct an argument. And, thinking about pedagogy, I wanted to know how this differed from what novices do. Thus my original purposes appeared to have more to do with the traditional essay form than with the narrative. As I collected the data, however, I began to notice the presence of narratives in the work of both experts and novices as they constructed their knowledge. The analysis reported in the following sections was intended to investigate this phenomenon, and the results suggest that it may be more appropriate to think of narrative not as something common to the thinking of novices and abandoned by experts but instead, as a way of thinking that can be significantly transformed by professionalization.

ANALYTIC TECHNIQUES

To examine the role of narratives in the construction of the participants' knowledge in the protocol transcripts examined in the last chapter, I located the narratives within these activities and examined their function in terms of the participants' developing position on paternalism. I began by selecting the most recurrent narrative for each participant. I then tracked its variations over the course of the participant's activities.

Recurrent narratives figured predominantly in all four participants' thinking, appearing repeatedly in protocols, interviews, and the final drafts of their papers. They were always what ethicists call "cases": situations in which agents are engaged in everyday situations that have ethical implications. In ethics, most narratives are "problem cases" that form the "data" to be explained or resolved by the proper use of ethical analysis. Other narratives serve as paradigm cases: cases that already have well-accepted treatments in the literature on ethics and that can be used to tease out features of the problem cases. A prototypic problem case in the issue of paternalism, taken from Roger's final draft, is as follows:

> Mister N, a member of a religious sect which strictly forbids blood transfusions, is involved in a serious automobile accident and loses a large amount of blood. On arriving at the hospital, he is still conscious and informs the doctor that his religion forbids blood transfusions. Immediately thereafter he faints from loss of blood. The doctor believes that if Mister N is not given a blood transfusion he will die. Thereupon, while Mr. N is still unconscious, the doctor arranges for and carries out the blood transfusion.

This case, told in historical present, contains the traditional linguistic signals for the presence of a narrative. Most obviously, it consists of a concatenation of clauses with verbs in the simple past or historical present tense that together form a backbone of story events (Becker, 1979; Labov, 1972; Polanyi, 1979). Intermixed with these "event" clauses are any number of clauses in a less well-defined time that serve as commentary on the events (Hopper, 1979; Labov, 1972; Polanyi, 1979; Smith, 1978). Holding together these events and commentary is the overarching perspective of a narrator responsible for making a point relevant to the context into which the narrative is inserted (Polanyi, 1979). This responsibility is fulfilled when the narrator has shown how events are causally related to each other and to the outcome (Journet, 1990). Overall, then, the aforementioned case of paternalism can be analyzed as a narrative linguistically as shown in Table 11.1.

In addition to being sets of events, narratives are also described by ethicists as sets of ethically relevant features. This Jehovah's Witness narrative for instance, can be described as a case of paternalistic interference where the

TABLE 11.1
An Analysis of the Linguistic Structure of a Narrative Case in Ethics

Events	Commentary
Mr. N *is involved* in an accident & *loses* a large amount of blood.	Mr. N's religion strictly *forbids* blood transfusions.
Mr. N *informs* the doctor.	Doctor *believes* Mr. N *will die* w/o blood transfusion.
Mr. N *faints*.	
Doctor *arranges* for & *carries out* blood transfusion.	
(Event clauses in simple historical present)	(Commentary provided by stative & conditional verbs)

patient's wishes are known (+ known wishes), the patient is competent (+ competent), the patient is unconscious (– conscious), the consequences are serious (+ serious), and the relationship between the parties is professional (+ professional). There is no limit to the number of features a case can be said to exhibit, although the literature in ethics usually points to a number of features that are relevant to any given issue.

Each of these features can be changed to produce variations on the original narrative. The purpose of thinking about these variations is to generate and test domain claims relevant to either the definition or justification of an ethical phenomenon. Suppose, for instance, Mr. N did not have time to tell the doctor about his religious beliefs (– known wishes)? Suppose Mr. N remained conscious and expressed a subsequent change of heart (+ subsequent wishes)? For each of these new narratives, it is possible to ask, Is the case still paternalism? Is the doctor more or less justified? Answering these questions helps ethicists to tease out the essential features of ethical phenomena.

My goal for the narrative analysis was to examine the function of narratives in the context of the participants' developing position on the domain content, the definition and justification of paternalism. More specifically, the following method was used:

1. *Narrative Selection:* A narrative was selected for each participant from those given in the final text each one produced.

2. *Final Draft Description:* Next, the use of the selected narrative in the final draft was described. For each occurrence of the narrative, I asked: What features were attributed to the narrative? With what domain content point was the narrative associated? To what author was this point attributed, if any? What was the relationship between the point, the narrative, and the author?

3. *Transcript Excerpted:* The protocol transcripts were next searched forward in chronological order to locate each instance in which the narrative or related domain content point was mentioned. A combination of computer search and simple reading of the transcripts ensured completeness. As participants introduced new variations on the narrative, new features, or new domain content claims, they were added to the search. Each instance was excerpted and a note was made of its surrounding context.

4. *Narrative Table:* A table for each participant was constructed listing the narrative excerpts chronologically along with the agent involved in the narrative and the features attributed to it by the participant.

5. *Distinct Narrative Analysis:* From this chronological table, a list of distinct narratives was developed. A distinct narrative was defined to be a narrative that had recognizably different agents and/or features. The case of Beaver's father, for example, was distinct from the case of God in Jeff's work because distinct agents were involved. The case of the doctor who gives the Jehovah's Witness

a blood transfusion was different from the case where the doctor lets him die in Leslie's work because the features were distinct (+/− intervention).

6. *Description of Overall Work:* A description of the participant's work was constructed. My aim was to construct an account of how each participant advanced toward the position expressed in the final draft. Particular attention was paid to how the case was described and its relationship to the participants' current domain content claims and plans. Whatever interpretations were developed were harmonized with the participants' own descriptions of their accomplishments provided in the interviews after each session.

The results of this analysis suggest striking differences. Quantitative results are presented first, followed by a qualitative description of each participant's work. Complete transcripts of participants' narratives can be found in Appendix I.

OVERALL PATTERNS

Table 11.2 summarizes the overall patterns of participants' use of narratives during their activities. The first row lists the narrative I selected to follow in the analysis. The next row gives the number of protocol excerpts in which this narrative or related narratives occurred. And the remaining four rows give the number of distinct narratives these excerpts represented and the activity in which they were first brought up by the participant. No data are given for organizing because no participant introduced a distinct narrative during this activity.

These quantitative data suggest two major differences between the ways the experts and novices used narratives. First, Janet and Leslie used a greater number of distinct narratives to develop their ideas. In fact, they used twice as many distinct narratives as Jeff or Roger did. Second, Janet and Leslie introduced distinct narratives throughout the activities of their working time. Jeff and Roger, by contrast, limited their introduction of distinct narratives to the activity of

TABLE 11.2
Quantitative Data on Participants' Use of Narrative During Their Activities

		Jeff	*Roger*	*Janet*	*Leslie*
	Case	*Father*	*Race*	*Drunken Parent*	*Unconscious Patient*
	# of Excerpts	16	14	37	34
Number	in Reading	0	0	2	13
of	in Reflecting	10	7	12	11
Distinct	in Drafting/Revising	0	0	10	6
Narratives	Overall	10	7	24	30

reflecting. The description of individual participants' work that follows confirms and elaborates upon these quantitative differences.

JEFF'S USE OF NARRATIVE

Jeff centered his attempts to develop domain content claims about paternalism on the father narrative. In this story, a father treats his child, usually a son, in a way that assumes superior knowledge and concern for the son's welfare and the father justifies this treatment on the grounds that he is helping his son grow up. By the time Jeff reached the activity of organizing, he had decided that this narrative was being used as an inappropriate standard by which to judge paternalistic behavior among adults. This inappropriate strategy, he argued, had led applied ethicists to endorse rather than question existing power structures. Jeff also suggested that this comparison had colored moral philosophy's entire view of the autonomous person and that a proper analysis of paternalism could help put ethics on a better footing. Although Jeff held this position stably throughout organizing and drafting/revising, it was far from stable during reflecting. In fact, at the beginning of Session 5, Jeff's position was roughly the reverse of that presented in his final draft. He began by believing that the father narrative was indeed the "root case" of paternalism.

Jeff's use of narratives played a major role in this reversal of domain content positions. As Fig. 11.1 indicates, Jeff rapidly introduced a set of 10 distinct narratives in the process of reflecting using two kinds of features. First, Jeff created one narrative from another by transforming the features listed in the second column that were incidental to paternalism. The narrative Jeff told about the father, for instance, can be transformed into his narrative about God simply by changing the feature +/− human, as the following excerpts from Jeff's protocols show:

Father: Father lets kid make great mistakes cause he thinks that it's good for the kid to go out and try this stuff and make these mistakes. He's basically thinking, "I remember when I was young and foolish. He just needs to work himself out of it." (+ human)

God: Maybe I just got what's involved in in a picture of a guy as the father the big father ... big daddy ... from God's point of view this is your best interest. (− human)

The other narratives can be produced by similar transformations: The narrative about God can be transformed into the daughter narrative by changing +/− male. The daughter narrative can be transformed into the narratives about Socrates and Jeff's philosophy faculty by transforming +/− family. Although the protocol

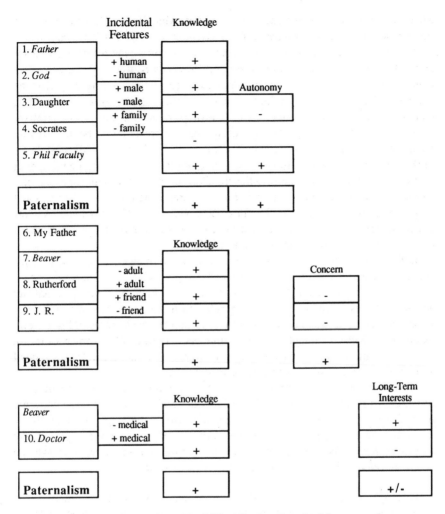

FIG. 11.1.   Distinct cases used by Jeff in reflecting. Cases in plain type are those
Jeff judged to be not paternalistic. Those in italics are those he judged paternalistic.
Full transcripts of these cases can be found in Appendix I.

transcripts do not show that Jeff was consciously aware of transforming these
incidental features, this set of distinct narratives is so closely interrelated that
some sort of systematic procedure must have been involved.

The transcripts do show Jeff to have been more consciously manipulating a
second set of more essential features given in the third and fourth columns of
Fig. 11.1. From the standpoint of his developing position, Jeff needed to ask two
questions about the narratives he had generated: If a narrative was paternalistic,

what feature made it paternalistic? If it was not, what feature eliminated it? The answers to these questions gave Jeff the essential features of paternalism.

As this figure indicates, Jeff discovered the essential features of paternalism by working in three stages to explore the differences between the narratives (in italics) he judged to be paternalistic and those (in plain type) he judged to be not paternalistic. He began in the first stage of reflecting, as shown in Fig. 11.1, with a hunch based on the paradigm case of paternalism, the father narrative: He guessed that knowledge of the victim's best interests might be an essential feature of paternalism (+ knowledge). As the rest of the figure indicates, Jeff's further explorations gave him no reason to doubt this hunch. It fit the remaining narratives he considered paternalistic: the God narrative, the philosophy faculty narrative, and the Beaver narrative. Furthermore, it helped him to understand why one of his noncases, the Socrates narrative, was not paternalistic. As Jeff put it, Socrates was not a paternalist because he was not even a good judge of his own best interests let alone anyone else's.

Jeff discovered his second essential feature of paternalism, autonomy, by once again considering a noncase of paternalism. By varying the incidental feature +/− male, Jeff created the daughter narrative, which was not paternalistic according to his intuitions. Because he believed that paternalism was inherently sexist, however, he was not surprised to find that the male cases did not easily extend to fathers' treatments of their daughters. Traditionally, women were not considered autonomous agents in their own right (− autonomy). Jeff thus judged autonomy to be an essential feature of paternalism.

Next, Jeff varied the incidental feature of +/− family to generate two narratives of paternalism outside of the family circle, both involving teachers. The narrative of Socrates, as we have already noted, confirmed the importance of the + knowledge feature by its absence. The narrative of Jeff's own graduate philosophy faculty confirmed both essential features he had discovered so far, + knowledge and + autonomy. Here is Jeff's thinking on this narrative:

> Philosophy Faculty: Teachers actually act paternalistically towards their pupils . . .
> Surely in philosophy departments they do . . . That is . . . the assumption is the
> faculty knows best what you should do, the problems you should worry about . . .
> They think they can tell better than you, student, what things to get wrapped up
> in and things to worry about . . . what things to read, what things to show confidence
> in . . . And that all has to do with your demonstrated lack of knowledge . . . If
> you're giving your consent to be trained . . . by this person . . . okay . . . That's
> really philosophy faculty . . . That's the basis for their paternalistic attitude—is to
> make you an autonomous . . . make you, against your will almost, into an
> autonomous thinker.

Thus, at the end of this stage in reflecting, Jeff felt he had a tentative definition of paternalism that included two essential features, + knowledge and + autonomy.

Having used these five narratives to verify his hunch that the father was an appropriate root case of justified paternalism, Jeff turned back in the next stage of his thinking to examine more closely the conditions for its justification. Just as he had attempted to embody the teacher narrative first in Socrates and finally in his own philosophy faculty, Jeff first tried to embody the father narrative first in his own father and then in the father in the 1950s sitcom "Leave it to Beaver." He rejected the narrative of his own father on the grounds that his father simply had not been paternalistic: "well let's see let's think about fathers and sons . . . I guess my father wasn't too paternalistic a father. . . . he kind of let me go." Beaver's father, however, seemed the consummate paternalist: Jeff remembered him letting Beaver take on projects that he knew would not work out—like trying to sell Christmas cards—simply because he believed that Beaver had to learn these things for himself. In acting this way, Beaver's father exhibited superior knowledge (+ knowledge) of his son's best interests at the same time that he actually did nothing to interfere with Beaver's actions, all on the grounds of what Beaver needed to learn in the long run to be an autonomous adult (+ autonomy). Thus the Beaver narrative seemed to have exactly the attributes Jeff was looking for.

Turning to consider cases of paternalism between adults, however, Jeff created a variation on the Beaver narrative that led him to reverse himself. Thinking about ways that Beaver's father treated colleagues at work, especially Mr. Rutherford, Jeff remembered Beaver's father thinking of Mr. Rutherford as particularly inept and thus assuming superior knowledge of Mr. Rutherford's best interests (+ knowledge). But, Jeff was surprised to realize, Beaver's father had not treated Rutherford paternalistically because he just was not concerned about Rutherford's fate (– concern). The Rutherford case, then, seemed to be a counterexample to Jeff's original definition of paternalism.

What was missing, Jeff realized, was a condition that the paternalist be concerned as well as knowledgeable (+ concern, + knowledge). To confirm this hunch about the need for a + concern feature, Jeff took the J. R. Ewing narrative from the television soap "Dallas": J. R. surely assumed superior knowledge about Cliff Barnes' best interests (+ knowledge) but just as surely was not paternalistic because he did everything in his power to destroy him (– concern). As a result of thinking through these narratives, then, Jeff reconfigured the father narrative to include both the + knowledge feature and the + concern feature and changed his definition of paternalism to include both features as well.

In the final stage of reflecting, Jeff explored the conditions for justifying paternalistic interference. He began by assuming that the features that characterized the Beaver narrative, his embodiment of the paradigmatic father narrative, would be relevant in adult–adult relations. He immediately realized, however, that his primary narrative of paternalism among adults, medical paternalism, was very different: Doctors only have the short-term interests of their patients in mind

(– long-term interests). With this realization in Session 9, Jeff's entire strategy of using the father narrative as the root case of justified paternalism fell apart. In subsequent sessions, he scrambled to reconstruct a viable domain content position, moving through a number of further reversals that ultimately led him to argue the position described earlier.

ROGER'S USE OF NARRATIVE

Roger's use of narratives in reflecting had several characteristics in common with the way Jeff used them. To begin with, Roger also reversed his domain content position and this reversal was motivated by working through a series of narratives. Unlike Jeff, however, Roger did not always generate these narratives by changing their incidental features. As Fig. 11.2 shows, he just as often held the incidental features constant while changing the essential features. As a result, Roger's set of seven distinct narratives were, if anything, even more tightly integrated than Jeff's. In Roger's work, the race narrative was central. In this narrative, A withdraws from a race that he is sure to win just to let B win. At first, as shown in Fig. 11.2, Roger thought this was not paternalistic because, although A acted for B's interests (+ beneficence) and crossed his will (+ crossing of will), his action was not something over which B should have legitimate control (– legitimate control) and therefore might not need to be justified. At

	Incidental Features	Beneficence to B	Crossing B's Will	Legitimate Control of B
1. Race				
	+ game	+	+	–
2. *Lottery*	+ game			
	– lying	+	+	–
3. Lying	+ lying			
	+ information	+	+	+
4. Withholding Information	+ information			
	– justification	+	–	–
5. Cornflakes	– justification			
	+ B's good			–
6. Refusal	– B's good			
		–	+	–

| **Paternalism** | | + | + | +/– |

| 7. Doctor | | | | |
| | | + | + | ? |

FIG. 11.2.   Distinct cases used by Roger in reflecting. Cases in plain type are those Roger judged to be not paternalistic. Those in italics are those he judged paternalistic. Full transcripts of these cases can be found in Appendix I.

this point, then, + beneficence, + crossing of will, and + legitimate scope of control were Roger's features for the definition of paternalism.

The subsequent series of narratives lead Roger to abandon this third feature. Roger first created the lottery narrative to share with the race narrative the incidental feature, + game, and the essential attribute, – legitimate control. In this narrative, A buys B a lottery ticket for B's good, but against his will. Roger decided this act was paternalistic even though he thought B did not have the right to control what A did with his money. Jeff next created the lying narrative, where A lies to B about the game, to get the + legitimate control feature: "A crosses B's will by lying to B for B's own good. A crossing of wills occurs in that. We presume that B's desire is that he not be lied to. Suppose that's true. Now, the object with respect to which the will is crossed is whether or not B is to be lied to. And that's something that's normally legitimately within B's control." Roger's next narrative, withholding information, is very similar to lying in that it involved information (+ information), but it was not within the legitimate control of B (– legitimate control). It was more like eating cornflakes for breakfast (– legitimate control), something that did not need to be justified.

At this point, as a result of working through these narratives, Roger began to wonder why any paternalistic action needed to be justified at all, and he created the refusal narrative to verify this hunch. If B asked A to withdraw so that he, B, could win the race and A refused (+ crossing of wills, – beneficence), no one would think that B had a legitimate right to complain (– legitimate control). So why did A's action suddenly become suspect when he acted for B's benefit (+ beneficence)? Based on this analysis, Roger decided that cases of paternalism need not involve acts within B's legitimate control and therefore need not be *prima facie* immoral. It was this analysis he took with him to consider the doctor case. At this point then, Roger had, just as Jeff had, reversed his domain content position as a result of thinking through narratives.

JANET'S USE OF NARRATIVE

Janet's use of narratives presents the greatest contrasts with the experts'. As noted earlier, both Janet and Leslie used considerably more distinct narratives than either Jeff or Roger, and they used them in activities other than reflecting. As shown in Fig. 11.3, Janet, in particular, introduced nearly half of her distinct narratives during the activity of drafting/revising. At this point, she was trying to illustrate features of paternalism that she had thought about earlier and wanted to incorporate into her final draft. Her organization of these narratives in that draft was typological—modes of paternalism, kinds of paternalism, parties in paternalism, types of paternalism—and the relationships among narratives within each type were loose associations rather than the tight feature-based variations used by Jeff or Roger. In fact, the narratives that appear together in clusters in

Reading

		Qualified (+)
1. Small Child	+ child	+
2. Drunk Parent	+ child +drunk	+

Reflecting

	Qualified (+)/ Belief @ Qualified (@)	Subsequent Consent (+)	Interference	Beneficence (+)	Moral (+)/ Belief @ Moral (@)
3. Helping	+ accident	+	(+)		
4. Transfusion			+		
5. Withholding			+		
6. Deception			+		
7. Fluoride			+		
8. Commitment			+		
9. Pills 1	+ wife		+		
10. Son			+	Beneficence (+)	
11. Witness	+ accident			-	-
12. White Lies					+
13. Denial					@
14. Older child	+ child			+	

Drafting/Revising

	Qualified (+)	Subsequent Consent (+)	Interference (+)	Beneficence (+)	Moral (+)/ Belief @ Moral (@)
15. Vegetables	+ child		+		
16. Robbery					
17. Pills 2	+ husband	+	+	+	-
18. Skiing	+ child	+	+	+	
19. Meal Plan	+ student				
20. Drunk Friend	+ drunk + car	+	+	+	
21. DWI	+ drunk + car			+	
22. Licensing				+	
23. Org Crime			+	+	
24. Dorms	+ student		+	+	

FIG. 11.3.   Distinct cases used by Janet in reading, reflecting, and drafting/revising. Full transcripts of these cases can be found in Appendix I.

Janet's final draft were often generated at different times during her work. Some were generated in reflecting, but many others were added during drafting/revising, sometimes in very late sessions.

Across clusters, Janet's narratives often appear to be united by incidental features that might have been salient for her but to which she did not call the attention of her readers. As Fig. 11.3 shows, many of her narratives involved being drunk (+ drunk), being a child (+ child), or being a student (+ student)—common concerns for a first-year college student. In addition, Janet treated these features as static characteristics of narratives rather than manipulable features as did Jeff and Roger. In those rare instances when Janet did vary a feature of a narrative, she appeared to be motivated by goals independent of the development of domain content. For example, she chuckled about changing a narrative she had encountered about a husband's hiding sleeping pills from his distraught wife (pills 1) into a story about a wife hiding pills from her distraught husband (pills 2):

Pills 1: If a husband were to hide pills from an upset wife who threatened to take an overdose, he would be acting paternalistically toward her. He is taking the authority to interfere in order to prevent her from harming herself. He considers himself to be in a more rationale state that she and therefore feels qualified to act.

Pills 2: You know what I think I'll do? . . . I think I'll be funny . . . I think I'll change the example around . . . I think I'll switch them . . . I think I'll change the example . . . I think I'll change the example around . . . I'll say . . . If a wife . . . ha ha ha . . . were to hide pills from an upset husband . . . ha ha ha . . . who threatened to take an overdose . . . she would be acting paternalistically toward him . . . ha ha ha . . . She is taking authority to interfere in order to prevent him from harming himself . . . He . . . She considers herself to be in a more rational state than he . . . and therefore feels qualified to act . . . ha ha ha . . . When the husband previously mentioned . . . When the wife previously mentions . . . mentioned before hides her husband's pills . . . she um . . . is doing it for a good reason . . . however . . . is not acting totally morally . . .

Although Janet appears to have been motivated by a sense that the original pills narratives was sexist, she did not use this realization to think about sexism in the issue of paternalism as a whole—as, for example, Jeff had done. That is, she treated the manipulation of this incidental feature as unrelated to the goal of determining the essential features of paternalism.

For the most part, Janet used the narratives in Fig. 11.3 to illustrate the domain content claims she had encountered in her readings and with which she agreed. But Janet did have her disagreements with the authors and they led to some of her most creative thinking. In particular, during reading and reflecting, Janet became aware of two areas on which she had disagreements with at least some of the authors she had read. First, she took issue with what she interpreted as the claim that children cannot act paternalistically toward their parents because they are not qualified to act; she thought they could be: " 'A small child cannot be said to be acting paternalistically toward his parents even when he satisfies all other conditions.' Someone younger reading this thing would have different opinions."

Later on, she took exception to Gert and Culver's claim that a small child cannot act paternalistically toward a drunk parent because the child is not generally qualified to act on the parent's behalf. First, she argued that a child could only help a parent who wanted to be helped: "Can that young child help the drunk parent and act paternalistically? I don't see how that relates cause paternalistically is when you help somebody and they don't want you to help. A young child couldn't help a drunk parent unless the drunk parent let him." Second, she reasoned that a small child would be qualified (+ qualified) because all he had to do was make a phone call to help the parent: "If child were to get help then he would be qualified to do so. Anyone who is qualified to dial a phone number is qualified to call for help."

These two lines of reasoning illustrate the priority Janet gave to constructing a coherent narrative at the expense of constructing a coherent domain content position. The first argument suggests that the small child is not interfering with the parents' actions and was therefore not acting paternalistically. The second argument, however, suggests that the child was indeed acting paternalistically. What makes these two lines of argument coherent are their application in the world of narrative. Both are descriptions that can hold true of the narrative of the drunk parent at the same time: The child can both be qualified to make the phone call and not interfere with the parents' wishes. What makes these two lines of argument incoherent, however, are their implications for domain content: The narrative cannot both be an example and a nonexample of paternalism.

Janet's second disagreement with claims she encountered in her readings is suggestive of the reality assumption that she brought to evaluating narratives. In this instance, she was concerned with an issue very similar to that with which both Jeff and Roger struggled: Is paternalism always immoral? Roger had asked the question, "Is paternalism always *prima facie* immoral?" thereby asking whether paternalistic acts are suspect on their face and therefore require justificatory effort. Janet had no such concept as *prima facie*, so for her the question was whether paternalistic situations were, in fact, always immoral. She was bothered, as Jeff and Roger had been, by the argument that they were because she could think of cases where it appeared to be very moral to take action.

Janet ultimately resolved this problem by arguing for a distinction between what the paternalist believes about morality (belief @ moral) and the actual morality of the act (moral). Paternalism, she suggested, is always of questionable morality, but the helper always believes in his own mind that he is doing the right thing. The paternalist can later turn this action of questionable morality into a moral one by arguing successfully in public that his action was justified. And, Janet suggested, the purpose of studying ethics was to learn how to make these public arguments. Here are Janet's notes on this point:

114: I think the reason why people are taught morality when they are young is so that they become aware of the importance of acting righteously, they must know there is a dif between right and wrong.

115: The purpose is *not* just to give the people a list of actions and thoughts that are right or wrong. They must learn to use their own minds to decide in each situation what is right and what is wrong.

116: Like an engineer learns to *think*, not memorize equations.

117: Lessons in morality are just another type of education. Is important that all people learn it. It is *then* that they may be *qualified* to act paternalistically.

118: If a person is qualified, then he will have a way to defend his actions later (at least he should). If a person was not very good at the art and logic of distinguishing between right and wrong he still acts paternalistically, because he tried, but the action may not be able to be justified by him later. He thought that he was qualified at that time but

119: his good intentions failed. It was still a pat. act though because he thought he was doing the right thing.

This position synthesized two features Janet had encountered in the literature, + qualified and + moral, and did so in a novel way that also addressed Janet's need to understand why she and her readers ought to study ethics in the first place. This synthesis is as close as Janet came to constructing an original position on paternalism and, like Jeff and Roger's positions, it was created in the face of disagreements with the literature. What Janet did with this position, however, is telling. Her final draft shows no evidence of what is in her notes and revealed in her protocols. When she returned to these notes in drafting/revising, she had difficulty making sense of them and so left out of her paper altogether the only original argument she had managed to construct.

LESLIE'S USE OF NARRATIVE

In many ways, Leslie was as different from Janet as Jeff and Roger were alike. Whereas Jeff and Roger seem to have been working with narratives using similar assumptions and strategies, Leslie worked quite differently from Janet. Under the influence of much more personal experience with paternalism, her work in some ways looked more "expertlike." Nevertheless, the ways in which she resembled Janet are even more interesting.

Leslie volunteered to work on this project in paternalism largely because she was bothered by recent events in her own family. Before she had even completed her first protocol, she introduced these events as the fifth narrative in her thinking:

Interfered Grandfather: I think if a patient says . . . like sometimes when they have um . . . patients who don't want to be on respirators and stuff like that . . . and you . . . some . . . like the family doesn't want them to be on . . . I mean . . . they wanta to have them alive as long as possible . . . but . . . when my grandfather was in the hospital . . . he said . . . before . . . when he got . . . before he got into the ambulance . . . he signed a paper that he wanted to be on a respirator . . . and still . . . I mean . . . I guess it was my family and doctor . . . decided to have him on one . . . because . . . we sorta decided . . . that we wanted to know . . . whether or not . . . he . . .

you know ... he could still ... it was ... they didn't know if he was brain dead
or not ... and we wanted to know for sure ... if he was or wasn't ... and I ...
I ... well I think people should know the truth about their own ... what's wrong
with them ... I think it's better all around that they know ... but ... I mean ...
if ... people request that they ... that they just don't want to know ... I think
it's up to them ... because it's their own decisions ... okay.

Thus Leslie came to the project with a narrative in hand as well as a sense of
its features as shown in Fig. 11.4: that her grandfather's wishes were known
through a living will (+ known wishes), that his decision had been interfered
with (+ interference), that it had involved the feelings of a family (+ family),
and that he had been brain dead (+ brain dead). All of this led her to suspect
that this interference had been unjustified.

Leslie's work on paternalism led her to repeatedly examine the narrative of
her grandfather to see whether features mentioned in the literature were relevant
to his case. Throughout, her understanding of the features of this narrative
changed, but the agents stayed the same. For the most part, Leslie's question
was, "Was my grandfather like that?" If a feature turned out to be inapplicable
to her grandfather's narrative, she more or less stopped thinking about it in terms
of the issue as a whole. Thus, she, like Janet, worked under the assumption that
narratives were descriptions of real events.

For instance, halfway through reading, she came across the feature of
competence and tried to think through how it applied to her grandfather:

? Competent Grandfather: It really makes me mad ... no not mad ... furious ...
makes me ... really makes me furious ... is to think ... that the doctor went ...
went against my grandfather's ... grandfather's wishes ... I really think it makes
me furious ... no ... no ... I know I really think ... it really ... Leave that there
... It really makes me furious to think that ... to know ... that the doctor went
against my grandfather's wishes ... when he was totally competent of deciding
... when he was totally competent ... He was a doctor ... doctor ... and knew
what the cause and what ... He knew what would happen to his body ... body
... if he ... wait ... compe ... He was totally competent in deciding ... wait
... He was totally in deciding ... He was totally competent of deciding ... He
was a ... he was a doctor ... and knew what would happen to his body if he had
... wait ... he had a stroke ... he had a stroke and ... and ... okay wait ... he
had a stroke and ...

I don't remember ... but I don't think he was very much affected ... I think
it ... one side of his body was paralyzed ... but I can't remember ... I was too
immature at the time ... It doesn't really matter ... I mean it does ... but it
doesn't now ... okay ...

he was a doctor and knew what ... knew what would happen to his body if he
had ... if he had another ... another stroke ... another stroke or he ... he ...
wait ... he knew what would happen if ... okay ... shit ... He knew what was
going to happen to ... He knew the process and ... He didn't know the process
... but he knew what went on ... what the effects were ... of a stroke ... how

Reading

	Known Wishes (+)	Interference (+)	Family (+)	Brain Dead (+)	Subsequent Wishes (+)	Competent (+)
1. Unknown J Wit	-	+				
2. Dead J Wit	+	-				
3. Christian Scientist	+		+			
4. Known J Wit	?					
5. Interfered Grandfather	+	+	+	+		
6. Dead J Wit w/ Family	+	+	+			
7. Changed Mind					+	
8. My Kid			+			
9. Alive J Wit	+	+			?	
10. ? Competent Person	+					?
11. Competent J Wit	+	+			+/-	+
12. Brain Dead Person	+	+		+		
13. Informed Grandfather	+	+	+	+		+

Reflecting

	Known Wishes (+)	Interference (+)	Family (+)	Brain Dead (+)	Subsequent Wishes (+)	Competent (+)	Angry (+)
14. ? Competent Grandfather	+	+	+			?	
15. Considerate Grandfather	+		+	+		+	
16. Angry Grandfather	+		+				+
17. Me Brain Dead	+		+	+			
18. Your Kid			+				
19. His Kid			+	+			
20. Me Competent			+	+		+	
21. They		-		-		+	
22. Resigned J Wit	+	-		-			-
23. Angry J Wit	+	-		+			+
24. Competent Grandfather	+	+				+	

Drafting/Revising

	Known Wishes (+)	Interference (+)	Family (+)	Brain Dead (+)	Subsequent Wishes (+)	Competent (+)
25. Dead Person		-				
26. Alive J Wit	+	+				
27. Regretful J Wit	+	+			+	
28. Interfered w/ J Wit		+				
29. Grandfather	+	+	+	+		+
30. Family Member	+	+	+			
31. Comatose Patient	+	+	+	+		

FIG. 11.4. Distinct cases used by Leslie in reading, reflecting, and drafting/revising. Full transcripts of these cases can be found in Appendix I.

it worked ... how the blood clots happened ... and things like that ... He knew that ... He understood it ... and ... I think he was totally ... he was competent ... He said he didn't want any life sustaining ... okay ... yeah ... okay ... He was competent ... okay ... I said that already ... He knew ... He knew that ... He knew that ... okay ... When he was totally competent ... of deciding ... he was a doctor and he knew what would happen to his body ... and he knew ... the process ... process ... not process ... but effects ... what the hell did I say ... he knew the process ... he knew the effect ... effects a stroke could have on him ... He signed a paper saying he did not want to be on any life sustaining machines ... machines ... machines ...

    I never thought of this ... thought ... but what if ... what if at the time he signed it ... it ... in the ambulance ... at his house ... at his house ... he was not competent ... but I really ... I do think ... think he was competent ... ah ... signed a paper saying he did not want to ... want to have ... be on any life sustaining machine ... I never thought ... but ... what at ... what if at the time ... he signed it ... the ambulance at his house he was not incompe ... he was not competent ... but I really think he was competent ... I mean ... he knew ... he knew he had high blood pressure ... pressure ... and he knew the effects it could have ... he knew the effects it could have ... I ... I feel ... wait ... I think ... I think my grandfather ... grandfather ... grandpa ... my grandpa thought about this situation.

Prior to her readings, she apparently had not considered whether her grandfather might have been incompetent at the time he signed the living will. Once she encountered the feature, however, she added it to her story: She decided that because her grandfather was a doctor himself, he must have been fully informed about the consequences of his decision and thus fully competent (+ competent). In fact, later on she decided that one of the reasons her grandfather had signed a living will was to relieve her family of the responsibility for making this hard decision. She was thus able to decide that this potentially relevant feature was finally irrelevant to justification and that what her family had done, no matter how hard it had been, was still unjustified. She thus transformed the narrative of the questionably competent grandfather into the narrative of the considerate grandfather in a way that unified her concerns about the living will (+ known wishes), the family (+ family), being brain dead (+ brain dead), and being competent (+ competent), all without changing her sense of what had been wrong about the situation to begin with. Thus, her work throughout these narratives served to reinforce and enrich her analysis, but not to reverse her position about what counted for justification.

    Although the reality assumption kept Leslie from engaging in the feature variation characteristic of Jeff and Roger's work, she did employ a kind of narrative variation that Janet did not use. Rather than thinking hypothetically about variations such as, "What if the patient is not competent?," she instead thought about variations by perspective: "What if it were me that was brain dead (me brain dead)? What if it were your kid (your kid)? What if it were his kid (his kid)?" By working through these shifting perspectives, she appears to have been testing whether her position on what should be done would make sense to all of the parties involved in the narrative: the doctor, the family, the patient. Such perspective shifting seems to suggest that the question "what is justified?" could not receive a single unilateral answer, but rather must be negotiated among the participants involved in the situation, a kind of situational ethics rather than the universal ethics that both Jeff and Roger were working toward.

In general, Leslie seemed to assume that ethical judgments were both more situational and more personal than either Jeff or Roger. Once she had worked through to a resolution of the grandfather narrative, she then went on to try to decide what this might mean in terms of paternalism in general. In her interviews, she clearly felt uncomfortable about making this transition, believing that whatever she had decided was strictly a personal decision that she would not want to impose on her readers. She resolved this discomfort again by shifting through perspectives: What would I want done to me (me competent)? What would they want done (they)? What do you want done to a member of your family (family member)? What should be done to a patient (comatose patient)? And, in the end, she presented only part of her own belief system ("Patients should be fully informed about what is happening to them") without mentioning the grandfather narrative or explicitly condemning paternalistic interference as unjustified. Her interviews make clear that this was a deliberate choice on her part: She did not want to get either too personal with her readers or too polemical about doctors. She simply wanted to suggest some of the things that readers should be aware of. Paternalistic interference changed from the "unjustified" act it was in her thinking into simply a "serious" situation in her text.

RELATIVE COMMITMENT TO FORMAL AND INDIGENOUS CULTURE

Stepping back from the last two chapters, we can say that all four participants in this study worked through a complex reading/writing task in ethics using the same sequential organization for their activities. Departing from the recursive pattern predicted by the cognitive process model (Flower & Hayes, 1981a), they completed their work using the following sequence:

Reading → Reflecting → Outlining → Drafting/Revising.

Nevertheless, though this important similarity unites their work, important differences separate them. Most obviously, Jeff and Roger's expertise appears to have been associated with the increasing regularization, specialization, and efficiency of their activities. That is, the activities data reveal less variation in the sequence and timing of the experts' activities than in the novices. Furthermore, both experts showed increasing specialization in what they attempt to accomplish with these activities, reserving reading other authors' texts for the early stages of their work and using knowledge development strategies, indexed by the introduction of distinct narratives, for the period of reflecting. Finally, they employed a minimal number of cases during this period, suggesting that their knowledge development strategies were highly efficient.

The novices, by contrast, showed neither efficiency nor specialization in their use of activities. Drafting/revising, in particular, was notably extended both in terms of the proportion of working time and in terms of the absolute length of protocol transcript. The novices also used other authors' texts and introduced distinct narratives during this activity. These three patterns—the length of drafting/revising, the use of other authors' texts in this activity and the introduction of distinct cases in this activity—all suggest that the novices were attempting to accomplish in this last activity what the experts have already completed earlier and more efficiently in reading and reflecting.

Underlying Jeff and Roger's advantage in knowledge development is their ability to construct and manipulate abstract representations of the narratives with which they worked. Both Jeff and Roger worked by making minimal feature variations to one narrative to produce another. Jeff, for example, changed the Beaver narrative into the Rutherford narrative just by changing − to + adult. Roger worked similarly.

Janet and Leslie did not make the same kinds of systematic transformations. Their narratives represent heterogeneous and scattered attempts to embody or illustrate features of paternalism, some taken from personal experience such as Janet's narrative of learning to ski, others taken from the readings such as Leslie's narrative of the pills. Although these narratives can be described using abstract features in the readings, they were not in any sense constructed to develop and test these features. Instead, Janet and Leslie appear to treat their narratives as stories of things that did happen, events that the telling could not change.

This difference between the experts and novices is consistent with the other work on expertise in ill-defined problems reviewed in chapter 3. As we noted there, a range of studies have shown that experts in such fields as physics (Larkin et al., 1980), radiology (Lesgold et al., 1988), and the social sciences (Voss et al., 1983) work with more abstract representations. Novices, by contrast, use more everyday representations. A radiologist looking at an X ray, for example, will see abstract three-dimensional working systems in the body whereas novices will see one-dimensional isolated blobs (Lesgold et al., 1988). In the same way, we can think of Jeff and Roger as "seeing" something different in narratives than did Janet and Leslie, something more abstract, something less everyday.

Studies of expertise have been less informative concerning a further interest of this analysis, the function of these abstract representations. In the case of Jeff and Roger, abstract feature-based variation seems closely tied to a second characteristic that sets their work apart from Janet and Leslie's. Both experts used feature-based variation to reverse the positions they held at the beginning of reflecting. Jeff changed his mind about treating the father narrative as the appropriate root case of paternalism. Roger changed his mind about defining paternalism to include violating the victim's legitimate scope of control. In making these reversals, both experts effectively moved away from common everyday understandings of paternalism and toward more specialized under-standings. They could thereby make an argument in their final texts to refute these common understandings, establish novelty, and garner argumentative success in the academy (Kaufer & Geisler, 1989).

We need to note that expertise in this study did not seem to involve the decision whether or not to use the resources of personal experience. Both Jeff and Leslie did; Roger and Janet largely did not. Rather the difference seems to lie in the direction of inference when it is used. When Jeff constructed narratives like the father case and the teacher case from specific situations from his personal experience—whether direct (my father; the philosophy faculty) or vicarious (Beaver, J. R. Ewing)—he chose situations toward which his own attitude was stable. That is, he did not try to use ethics to help him work out his own personal problems. His philosophy faculty, for example, were, without a doubt in his mind, justified in how they were treating him. Leslie, however, chose a situation that was highly problematic for her and she hoped to work out a way to live with it at the same time that she worked out a position on the domain content.

To philosophers, personal involvement of the kind that Leslie exhibited is considered highly inappropriate; they believe that it will undoubtedly color whatever domain content claims that are produced. In some sense, this is exactly what happened to Leslie. Anchoring herself to the narration of her grandfather, she did not consider the full range of situations with which philosophers feel obligated to deal: patients who, because unconscious or mentally incompetent, cannot be "fully informed" as she recommends. But it is just as important to say that because Jeff and Roger anchored themselves to the domain content of ethics, they did not consider the full range of features that Leslie found to be important (What do you say to the family? How do you live with that family afterward?).

Thus a difference in the abstractness of their representations is not the whole story of what separates these experts and novices. Underlying this difference appears to be a difference in their relative commitments to the formal culture of the academy. Both Janet and Leslie's primary commitments were to the narratives of everyday life. It was in these narratives that they pursued coherence. For Janet, this meant deciding that a small child can both be competent to act and not interfering even though this combination of features made the narrative, from the standpoint of professional ethics, irrelevant to a discussion of paternalism. For Leslie, this meant figuring out how to understand the feelings of her own family while at the same time maintaining her basic intuition that her grandfather's final wishes should have been honored—even though, from the standpoint of professional ethics, her family's feelings were irrelevant to the issue of justification. Because the novices were committed to seeing these narratives as situations in the world in which they lived, real situations, they could not ignore these professionally irrelevant features. They both expected that the domain content positions they developed would have application in indigenous cultures in which they themselves lived and thus that they had to account for the world as they found it.

Jeff and Roger's commitments lay elsewhere, in the development of a coherent domain content knowledge and in the development of an argument that would put them at the "cutting edge" of the current discussion on paternalism as they conceptualized it. For both of them, it was important to acknowledge the relationship between the issue of paternalism and other domain content issues (domain content of which Janet and Leslie were largely unaware) and to create an argument that explicitly pointed out the weakness in previous positions. As a result, Jeff and Roger treated narratives as fundamentally negotiable: Features could be changed at will to better illustrate a point; cases could be summarily dropped if they did not contribute to the domain content (if my father wasn't a paternalist then I won't think about my father).

The results of this analysis suggest, then, that it may be more appropriate to think of narrative not as something common to the thinking of novices and abandoned by experts, as many theorists have argued. Instead, narrative appears to be a way of thinking that can be transformed by expertise. In the work of the experts participating in this study, narratives formed a small but significant component of their literacy practices. The experts used abstract representations of these narratives as a way of testing and developing their domain claims in the service of developing their own position. Consequently, both the narratives themselves and the domain claims to which they were linked were negotiable: Intuitions about the narratives could change the expert's position on a domain claim; analysis of a domain claim could change an intuition about a narrative. This manipulation of narratives was possible because the experts saw them not simply as episodic structures organized to make a point, but also as abstract sets of features that could be independently varied. By having repeated recourse to a small number of narratives with well-understood sets of features, the experts assured themselves that the position they eventually developed would be coherent in terms of domain content at the expense of coherence in the narrated world of their everyday lives. Janet and Leslie did not know about and perhaps would not have been willing to make the same compromise.

CULTURAL SLIPPAGE AND THE PROFESSIONALIZATION OF SELF

Traditionally, studies of expert–novice differences such as the ones reported in this book have been viewed as providing a means of examining contrasts along a developmental continuum, with experts representing the goal of development and novices representing the starting point (Flower & Hayes, 1981b, 1981c; Larkin et al., 1980; Lesgold et al., 1988; Lundeberg, 1987; Newell & Simon, 1972; Schumacher, Klare, Cronin, & Moser, 1984; Sommers, 1979; Voss et al., 1983). The hope, then, was that expert-novice studies would provide some clues about what knowledges and skills experts actually possessed and what misunderstandings and assumptions novices harbored. With this knowledge in hand, educators could then develop curricula to bridge the gap.

This cognitive approach to the study of expertise, however, has overlooked the social function of the expert in society. A more critical perspective can be provided by thinking of the participants in expert–novice studies not simply as representatives of two ends of a developmental continuum, but also as representatives of two camps in a professionalized society, the professions and the lay public. As we noted in chapter 4, the last 100 years have witnessed an increasing professionalization of Western life (Haskell, 1984). Traditionally, members of a profession have controlled entrance to and evaluation of their membership in exchange for the production of a disinterested knowledge contributing to social progress (Hollinger, 1984). The general public allowed and even mandated professionalization in many areas on the grounds that individuals would not invest in the long-term training necessary to master the required technical knowledge unless they were provided the guarantees afforded by market protections (Freidson, 1984).

Universities have played a significant role in this process of professionalization by serving as gatekeepers overseeing a wide range of degrees in everything from landscape architecture to high-energy physics (Oleson & Voss, 1979). A less obvious but no less vital role has been their service in training an educated public of laypersons receptive to these professional services (Halloran, personal communication, 1992). That is, in order for the professions to market their expertise successfully, the general public must be made aware of its own inadequacies in areas that are nevertheless relevant to the conduct of daily life. They must be predisposed to look toward certified professionals for advice in these areas. And they must be willing to have the adequacy of this advice evaluated on specialized rather than obvious grounds. Training to be receptive in these ways probably begins in the very earliest stages of elementary education when children are encouraged to augment if not replace personal experience with book learning (Edwards & Furlong, 1978; Edwards & Mercer, 1987); but it undoubtedly culminates in the general education curricula of most undergraduate programs, which aim to provide students with an appreciation of fields outside of their speciality, but not with the specialized knowledge that would be required to make a contribution.

Thus differences between experts and novices that, from one perspective, look like temporary differences between those in and those moving into the professions, must also function as a more permanent great divide between professionals and laypersons. The way this happens can be illustrated by considering one final difference between the experts and novices studied here. The professionalized strategy identified in this analysis—pursuing coherence in a problematized world of domain content while sampling selectively from a relatively unproblematic but manipulable world of indigenous narrative experience—can never be more than a paradigm of professional behavior to which professionals try to assimilate their own activities. Each individual will, in fact, find themselves falling short of this ideal—unable to achieve coherence in the world of domain content, unable to stabilize their personal lives. In the face of this inevitable cultural slippage, professionals must develop strategies for handling and even capitalizing upon their difficulties.

As noted earlier, Leslie's work exhibited slippage. The argument in her final draft was only a partial presentation of the beliefs that she had worked out over 26 sessions. It failed to mention her grandfather; it did not include her basic belief that paternalistic intervention was unjustified. Leslie apparently accounted for this partial presentation of beliefs along a divide between the private and the public. Some beliefs, she felt, are private beliefs not to be imposed on others; others have a public character that can be presented to readers.

Like Leslie's paper, Jeff's paper was only a partial presentation of his full set of beliefs. His interviews clearly suggest that he thought moral philosophy was sexist and that autonomy should be reconceptualized along the lines of friendship rather than paternal power. His interviews also show that he originally intended to take his paper further and explore the implications of this belief. But eventually he abandoned this intention for lack of time. But rather than account for this partial presentation of beliefs along the private–public split as Leslie had, Jeff assimilated his situation to the main path/faulty path structure of the philosophic essay. That is, though he characterized his paper as a description of a problem and did not go on to suggest a solution, he justified this incompleteness by thinking of it as the first article in a series rather than just an isolated piece.

This professionalized strategy transformed what was essentially a private problem (I don't have time to do more than this) into an analysis of the state of the public (This is all my readers are ready to hear now; a second article will find them ready for the rest). Thus, in Jeff's framework, splits between private and public knowledge are temporary. He assumed that the public would eventually come to share in his entire knowledge structure, if not in the space of a single article, then in the space of a series of articles. Leslie's conception, by contrast, is that such splits are permanent and appropriate. Some of what she believes she should keep to herself.

Jeff's strategy was possible only because he had a concept of himself as a professionalized self—a self whose state of beliefs was of concern and importance to the public because he was an expert. That is, he assumed the public ought to be concerned with his beliefs because he had the special knowledge and time to think them though in a way they did not. Leslie, by contrast, did not assume a professionalized self. She saw herself as having no special abilities that justified her imposing her own views on her readers. Readers must, in her opinion, judge things for themselves.

Process-wise, Leslie's layperson's framework required her to understand her complete position in advance of writing so that she could determine which parts of it were appropriately public and which were appropriately private. Jeff's strategy required no such work. He only had to figure out exactly what he would write because he was secure in the belief that anything he did work out would be appropriate material for public presentation and anything that he had not yet worked out would eventually become appropriate. Leslie's layperson framework thus required her to do a lot more work prior to "publication" than Jeff's and ensured that a good deal of her work would not be publishable under any condition. Jeff's professionalized strategy, on the other hand, ensured a quick capitalization of whatever knowledge he had managed to produce thus far and, furthermore, developed a line of work that ensured further publication.

Ultimately, the two analytic perspectives on expert–novice differences, one cognitive, the other social, cannot easily be untangled. People acquire the knowledge and attitudes necessary to be members of the general public—a sociological indoctrination—at the same time that they acquire knowledge and skills—a cognitive development. Studies of other cultures on the edge of Westernization have be helpful in pinpointing the kinds of training required to bring otherwise functioning adults into a professionalized society (Goody, 1983; Luria, 1976). But expert–novice studies such as this one are essential to understanding how cognitive development and professionalization are bound together in our own culture. For this reason, we have paid particular attention to differences along both dimensions.

Differences between Jeff and Roger and Janet and Leslie must be understood as both differences in cognition and differences in value. They saw different things in the narratives they constructed, and in this seeing, they made different assumptions about what was important and had different criteria about what counted as coherent. Jeff and Roger belong to a profession that prizes coherence in the world of their domain knowledge at the expense of narrative coherence; Janet and Leslie belong to a lay public that reverses those values. When put in this perspective, I would suggest, educators can no longer easily assume that Janet and Leslie ought to be made by the educational system to resemble Jeff and Roger. Instead, we must begin an open dialogue in which both sides of the professional–layperson divide must articulate and defend their epistemic and moral values. And, as we see in the next chapter, we are very far from achieving this in our current classrooms.

12

AT THE BOUNDARIES OF EXPERTISE: TRANSFORMING APPRENTICESHIP IN AN INSTRUCTIONAL SITUATION

The commonplaces of our culture have led us to believe that being an expert in an area means knowing a lot. In the early years, as children, we strive to achieve this expertise on our own—trying, for example, to master everything about dinosaurs. Later on, we often rely on the expertise of others: To understand the implications of a split vote in an upcoming election, for instance, we search out experts on the electoral college. The common assumption running through both these examples is that expert practice—what an expert does—is what an expert knows. And under this assumption, as we have seen, literacy is incidental rather than central to the development of expertise in the academic professions.

As we have noted in chapter 1, however, recent research on the literacy practices of the sciences gives us reason to question this assumption. According to a growing body of research, expertise cannot simply be equated with the increasing mastery of facts. Instead, an important component of expertise is attention to the rhetorical processes by which these facts are created and disseminated in texts. In physics, for example, rather than reading everything in a given area, active researchers use authors' names and research affiliations to decide which experimental reports to peruse (Bazerman, 1988).

In areas outside of the sciences, this pattern appears to hold as well. In law, for example, experts attend to the date, place, and parties involved when reading appellate court cases, and often question judges' decisions rather than accepting them as legal facts (Lundeberg, 1987). In literature, experts appear to consider the intentions of authors when constructing literary interpretations (Vipond & Hunt, 1984). And, as we have just seen in chapter 10, even experts in academic philosophy appear to attend to the authorship of texts in analyzing the strengths and weakness of philosophic arguments.

This evidence suggests, then, that academic experts pay as much attention to the rhetorical processes by which texts are produced and read as they do to the domain content these texts contain. These results are consonant with a larger body of work from the fields of philosophy (Bernstein, 1983; Rorty, 1979), rhetoric (Bitzer, 1978; Farrell, 1976; McCloskey, 1985; Nelson, Megill, & McCloskey, 1987; Scott, 1967; Simons, 1989; Toulmin, 1958), and sociology and anthropology (Bazerman, 1988; Brodkey, 1987a; Gilbert & Mulkay, 1984; Latour & Woolgar, 1979; Myers, 1985) that has suggested that what is accepted as true in a given field—the domain content—is not a set of facts simply "found" by the discipline. Instead, it is socially constructed by the discipline's members and intimately related to the rhetorical processes underlying the reading and writing of texts. That is, as we noted in chapter 5, across the great divide, expert practice integrates both knowledge of domain content and knowledge of rhetorical process.

If expert practice integrates both of these kinds of knowledge, it becomes important to ask, how does an expert who enters the classroom transmit this integrated practice to students? How, in other words, do students ever learn to cross the great divide, to rediscover the rhetorical aspects of knowledge making, and reconstruct the practice whole? Schooling, as we noted in chapter 4, is not generally aimed to achieve this outcome. For the vast majority, schooling, particularly in the early years, succeeds in reifying the distinction between expert and layperson. Students like Janet and Leslie, whom we examined in the last two chapters, appear to operate with a disjoint practice, a conversational way of interacting with nonconversational texts, a practice best designed for knowledge getting rather than knowledge making.

But some students do eventually pass over the great divide, reintegrating the rhetorical aspects of expertise with their conceptions of the domain content of their fields. They become, in short, the experts of the next generation. How does this happen? Often, it seems to occur in the one-on-one mentoring situations of graduate school advising. Occasionally it seems to occur in the extracurricular experiences of advanced undergraduates (Haas, 1994). But sometimes, as in the situation studied here, it happens in the classroom.

In general, previous research on reading and writing has not examined this integration of rhetorical process and domain content. Instead, these studies have treated domain content as a fixed entity—present, missing, or incorrect at the outset of composing and comprehending—and unaffected by subsequent activities. That is, the domain content was assumed to remain the same throughout the task. Readers and writers have not been attributed the power to change it. Studies by Gradwohl and Schumacher (1989), Langer (1984), McCutchen (1986), and Schumacher, Gradwohl, Brezin, and Parker (1986) have suggested, for instance, that writers who have prior knowledge about a topic may produce better writing on that topic. Studies by Alvermann and Hague (1989), Alvermann et al. (1985), Dole and Smith (1989), Lipson (1982), and Voss (1984) have suggested that readers who have incorrect prior knowledge about a topic will be poorer readers and learners. Even those who wish to avoid an information transfer model have been trapped by their own language: A recent article by McGinley and Tierney (1989), for example, describes serious reading/writing activities as traversals of a "topical domain," thus suggesting the existence of an already-defined territory of domain content.

Outside of expert practice, of course, domain content does appear to have the fixed quality these studies take for granted. In fact, domain content is often defined as abstract concepts standing in permanent logical relationships to one another: being part of one another, causing one another, opposing one another, and so on: We say, "paternalism is" or "the causes of the Civil War were" or even "the rights of the individual must always be balanced against the interests of the common good." In everyday discourse, these abstract relationships are considered to be more or less unchanging: The definition of paternalism will remain the same; the causes of the Civil War will remain unchanged; and the relationship between the individual and the common good will always be in precarious balance. In this discourse of the laity, the world of academic knowledge, what Popper (1979) called the objective world, is expected to be universal and timeless.

Inside expert practice, however, this status of immutability is seen to be a hard-fought achievement rather than an inherent property. In the disciplines, as we have seen, domain content claims like "paternalism is" are routinely embedded in a framework of rhetorical process. This framework gives them a specific location in place and time and thus suggests their conditional status. Academic philosophers seldom say, "paternalism is" without also suggesting the context of rhetorical processes by which such claims must be qualified. Thus they say "Carter argues that paternalism is" or "I once believed that paternalism was" or even "At the upcoming meeting, Michaels will argue that paternalism is." With such metadiscourse, they illustrate the close connection between domain content claims and the rhetorical processes by which they have arisen.

Knowledge of rhetorical processes, then, is knowledge of an active and changing world in which authors agree or disagree, make alliances and dissolve them, make progress on a problem or get distracted. It is by such rhetorical processes that domain content claims come to be. Once claims achieve the status of fact, however, their connection to rhetorical process is often broken. Author attributions and hedges fall away and statements like "Carter claims that paternalism is" become reduced to "paternalism is" when they move outside their disciplinary boundaries (Fahnestock, 1986). Readers can then only guess the context of their creation (Haas & Flower, 1988), and even writers often no longer remember the choices they made (Rymer, 1988).

In schools, in particular, the connection between domain content and rhetorical process is almost completely broken. In textbooks, knowledge claims are usually divorced from the rhetorical processes of authorship, and students are seldom expected to evaluate them (Luke, de Castell, & Luke, 1989). In this kind of decontextualized prose, domain content is presented as autonomous of the rhetorical context in which they have been constructed. According to Olson (1977), readers need only carefully attend to their syntax and semantics to assess their meaning. In other words, we should be able to understand the statement, "paternalism is," without knowing that Carter argued it.

As we have already noted, Olson's (1977) views have been widely criticized for assuming that decontextualized school textbooks provide an appropriate model for students (Applebee, 1984b; Cazden, 1989; Street, 1984; Walters et al., 1987). Many have suggested that autonomous texts provide poor preparation for more advanced work in the disciplines. Indeed, in a recent article drawing on studies of disciplinary discourse such as those reviewed earlier, Cazden (1989) characterized the notion of autonomous text as a "myth" that only serves to support and justify the status quo. In other words, it provides a rationale for the current knowledge-telling practices in our schools. Cazden ended her critique by calling for a new educational practice in which students are provided authentic opportunities to participate in disciplinary "conversations." Echoed by many others (Applebee, 1984b; Bereiter & Scardamalia, 1987), the suggestion is that we ought to direct students' attention not only to the domain content of an area but also to the rhetorical processes by which this content is created and manipulated.

One might assume that Cazden's (1989) recommendation would be routine practice at the university level where already-expert teachers teach those seeking entrance to the disciplines. Yet despite the prevalence of writing-across-the-curriculum programs across the country (Griffin, 1985; McLeod, 1988), courses that deal with both content and process at the same time are far from common at the university (Knoblauch & Brannon, 1983; Schön, 1983). In most undergraduate courses of study, students deal with domain content in one kind of course and rhetorical process in another: lecture courses versus laboratory courses in the sciences and social sciences; lecture courses versus seminars in the social sciences and humanities; lecture courses versus studio or design courses in the arts, architecture, and engineering sciences. Thus, despite its acknowledged importance in expert practice, little has been done to show how the integration of domain content and rhetorical process can be achieved in the classroom.

The study to be reported in this chapter is an examination of one classroom situation in which this integration was attempted. A case study of the dynamics of interaction between the teacher and students introduced in chapter 8, it was part of our larger effort to develop a pedagogy for argumentation in philosophy. It thus went beyond the standard expert–novice paradigm with which we have been concerned in the last two chapters to include a study of an instructional situation. That is, we observed not just experts and novices working alone on a task in philosophical ethics, but also the classroom conversations between a teacher and his students engaged in transmitting expertise from one generation to the next.

To focus our analysis, we compare the conversations that occurred between this teacher and his students with the indigeneous form of apprenticeship. In the ideal scenario first proposed by Vygotsky (1962), apprenticeship situations make expert practice—normally the private concern of an individual expert—manifest in the joint activity of teacher and students at their proximal zone of development. Eventually, the theory goes, students internalize this distributed practice and are able to function as experts on their own. If, as many educators are now claiming (Brown et al., 1989; Bruner, 1983; Rogoff, 1990; Wood et al., 1976), instructional situations in the academy are like apprenticeships, then we should see evidence in this one classroom of how expert practice, normally kept private, was made explicit in the teacher's public conversations with his students.

THE CLASSROOM SITUATION

As described in chapter 8, 24 students enrolled in the upper level writing course in an English department were observed for this study. In this instructional situation, they were—like the experts and novices we examined earlier—asked to read from the philosophical literature on the ethical issue of paternalism and create an original argument defining paternalistic interference and outlining the conditions, if any, under which it could be justified. For the first four fifths of the course, they completed writing assignments weekly, summarizing and analyzing arguments presented in the readings, first on the definition and then on the justification of paternalism. In the final fifth of the course, they drafted and revised a major paper on the definition and justification of paternalism.

These students were divided with respect to their preparation for the course. A number (10) felt prepared by a background in philosophy: Some had completed undergraduate majors in philosophy (3), taken advanced philosophy courses (4), or at least completed an introductory freshman philosophy course (3). On the other hand, a large number (9) felt that they had never taken a course that prepared them for this one. Nevertheless, all expected to acquire new rhetorical skills—for argument (6), for writing (9), for thinking (2) and for reading (3). Only three students reported an expectation to learn theory and two students were unsure what they would learn.

As described in chapter 8, the teacher in the course was an associate professor of rhetoric with additional training in philosophy, linguistics, and computer science. At the time of this course, he had published extensively on the rhetorical tropes, particularly metaphor, and on argumentation. As coprincipal investigator of the WARRANT project, he was teaching this course for the first time in order to develop a pedagogy. He allowed me, in my role as director of the research component of the same project, to observe his class and conduct interviews.

Transcripts of 25 class sessions were collected, usually 2 per week, for 15 weeks. Forty-four interviews were conducted with the teacher following the guide given in Appendix D, usually 1 before and after each of the two class sessions, roughly 4 per week, for 15 weeks. Twenty-eight interviews were conducted with students following the guide in Appendix E, in random order, roughly 2 per week, for 14 weeks. Two of the students also agreed to be interviewed twice, once early in the term and once later on. A full list of the data collected is given in Fig. 8.4.

The analysis reported in this chapter was undertaken in two phases. In the first phase, I was interested in characterizing the conversation of the classroom. I coded the class transcripts for pattern of participation, pattern of interaction, and world of discourse according to the techniques described next, using quantitative methods to describe the resulting patterns. In the second phase, I used a more qualitative narrative analysis to examine the relationship between these public conversations and the private thoughts of the teacher and students as revealed by the weekly interviews. This combination of methods thus enabled me to explore the relationship between the private reflections of the participants and the public interactions by which they jointly constructed their instructional situation.

QUANTITATIVE ANALYSIS

Using techniques of conversation analysis (Edwards & Westgate, 1987; Heritage, 1984), I segmented the transcripts of the class sessions into independent clauses and then coded each clause along the three dimensions described in the following sections.

Pattern of Participation

Following suggestions by conversation analysts, I examined the class transcripts to determine the relative control of the floor by teacher and students. In general, previous studies of classroom discourse have shown a predominance of control by the teacher (Heritage, 1984; Mehan, 1979).

Pattern of Interaction

Conversation analysts have also suggested that the conversational interactions may take a variety of structures, some of which are more participatory than others. In monologue, for example, a single speaker controls the floor, not only contributing the majority of the discourse, but also controlling the introduction of topics and the allocation of speaking roles to other participants. In ordinary conversation, monologic discourse is often story telling (Polanyi, 1982), but in educational institutions, monologues are often "lectures" on course material.

The typology of interaction type used here was developed inductively by aggregating clauses into interchanges according to the rules given in Appendix J and then coding each interchange as either interactive or monologic. *Interactive* interchanges were interchanges in which two or more speakers participated. *Monologic* interchanges were interchanges in which one speaker held the floor and received no participation by other speakers. A reliability check of our aggregation in a subsample of the data, Class 5a with 391 clauses, showed an 88% agreement between two coders.

World of Discourse

The final dimension for coding the class transcripts was the world of discourse. As discussed earlier, a great deal of the literature in sociology and rhetoric has suggested the existence of at least two worlds of discourse, the world of rhetorical process and the world of domain content. The coding scheme in this study included, in addition to these two worlds, one other world of discourse that became obvious in the study of experts and novices described in chapter 11: the world of narrated cases of paternalism. Thus, the final scheme, found in Appendix K, included the following categories:

1. *The World of Rhetorical Process:* The world in which people make claims and counterclaims, the world of texts in which authors take approaches which may agree or disagree with one another. A paradigmatic statement in this world might be, "Dworkin claimed that paternalism is action without consent. Carter disagreed by arguing that, at least in cases of justified paternalism, consent is present, but in an implied form. I believe we should abandon the notion of implied consent altogether and confront head-on the question of justification."

2. *The World of Domain Content:* The world of possible "eternal" truths about paternalism, considered to stand independently of the authors who created or contested them. This is the world of concepts and their relationships such as the following definition: "Interference with a person's liberty of action is justified by referring exclusively to the welfare, goods, happiness, needs, interests, or values of the person being coerced."

3. *The Narrated World of Cases:* The world of people interacting with each other, taken to exist independently of the concepts of paternalism but that can potentially be characterized in terms of paternalism. This is the world of narratives such as the following: "Imagine the case of some ordinary person showing up at a hospital in need of a blood transfusion, a person with no religious, moral, or other scruples against this, a person who positively lusts for a blood transfusion. But, as it happens, the doctor on hand that night has recently suffered a conversion to Jehovah's Witness himself."

Agreement between two raters using the final coding scheme on a subset of the data, Class 10a with 518 clauses, was .84 which, corrected for the proportion of agreement expected by chance, yields .77 using Cohen's (1960) kappa. Sample codings using this scheme can be found later in the narrative analysis.

Results

The results of this first quantitative analysis suggest that the students and the teacher in this class differentiated between the worlds of discourse in a complicated pattern of participation and interaction. This pattern, furthermore, appeared to shift over time as teacher and students jointly negotiated their expert practice.

Specifically, the course appears to have fallen into three distinct periods, Period I (Weeks 1–5) in which the teacher dominated classroom interaction with monologues about rhetorical process, Period II (Weeks 6–11) in which the teacher and students shifted to a dialogue about domain content, and Period III (Weeks 12–15) in which the teacher and students returned to discuss rhetorical process in a more interactive manner. These results are described next.

The data indicating the interaction among the pattern of participation, pattern of interaction, and the worlds of discourse are given in Table 12.1. In this table, the total number of clauses in each discourse world have been taken as a baseline (4,607 for rhetorical process, 1,606 for domain content, and 460 for narrated cases), and percentages have been computed to show the distribution of the clauses within each world across participant (teacher or students) and interaction type (monologic or interactive).

As these data suggest, the three worlds of discourse had different frequencies in this class. Talk about rhetorical process clearly prevailed; fully 69% of the clauses (4,607 of 6,673) in all the classes were in the world of rhetorical process. Talk about the domain content of paternalism was the second most frequent, taking 24% of the class time (1,606 of 6,673 clauses). Talk about cases of paternalism was least frequent, occupying about 7% of the class time (460 of 6,673 clauses).

These data also show that this classroom, like so many other classrooms documented in the education literature, was largely controlled by the teacher's discourse. In fact, 77% of the classroom discourse was controlled by the teacher as participant and only 23% by the students.

Paralleling this effect of speaker was the effect of interaction type. About half of the class time (47%) consisted of monologues in which one speaker, nearly always the teacher, took and held the floor for extended periods of time without receiving the participation of others.

The relationship among the pattern of participation, pattern of interaction, and world of discourse was not straightforward, however. It was complicated in two ways. First, the teacher as participant tended to dominate talk about rhetorical

TABLE 12.1
Results of the Quantitative Analysis

	% Monologic	% Interactive	Total
		Rhetorical Process	
% Teacher	.48	.33	.81
% Students	.02	.17	.19
Total	.50	.50	1.0
			Total = 4,607
		Domain Content	
% Teacher	.34	.33	.67
% Students	.03	.30	.33
Total	.37	.63	1.0
			Total = 1,606
		Narrated Cases	
% Teacher	.47	.24	.71
% Student	.04	.25	.29
Total	.51	.49	1.0
			Total = 460
		All Worlds	
% Teacher	.45	.32	.77
% Student	.02	.21	.23
Total	.47	.53	1.0
			Grand Total = 6,673

process more than he did talk about either domain content or narrated cases (81% for rhetorical process vs. 67% for domain content and 71% for narrated cases). Second, the students as participants tended to engage in more interactive discourse when the talk was about domain content or narrated cases than when it was about rhetorical process (30% for domain content and 25% for narrated cases vs. 17% for rhetorical process). Taken together, these two effects combine to suggest that the teacher was more likely to contribute monologically to talk about rhetorical process whereas the students were more likely to contribute interactively to talk about either domain content or narrated cases.

Interestingly, this pattern of differential contribution to the worlds of discourse was significantly affected by the time of the semester. As Fig. 12.1 indicates, the percentage of independent clauses given to a particular world of discourse shifted dramatically over time. Overall, a tradeoff appears to have existed between concerns about rhetorical process on the one hand and concerns about the domain content and narrated cases on the other. Concern about the domain content and cases of paternalism clearly clustered in the middle session of the semester,

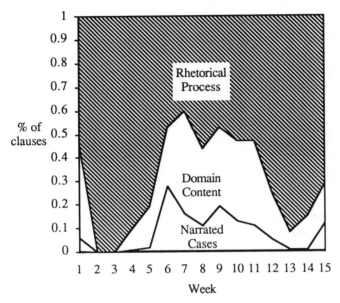

FIG. 12.1. Distribution of the worlds of discourse over time. The totals are given for teacher and student combined because the differences between participants remained stable over the time.

Period II (Weeks 6–11). Concern about the world of rhetorical process clustered at the beginning and ending sessions: In Period I (Weeks 1–5), it surfaced primarily in monologic discourse dominated by the teacher; in Period III (Weeks 12–15), it shifted to interactive discourse more evenly shared by both teacher and students.

NARRATIVE ANALYSIS

The results of the initial quantitative analysis of the classroom transcripts thus suggested that the activities in this course fell roughly into three periods, each characterized by a distinct pattern of participation, pattern of interaction, and world of discourse. The second and more qualitative phase of analysis attempted to account for the nature and development of these phases by building a week-by-week narrative analysis that collated the incidents and reflections reported across all three data sets: the class transcripts, the teacher interviews, and the student interviews. Specifically, for each week, this narrative construction began with my notes on the teacher's and students' responses to interview questions and was followed by a one-paragraph summary that attempted to develop a relationship between this interview data and the actual events of the classroom. Throughout, I attempted to maintain the participants' own language.

The results of this analysis suggest that the pattern of shifting concerns revealed by Fig. 12.1 was the result of a negotiation process by which the students and teacher tacitly distributed the components of expert practice, rhetorical process and domain content, across the public and private spaces of the instructional situation. A condensed version of this analysis is given in the following sections. A more complete report is given in Appendix L.

Period I: Monologues on Rhetorical Process

In the first 5 weeks of the semester, students and teacher worked on summarizing and evaluating scholarly articles on the definition of paternalism. The teacher saw his responsibility as providing the students with heuristics to complete these tasks and this concern for rhetorical process became manifest in the classroom discourse. In his private preparations for class, the teacher used his expert reactions to the domain content in students' weekly assignments to generate heuristics for rhetorical process, which he then presented publicly in class using largely monologic discourse. In such monologues, the teacher's tag questions ("right?"; "okay?") served to break up the flow of discourse, but were not taken by the students as serious invitations to contribute. When students did participate in this world of discourse, it was most often to seek clarification on what they should be doing.

The teacher was dissatisfied with this level of participation and tried various strategies to increase it without success. In the 4th week, however, he inadvertently shifted his focus to domain content when he asked students to make a list of confusions that remained thus far unresolved in their minds. In class, he intended to use these confusions to illustrate the rhetorical skill of assessing one's own metaknowledge. The students, however, reacted enthusiastically to this introduction of domain content and the ensuing discussion, spilling over into Week 5, repeatedly moved both teacher and students away from rhetorical process and toward domain content.

The following example illustrates the way that students used their level of conversational participation to affect the teacher's choice among the worlds of discourse in this period. At first, when the teacher requested a rhetorical process account of the students' difficulties with the term *nonacquiesce*, he was met with silence (In this and following examples, I have provided the coding in the margin as follows: RP = rhetorical process; DC = domain content; NC = narrated cases):

RP   T: Many of you thought by "nonacquiescence" that Childress is just being negative, taking the easy way out, only telling you what the paternalist doesn't do, but not what he does do. Is that true? Is he taking the easy way out? I mean if I tried to explain what it's like to be a certain person and I say, "Well, you don't go to the drug store on Sundays," that doesn't tell you much. But is he really being that noncommittal? What is the problem? I don't know what the problem you have with

the word is. I honestly don't know.
[silence]

RP   T: I agree that it is the negative of "acquiesce."
[silence]

When the teacher shifted, however, to providing a domain content definition with narrative case examples, the students joined in and the mood of the class improved:

DC   T: What are the circumstances under which you can nonacquiesce?
NC   If I live in another city and don't know you and all your life you've wanted various different things,
DC   have I spent a life nonacquiescing to your wishes?
RP   S: I never looked it up cause I always assumed that
DC   "acquiesce" means go along with and nonacquiescence means "won't go along" implying some kind of knowledge.
       T: Okay.
NC   S: And you couldn't reasonably know what I want cause I've never told you. I want a SAAB.
DC   T: Well, now I can really nonacquiesce.
[students laugh.]
(Interactive Discourse, Tuesday, Week 5)

Such selective participation on the students' part appears to have been one of the primary mechanisms by which they influenced the choice among otherwise teacher-controlled worlds of discourse. In fact, this entire discussion of student confusions became a watershed for the participants in this class, marking a transition from Period I, where the focus had been on heuristics for rhetorical process, to Period II, where the focus shifted to domain content.

Period II: Dialogues About Domain Content

During the middle period of the semester, the teacher appears to have shifted to the discourse of domain content in order to compensate for—rather than develop—the students' expertise. As he articulated in an interview before Tuesday's class, Week 9, he had come to feel responsible for constructing an interpretive framework for the domain content himself on his own time and then providing that framework readymade to students in class. In the following excerpt, the teacher contrasted his own expert practice, assumption digging, with what he had come to believe was within the students' current reach, knowledge digging:

T: For an expert ... for an expert to do assumption digging, it probably means moving back and forth between the text and the library, you know—scholarship—to keep making assumptions about how you can continually induce that structure. When you go to the library and you go to other articles, that helps shape your knowledge base, you know, in the way that becomes very top down. But then you read other articles and that can shake your conception of the knowledge base. That drives you back to specific articles. That drives you back to the card catalogue system. That drives you back to lists of articles. So, for an expert, that induction is very interactive and fluid.

I think in the scope of a . . . course, the most you can hope for is knowledge digging as you can't assume students can induce anything from these articles. What you can do is sort of present them with this structure or at least, you know—pacing this thing—you would quibble with them and you can certainly . . . you can . . . you can try to lead them to induce the structure after they've read certain things, you know, and ask them questions of what invokes the problems, build the structure, and then, carefully, you know, gingerly, do questioning after different articles. The combination of different articles . . . through a combination of questions after articles and then a little bit of exposition, you know, help them induce the structure.

As a result of the resistance he met in Period I, then, the teacher had decided that he could not expect students to handle the whole of his expert practice. Instead, he opted to distribute responsibility for it, reserving the generation of a framework from the literature for himself using rhetorical processes, and leaving to students the task of inducing this framework given carefully crafted questions about the domain content.

This change in strategy not only shifted the public classroom discourse from rhetorical process to domain content, but also affected the teacher's private reflections: In order to provide them with a workable structure, the teacher had to work out his own position on paternalism. This expert effort led him to make repeated changes to his own interpretative framework as he moved "interactively and fluidly" between the texts in the course and the available scholarship. This process involved a number of stages in which positions entertained hypothetically at one point were reinterpreted, modified, and even abandoned at later points.

For instance, at the beginning of Week 6, the teacher had recognized that the philosophers he had been reading were working in the British analytic tradition. To his own satisfaction, he could show how all of the authors he had read so far fit into this tradition and he had decided to work within that tradition as well. By the end of the following week (Week 7), however, he had decided that he had wrongly characterized one of the authors. After 2 more weeks and a discussion with a Kantian scholar (Week 9), he had abandoned the analytic tradition altogether and decided to work out a position in a more continentally inspired cultural framework. The end of Period II, then, saw the teacher *qua* expert in possession of a fully developed characterization of the "faulty paths" taken by the other authors he had read and his own "main path" that overcame these faults.

Ironically, the teacher's exercise of this rhetorical expertise undermined his ability to achieve his pedagogical objective of providing students in class with a structure for domain content. Under pressure to teach as well as think, he presented his current conception of paternalism to students as "the framework" that they were to use in their own work. Each time his conception shifted, however, he had to publicly abandon his previous commitments and ask students to replace their prior framework with his new conception. Looked at rhetorically, such repeated revisions may be an inevitable characteristic of experts trying to develop points to make with their own readers. Looked at pedagogically, however, such back pedaling might seem inept and, indeed, the teacher feared that students would interpret things this way:

> T: There's one response I hope for and one response I dread. And the response I hope for is that people get awakened and say, "How can I get deeper into the issue?" The response I dread is people will say, "Oh God, the guy's pulled the rug out from underneath us again. Why?" In other words, they are utterly weak. They think that's going to be the [answer]. The real structure is going to come out. What is the purpose of doing it. And the next day comes and all the guy does, he just pulls the rug out from under us again. He just comes across as a person who clearly doesn't know what he wants to teach, just fumbling around and just getting us through in any way he can. (Interview after Thursday's class, Week 5)

Although interviews in this period show students aware of the teacher's changes of mind, they do not, by and large, reveal the "response I dread." In fact, it appears as if the teacher's shifts enabled the students to see domain content as something less than monolithic and thus as something on which they might have something to say. In class, interactions on domain content in this period could be lengthy, involve multiple speakers, and often contained arguments against the teacher's position. For instance, one interaction on the distinction between a priori and actual rights, which had been introduced in an article by Rosemary Carter, evolved to include a total of 263 clauses and 13 different speakers:

RP	S1:	I mean,
DC		what are the *prima facie* rights in that case and what are the actual rights?
RP	T:	I think you only get very confused when you try to think that way. . . . I don't think it matters. I just don't think it's that important. All she ever talks about . . . After the first paragraph, she's only considering what she calls *prima facie* rights which normal people call rights. I mean if you want to say that
DC		the meaning of a right is that you can't violate it, you can do that, right?
RP		But then you're only going to spend the rest of your life talking about *prima facie* rights. Those are the only rights I know about. In other words, I only know about rights that you can violate.
RP	S1:	Can't you think of a right that can't be violated?

DC T: Well, is there any right more important than the right to life?

S1: Yes. [garbled]

DC T: So under the right circumstances, there's no right that can't be taken away. You know, your right to life, to liberty, to justice ... Well, your right to justice—Can you take away your right to justice? You have a right to due process. Maybe that's an actual right. Maybe the right to due process is an actual right.

DC S1: Oh. You can take away a person's right to due process.

DC T: When? Yeah, but justifiably, can they ever alienate their right to due process?

NC S1: What about streakers?

DC T: No, I've still got to try them. You know, maybe there are some actual rights. [laughter]

DC S2: Part of due process is not being roughed up by the cops. You argued that it's really justifiable [a reference to the teacher's earlier analysis of *Dirty Harry*]

NC T: Yeah, I know. But that was a movie. That was Hollywood. Yeah?

DC S3: Actual rights have to do with moral principles. *Prima facie* rights are something [garbled]

RP T: That may be productive but I don't think that's going to get very far. I don't think trying to represent it—the distinction—is going to help you understand this article one whit. And I've already seen plenty of examples in your papers of how it can screw you up. [laughter]

RP T: So I'd rather put an end to that distinction.

RP S4: Maybe she's just trying to get away from the idea that

DC   we can violate rights

RP T: Right. I would say

DC   the right to due process you can't violate.

RP   I'd probably say that.

RP S4: You can't give it up?

NC T: Well, actually, what if you're in death row, okay? And you kill somebody. I don't think you have to be tried again, do you? No. If you're in death row and you kill somebody, I don't think you have to be tried again.

DC   You don't have to have due process.

    S4: [garbled]

DC T: There's no circumstances where it's inalienable.

    S4: [garbled]

RP T: What I'm saying is, let's say

NC   a guy was going to be electrocuted in three days and he gets smart and says, "Hey, if I kill two guards, they'll need another six-year trial and that could delay the execution." So he kills the person and he says, "Okay, I want a trial. I want due process," okay? He won't get the trial. (Tuesday's class during Week 9)

Typical of Period II, this dialogue exhibits two important features. First, it illustrates how the teacher's treatment of domain content implicitly showed students the hypothetical thinking and use of narrative cases that are the hallmarks of rhetorical process in ethics. By running through a number of cases (right to life, to liberty, to justice), he not only illustrated his claim that all rights can be alienated under some circumstances, but also came up with one case (due process) that nearly caused him to abandon his argument. Just as quickly, however, he constructed a narrative case to negate the counterexample (a murderer on death row is not entitled to due process) and thus was able to reassert his claim. Although such interactions explicitly worked through the discourse world of domain content, the teacher's shifts of claims in that discourse provided students with implicit lessons about rhetorical process.

Second, this selection illustrates the complex relationship that was developing between the teacher's private rhetorical processes and the public lessons he attempted to teach about domain content. The teacher opened and closed this discussion by trying to make a point about domain content: The distinction between a priori rights and actual rights was meaningless. Such lessons on domain content, however, were deeply embedded in the teacher's own private reflections, for the interviews show that he was only able to say that this distinction was meaningless as a result of being unable to make meaning of it himself.

To sum up, Period II can be characterized by the teacher's attempt to compensate for students' lack of expertise by moving rhetorical process out of the classroom and onto his own shoulders. Thus, contrary to the evidence in the transcripts, rhetorical process did not disappear in this period; it simply moved out of the public space of the classroom and into the teacher's private reflections. The classroom was then left as a forum for the discussion of domain content. Furthermore, although the teacher's rhetorical processes were the source of classroom discourse, it was also segregated from that discourse, at least as an explicit topic. As we see, Period III was characterized by the reverse. In the final period of the course, the teacher's conception of the domain content became the unacknowledged force behind the class's return to the discourse world of rhetorical process.

Period III: Dialogues About Rhetorical Process

In the final 4 weeks of the course, the teacher, realizing that the semester was almost over, turned the students' attention back to rhetorical concerns: the final essay they were required to write on paternalism. The students, for their part having a better understanding of the domain, showed greater willingness to participate in discussions about rhetorical process. In fact, in this period for the first time, students' contributions to classroom discourse nearly equaled the teacher's.

This return to the discourse world of rhetorical process and initiation of an interactive pattern of participation corresponded to the teacher's decision to move the class into "workshop" mode. During the preceding 2 weeks, he had given them the general progression he expected in their papers: Establish the problem, review the scholarship, show the limits of the scholarship, restructure the issue. He assumed that the final section of the paper—the one in which students were to "situate themselves" and make a point—would be based on their personal response to the literature.

As a teacher, this seemed to bring him, for the first time, a period of comparative rest as he watched for students to develop their own positions. As an expert, however, his activity was not at an end. The relationship between the teacher's own expertise and his pedagogical goals remained complex as his fully developed position on domain content began to influence his lessons about rhetorical process. Privately, he saw his own position as the best answer to the inadequacies of the previous scholarship as he saw them: If he could have thought of counterarguments to his own position, he would have changed his mind; if he could not have thought of counterarguments to alternative positions, he would have given them serious consideration. Thus his expertise seemed to make him unable to imagine his students taking any position on paternalism other than his own. This position on domain content in turn shaped the advice he gave students about rhetorical process. When I questioned him in an interview before Tuesday's class, Week 14, he described his pedagogical stance this way:

> G: Is that where you think all the students should be, working there too, or is that just an exemplar of what you said?
> T: It's an exemplar, but it's going to be hard to beat. And so the point is that they ought to be generating their own stuff and exploring their own paths but as . . . they see a path toward this pivotal problem, they're going to have to have dam good resistant arguments to continue exploring in THEIR directions. . . . (Interview before Tuesday's class, Week 14)

Although the teacher was incapable of imagining his students constructing rhetorical plans different from his own, he was fully capable of revising them for himself. Just as he had revised domain content during Period II, his rhetorical plans became subject to revision during Period III. In class, he presented these rhetorical revisions to students in highly interactive discourse. The interviews suggest that, in response, the students began to develop their own rhetorical plans, which, nevertheless, echoed the rhetorical plans of the teacher. Instead of being confused by the teacher's changes of mind, they appear to have interpreted his actions as symptomatic of the choices that they had to work out for themselves. At the end of Week 14, one student described it this way:

> I: Situating yourself—well, what does that mean?

S: It ... it took a couple ... It took probably a month and a half to figure out what it was—a pretty well thought mental structure to these things that he was talking about—because I didn't get the ... I really didn't get the impression firsthand. You know, you come in very skeptical and you're not sure where you're going. And sometimes you see things that ... that you believe that he's not sure where he's going either because kind of the structure will break down sometimes—what's your crucial questions. And after a while, you learn that he's willing to be stumped on an issue and pause and think about it rather than say, "Well I have an approach that ..." But it ... it seemed overall that—maybe I just had some really good tools going in in terms of being ready for this kind of thing—but it was challenging and it was unstructured—maybe a little bit too unstructured. But you have to have kind of a lack of structure plus principles that you talk about over and over to really do critical thinking. Otherwise, it's just, you know, learning, like he says. (Interview with S14, Thursday of Week 14)

In retrospect, the teacher of this course found many things he would have liked to do over and, indeed, he has done them over many times since he first taught this course. He was particularly aware of the way that his continuous changes of mind had affected the students:

G: Can you describe to me how you ... what you think happened ... what you saw happening with the students in class?
T: A bunch of students saw me fumble trying to understand a question. They got lost, found themselves, got lost, found themselves, got lost, found themselves, never knew what the question was about because I kept upping the ante. (Interview before the final class, Tuesday of Week 15)

Nevertheless, this course taught the students important lessons about expert practice. Interviews during the final period show that all of the students had come to understand the teacher's pedagogical goals as rhetorical process goals and to see the domain content of paternalism as secondary to these goals. Furthermore, they understood that they were expected to build a connection between the academic scholarship and their own personal positions. Many, in addition, could describe the main path/faulty path structure typical of philosophic discourse and aimed to incorporate it into their final papers as one student described in an interview at the beginning of Week 14:

S: I'm kind of going to introduce the scholar literature and say, "See, there's these really bright people that have thought about this already" and kind of manipulate their ideas too ... with my ... not ... not saying what I feel yet, but knowing that I have to kind of piece together my idea through the scholarly literature. Introducing that and then going beyond that, saying, "But see, this is what it really ... This is what it really is" and kind of putting forth my definitions, you ... you know, with support from the scholarly literature. (Interview with S30, Monday of Week 14)

THE TACIT INTEGRATION OF ACADEMIC EXPERTISE

One of the most important lessons of recent scholarship on literacy in the professions is that whenever expert practice is truly present—when knowledge is treated as something to be constructed rather than something to be found—both rhetorical process and domain content will necessarily be involved. The data presented previously indicate, however, that the relationship between the two can be complex when distributed across the various spaces of an instructional situation. As the schematic diagram in Fig. 12.2 represents, when the discourse of one world dominated the public classroom discussion in this classroom, the other moved "off stage" into the teacher's private reflections. In Period I, when the classroom time was filled with heuristics on rhetorical process, the discourse of domain content moved into the teacher's private thoughts. In Period II, when domain content issues came to dominate the classroom interaction, the discourse of rhetorical process, in turn, retreated into the teacher's reflections. And, in Period III, when rhetorical concerns once again moved center stage, the teacher's recommendations concerning a rhetorical plan for the final paper were irremediably colored by the position he held privately on domain content.

In this classroom, then, the two components of expertise, though present throughout the semester, appear to have remained segregated. As a result, outsiders who looked only at the progression of concerns represented in public spaces of classroom discourse—the white spaces in Fig. 12.2—would notice a remarkable linearity. On the surface, that is, it looks as if the class resolved domain content issues prior to and independently of rhetorical process even though, in effect, both discourses were simultaneously albeit tacitly distributed across the classroom floor and the teacher's own private reflections. This instructional situation, then, appears to have reproduced rather than challenged the cultural myth of the autonomous text by making the relationship between the two components of expert practice appear linear rather than interactive. That is, the public facts of the instructional situation seemed to support the idea that the generation of ideas about the domain content is prior to and independent of their expression in text.

This lack of explicit integration seems to have occurred for two reasons. First, in this class, the students used the relative level of their participation in classroom conversation to influence the teacher's focus. As the teacher was well aware, he could not operate as a free agent in determining how to make his expertise available to students. By their minute-by-minute responsiveness in classroom conversation, the students encouraged the teacher to separate rhetorical process and domain content and attend to them in an order that matched their expectations: domain content first, rhetorical process later.

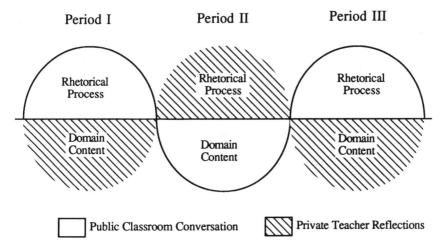

FIG. 12.2.   The distribution of the components of expertise across the public and private spaces of the instructional situation.

Second, the teacher's own expertise contributed to the lack of explicit integration. Though tacitly aware of the need to shift between domain content and rhetorical process in his own construction of knowledge, the teacher nevertheless did not make this shift a public fact for students. Instead, once he had decided, in Period II, to do the task himself in order to compensate for students' lack of expertise, he took on, as well, the expert requirement to be convinced of what he decided. *Conviction* appears to be an important component of expertise in argumentation. An expert's conviction can easily shift in the face of new counterarguments or unanticipated positions and this accounts for the teacher's repeated changes of mind in the face of new readings, discussions with colleagues, and interactions with students. Nonetheless, at any given time, the teacher strove to be convinced that he was right, whether about the domain content (Period II) or about the rhetorical situation (Period III).

However important this state of conviction was to the teacher *qua* expert, it worked against explicit pedagogical integration. Specifically, studies of the role of writing in the professions and disciplines, science in particular, have suggested that experts routinely suppress accounts of rhetorical process once they develop convictions about domain content (Gilbert & Mulkay, 1984). Thus, once the teacher in this class had developed convictions as an expert, a task he took on to support students' work, he was unable to discuss with students ways in which those convictions could be altered.

Nevertheless, behind the public appearance of linearity was a tacit integration of rhetorical process and domain content. When faced with new arguments or counterarguments, the teacher's convictions were repeatedly destabilized and the relationship between the two components of expert practice was demonstrated rather than articulated for students by his changes of mind. Thus, in periods of high interaction (II and III), the teacher's own actions amounted to showing rather than telling students that both kinds of knowledge played a role in the exercise of expert practice in philosophical ethics. In the end, then, this teacher did succeed in transmitting his integrated practice to students, but this integration continued to operate for them as it had for him—at the tacit level.

PROBLEMS WITH THE APPRENTICESHIP MODEL

Despite calls for reform (Applebee, 1984b; Lampert, 1990), few teachers at the undergraduate level and even fewer at the secondary and primary level attempt what the teacher in this class attempted: to show students how to cross the boundaries of expertise by making the crossing himself. In traditional domain content courses, rhetorical processes have usually been completed in advance of teaching by expert teachers who, following the conventions of the autonomous text, have removed all traces of the process once they have constructed their positions. In this manner, rhetorical processes do not normally become the topic of classroom discourse. In a parallel fashion, domain content does not normally have a place in the classroom discourse of traditional writing courses. Without a commitment to any particular domain content, writing teachers most often allow students to choose their own topics and struggle with domain content on their own time.

This classroom thus provides an unusual case study of an instructional situation in which rhetorical process and domain content met. In large measure, this was the result of the teacher's belief that his expertise lay as much or more in the rhetorical processes he knew how to employ as in any domain content he had come to believe. In this, he echoed much of postmodern thinking, reviewed earlier, about the nature of knowledge and the role of rhetoric in its construction. Yet, as this analysis has shown, his commitment to teach an integrated practice did not translate unproblematically into instruction. In point of fact, what happened in this classroom can be understood as the result of the students' firm belief in the myth of the autonomous text and their insistence, via the mechanism of conversational interaction, that the teacher organize instruction accordingly. By distributing expert practice over the public space of the classroom and the private space of the teacher's reflection, this instructional situation left the cultural myth of the autonomous text unchallenged even though the expert himself did not believe it or act according to it.

A simple model of instruction as indigeneous apprenticeship does not lead us to anticipate this result. Taking for granted that one generation wants to pass on its expertise to the next, the indigenous model ignores the powerful impact of professionalization: All professions do indeed want at least some of their students to become apprentices and, through interaction with them, cross the great divide. But they also need other students to remain on the other side. The apprenticeship model ignores these sociological facts. Indeed, it seems to suggest that teachers can overcome educational inequities through simple efforts to open up their practices to students.

This study suggests that such simple prescriptions for reform are problematic. In particular, experts who attempt to teach an integrated practice ultimately have an unsatisfying experience. They feel accountable when they do not live up to their students' demands to pass on knowledge and seldom persist in this effort. With no metalanguage with which to rise above their own convictions, they have no way to teach their practice except through actual demonstration, but this very demonstration often puts them at risk in the classroom—at risk of losing face, at risk of losing control. We cannot expect too many to be willing to take these risks. Indeed, when presented with an earlier version of this article, the teacher in this study felt that I had been too kind to him: He blamed himself for not keeping his own knowledge of the domain content more firmly under control and for failing to provide students with the basic conceptual knowledge they initially required. That is, he himself believed that he should have settled domain content issues as much as possible in advance of teaching.

This teacher's decision to maintain a more segregated practice may seem regrettable, but articulated alternatives are hard to find. The basic problem, as Applebee (1984a) pointed out, is that a practice and discourse that fully integrates rhetorical process and domain content simply does not exist at this point in our culture. Thus, in language and practice, all members of the academic community are experts just as much as the teacher in this study. This teacher's decision thus challenges us to reconsider our questions. When I started these studies, I was asking what I thought was a question about instruction: What can I do as a teacher to help students write the kinds of texts required by their courses? Although I still think this is an important question, I now also want to ask questions about the expert practice itself: Why do I want them to write these kinds of texts? And, perhaps more significantly, Why do I want to? It is to questions like these—questions of reflection and reform—that we finally must turn in the closing chapters of this book.

REFLECTION AND REFORM

13

REFLECTING ON ACADEMIC LITERACY

In 1990, the Research Network (Bazerman et al., 1989) asked me, as one of a group of young scholars, to produce an account of my research. They asked, in particular, that I describe how I saw my research as being multimodal and what I saw as the benefits and hazards of adopting a multimodal approach. The texts that I and others produced in response to this charge were intended to form the basis of a daylong preconvention workshop during the upcoming Conference on College Composition and Communication.

As soon as I put pen to paper, my text—which forms the kernel of the following chapter—began to take shape as a series of layers, each of which appeared to be an indispensable component of answering the charge I had been given, yet each individually remaining inadequate to the task. The first layer, a summative *scientific report*, described the goals of my research, its methods, data, and results. This traditional description justified the decisions I had made in terms of the knowledge they had produced. Next, a *reflective analysis* took the research apart, describing how I saw it as multimodal and what I saw as its benefits and hazards. Here decisions were explained through contrasts with alternatives I had rejected. Next, a *personal history* traced the events and influences that I believed had shaped my research. Such personal historicizing, though inevitably selective, seemed important to accounting for my decisions. Finally, a *deliberative appeal* enclosed the whole, first warning readers about the struggle they might encounter in digging through the text, and finally urging them to consider the implications of this struggle for the future of our field.

Each of these layers was comprehensible to me in its own terms, but when put together, I found the combination to be unreadable—at least within the conventions of the academy. In particular, although I was making an argument as required by academic conventions, my "point" was elusive: In every layer, meanings seemed to accumulate rather than culminate. Whenever I tried to move things around, eliminate the superfluous, and consider my reader (the one in my mind looking over my shoulder), I squirmed with the results. I had not got it right. Finally, I just let it go as written.

As the text has companioned me over the last 4 years, however, I have begun to understand what I was trying to say. As one of my readers put it, "the ideology being proposed is that the experiences, understandings, ideas, and mentalisms of the researcher/writer/author/person need to be accounted for if there is to be a good (better?) understanding of what is being written and how." This ideology had forced me to start with myself as a writer, admitting the multiple worlds within which I composed myself. But it also meant starting with myself as a reader, recognizing how the text that I wanted to find myself writing repressed the very multiplicity that enabled its composing. And this reflexivity began to make a point for me that was more than personal: If we, as a community centrally concerned with composing, fail to recognize that we do not value what we actually do to compose the texts we make, then we will not be able to do justice to those who do not manage the negotiation quite as well as we ourselves do—or manage it differently—and we will continue to allow ourselves and others to behave as badly as Peter Elbow (1991) said we so often do.

Making this point is ultimately the purpose of this chapter, but as a preliminary, I first invite readers to read through the original text I wrote for the Research Network. Then, with the results of this experiment in composing in hand, I turn to consider the tensions among the possible accounts of our research that we might compose and what these tensions tell us about the reading and writing practices of the academy. I need to apologize in advance, however, for placing myself so much at the center of the text that follows. Fundamentally, this text needs four characters to act it out: I as a writer, you as a writer; I as a reader, you as a reader. Unfortunately, the only characters for which I could write the dialogue were the ones with my name attached. But the text will not work unless the ones with your name attached speak up as well.

MARCH 1990: A FOUR-LAYERED ACCOUNT OF RESEARCH

Because I have been asked by the Research Network to offer an account of my research, it will be helpful to begin this chapter with a discussion of what it means to offer an "account." This small definitional journey may not only help me to speak to my charge, a "metacommentary on the methods of inquiry you have used in recent projects," but also illustrate the issues and modes of inquiry involved in my research.

We can begin by placing the activity of "accounting" within the context of conversational interaction. People offer accounts when something in the normal run of conversation is disrupted, when an exigency makes manifest a lack of common ground for understanding. This use of the term account has been strongly shaped by John Heritage's treatment in *Garfinkel and Ethnomethodology* (1984). Drawing on the theoretical work of Harold Garfinkel (Garfinkel & Sacks, 1970), Heritage claimed that accounts, as situated actions, cannot be interpreted without asking, "(1) why is the speaker referencing that object, (2) in that way, (3) right now?" (p. 151). Heritage then described the role of accounts in the turn-taking sequences patterning everyday conversation. In these conversations, according to Heritage, actors feel morally obliged to supply accounts for their actions whenever they respond with dispreferred, usually disafilliative, responses (see also Pomerantz, 1984a, 1984b)—that is, whenever an interlocutor responds with what a first speaker did not want to hear.

Thus, accounts are stories we tell each other about who we are, where we have been, and how things appear from our perspective. When we know each other very well, we do not need these accounts. When we are strangers, such accounts enable us to begin the conversation. Understood in this way, I can only applaud the request for an account of my research. Indeed, as chair of last year's Research Network, I myself asked for such accounts from others and, in my observation, the process had enormous benefits. An account is, by definition, historical, local, particularized: To account for one's research, one has to explain the history and circumstances of one's identity as a researcher and how one's work arises out of those particularities. These accounts can help us to see reality in the shoes of another researcher whom we initially fail to understand and to explain how differences in approach and belief are the result of normal differences in such factors as undergraduate and graduate training, institutional role, and cultural heritage. Accounts, in short, help to normalize and humanize our differences rather than escalate them into full-scale confrontations. I am all in favor of this.

My own work on the relationship between the conventions of everyday conversation and the literate interactions of academic literacy cautions me, however, about the activity of accounting for one's research in print. Whereas people tend to use accounts in oral conversation to diffuse difference and build a common understanding, the conventions of academic literacy often force upon us an interpretation of accounting that is less than flattering. According to these conventions, the only positions or claims that need to be "accounted for" are those that are inadequate, false, or misleading. For instance, if I write this account, "My analysis of academic literacy reflected the ambivalence of someone raised in an antiintellectual tradition," as I do later in this chapter, academic reading conventions easily suggest that the analysis in question was improperly colored by personal bias. If I write, however, that, "Expertise in academic literacy can best be conceived as the ability to negotiate among distinct worlds of discourse," as I do in another place in this chapter, these claims read with more validity. Stripped of metadiscourse, they appear to be the result of a process of universalization in which we use special disciplinary techniques to pull abstract truths out of the mundane details of everyday life (Gilbert & Mulkay, 1984).

As a consequence of these conventions, whenever we venture to account for our research and place this account in print, we run the risk of being taken as less than serious, of having our claims assessed as less than valid, and of being accused of methodological impurity. This will happen to some extent, no matter how good our intentions are, and it is particularly likely to happen when the person giving the account has not "earned" the right of personal reflection by a long and distinguished career as I certainly have not.

Nonetheless, as organizations of people, research communities cannot do without accounts. Not only do they help to explain us to each other, but they also help to explain us to ourselves. People need particular and localized accounts of how something is actually accomplished in order to become actors themselves. Simply looking at the products will not suffice. Although these accounts have traditionally been provided through graduate education and conversation at professional conferences, an increasing number of attempts have been made to open up knowledge-making practices beyond these circles of interpersonal contacts. It is in this light that it is important to share individual accounts of research as I have done in what follows.

Nevertheless, we have little experience and less success in doing this easily. It takes a struggle on the part of both the writer and the reader to be self-conscious of tradition and willing to suspend expectations. Having said all this by way of preface, however, I propose to fulfill my charge. However imperfect and jarring the resultant discourse might be, such experiments in composing must be conducted in order to forge a more appropriate discourse for the diversity of multi-modal inquiry which, as I argue later, it is our privilege to help the academy develop.

Layer I. Scientific Report: "The Nature of Expertise in Academic Literacy"

I have for the last few years been involved in developing a characterization of expertise in academic literacy. My concern has been to use my case studies of argumentation in philosophical ethics to develop a model of expertise that would do justice to the cognitive complexity of this practice, its function in society, and its future in our culture.

The data for the research came from a project I began in January 1985. Supported by the Fund for the Improvement of Postsecondary Education, the research design included three sites for observing the reading, writing, and thinking of individuals engaged in practices of academic literacy: (a) two PhD-level philosophers working to develop an original essay on the ethical issue of paternalism, (b) two college freshman asked to do the same task, and (c) one classroom in which students were engaged in learning how to do the same task.

The experts and novices worked on the task for between 30 and 50 hours over a 15-week semester. The classroom situation developed over the same time period. The data from these participants included think-aloud protocols from the experts and novices whenever they worked on the task, tape recordings of the classroom interaction between teacher and students, interviews with all participants at regular intervals throughout their working time, and copies of the intermediate and final texts they produced. This corpus of data added up to well over 2,000 pages of text and transcript.

These data were analyzed using analytic induction to develop coding categories (Goetz & LeCompte, 1984) and multiple coders to achieve reliability in coding. Details of the analysis varied with data type. Textual data have been analyzed using a modified version of Langer's system for the analysis of structure. Protocol data have been analyzed following methods pioneered by Newell and Simon (1972) and applied to writing by Flower and Hayes (1981a). The classroom discourse has been analyzed for structure in the tradition of conversation analysis (Mehan, 1979) and for content using the system described later.

The characterization of expertise in academic literacy put forward here builds on suggestions by earlier researchers that writing involves the cognitively and socially complex task of negotiating among several worlds of discourse. In *The Psychology of Written Composition* (1987), for example, Bereiter and Scardamalia suggested that writing requires thinking in two "problem spaces" (a term borrowed from Newell and Simon's (1972) work), one for content, the other rhetorical. A writer, according to Bereiter and Scardamalia, has to translate problems in the rhetorical problem space into subgoals to be achieved in the content problem space. For example, the rhetorical awareness that readers will not understand a term will be translated into a subgoal in the content space to search for an existing definition and, if necessary, to construct one. According to Bereiter and Scardamalia, the power of writing to transform knowledge lies in the writer's openness to moving back and forth between these two spaces interactively—allowing developments in one's beliefs to change one's goals with respect to audience; allowing one's goals with respect to audience to shape the development of one's beliefs.

A second line of research that has also drawn on the idea of multiple worlds is the study of children's acquisition of narrative structures. It is tempting to take this earliest form of discourse as relatively unproblematic. But the work of Dyson (1988) suggests that children learning to tell stories must struggle to develop a boundary between the everyday world of their experience and the world of text. Thus a child who is angry with her brother may tell a story about a little girl who has a fight with *her* brother. Incoherences in tense and personal pronouns reveal a struggle to maintain a boundary between worlds: "Once there was a girl. I like the girl. I Hate the Girls Brother a Lot. The End." Dyson's point about these two worlds of discourse is similar to that made by Bereiter and Scardamalia (1987). Although well-formed written discourse must keep the worlds separate, from a process point of view the boundary must be permeable: Children draw inspiration for their stories from everyday life and the stories can, in turn, help them understand and work out difficulties in that life.

The practices of academic literacy appear to be even more complicated than the two-world models proposed by Bereiter and Scardamalia (1987) and by Dyson (1988). Academic literacy first appears to be cognitively more complex than narrative literacy because it involves the addition of another world of discourse—the discourse of logically related domain concepts. In ethics, for example, concepts such as "paternalism" and "autonomy" are defined in domain-specific ways. Second, academic literacy is cognitively more complex than the school writing described by Bereiter and Scardamalia because it involves the abstraction of an interpersonal problem space into an intertextual world of interaction among "authors" taking various "approaches" to an issue for an "audience." Such authors are not identical with the persons who compose essays. Approaches are not the sum of claims made by particular persons. And the audience is not simply a collection of actual readers. Instead, these concepts are abstractions from more everyday interpersonal entities according to different conventions and different purposes. One of the differences, as I mentioned earlier, lies in the differing role of accounts.

Looked at in its entirety, then, expertise in academic literacy can best be conceived as the ability to negotiate three distinct worlds of discourse: the *domain content world* of logically related truths (what Bereiter and Scardamalia (1987) called the content problem space), the *narrated world* of everyday experience (the everyday world of Dyson, 1988), and the *rhetorical world* of abstract authorial conversation. The protocol data, then, were looked at for the world of discourse involved in each segment of the transcripts and for the patterns of movement across segments. Early analysis given in chapter 10 suggested that the experts located their activity within a discourse of authorial interaction based on differences in approach, whereas the novices tended to discount or resolve differences in favor of a more topically organized and logically related set of concepts. More recent analysis given in chapter 11 suggests that the novices were also using the narrated world of everyday experience in a less hypothetical way than the experts. The two philosophers, for example, paid attention to the stories of paternalism given in the readings, manipulated them along ethically salient dimensions, and created new stories to develop, test, and, finally, illustrate their arguments. The freshmen, on the other hand, used these stories, first, to understand the claims being made by the readings, and, second, to illustrate claims in their texts. What they did not do is engage in hypothetical thinking: They neither manipulated these stories to develop new arguments nor tested them to find logical problems in extant arguments.

Conceiving of expertise in academic literacy as the ability to negotiate among multiple worlds of discourse has implications not just for those concerned with literacy but also for those concerned with the notion of expertise in general.

Current theorists, as we have noted in chapter 3, have seen expertise as the replacement of everyday entities with more abstract representations or mental models. Such a conception, however, overemphasizes the arcane quality of expert knowledge while overlooking its social utility. To be socially useful, experts must translate arcane domain knowledge back into the everyday discourse of the public domain. This requires the expert to maintain multiple representations that, even though incommensurate, actually touch and transform each other. An expert who simply replaces everyday discourse with abstract discourse will not be able to manage this transformation.

The analysis of the third set of data in this project, reported in chapter 12, clarifies the difficulties students face in learning this transformation, difficulties both cognitive and cultural. Coding the classroom interaction for both structure and content revealed an interaction between speaker, content, and structure over time. In essence, the teacher and the students moved from an initial period of conflict over their conceptions of expertise to a period in which the teacher followed the students' lead in becoming immersed in a discussion of domain content that was, in turn, followed by a period in which the students more amicably followed the teacher into discourse on rhetorical process. These results suggest that whereas many have argued for a more rhetorical understanding of expertise, we have yet to face and resolve the difficulties that arise when we try to pass this new understanding on to students who believe expertise lies in having true content knowledge divorced from rhetorical process.

Layer II. Reflective Analysis: "Benefits and Hazards of Multimodal Research"

I see my study of academic literacy and the nature of expertise as multimodal, first, with respect to design and data acquisition. The design extended the traditional expert–novice study in cognition to a more real-time reading/writing task of weeks rather than hours. The protocol data were triangulated with interview and textual data. And the study of classroom discourse allowed me to examine the problematic social and cultural dynamics involved when an expert teacher tries to transmit expertise to novice students. All of these modifications enabled me to bring a cultural and social frame of reference to issues of cognition in literacy. This experience has framed my own understanding of research as a process of systematically acquiring experience from multiple perspectives at the site of a single practice of literacy.

The research has also been multimodal with respect to the analytic activities used once the data were collected. I consider my research useful, not in and of itself, but for the help it gives in uncovering the world or worlds in which readers and writers act and in which I as a researcher and teacher act. For me, then, data and claims made about the data are an integral part of the self reflection and cultural reflection that my more humanistically trained colleagues find so valuable. Thus, in my own work, I have tried to balance my days. Sometime weeks go by in which I do nothing but look at transcripts and try to get interrater reliability on my coding scheme as a way of helping me to articulate exactly the concepts I am after. Then there will be periods of number crunching: correlations, transition probabilities, chi squares, graphs. And there are the days spent reading, conceptualizing the approaches taken by other authors, manipulating them, testing them, arguing with them. And finally there are the days of writing, model building and model dismantling, trying to make myself smarter and my readers smarter about what academic literacy is and what it is not. Thus I have used both the analytic and critical techniques of the humanities and the quantitative techniques of the social sciences. I like this mix and I believe in its power.

I see the power of quantitative analyses as their ability to provide one more way of confirming or disconfirming my assumptions. Just to give one example from my own work: I had read and many times thought that more experienced readers would engage a text more interactively than those less experienced. But I decided to see if this was played out in my own data. I decided to examine the reading portions of my protocols as interactions between the author and the reader—as a conversation—and count the amount of time that the reader let the author "take the floor" by simply reading and the amount of time the reader took the floor for him or herself by voicing thoughts or reactions. To my surprise, both the philosophers and the freshmen let the authors have the floor to an equal degree during reading. Although I have never been able to make a positive claim about this simple calculation, it has kept me from blithely reaffirming something that seemed intuitively true until examined quantitatively.

For me, the power of analytic and critical analyses lies in their ability to provide a way to go beyond the here and now to what might have been or what should be. Studying ethicists has given me tremendous respect for the value of such hypothetical thinking and I see it as the crucial link between my expertise as a descriptive researcher and my responsibility as a citizen. Thus I do not think it would be right for me to study expertise in academic literacy without taking a critical look at its practices: to imagine a world without this expertise, a world without schools, a world without reading and writing, a world without experts. These thought experiments have lead me to question the benefits of expertise at the same time that I take issue with utopian calls for a return to a more public forum without experts. To make such arguments, however, I have had to be at pains to be understood by communities with different standards for evidence and different starting assumptions. I believe, however, that this perspective shifting is necessary to understand why we as educators might want to teach academic literacy at the same time that we call for its reform.

A third way in which my research is multimodal lies in how I have deliberately tried to address my arguments to more than one academic community. I have presented my research not only at the Conference on College Composition and Communication and the National Council of Teachers of English, but also at the annual meetings of the American Educational Research Association, the National Reading Conference, the Society for the Social Studies of Science, and the Speech Communication Association. The benefits of participating in more than one academic forum seem obvious to me: Each one brings its special concerns and ways of validating claims. By attempting to frame my ideas in ways that can be understood by all of them, I think I achieve a broader conception. People in education, for example, think primarily about school children and I have found it illuminating to consider the parallels described earlier between narrative literacy and academic literacy. Such parallels would be lost if my exclusive focus were on college composition. On the other hand, those concerned with schooling often lack an understanding of mature practice, and it becomes all too easy for K–12 educators to think of the analytic essay as a final achievement rather than a special genre of schooled literacy.

I see the benefits of multimodal inquiry in these three ways—in data acquisition, in analysis, and in presentation. Further, I believe that the field of rhetoric and composition is one of the few where I can take advantage of them without seriously jeopardizing my academic career. However, I do think there have been and may be costs—in terms of my time, the comprehensibility of my work, and the evaluation of my work.

Personally, the biggest cost of multimodality is the time it takes. To do a text analysis, for example, I do not just read in depth; I also segment the text using techniques from linguistics, and code it using techniques from discourse analysis. When I am done, I am fairly sure of my conclusions and I can explain and defend them both to someone who wants numbers and someone who wants exegesis. But the one who wants numbers does not care about exegesis; the one who wants exegesis does not understand the numbers. Sure, I can talk to both, but it takes twice as long to get something to say.

The second highest cost comes in terms of comprehensibility. By building an argument across multiple methods and traditions, it becomes inevitable that some parts of the logic are simply incomprehensible to some of the people to whom I think the conclusions should be important. It is easier to translate technical terms across disciplines than it is to translate fights. Take, for example, the discussion in composition circles for the past few years about the conversational nature of reading and writing (Bartholomae, 1985; Bazerman, 1980; Bizzell, 1982b; Bruffee, 1984). My argument about the abstract nature of this conversation is aimed as a corrective to what I have seen as this too simplistic mapping of indigenous conventions onto academic literacy. People in composition know what I am talking about. A friend in education, however, wondered why I was making the argument: Surely, she said, nobody believes that "conversation" stuff anymore. Unfamiliar with the disagreement, she could not value my contribution.

The final cost of multimodal inquiry comes in the evaluation of my work. Whenever a researcher reaches out to other disciplines, efforts in that direction are inevitably valued less than whatever the home field considers mainstream. I have wonderfully multidisciplinary colleagues and this cost has not been high for me. But I think it is inevitable that publications or outsider reviewers in one field may be more highly valued than those in another.

Evaluation also gets tricky when I borrow concepts from various disciplines. I have to think, for instance, before I use the term *expertise* in composition circles; among my psychologist friends, I have to find another way to talk about ethics. Of course, I have developed alternative ways of talking about my concerns and can use them when I need to. But I must confess that as I become more immersed in my project, I become less patient with the need to explain everything I do not mean before I can explain what I do mean. At these times, I yearn to work in a well-defined tradition where I could say "I was so-and-so's student" and everyone would know what I thought about, what techniques I used, and what assumptions I made. I am not sure that such disciplinary utopias actually exist, but I sure understand why people want to think they do.

Layer III. Personal History: "A Postscript"

In drafting this chapter, the first section I completed was a personal narrative that located my intellectual position in my personal history. But the first thing I did to my completed draft was cut it out as being too personal, too loosely connected to the argument of the essay, and—anyway—too long. But I recognize that this push toward coherence at the expense of the local account is part of what we should be resisting. The trouble is I can not make it fit in comfortably. My best solution is to append it here as a kind of postscript to the argument and ask you as reader to consider how it could have been integrated. Here it is:

> One way to start the story is with high school. In 1972, when I was a senior, several considerations added up to my decision to attend Carleton College in Minnesota. But when I stepped off the plane in the fall of 1972, I certainly had no clue about the normal preprofessional life plan of most students attending Carleton. No one in my family had been to college, let alone a liberal arts college. In retrospect, I can see my freshman year as a jarring clash between my fundamentally middle-class anti-intellectual heritage and the liberal arts tradition. I flourished in my courses, but had grave doubts about spending all my parents' money on something that, although so much fun, didn't look at all practical. At the end of that year, I reconciled these opposing forces by deciding to earn my living by teaching English. It mattered little that I had not taken one college English course or one education course up to that point: It was a plan that I could live with. I didn't know about graduate school; I couldn't imagine affording something like law school. I had always liked school; I had always liked teaching.
>
> Although I didn't realize it at the time, Carleton in those years was unusually filled with interdisciplinary and postdisciplinary activity. In my courses, I devoured texts on the philosophy, history and sociology of science, reading Kuhn (1962) among others, and incorporating them into my own epistemology of knowledge making. In physics courses, I learned that the difference between Aristotle, Newton,

and Einstein was not so much a matter of accuracy as of simplicity and perspective. Stumbling onto the nascent field of cognitive psychology through the work of Frank Smith (1971) in my senior year, I quickly absorbed the emerging research on perception into a nonfoundational framework. Then I graduated.

During a practical master's degree in secondary reading and several years of teaching that followed, I became disillusioned with academics, swearing I could never pursue something like a PhD. During a particularly disheartening encounter with disciplinarity in a year of graduate school in 1979, however, I began to hear-tell of a new field of rhetoric that offered a combination of language, cognitive science, and a link with the practical world. Some 3 years later, I found myself starting out in the PhD program in rhetoric at Carnegie Mellon University.

Trite as it may sound, I found graduate work to open up a whole new world of intellectual life, one that I had not even known existed. I was determined to cross the divide between consumer and producer of knowledge once I saw that it was there. I felt privileged to be at Carnegie Mellon at a time when rhetoric and psychology could offer so much. I took not only the courses offered by Richard Young, Linda Flower, and Dick Hayes in my own program, but also courses with John Anderson, Herb Simon, and Jill Larkin in psychology. I also felt privileged to have the opportunity to work with an advisor whose scholarship in argumentation was firmly established and who was now moving into the area of composition.

As I became immersed in my graduate training, I became aware, as did everyone else in my program, of the controversies raging in the composition journals about protocol analysis, cognitive versus social perspective, quantitative versus qualitative research. To those of us in graduate school in 1982 and 1983, Flower-and-Hayes bashing seem like the latest indoor sport. Critical reviews by Bizzell (1982a), Berkenkotter (1983), Emig (1982), Cooper and Holzman (1983), Connors (1983), Clifford (1983), Petrosky (1983), and Voss (1983) all appeared in short order and with a ferocity that still warrants investigation (Berkenkotter, 1991). When I read the published characterizations of cognitive work on writing, I could hardly recognize my own experience. When I read descriptions of alternative programs of research, I knew I did not understand them. Thus I began a program of reading and study aimed at understanding the controversy, aimed at defending what I understood to be my approach to research. I soon realized that the parries and thrusts in the composition literature were echoes of raging arguments in the fields of sociology, anthropology, linguistics, education, philosophy. . . . As I read on and on, I began to see the intellectual oppositions disappear. I thought that much of what I heard was the anger of the dispossessed and the boundary marking of a field in the making. Thus, when it came to finalizing the details of the study on philosophical ethics I described earlier, I was working to integrate two traditions that many at the time considered opposed.

I can see my developing analysis of the nature of expertise in academic literacy as a product of this history I've just told. Carleton made me a Kuhnian before I'd ever heard the word: I just naturally understood cognitive science in a nonfoundational framework, as another attempt at human meaning making situated in a particular culture at a particular time—I probably couldn't have seen it any other way. My analysis of the multiplicity of academic literacy practice probably reflects the ambivalence of someone raised in an anti-intellectual tradition who, nevertheless, loves the intellectual life—I am just naturally aware of the contradictions involved in a practice I was not born to. My incorporation of multiple modes of inquiry into the design of the study resulted from my attempts to find intellectual comfort as a graduate student. And my determination to stay within the field of rhetoric and composition probably reflects my practical bent—I would never be comfortable in a purely intellectual field. I love the literate life—but I still take delight in admitting an improper fondness for watching "Dallas" on Friday night.

Layer IV. Deliberative Appeal: "Choices for the Future"

As a field, literacy research—if that is what we would call ourselves for the moment—has been brought into existence by society to offer an "account" of the "crisis" in reading and writing in this country. As I indicated in my introduction, such accounts are required only in the face of difficulties. Thus, as a profession, we are located right at the point where society is trying to adjust an educational system based on the restriction of literacy to one that has an interest in diversity. In my own institution, we talk of recruiting women and minorities not out of any moral considerations but because we feel that we can no longer allow such a large segment of the population to be marginalized. But the practices of academic literacy that we try to open up simply do not reflect diverse experiences and heritages. Indeed, the "disruption" in conversation that gave rise to a request for this account of my own work is, I believe, symptomatic of less obvious but no less real difficulties in the academy in general, difficulties with universalism, disciplinarity, and divisiveness. This is where I would locate the importance of an account such as I have tried to construct.

I think we can be at the vanguard of changing the nature of reading and writing practices in the academy, of inventing a new discourse of knowledge making, one less reliant on the conventions of polarizing approaches, discounting interdisciplinarity, and devaluing local knowledge. As a group, however, we are privileged in our opportunity to develop a new way of being in the academy, first, because of our problematic status within the academy and, second, because of our understanding of the role language has to play in the construction of that status. Our status is a problem and a benefit for us because we cannot easily mold ourselves along disciplinary and professional lines without a loss of many of our most important values and concerns: our practical concern with day-to-day teaching, our privileging of issue over methodology, our esteem for multiple perspectives. Each of these values runs contrary to the standard paradigm for disciplinary endeavor, yet each is a source of strength in our intellectual life. If we accept the challenge of building a new framework, a new way of talking, that allows these values to be incorporated within rather than shunted aside in our intellectual work, then we will have an accomplishment that will not only ensure our own survival and respect, but also have something that we can teach to those other disciplines toward which we sometimes look so fondly.

This idealistic scenario requires that we resist the temptation to mold ourselves to existing conventions in the academy and that we develop an alternative. To succeed, however, I think we have to understand the hazards faced by the growing number of junior people who have come to this field with graduate training in the area and with aspirations for a "normal" academic career. I have already described some of the costs in terms of time, comprehensibility, and evaluation, costs that thus far have been outweighed for me by the benefits of multimodal inquiry. But it is not hard to imagine the scales tipping in the other direction. Some may simply drop out of the field in the face of bitter controversy or difficult promotion and tenure processes. Others may develop professional schizophrenia, carrying out teaching and administrative duties at odds with their intellectual values. And the day may come when it will be a faux pas to admit the impact of our daily experience on our intellectual lives or when it will be taken for granted that our research has no direct bearing on our teaching, administration, or living. Any of these developments would signal our acceptance of the conventions of the academy at face value and our failure to accept the challenge of developing an alternative. Although we often find it hard to say, as a group, what we agree on, I think we would all agree that this is a future we would like to avoid. Now we have the task of creating the alternative.

SUMMER 1993: REFLECTIONS ON ACADEMIC LITERACY

The essential problem for those who wish to take research in literacy as a serious life's work within the academy is the quandary of reflection. Although reflection is a very slippery term to pin down, my own interpretation, influenced most recently by the work of Richard Bernstein, characterizes as reflective the process by which each of the multiple worlds in our lives acknowledges and plays off against all of the others, generating a potential for change. The layers of my essay for the Research Network, I now see, each embody one of the worlds in which I live, but it was only when set grinding against each other that they came to feel, to me, complete. For me, accounting for my research had to include the claims I make (Layer I), the reasons I make them (Layer II), the history that lead me to make them (Layer III), as well as the deliberative frame (Layer IV) that I constructed to place them within the context of a scholarly community.

Nevertheless, this completeness runs against the grain of academic conventions in ways I tried to warn readers about in my introduction. In print at least, we are supposed to cast ourselves as part of a public we, not a "self-centered" I. We are supposed to construct a course among issues and projects that is carefully detailed, not dense and "unpacked." And our prose is supposed to be deliberate, not ragged and "hastily put together." These quotes, all reactions I have gotten from readers, amount to a demand for greater coherence. And more than once I have dutifully tried to respond: opened the file, poised hands above the keyboard, ready to beat the edges of my prose into a seamless unity. Each time, however, something stops me; I play about the edges, change a word or phrase, but then I change it back, close the file, go away.

Stopping my hand in midtype is an understanding of how academic literacy works. In every layer, this text demonstrates a multiplicity of incommensurate yet overlapping discourses that make up composing within the academy. Layer I is where I gaze, the phenomenon and the model I build to understand that gazing; Layer II is how I gaze, my methodology and its rationale; Layer III is why I gaze, personal history understood as motivating force and serendipity; Layer IV is when I gaze, my appeal to the public moment as I understand it. In the intersections and overlappings of these discourses, I have happily beat the necessarily crooked path of rhetorical invention. Thus each attempt at revision—pressing for greater coherence—feels like the act of a collaborator: We—I as writer working toward coherence; you as reader wanting that coherence—stand implicated in the very cultural myth of the autonomous text that this research reveals.

For the time being at least, we must resist. Otherwise, the resulting text would cut out much that is indispensable to our well-being. If the problem were simply how *I* can get through this day, this year, this life, then the reflective process of composing and juggling multiple accounts of ourselves could remain a private affair, better shared just with our students and the colleagues we manage to keep in touch with through the years. But for researchers and scholars in literacy, the problem is larger because we not only have the responsibility as individuals to be privately reflective about our literacy practices, but also the responsibility, as a community, to characterize these practices for those outside the academy. That is, we are responsible not only for composing accounts of ourselves in the academy but also responsible for composing accounts of what it means to compose within the academy. Furthermore, we must begin to investigate the implications of this composing for ourselves and others. The writer who returns to school after 20 years in industry and resents the "student" role, the pregnant graduate student whom no one takes seriously, the colleague who rails about his students' illiteracy, the shop clerk afraid to write us a note with misspellings—all of these and many more both within and outside of the academy need our reflections on how the multiple worlds in which we live sometimes complicate but oftentimes animate our knowledge making.

What this all means for how you and I read and write is not yet settled. As I suggested 4 years ago, some will want to see developed a new and more coherent discourse, one that can be fully expressive of the range of human experience now in the academy. Others, however, will want to see multiplicity maintained and celebrated with newfound consciousness. I now find myself somewhere in the middle, doubting that our current practice can serve as the foundation for a coherence that is anything other than superficial, . . . outraged at the results of our lack of reflection on this practice, . . . yet very much at home in the practice. Minimally, it comes down to this: We cannot claim to construct a full account of literacy practices within the academy without understanding the pressures within our very own reading and writing that tend to shape these accounts and—whenever we find ourselves under their weight—we should ask ourselves why, and—occasionally—do our best to do something different. These experiments in composing, while seldom successful and sometimes enraging, can enrich our studies of what it means to be literate, deepen our commitment to their pursuit, and, at the same time, point in the directions of reform we explore in the next chapter. It is for this reason and with these hopes that I have put my accounts before you this hot summer day, nearly 4 years after their composing.

ACKNOWLEDGMENT

Portions of this chapter are from "Exploring Academic Literacy—An Experiment in Composing" by C. Geisler, 1992, *College Composition and Communication, 43*(1), pp. 39–54. Copyright 1992 by the National Council of Teachers of English. Reprinted by permission.

14

REFORMING ACADEMIC
LITERACY

The studies of philosophy reported in the preceding chapters have implications that extend beyond the narrow territory of a single academic discipline. Despite its humanistic resistance to the professionalization movement and its concern with what William James called the most universal of human truths, academic philosophy appears to create and recreate the great divide between expert and layperson. Academic practice in philosophy, that is, seems to work itself out through the dual problem spaces of expertise, separating the apparently timeless truths of domain content from the temporal rhetorical processes that give them life.

As these studies have suggested, however, the formal culture of academic philosophy does not represent so much an abandonment of the resources of everyday indigenous culture as a transformation of them. Philosophic expertise, in fact, is solidly build upon a foundation of indigenous practices: conversation, narrative, and apprenticeship. Abstract interactions with texts represent transformations of conversations with colleagues. Abstract sets of ethical features represent transformations of everyday narratives. Formal classroom instruction represents a transformation of apprenticeship training. In each of these cases, the original and transformed practices seem to remain side by side as the multiple and unacknowledged worlds of academic composing. Real expertise thus seems to requires a tacking back and forth between these worlds, a movement like Alice through the looking glass where, on either side, the world seems to be the same, but not the same.

The success of this tacking back and forth seems to depend, however, on having things in the everyday world well in order. If things are not well in order—if one's grandfather has died—then the tacking back and forth may become more problematic and the required balance of commitments may become harder to sustain. People with differences in race, class, and gender almost invariably do not have their everyday lives well in order according to the traditional standards of the academic professions. These professions were created out of one particular indigenous culture, that of the upper-class eastern elites, who took as their problem the erosion of control arising from the influx of ethnic cultures at the turn of the century. Academics whose indigenous culture is not the indigenous culture of the upper-class elites—who, in fact, may come from the "ethnic" cultures they are trying to control—may feel an underlying disjunction between the culture of their everyday life and the formal culture of the academy.

Perhaps this sense of disjunction explains why most of the alternatives for academic practice now being offered represent a return to more indigenous practices. Narrative, conversation, and apprenticeship may be appealing as a way out of the elitist agenda of the professions, a way of avoiding the negotiation of these multiple worlds. But this attempt to return to indigenous cultural practices, though understandable, does not present a real alternative for academic expertise. To begin with, it does not help us to resolve the dilemma of choosing whose home culture to return to in a multicultural society. We neither can nor want to give up our differences, particularly because they seem so generative of new insights.

The call for a return to more indigenous practice also ignores the real beauty and achievement of formal abstractions. There are marvels to be had in thinking in timeless space rather than always living in relentless time. Academic literacy appears to provide a "time out" from time by favoring spatial thinking, but it does not foist this spatial dimension on us. As a technology, it only takes advantage of the ways we already move and think in space. In other words, like the gardener who takes advantage of the tilt of the earth's axis to plant roses in the sun and hostas in the shade, academic literacy takes advantage of our biological nature. Our problem, then, is not how to change our nature, but how to use it in the right way. For this reason, an agenda for the reform of the academy is probably much more complicated than simply going back to a preprofessionalized utopia. In these closing pages, then, we take up some of the possible directions for reform.

RETHINKING LITERACY RESEARCH

A recurrent theme throughout this study has been the way literacy researchers have often taken at face value the cultural myth of the autonomous text. By mistaking the virtual spatial experience of participants' texts for the actual and temporal experience of their composing, these accounts often ignore the material and biological factors that shape what people do and think.

In order to build more adequate models, then, literacy researchers must move away from modeling academic literacy as a single coherent practice that works itself out primarily in the spatial dimension of participants' representations. In these representations, virtual authors are presented as professionalized agents moving with rational purpose toward the progress of the community. Real authors, however, eat, go to the bathroom, worry about their career, and get interrupted by the noise on the street. Academic texts never acknowledge these human aspects of their real authors for to do so would jeopardize their claim to timeless truth. But researchers of academic literacy cannot afford to make the same mistake. Instead, we must make efforts to gather data on how participants' texts, representations, and activities change over time, and then we must look at the relationship among these temporal changes. In this analysis, we need to be prepared to see divergences and incoherencies as well as seamless wholes, and we must equip ourselves theoretically to explore their functionality within a larger framework of practice.

Such a methodology neither takes participants' own accounts at face value nor dismisses them as irrelevant. Because they always reside in some world at any given time, participants will have some conception of what they are up to, but from moment to moment, working session to working session, we should expect this conception to shift in ways of which they cannot be fully aware. The job of the literacy researcher, then, is to mark the interrelationships among these multiple worlds as they unfold and interleave over time.

Within this framework, as well, distinctions between individual cognition and social interactions can neither be accepted as a natural fact nor dismissed as a misrepresentation. Instead the boundary between the individual and the social needs to be investigated as a cultural resource. For any given practice, we need to ask, what is left for individuals in this practice to do on their own? What is left to be accomplished in groups? And what kind of information passes and does not pass from one world into the other? Think-aloud protocols and other methodologies for investigating the private reflective space of the individual are thus just as indispensable for investigating academic practices as the interviews and observations that document the more social world. We need both.

REFORMING ACADEMIC PRACTICE

Just as literacy researchers cannot afford to mistake the apparently powerful virtual experience of text with the actual experience of readers and writers, academic practitioners themselves need to acknowledge the difference between the two. Academic texts provide the experience of moving forward into a communal future, but that experience is a virtual one with all that the term virtual implies. We can think of it this way: Fiction gives readers a virtual experience marked with distinct borders on the actual. Academic texts, on the other hand, blur these borders by populating its virtual experience with objects from actual experience: colleagues and claims. As a consequence, the two experiences become intertangled in the Alice-through-the-looking-glass phenomenon, but with a strong preference for the virtual experience. For this reason, academics often lose all sense of the temporal experience of composing, but less often lose track of their lines of argument. The spatial experience of text obscures the temporal experience of textmaking.

Academic practitioners need to escape from this entanglement, to recognize that real readers are often unaffected by the virtual experience created by academic texts. Following the conventions of the main path/faulty path structure, academic texts routinely sidestep the rhetorical burden of addressing alternative perspectives and instead, from the start, place virtual readers on the same main path, already agreeing, already in consensus. But, as we have seen in the sciences, real readers, even those in the same disciplinary community, often explicitly resist the virtual experience of consensus created by their colleagues' texts. How much poorer must be the chances of convincing readers outside of the academy to follow our reasoning?

If our colleagues resist our texts and lay persons do not read them—or when reading them, fail to be convinced—why do we write them? The traditional answer has been that we are trying to archive knowledge, to make universal statements that can stand for all time. But we cannot take refuge in this invocation of the myth of the autonomous text any more. Too much evidence tells us that texts and knowledge making do not work that way; that facts become facts through rhetorical processes rooted to specific times and places. A better way would be to more openly acknowledge the burden of rhetorical persuasion that our expertise places on us, to make a point of addressing the two equally compelling audiences to whom we are beholden: our professional colleagues and the general public. That is, if we want to reform academic literacy, to make our texts more pluralistic, to reconnect expertise to the arena of civic action, we—like William James—must find our general readers and talk to them.

The barriers to talking with and listening to the general public in the course of academic work are, of course, tremendous and not simply to be overcome by solitary individuals. The pressures against writing for the general public have, if anything, increased since the days that James fretted over the issue. Few if any researchers today could afford to split their textual output as evenly across the great divide as James apparently did, if not for lack of time, then for the danger of being called a "popularizer." As a consequence, most academics do not even know where to find lay readers, let alone begin to talk to them.

RESHAPING AMERICAN SCHOOLING

James found his general readers among the amateurs that packed his public lectures and sent his popular essays into multiple editions. He regarded them as his hardest critics: They were unlikely to be distracted by technical virtuosity, were in touch with the everyday experience, and were willing to sustain interaction with his discipline. Though amateurs still exist today in our society, especially in the growing readership of popular science journals, their activities for the most part remain extracurricular, outside the reach and interest of academic experts. American schooling needs to bring them back in. That is, we need to reconceptualize general education as the creation of disciplinary amateurs like those James addressed, lovers of the truth pursued in the academic professions, but not members of the professions themselves.

As Veysey (1979) pointed out, general education was originally conceived as the result of a compromise between proponents of the professionalization movement and the defenders of liberal culture. Staffed by the remnants of the faculty from the preprofessional liberal arts days, these courses soon fell into the hands of junior faculty whose professional training had given them no good reason to want to teach those outside their profession. Sometimes these courses evolved into recruitments campaigns, a way of identifying potential majors. Other times, they developed into "service" courses of no intrinsic value to the discipline itself. But in both cases, no serious effort was given to creating a dialogue between the expert and nonexpert. The emphasis was on delivering knowledge, covering the domain content.

The apprenticeship movement has attempted to remedy this state of affairs by making everyone into a cultural producer. Indeed, the original conception for the WARRANT project shared this assumption. Following in the cognitive process tradition, we originally believed that our curriculum for "critical reading, reasoning, and writing" would consist of advice to students. We took as our paradigm the process of teaching someone to play a game: Our study of the experts would help to clarify how best to win the game. Our study of the novices would show us how they were currently playing. Our study of the classroom would help us to develop advice that could move students closer to the strategies of expert play. Such advice, we assumed, would be largely strategic and adaptive.

This image, though obviously oversimplistic, is not far from current apprenticeship models of teaching and learning. These models see students as apprentices to a culture, assisted in learning by mentors who already posses the skill. Descriptions of this kind, for example, are common in the literature on language learning (Geisler, 1991):

> Young children learn language in the process of using it in supportive contexts. Adults ... listen to them, ask appropriate questions about what they are saying, and expand upon their children's beginnings to build a fuller meaning.... [T]his process can itself be taken as a model for the instructional interaction of the classroom. The teacher's role becomes one of providing instructional support or *scaffolding* ... that will allow the student to undertake new and more difficult tasks. These tasks are purposeful for the student because they grow out of what the student wants to do, but cannot do without the teacher's help.

> With Vygotsky (1962, 1978), we believe that individuals gain access to the store of cultural knowledge through the social process of interaction, and during the process gradually make that knowledge their own. From this perspective, the role of instructional scaffolding is to provide students with appropriate models and strategies for addressing new problems; these are in turn internalized by the students, providing them with the resources to eventually undertake similar tasks on their own. (Langer & Applebee, 1984, p. 176)

The problem with this model, however, is that it makes the assumption that adults participate in a single homogeneous culture into which all students are to be brought. But, as we have seen, academic expertise is a culture into which all students neither want nor need to enter.

For this reason, we need to use the curriculum to find a way to interact with those who are different than us and intend to stay that way. A reconceptualized general education would acknowledge the difference between expert and amateur perspectives and give as much attention to educating the one as the other. We need to grant the lay perspective respect, to say: "I know that you have something I do not have. I need you to understand what I am saying, but I need to know what you think as well. My profession depends on it." Indeed, the academy depends on it. Only through this reconceptualized general education can we change the social facts behind academic literacy, build into our disciplinary knowledge the need to listen to those not so "disciplined," and thereby remake the nature of expertise.

A

CHRONOLOGICAL BIBLIOGRAPHY OF THE COGNITIVE PROCESS TRADITION

A chronological listing of the published research of the team of Flower and Hayes, spanning the years from 1980 to 1990, can be found in the following sections. It can be divided into a number of strands. The most often cited work is associated with their cognitive process model of writing that was introduced in 1980 and 1981 (Flower & Hayes, 1981a; Hayes & Flower, 1980a, 1980b). Associated with this model were a number of studies elaborating on the major processes from the original model: planning (Flower, 1988; Flower & Hayes, 1980a, 1980b; Flower and Hayes, 1981b, 1981c), translating (Kaufer, Hayes, & Flower, 1986), and revision (Flower et al., 1986; Hayes et al., 1987). Two book chapters in the middle years attempted to characterize protocol methodology (Hayes & Flower, 1983; Swartz, Flower, & Hayes, 1984) and several articles were devoted to what I call issues of representation (Flower, 1988; Flower & Hayes, 1984). Finally, Flower's more recent work has concerned writing in academic contexts (Flower, 1988; Flower et al., 1990; Haas & Flower, 1988).

Following this chronological listing of the Flower and Hayes' work is a chronological bibliography of the critiques and defenses that have been made of the cognitive process tradition and protocol methodology.

THE WORK OF FLOWER AND HAYES

1980

Flower and Hayes (1980a)
Flower and Hayes (1980b)

Hayes and Flower (1980a)
Hayes and Flower (1980b)

1981

Flower and Hayes (1981a)
Flower and Hayes (1981b)
Flower and Hayes (1981c)

1983

Hayes and Flower (1983)

1984

Flower and Hayes (1984)
Swartz, Flower, and Hayes (1984)

1986

Flower, Hayes, Carey, Schriver, and Stratman (1986)
Kaufer, Hayes, and Flower (1986)

1987

Hayes, Flower, Schriver, Stratman, and Carey (1987)

1988

Flower (1988)
Haas and Flower (1988)

1989

Flower (1989)

1990

Flower, Stein, Ackerman, Kantz, McCormick, and Peck (1990)

CRITIQUE AND DEFENSE

1971

Berthoff (1971)

1982

Bizzell (1982a)
Emig (1982)
Hairston (1982)

1983

Berkenkotter (1983)
Clifford (1983)
Connors (1983)
Cooper and Holzman (1983)
Gebhardt (1983)
Humes (1983)
Petrosky (1983)
Voss (1983)

1984

Afflerbach and Johnston (1984)
Flower (1984)
Selzer (1984)
Tomlinson (1984)

1985

Cooper and Holzman (1985)
Flower and Hayes (1985)
Reither (1985)
Rose (1985)

1986

Cooper (1986)
Dobrin (1986)
Faigley (1986)
Hairston (1986)
Steinberg (1986)

1987

Arrington (1987)
Berlin (1987)
Fitzgerald (1987)
North (1987)
Witte (1987)

1988

Phelps (1988)

1989

Berkenkotter (1989)
Brooke (1989)
Flower (1989)
Haas and Flower (1989)
Ray and Barton (1989)
Smagorinsky (1989)

1990

Carter (1990)
Greene (1990)
Stotsky (1990)

1991

Berkenkotter (1991)

B

Directions for "Thinking-Aloud" Protocols

As you work through this work on medical paternalism, we ask that you do all of your thinking out loud. "Thinking out loud" is probably new to you, but most people do not have trouble once they get started.

When you think out loud, you simply say whatever is on your mind. If you are reading something, you simply say the words as they go through your mind—you will probably skip words, reread things; you would not make sense to someone if they were listening. If you are thinking, you will jump around alot.

Thinking out loud is *not* the same as talking with someone else. When you read for someone, you pay attention to how fast and expressively you read. When you explain to someone, you try to make your story coherent and think about what your listener knows and does not know.

In thinking out loud there is no audience. At least at first, of course, one of the people on this project will be nearby to see that you do not have any problems. But they are *not* listening to you. They are *not* there to answer your questions. They will pay attention only to the sound of your voice—if you stop talking, they will remind you to "keep talking." But other than that, you are on your own.

The following are some guidelines for thinking out loud that many people find helpful:

1. Begin by turning on the tape recorder and saying your name and the date. Replay it to make sure the recorder is working.
2. Say whatever is on your mind. Do not hold back hunches, guesses, wild ideas, images, intentions.

3. Speak as continuously as possible. Say something at least once every 5 seconds, even if only, "I'm drawing a blank."

4. Speak audibly. Watch for your voice dropping as you become involved.

5. Speak as telegraphically as you please. Do not worry about complete sentences and eloquence.

6. Do not overexplain or justify. Analyze no more than you would normally.

7. Do not talk about the past. Say what you are thinking now, not what you were thinking a few seconds ago.

8. When you are finished working for a session, say, "This is the end of my work for today" followed by your name and date.

C

Interview Guide for Experts and Novices

1. At what point did you stop in your last session?
2. Can you describe the process you went through?
3. Where does what you have done so far fit in with your overall plans?
4. Where do you see yourself headed from here?
5. What problems did you encounter in your last session?
6. Why did you stop your last session?
7. Has anything new occurred to you since you stopped?
8. What are you going to do in your next session?
9. Do you anticipate any problems?
10. Do you have any other comments you want to make?

D

INTERVIEW GUIDE
FOR THE TEACHER

BEFORE CLASS

1. What do you plan for class today? (your actions? your students' reactions?)

2. What are your objectives for this class? What do you intend for them to learn/realize?

3. What did you realize/learn from preparing for this class? (about your students? about the subject matter?)

4. As of this moment, how do you see the rest of the course developing?

5. Can you describe for me what you think of as the one or two "prototypical" students in the course right now?

AFTER CLASS

1. Could you describe in detail what you saw happening in this class today?

2. In what ways did this differ from what you had planned?

3. What was the source of these differences?

4. What do you think you accomplished in this session?

5. How does this compare to your initial objectives for the class?

6. How does what happened today change the way you will plan for future classes?

E

INTERVIEW GUIDE
FOR THE STUDENTS

PERSONAL INFORMATION

1. What program/major are you in?
2. How many semesters have you been here?

COURSE EXPECTATIONS

1. Why did you decide to take the course in . . . this term?
2. What other courses or experiences have you had that might be related to this course?
3. What did you expect to get out of this course when you signed up?

MOST RECENT ASSIGNMENT

1. When you were working on the assignment you turned in on Monday, how did you conceive of it?
2. What steps did you take to complete it? [probe for completeness]
3. Could you describe for me as fully as you can what happened in the class meeting(s) on this assignment?
4. How did this/these classes change your conception of what you were supposed to do?

5. How would you go about it if you had to do it again? [actions]

6. Overall then, what do you think you were supposed to learn from that assignment and its discussions?

7. Suppose someone were to do that assignment for the first time—what advice would you give them?

COURSE OVERALL

1. Overall, how is this course going for you personally?

2. How does this compare with your original expectations?

3. How is it going for other people?

4. What do you think you will have learned when you finish the course?

5. Is there anything else you would like to say about the course?

THE CAREER OF
WILLIAM JAMES

TABLE F.1
Chronology of James' Professional Activities

Publications	Year	Professional Advancement
five unsigned book reviews in *The Nation,* *Atlantic Monthly,* and *North American Review*	1868	
reviews E. Sargent's *Planchette* for *Boston Daily Advertiser*	1869	completes thesis and requirements for MD
	1870	
	1871	
Review of Raine's *On Intelligence* in *The Nation*	1872	
	1873	begins teaching undergraduate physiology at Harvard
writes seven unsigned reviews for both professional and general journals	1874	helps found the Metaphysics Club
article defending vivisection in *The Nation* tribute to Chauncey Wright in *The Nation*	1875	begins teaching graduate physiology at Harvard
article on Bain and Renouvier for *The Nation* anonymous letter on neglect of philosophy in *The Nation*	1876	appointed assistant professor of physiology at Harvard
	1877	considers offer of professorship at Hopkins begins teaching psychology classes in Philosophy Department at Harvard
Brute and Human Intellect in *Journal of Speculative Philosophy*	1878	delivers ten lectures at Hopkins on physiology

(Continued)

TABLE F.1
(Continued)

Publications	Year	Professional Advancement
Remarks on Spencer's Definition of Mind in *Journal of Speculative Philosophy* Quelques Considérations sur la Méthode Subjective in *Critique Philosophique*		
Are We Automata? in *Mind* The Sentiment of Rationality, Version I, in *Mind*	1879	decides to stay at Harvard
The Association of Ideas in *Popular Science Monthly*	1880	appointed assistant professor of philosophy at Harvard
Reflex Action and Theism at Unitarian Ministers' Institute at Princeton, MA	1881	
On Some Hegelisms in *Mind*	1882	begins attending meetings of "Scratch Eight" philosophy discussion group in London
	1883	
The Dilemma of Determinism at Harvard Divinity School *The Literary Remains of the Late Henry James* Some Omissions of Introspective Psychology in *Mind*	1884	becomes corresponding member of the English Society for Psychical Research and organizes informal Boston branch
	1885	promoted to full professor of philosophy at Harvard
The Perception of Time in *Journal of Speculative Philosophy* report on séances conducted by Helen Berry and by Mrs. William Piper appears in *Proceedings of the American Society for Psychical Research*	1886	
The Perception of Space in *Mind* The Laws of Habit in *Popular Science Monthly* Some Human Instincts in *Popular Science Monthly* What Is an Instinct in *Scribner's Magazine*	1887	
	1888	
	1889	becomes first Alford Professor of Psychology at Harvard
The Principles of Psychology	1890	
	1891	
Psychology: Briefer Course	1892	receives honorary doctoral degree from University of Padua
	1893	elected President of the American Associate of Psychologists declines editorship of *Psychological Review*
letter to *Boston Evening Transcript* opposing bill to restrict practice of mental therapy to licensed medical doctors notice of Freud and Breuer's first article on hysteria for *Psychological Review*	1894	begins teaching at Radcliffe (until 1902)

(Continued)

Publications	Year	Professional Advancement
The Knowing of Things Together in *Psychological Review* Is Life Worth Living? to Harvard YMCA, published in *International Journal of Ethics*	1895	
The Will to Believe at philosophical clubs at Yale and Brown	1896	
The Sentiment of Rationality, Version II, in *The Will to Believe and Other Essays in Popular Philosophy*	1897	declines Gifford Lectureship at Aberdeen
Human Immortality: Two Supposed Objections to the Doctrine Philosophical Conceptions and Practical Results at University of California, Berkeley	1898	accepts Gifford Lectureship at Edinburgh heart damage
Talks to Teachers of Psychology: and to Students on Some of Life's Ideals	1899	
letter criticizing U.S. policy in the Philippines in *Springfield Republican*	1900	
	1901	begins Gifford Lectures at Edinburgh
The Varieties of Religious Experience: A Study in Human Nature	1902	completes Gifford Lectures at Edinburgh receives honorary LL.D. from University of Edinburgh
The PhD Octopus in *Harvard Monthly* Address on the Philippine Question for the New England Anti-Imperialist League Radical Empiricism as a Philosophy for Glenmore School The True Harvard in *Harvard Graduates' Magazine* letter against lynching in *Springfield Republican*	1903	resigns from Harvard
The Chicago School in *The Psychological Bulletin* Does 'Consciousness' Exist? in *Journal of Philosophy, Psychology and Scientific Methods* A World of Pure Experience in *Journal of Philosophy, Psychology and Scientific Methods* The Experience of Activity as presidential address at American Psychological Association	1904	persuaded to continue at Harvard with reduced load
How Two Minds Can Know One Thing in *Journal of Philosophy, Psychology and Scientific Methods* Humanism and Truth Once More in *Mind* Is Radical Empiricism Solipsistic? in *Journal of Philosophy, Psychology and Scientific Methods* The Place of Affectional Facts in a World of Pure Experience in *Journal of Philosophy, Psychology and Scientific Methods*	1905	

(Continued)

TABLE F.1
(Continued)

Publications	Year	Professional Advancement
On Some Mental Effects of the Earthquake in *Youth's Companion* *Pragmatism: A New Name for Some Old Ways of Thinking* as Lowell Lectures in Boston	1906	receives one-semester appointment at Stanford
The Energies of Men in *Philosophical Review*	1907	resigns professorship at Harvard given pension by Carnegie Fund
The Social Value of the College-Bred in *McClure's Magazine* Pluralistic Universe as Hibbert Lectures at Manchester College, Oxford	1908	receives honorary D.Sc. degree from Manchester College receives honorary Litt.D. degree from University of Durham
Report on Mrs. Piper Hodgson-Control in *Proceedings* of the English and American Societies for Psychical Research *The Meaning of Truth: A Sequel to "Pragmatism"* The Confidences of a "Psychical Researcher" in *The American Magazine*	1909	
Bradley or Bergson? in *Journal of Philosophy, Psychology and Scientific Methods* A Suggestion about Mysticism in *Journal of Philosophy, Psychology and Scientific Methods* The Moral Equivalent of War for Association for International Conciliation, Leaflet No. 27A Pluralistic Mystic for *The Hibbert Journal*	1910	dies of heart failure
Some Problems in Philosophy	1911	

TABLE F.2
Analysis of James' Publications

General Texts	Year	Specialist Texts	
5 reviews	1868		
1 review	1869		
	1870		
	1871		Period I, 1868–1877
1 review	1872		11 general texts
	1873		0 specialist texts
	1874*		
2 articles	1875		
1 article & 1 letter	1876		
	1877		

(Continued)

TABLE F.2
(Continued)

General Texts	Year	Specialist Texts	
	1878	. . . . 3 articles	
	1879	. . . . 2 articles	
1 article	1880		
1 article	1881	. . . . 1 article	
	1882		
	1883		
1 article & 1 book	1884	. . . . 1 article	
	1885		
	1886	. . . . 2 articles	**Period II, 1878–1896**
3 articles	1887	. . . . 1 article	8 general texts
	1888		14 specialist texts
	1889		
	1890	. . . . 1 textbook	
	1891		
	1892	. . . . 1 textbook	
	1893		
1 letter	1894	. . . . 1 review	
	1895	. . . . 1 article	
	1896		
1 book	1897		
1 book	1898	. . . . 1 article	**Period III, 1897–1901**
1 book	1899		4 general texts
1 letter	1900		1 specialist text
	1901		
	1902	. . . . 1 book	
4 articles	1903		
	1904	. . . . 4 articles	
	1905	. . . . 4 articles	**Period IV, 1902–1911**
1 article	1906		9 general texts
1 book	1907	. . . . 1 article	15 specialist texts
1 article	1908	. . . . 1 book	
1 article	1909	. . . . . 1 book & 1 article	
1 pamphlet	1910	. . . . 1 article	
	1911	. . . . 1 book	

In 1874, James published seven unsigned reviews for both general and specialist journals, but James (1987) did not specify how many of each. These texts, therefore, have been left out of this analysis. When they are added back in, they show James producing a total of 69 texts in 44 years, rather than the 62 enumerated here.

G

PARTICIPANTS' FINAL TEXTS*

JANET'S TEXT

This paper will define paternalism and discuss its justification. Paternalism is the action of one person interfering with another person's actions or thoughts to help him. The person who interferes, called the paternalist, breaks moral rules of independency because he restricts the other person's freedom without that person's consent. He does it, however in a fatherly, benevolent way, and assumes that the person being restrained will appreciate the action afterwards.

A common place for paternalism is within the familty. Parents restrict their children's activities, such as playing in the sewers, to prevent them from harming themselves or others. Paternalism extends to many other people in society such as adults, professionals, administrators, and law enforcers. It is very common in medicine where the doctors act paternalistically to the patients.

Paternalistic acts are not simply actions that supply the needs of others, such as helping a cripple across the street. Rather they are authoritative actions that deceive or restrict freedom of the other person. A mother who orders her son to not go to the marines is acting benevolently, because she is possibly saving his life, but also unfairly, according to him because she is taking away his freedom. A doctor who gives a blood transfusion to an uncontious man who previously said that he did not want it because of religious beliefs is acting paternalistically. He is overriding the patient's protest in order to do what he feels is right, to save the patient's life. Another type of paternalistic acts involves witholding information. A nurse who

---

*All material in this chapter is reproduced verbatim. Therefore, all grammatical and other errors have been retained to preserve the original text.

does not reveal bad news to a sick patient is protecting him from additional stress, but is also hiding the truth. These are three examples of acts which illustrate the system of paternalism.

Paternalism can exist between different types of people. A father may force his daughter to practice skiing so that she can become a good skier. Although he forces her to practice against her will he hopes that she will appreciate the learn skill later. Another example is that a concerned adult may prevent another adult from driving home drunk after a party. The first one takes the authority to control the actions of the other. In a different case, a doctor may force a person to be hospitalized so that he does not infect others with his sickness. In a university establishment, the administrators may require Freshmen to live on campus so that they can adjust to college life successfully. These are four more of many cases of paternalism.

Paternalism does not always include actions that restrict the same people who are being helped. Often it restricts one group's actions to protect a second group. This is called impure paternalism. Law enforcers prohibiting organized crime protect the general public from criminals. The law makers restrict the freedom of the criminals to protect the general public. Very often paternalistic acts help the party that is restricted also. This is called partially pure paternalism. Lawmakers who forbid drunk driving prevent drunk drivers from injuring themselves as well as injuring the other drivers on the road. The law protects everyone, but only directly affects the people who are intoxicated. Of course everyone who drinks alcohol is restricted from driving at one time or another, but in a specific case, the ones who are inebriated at that time are the ones who are restricted.

In the first part of this paper I gave descriptions of factors that make an act paternalistic. In this part I will discuss ways for a paternalist to determine if his acts are justified, ie. that his actions are accepted by others and considered to be, all together, moral.

In order for a paternalistic act to be justified, the person whose freedom is being interfered with must be incompetent. Incompetence is the inability to make decisions relating to ones self after all information necessary to make the decision has been received. A person who is incompetent, such as a mental retard, is "unable to understand or practice the basic requirements of survival successfully." Their "lives would be horrible if others do not intervene to help them." Of course, not all cases of incompetency are permanent, as with mental retardation. Some are results of emotional stress, compulsion, or drug addiction.

Before the paternalist acts he must be sure that the subject is actually incompetent. He must understand the subject's morals, values, and long term expectations of himself and "place appropriate weights on them." A paternalist should not base his evaluation of another's ability to survive w/out help on his own rules of behavior. In the case of a child, the child is incompetent because he is young and inexperienced.

In order for the paternalist to decide if a person is incompetent, he must be sure that the subject has received all the pertinent information and all the *correct* information. If a father is falsely told that a tornado is approaching his town, he might force his entire family to stay in the cellar until it passes. Instead of labeling him incompetent because of his irrational behavior, the paternalist should realize that he has been lied to and should reveal the truth.

In order for the paternalist to be justified, the subject must not only be incompetent, but also in risk. A person who is not in potential danger must not be bothered, no matter how incapable he is.

Another restriction to paternalism is that the paternalist believes that the subject will give him consent after the act. If the subject is adverse to the act before hand the paternalist must believe that brainwashing, lack of information, or temporary incompetence caused him to be. Hopefully, during or after the act, the subject will be enlightened and will be thankful for the interference. If he is not, except if he is permanently incompetent (ie. mentally retarded) then the act is not beneficial to him, and not justified.

In order for the act to be justified, the paternalist must weigh the magnitude and probability of the harm prevented and the magnitude and probability of the harm caused before deciding whether or not to act. The magnitude of the moral rules broken, the emotional strain that the subject will experience by his interference, and the effects that his act would have if they were universally practiced in similar situations must be included. If the harm that the paternalist wants to prevent outweighs all these factors then he is justified to act.

An additional way for a person to decide if he is justified to act paternalistically is to imagine advocating his actions in public. If he predicts that he would be supported by other people, then he is justified. If not, then he is not justified.

Once that paternalist decides that he is justified he must make sure that he does not overact. He must adjust the amount of interference according to the capabilities of the subject. The more independent and competent the subject becomes, the less he should be helped. He should be forced to be self-reliable as soon as possible. In medicine, a doctor should be continuously aware of his patients competence so that he does not over interfere. He would not be justified to make decisions for a patient once the patient is well enough to make them himself.

The methods mentioned throughout the second part of this paper can be used by the paternalist to decide when to act and how much to act. They can also be used by others to determine whether or not the paternalist is justified.

LESLIE'S TEXT

Paternalism: What Could It Mean to You

While Medical paternalistic acts effect a wide variety of people, under a wide variety of circumstances, it is an issue that is unnoticed in our lives. The moral questionability and the justification of paternalism make this issue important to all of us, due to the effects of medical paternalism. Therefore, I hope this article helps you to understand societies accepted definitions and the accepted conditions for the justification of paternalistic acts.

Paternalism as defined by Gerald Dworkin a philosopher is the "interference with a person's liberty of action justified by reasons referring exclusively to the welfare, good, happiness, needs, interests, or values of the person being coerced." An example given by Dworkin is the law requiring motorcyclists to wear safety helmets when operating their machines. This law has the motorcyclist's safety in mind by its enforcement. Wearing a safety helmet can result in fewer damages to the skull if and when a motorcyclist is involved in an accident. Some states do not require helmets to be worn, therefore, giving a choice to those who operate motorcycles, to wear a helmet or not to. Because some states give this choice it makes state laws that require helmets paternalistic.

Equally important, is the definition of paternalism given by James Childress; "paternalism attempts to meet the needs of another person even against that person's wishes. This does not including material objects. An example may be buying a car for your child because, he says he needs one. The first feature of paternalism is altruistic beneficence—the aim to benefit another person. The second feature is a refusal to accept that person's wishes, choices, and actions in some circumstances." In brief, paternalism may be defined as a refusal to accept or to acquiesce in another person's wishes, choices, and actions for that person's own benefit. To demonstrate his definition of paternalism Childress gives the following example. A member of a religious sect, who is in need of a blood transfusion, is administered to a hospital. Before the patient faints from loss of blood, he informs the doctor that his religion forbids this type of action. Even after the patient gives this information the doctor performs the transfusion in order to save the man's life. By doing so the doctor disregarded the patient's wishes, therefore, acting paternalistically. To demonstrate a non-paternalistic action Childress has changed how the doctors could have acted. A member of a religious sect that does not believe in blood transfusions, is involved in a serious automobile accident and loses a large amount of blood. On arriving at the hospital, he is still conscious and informs the doctor of his religious beliefs, and states he would rather die than go against his religion. Immediately thereafter he faints from loss of blood. The doctor believes that if the man is not given the transfusion he will die. After the doctor thinks the situation through, he calls in the leader from the man's religious sect to administer final rites to his patient before he dies.

In conclusion to the above definitions of paternalism, I feel paternalism is when a person makes a decision, whereupon affecting another person in a way he or she did not wish to be affected. An example may be when a doctor disregards a patient's requests for certain procedures or treatments, such as giving a pregnant woman something to ease her labor pains after she's informed her doctor she is against this. By not following the patient's requests the doctor makes a decision which affects the patient in a way he or she does not wish to be affected. Often, there is little time to inform the patient of his or her choices in the matter. Nevertheless, I feel every patient has the right to a clear explanation of the causes and effects of the treatment(s) he or she has chosen or has been given. In a case where time was limited the patient should be given an oral report by the doctor. Thereby justifying his reason(s) for treatment(s).

Besides, the definition of paternalism there is another controversial aspect of this topic. The moral questionability of paternalism is one such aspect. The definition of morally is acting in a moral manner. Moral defined is relating to, dealing with, or capable of making the distinction between, right and wrong in conduct. Paternalism becomes morally questionable when a person doesn't conform with accepted morals. One accepted moral is lying. The questionability of morals in paternalism appears when lying is used to deceive a person. To demonstrate this questionability an example given in The Warrant Project's (Spring, 1985) Corpus on Paternalism is as follows.

One evening five victims of an automobile accident were admitted to the ward of a small rural hospital. The nurse in charge knew the woman who had been driving and her four children who were also injured. Three of the children survived, but the oldest child, a daughter, died shortly after admission. The mother suffered minor contusions and abrasions, and she was understandably concerned about the condition of her children. The nurse asked the doctor, who was lounging in the operating theatre, what she should tell the mother about the daughter's death. The doctor told the nurse to reassure the woman at all costs because he thought she had had a stressful enough day already and her husband would be there the next day to give his support. All through the night the mother constantly asked the nurse about the children. As the nurse put it, "it went strongly against my conscience to have to look her in the eye and repeat a lie of such magnitude." The next day, the doctor told the woman that he had ordered the nurse to lie to her "for her own good."

Obviously, the above example questions the doctor's decision to lie to his patient. Should he have told the truth rather than lied? Was his decision really beneficial to his patient? This moral questionablity leads us to another topic; under what conditions can the doctor's paternalism be justified and under what conditions can paternalism itself be justified?

As I have noted, paternalism violates a person's rights to knowing the truth, to being left to his or her own decisions, and to not being judged by others about these decisions. However, paternalism requires conditions for justification. Rosemary Carter states that paternalism can be justified when a person who acts paternalistically was priorly consented to do so. For instance, Bill has resolved to quit smoking. Knowing that once tempted to smoke he will probably break his resolve. Therefore, he asked Jim to prevent him from doing so. This alienates Bill's right to non-interference. Under this specific circumstance Jim's action is justified. When Jim actually does prevent Bill from smoking, his act is justified.

Although this is true, another question of this being justifiable comes to mind. Was Bill competent at the time he endorsed Jim to act paternalistically? If we accept following the descriptions of incompetence given by Rosemary Carter, Bill is considered competent. There is a group of people who we as society lable as being incompetent, therefore justifying paternalistic acts toward them. These people are discribed and labled as the following: those who are unable to understand or practice satisfactorily the basic requirements of survival, and so whose lives would be at worst in constant peril, and at best grossly unhappy, if not for the intervention of others. Those suffering from mental retardation, below a certain level, and those suffering from certain kinds of insanity are included in this class.

Rosemary Carter's description of competentence as a means for justification also speaks for both James Childress and Gerald Dworkin, with the following exceptions: Childress' justifies paternalism by probability of harm to that person unless there is intervention, e.g. a man attempting to commit suicide which if achieved would ultimatly result in his death. Dworkin justifies paternalism toward people who are considered to be making decisions that are far-reaching, potentially dangerous or irreversible. One example of these types of actions may be a person's decision to smoke, while being unaware of the harmful effects e.g. smoking 1 or 2 packs a day shortens the life expectancy 6.2 years. Altogether, these people tend to describe the same conditions for justification, but in a different manner with different examples.

While these conditions for justification are accepted by some of today's society, I feel that paternalism can be justified under only one condition, that of prior consent giving someone an OK for pat. action. The conditions of mental retardation, and insanity, do not give justification for paternalistic actions. These persons should have the right to incorporate their views and feelings into medical decisions. After all these people do have the ability to communicate to certain extents. Why should the views of these people be carelessly disposed of.

Altogether, paternalism can be a very serious matter, with very serious effects. Especially when it is applied in a situation of life or death, or in a situation of comotose patients. Many times patients who are seriously ill or who are suffering from brain damage are subject to having their prior consent disregarded by their family and their doctors. People don't realize that everyday a doctor or a patient's family make paternalistic decisions. These decisions might not be what the patient wanted, but are usually what the family members feel are for the patients own good. Many times disregarding prior decisions by patients, is done in order to prolong a patient's life. The condition in which a patient may have to live is a minor factor, the family just wants them to breath air, communication is often lost. Paternalism is an important issue because of the serious affects it can have on you and on members of your family. Paternalistic decision are on a scale of life to death, often people aren't given the choice to choose their fate.

JEFF'S TEXT

Physicians are routinely required to make decisions effecting the welfare of those in their care. While the patient is often content to 'let the doctor decide' the most appropriate course of treatment, it sometimes happens that the patient's expressed desires concerning treatment are in conflict with the considered medical opinion of the attending physician. Sometimes a doctor feels compelled to override the desires of her patient and to do so for the patient's own good. Consider the following rather extreme example of such a situation.

Mr. Jones is pacing back and forth on the roof of his five-story apartment house and several times appears to be about to jump off. When questioned by the police, he sounds confused. When interviewed by Dr. Smith in the emergency room, Jones admits being afraid he might be losing his mind. He speaks of the depression he has been experiencing the last several months and begins weeping uncontrollably. He claims not to know the source of his despair but says he can stand it no longer. He adamantly refuses hospitalization but will not say why. Dr. Smith decides that she must commit Jones to the hospital for a six-month observation period for Jones' own protection.

When considering cases such as this we are naturally led to ask such questions as

Has Dr. Smith done the right thing?

This could be a relatively straightforward questioning of the 'medical appropriateness' of Dr. Smith's enforced confinement of her patient. We might well question whether, given the evidence at hand, Smith's decision conforms to certain standards of 'good medical practice.' We could, however, be questioning the *moral* appropriateness of Smith's treatment of Jones. Smith is, after all, not merely a doctor, but a moral agent, and Jones, even while playing the role of 'patient,' is a moral actor in his own right. Assuming that Smith's conduct constitutes good doctoring, we can still question the moral value of her actions.

Has Dr. Smith done the *morally* correct thing by Jones?

Increasingly, moral philosophers have attempted to apply their theories of right and wrong to concrete, sociologically complex human situations. They have begun to examine such social relationships as that between a medical doctor and the patients in her care, and have begun, sometimes in cooperation with practicing health professionals, to bring moral issues to bear in considerations of medical practice and procedures. Those involved in health care are now more likely to call into question the moral appropriateness of their actions. 'Application' of moral theories to specialized contexts such as the interactions between doctors and patients thus plays on the undeniable fact that doctors and patients are, in addition to the 'roles' they play in the medical context, moral agents. We can ask not only whether a doctor has done the right thing as determined by the standards of proper doctoring, we can also ask whether she has done right by 'ordinary' moral standards. A doctor 'treats' not just a 'patient' but also another moral agent, and thus should be sensitive not just to the special obligations she has to the patient based on their respective contextually defined roles, but also to the 'general' obligations she has by virtue of being a moral agent.

It is clear that one goal of a project of questioning the *moral* appropriateness of particular instances of medical decision making is an eventual rethinking of medical practice. Taking general moral considerations seriously, philosophers and health professionals together may eventually reform the standards of health care delivery. The point of asking

Has Dr. Smith done the right thing?

is ultimately a rethinking of a doctor's responsibilities towards those in her care. The point of moral philosophizing about doctoring is to put medical practice on a more secure moral footing.

The point of this essay will be to question this conception of 'medical ethics.' I will consider how moral philosophers have dealt with cases such as our example of Smith and Jones, where a doctor apparently overrides the expressed preferences of her patient and seems to do so for the patient's own good. I shall suggest that the strategy employed by most moral philosophers in 'applying' their general moral theories to such cases both prevents them from engaging in anything like a true and deep reassessment of medical practice and blinds them to the general moral importance of such cases. Assumptions are made prior to the 'application' of moral theory that ensure both that the underlying social practice remains unquestioned and that moral issues that could be drawn from consideration of such cases remain unnoticed.

Consider another specific mdical case.

Jane, a seventeen year-old woman, unmarried and in her second month of pregnancy, is treated for symptoms of abdominal pain, weakness and swelling of the angles. Her doctor believes that her illness is pregnancy related, though not serious. Still, he believes she will get better faster if she has her parents to nurse her. However, Jane has not yet told her parents she is pregnant and had intended to get an abortion before they find out. She pleads with the doctor that it will "just ruin everything" if her parents find out, but he insists—and he calls her parents and informs them of their daughter's pregnancy.

Has Jane's doctor done the morally correct thing?

One sort of answer to this question would consider the actions of the doctor in light of certain general principles or 'rules' of moral behavior. According to some moral philosophers, it is a question concerning the 'nonmoral' value of the consequences of the doctor's actions.

Has he through his acting brought more happiness into the world than he would have had he refrained from acting?

Taken this way, the question is no different than any question concerning the moral appropriateness of an action. Furthermore, no specifically *medical* considerations are especially relevant to the general moral question.

However, philosophers whose concern is to 'apply' their general theories to *specific medical cases* often proceed in an entirely different manner. They note the sociological similarities between this case and others, for example that of Smith and Jones. In both cases, a doctor, that is, a highly trained specialist bound by oath to act in the best interest of his or her patient, makes a decision based on this blend of specialized knowledge and selfless concern that conflicts with the expressed desires of the patient, who is not only 'sick' but also lacks the special knowledge of the physician. Such situations, where one person's greater knowledge and genuine concern for the welfare of another lead him to act in ways contrary to the wishes of the less knowledgable and impaired other are common. Teachers often act in this way toward their students. Kings, dictators and the impersonal State act in this manner towards their subjects and most importantly, facthers act this way towards their children. Taking this last example as the paradigm case of this sort of relationship, some moral philosophers identify the actions of Dr. Smith and Jane's doctor as 'paternalistic.' These doctors have treated their pateints in ways significantly like the manner in which a powerful father treats his children. They have both exercised something like 'paternal power' over their patients.

To act paternalistically, according to one such philosopher is to refuse to "accept or to acquiesce in another person's wishes, choices, actions for that person's own benefit." Given this defitnion it is clear that doctors often act paternalistically towards their patients. To be a doctor in this society is, in part, to wield a power over others. This power flows both from a tremendous epistemic advantage based on years of specialized training, and a genuine and usually self-less concern for the best interest of others. To be a patient is both to be at a relative epistemic disadvantage and to *acknowledge* this lack of power through the very act of seeking medical attention. Patients see themselves as 'sick' and are thus acknowledging not only that they lack the best knowledge of what is in their best interest, but also that they may even lack the proper concern for their own welfare. Doctors, teachers and the State often find themselves acting to protect their patients, students and citizens from themselves.

In defining a concept of 'paternalistic action,' and seeing specific cases of medical treatment as exemplifying 'paternalism,' medical ethicists are following something like this strategy. They have, in effect, identified certain *sociological* features that many medical situations share, and share with other social settings, particularly with the complex interactions between a father and his son. They go on, however, to assume that these shared features are also *precisely* the features of moral relevance. They assume that the structure of power relations that serve to mark these situations as instances of 'paternalism' are also the features that will play a role in a moral justification of the actions. The question

Has Dr. Smith done the morally correct thing?

becomes, for those following this strategy, a question of the moral appropriateness of Smith's exercise of paternal power. Once an action has been identified as 'paternalistic,' its moral justification will turn on the answers to such questions as

Is Smith a better judge than Jones of Jones' welfare?
Does Jones' behavior show that he has lost the proper concern for his own welfare?

The moral evaluation of 'paternalistic' action is made in terms of the power relations structuring the interactions of doctor and patient.

Smith did the right thing if she correctly exercised paternal power over Jones. In this case, it seems, Jones has demonstrated precisely the sort of 'incompetence' that would tip the 'balance of power' towards Smith. Like a child, Jones lacks the kind of power over himself that underlies his 'autonomy' as a moral agent. Jones' diminished autonomy justifies Smith's acting to commit him against his wishes; Jones is simply not in a position to determine his own best interest. On the other hand, Jane's doctor, it seems, has overstepped the proper limits of paternal power and has infringed unjustifiably on Jane's autonomy.

An action identified as paternalistic is justified morally to the extent that the exercise of paternal power by one party over another is licensed by such things as the demonstrated incompetence of the other. The justification of paternalistic action is always a matter of the proper balance of power between two moral agents. Paternalism is first defined in terms of sociological features relating to the balance of power between two persons. The nature of the power relationship is then used to determine the moral appropriateness of the exercise of paternal power.

Following this strategy, however, severely limits the extent to which medical ethicists can influence or reform medical practice. The contribution of these moral philosophers to the actual constitution of medical practice is limited to that of clarifying and refining the morally accepted limits on the exercise of *paternal power*. Those following this strategy have assumed that the features that mark a specific medical situation as involving an instance of paternalism are the very features on which any justification of the actions and decisions of the doctor are to be based. This assumption carries with it the implicit recognition of the doctor's essentially paternal relation to his patient. Medical ethicists following this strategy cannot question whether doctors are best thought of as father-figures. On the contrary, they assume, by focussing their moral evaluations of the actions of doctors on the power relations between doctor and patient, that doctors *rightly* exercise a power over their patients not unlike that of a father over his children. They can merely go on to refine the conditions under which the exercise of this power is morally appropriate and cannot question the moral value of the underlying conception of the role 'doctor.' Indeed, in making this assumption, they have endorsed this conception.

The assumption of the *moral relevance* of the sociological features marking an action as paternalistic changes our question from

Has Dr. Smith done the morally correct thing?

to

Has Smith appropriately exercised paternal power?

and in so doing blocks any genuine moral inquiry into the nature of the doctor–patient relationship. In adopting this strategy, medical ethicists have, to put it rather bluntly, become mere apologists for the *status quo*. Instead of investigating the moral implications of the nature of the underlying power structure, they can merely give to those who wield this power suggestions as to its appropriate employment.

One aim of 'applying' moral theory to specific medical contexts is to eventually put medical practice on a sounder moral footing. That this project is, in principle at least, the ultimate goal of 'medical ethics' is demonstrated by the interest of practicing health care professionals in the discipline. Hospital administrators and others who fund work in medical ethics have no interest *per se* in 'theoretical' questions of morality. Their official goal must be to bring moral issues to the forefront in a genuine re-evaluation and eventual reform of their own *practice*. This project requires of medical ethicists the will to submit the deep-structure of medical practice to close moral scrutiny. This task involves, among other things, an investigation of the social roles 'doctor' and 'patient' and of concepts such as 'sickness' and 'health.' Those who focus on 'paternalism' in assuming that the moral evaluation of a doctor's decision making is primarily to be made in terms deriving from his father-like power relation to his patient, are unable to pursue such an investigation. They have 'endorsed' and given moral sanction to the very social structures they were meant to question.

This is not to deny that considering cases of paternalism is a valuable thing for moral philosophers to do. Indeed, such cases involving a conflict of paternal power and autonomy give the moral philosopher a chance to re-examine the nature of 'autonomy' and its conceptual relations to paternal power. An autonomous agent has just the kind of special knowledge and concern for his own welfare that enables him to have what amounts to a father's power over *himself*. Considering cases of paternalism may shed light on the complex relations between such fundamental moral notions as 'autonomy' and the underlying power structures. It is perhaps no accident that a morality that values 'rights' and 'autonomy' above all else and which sees moral conflict in terms of a struggle for power developed in a society where the role of the powerful father is so pervasive and so dominant. These cases of 'medical paternalism' are especially important for moral philosophers to consider precisely because the underlying power structures are so close to the surface. Again, however, 'medical ethicists' by their adoption of a strategy aiming at the legitimization of the existing structures of power remain blind to the extent to which those very structures color the moral theories they are 'applying.'

To a practicing 'general' moral theorist, specific actions in a social context, such as the cases we have been considering, are morally evaluated according to the general principles of right and wrong thought to apply 'universally.' These specific cases are of interest in part because of what they may reveal about the concepts employed in the general theory. As we have hinted here, the doctor–patient context may be especially helpful in examining the role of paternal power in moralities centered on the notion of an agent autonomy. An open-minded moral philosopher might learn from such cases the extent to which the power an autonomous moral agent has over her own actions is modelled on the blend of power, knowledge and concern a father has over his children. A moral philosopher concerned especially with the reform of medical practice might also gain from consideration of these cases the kind of insight into the complex conceptual interactions of 'power,' 'knowledge,' 'sickness,' and 'health' that would be a first step in a deep reconceptualization of the role and responsibilities of doctors and eventually to a general reform of health care.

An applied ethicist on the other hand, is interested in these cases *because* they are taken to share morally relevant features. The 'business ethicist,' for example, assumes that actions of, say, presidents of major corporations are to be morally evaluated according to common features—in terms of, say, the power and responsibilities of persons playing the social role 'president of a major corporation.' Medical ethicists assume that the moral evaluations of a doctor's actions are to be made in terms of specific features of the social role 'doctor.' This, however, is not to examine the social context in a way that may eventually lead to a practice becoming more in line with general moral principles, but to do nothing less than to incorporate the social *status quo* into one's moral theory.

I have attempted to show how the strategies of the 'applied ethicist' prevent him from both gaining insight into the workings of the general principles of morality and having any real influence on the moral status of the practices he is investigating. Moral philosophers have an indispensable role to play in making our world a better place, but it is a role they can only play by resisting the temptation to become an 'applied ethicist.'

ROGER'S TEXT

Consider the following situations:

Situation One: Mister N, a member of a religious sect which strictly forbids blood transfusions, is involved in a serious automobile accident and loses a large amount of blood. On arriving at the hospital, he is still conscious and informs the doctor that his religion forbids blood transfusions. Immediately thereafter he faints from loss of blood. The doctor believes that if Mister N is not given a transfusion he will die. Thereupon, while Mister N is still unconscious, the doctor arranges for and carries out the blood transfusion.

Is the doctor right in doing this?

Situation Two: The legislature of state S considers a law requiring bicyclists to wear football gear (helmets shoulder pads knee pads). Safety experts and insurance company witnesses insist that the incidence of serious injury to riders in crashes can be significantly cut by such a measure. Adult bicyclists and parents insist that the risks involve are small in the first place, but the gear is prohibitively expensive for the poor, and that riding in such outfits is uncomfortable and no fun at all. The legislature is shown gory graphs of mangled children and their mangled bicycles under the wheels of large trucks and passes the law for the good of the riders quite against their will.

Is the legislature right?

Situation Three: Peter and Paul Jones are both avid swimmers. A race is to be held at their junior high. Peter, the faster of the two, finds out that Paul has entered. Having won several previous races in which Paul has entered, Peter, not willing to demoralize Paul any further, does not enter the race, in the correct belief that this virtually ensures Paul's victory; and that, were Paul to know of his action, he would oppose it.

Is Peter right? Does it matter if Paul finds out what he's up to and says he wants Peter to compete, given that Paul would certainly lose the race in that case?

In each of these cases someone or some group behaves paternalistically toward another person or group. Generally, the public is concerned about paternalism only in either the medical or the legal contexts; but Situation Three reminds us that it can occur in non-professional contexts, among private persons, as well. Sometimes paternalistic actions seem justified, and sometimes not; but always, paternalism seems at least to be a bit disquieting. Inevitably, the pheonomena involves a clash of wills, and the fact that the thing is done to someone who opposes it for his own good only seems to make it all the more questionable.

Regarding legal and medical paternalism in particular, the clash of will has given rise to disputes about morality of such action. A few people think all paternalism is wrong apparent (e.g. few oppose involuntary treatment for extremely deranged persons, even in cases where they are not dangerous to others) but nearly everyone believes that some paternalistic actions are or would be involved. The authors whose efforts will be reviewed here have undertaken the task of trying to spell out coniditons which must be satisfied for a paternalistic action to be justified.

The problem is complicated by the fact that paternalism as it is commonly used is more than a little fuzzy. That is because there are some actions that are clearly paternalistic and others that are clearly not. But there are also actions about which one is not sure what to say so a preliminary task is that of giving an account of what are paternalistic actions; that of settling on a definition in order to gain a clearer notion of what we are talking about and of what, if anything, has to be justified. Examples, in consequence, play a great role in writings about paternalism. They serve both to inspire insight and to correct mistaken definitions. So each of our authors is forced in the nature of the case to perform two tasks—each first provides a definition, making illlustrative and/or polemical use of examples and each then provides an account of how paternalistic actions so defined are to be justified. What we have to consider then are different definitions of paternalism and different justifications as well.

Definitions of paternalism are intended to point up a set of characteristics of actions so that any paternalistic act necessarily have them and any act that has them is necessarily paternalistic. Such characteristics are suggested by more or less generally accepted (or acceptable) examples of cases of paternalism such as those given at the outset and the following.

Example One: Mister K is pacing back and forth on the roof of his five story tenement and several times appears about to jump off. When questioned by the police he sounds confused. When interviewed by Doctor T in the emergency room, Mister K is afraid he might be losing his mind. He speaks of the depression he has been experiencing in the past several months and begins weeping uncontrollably. He claims not to know the source of his despair but says he can stand it no longer. He refuses hospitalization but will not say why. Doctor T commits Mister K to the hospital for a sixth month observation period for his own protection.

Example Two: Many states have laws requiring motorcyclists to wear crash helmets for their own protection.

Example Three: Laws forbidding the general sale of various drugs for the good or potential (or actual) users.

The prominence of such examples as these in the discussion of the moral status of paternlaism suggests to Dworkin (source one, above) the following "rough" definition (pg. 7):

D1: "Paternalism is the interference with a person's liberty of action justified by reasons referring exclusively to the welfare, good, happiness, needs, interests, or values of the person being coerced."

The definition D1 is faulty in several respects, and is not made any better by Dworkin's admission that it is "rough". First, as it stands, if the definition is right, there can be no unjustified (i.e. wrong) paternalistic action for D1 says paternalism is justified. Doubtless this is part of the "roughness". Perhaps what Dworkin intends is something more like the following:

> D1': "Paternalism is interference with a person's liberty of action of such a sort that if justified at all it is justified exclusively by its positive bearing on the welfare, good, happiness, needs, interests or values of the persons being coerced."

But this will still not work, as can be seen from Example Three above. In the case of the drug laws, potential buyers who can't buy because the product is not on the market are not coerced at all though they are the ones whose benefit is intended.

There remains, however, the question of interference with liberty of action; for surely the potential buyer is no longer free to buy when the sale of the product is outlawed. Buchanon, too, thinks this feature important, if not universally present. He offers (cited in Childress, source seven, pg. 17).

> D2: "Paternalism is interference with a person's freedom of action or freedom of information or the deliberate dissemination of misinformation where the alleged justification of interferring or misinforming is that its for the good of the person interfered with or misinformed."

But here we can kill two birds with one stone. Suppose, in Situation Three, that Peter tells Paul in advance that he will not compete. There is no interference with freedom of action or information, nor any misinforming; so D2 is wrong as is D1'. Besides any case where a patient is just lied to for his own good is a counterexample to D1'. Paternalism sometimes involves coercion, or at least deprivation of liberty. But by no means does it always do so. For these reasons, Carter's definition (pg. 44, source 6) is also faulty:

> D3: "Paternalistic acts are those in which the protection or promotion of a subject's welfare is the primary reason for attempted or successful coercive interference with an action or state of that person."

In ordinarily life we require justification only for actions that we have reason to think are wrong. Someone out to justify an action is usually out to show that it isn't wrong after all; to rebut a presumption of wrongness. Perhaps taking a hint from this, or perhaps just displaying a bias descended from Mill, or perhaps being overimpressed with cases of paternalism that generate controversy, most of our authors seem to suppose that paternalism requires justification in this way.

They suppose that paternalism requires justification because there is always at least some reason to think it wrong. If this is so, then of course all acts of paternalism must share some defining feature which generates the presence of a reason to think them wrong. Paternalism must be a suspect class of actions.

Gert and Culver (source 2, above) take a peculiarly direct approach to ensuring that a presumptive wrong attaches to paternalism. The definition they offer is (pg. 13.)

> D4: "A is acting paternalistically toward S if A's behavior (correctly) indicates that A believes that:
>
> (1) his action is for S's own good,
> (2) he is qualified to act on S's behalf,
> (3) his action involves violating a moral rule (or doing that which will require him to do so) with regard to S,
> (4) he is justified in acting on S's behalf independently of S's past present or immediately forthcoming (free, informed) consent,
> (5) S believes (perhaps falsely) that he (S) generally knows what is for his own good."

D4 is objectionable on a number of grounds. First, nothing in it excludes actual consent at or before the time of action, though Gert and Culver clearly seem to think it does (pg. 15, source two). And it is generally agreed that opposition by the beneficiary is in some way essential to paternalism. Second, the definition excludes parental care of the very young (vide clause (5)), though such cases are routinely cited by writers in the field as pardigmatic of (justified) paternalism. And third, the reference to qualifications too narrowly restricts the definition to professional contexts.

But apart from all this, the immorality clause (clause (3)) is itself out of place. Situation 3 (Peter and Paul) should make that clear; and if it does not, any case in which a doctor delays telling a patient the bad news for a few moments, until he calms down and is able to handle it, certainly should.

These counter examples have a broader significance. They are illustrative of whole classes of paternalistic action that are not suspicious on their faces. They show that there are paternalistic actions for which there is not necessarily present any reason to think them wrong. If this is so, then no correct definition of paternalism can attribute to them any feature such that any action with that feature is on that account suspect.

I will have more to say of this shortly. For now it is enough to point out that plausible definitions satisfying this requirement are in the field. Here, for instance, is Childress' definition (pg. 17, source 3):

D5: "Paternalism is nonacquiescence in a person's wishes, choices and actions for that person's own benefit."

The definition is not without flaw (surely he means "or" not "and", and "nonacquiescence" is even fuzzier than "paternalism") but it illustrates the point.

The task of supplying the justification of paternalism can be conceived in any of (at least) three ways: (a) That of showing how individual acts of paternalism are to be justified in the face of (rebuttable) reason to think them wrong; (b) that of supplying a way of sorting the class of patrnalistic action into 2 non-empty subclasses: those that are at least presumptively wrong and those that are not; and, (c) that of supplying a blanket justification intended to show that all acts of paternalism (large blanket) or all of a specified type (small blanket) are morally okay. Only if we suppose that the first type is necessary for paternalism do we have to incorporate in our definition of it something to guarantee that *each* act of paternalism is suspicious.

Gert and Culver are not alone in making this suposition. So does Ms. Carter (source 6) who defines paternalism in this way:

D3: "Paternalistic acts are those in which the protection or promotion of a subject's welfare is a primary reason for attempted or successful coercive interference with an action or state of that person."

Ms. Carter sees that the problem of paternalistic acts *so defined* is the problem of justifying the coercive interference with another person's action or state. This, she says, is always in conflict with the intended beneficiary *prima-facie* right to non-interference. If, in a particular case, the paternalistic act is in fact justified, this will be because the prima-facie right was not, in that case, an *actual* right of the beneficiary. Taking this as her starting point, she sees the problem as one of laying out conditions for the prima facie right to fail to be actual (source 8, pg. 44).

This happens, she says, when we are in one (or more) of these cases:

"(1) when the prima facie right conflicts with some other person's more important prima facie right;
(2) when the prima facie right is alienated by its possessor;
(3) when realizing the prima facie right would result in sufficiently large disutilities for others." (source 8, pg. 44)

Apparently taking for granted the professional context in which neither condition (1) nor (2) will hold, she focuses in the remainder of her piece on (2), providing a discussion of alienation by consent.

It seems to me that there are three things wrong with Ms. Carter's account. First of all, the boundaries and weight of the right to noninterference are terribly vague; but, I will not place much emphasis on this because most moral considerations are at least equally vague. More importantly, her account gives no role at all to the (intended) welfare of the interferee in justifying paternalism, and it gives far too great a role to his prior or subsequent consent. Secondly, there are cases where the benefit intended would be so great as to dwarf worries about the subject's consent, and in which this benefit does all the work, in one way or another, of supplying what justification is needed for interfering with a beneficiary's actions or state. If it were true, for instance, that only by believing that God created the world in six days could one avoid eternal hellfire, then seeing to it that someone did believe this by coercive interference with his reading and education would be justified primarily by the benefit intended, and quite regardless of whether or not the subject ever consents to the interference itself.

There is, however, further difficulty of any account relying on the actual consent of the subject: the fact that he simply might not give it, however much information we might supply him about the circumstances of the case that seem to us to call for paternalistic action. Some writers, well aware of this, advert to hypothetical consent. Dworkin and Gert and Culver, for instance, do this.

Though their treatment of the problem is fairly detailed and elaborate, I take it that what Gert and Culver have to say about justified paternalism comes roughly to this (vide, pgs. 37, 38, source 5)

(Gert and Culver): A's doing X, a paternalistic act with respect to S, is justified iff:

(a) it prevents more evil to S than it causes for S
(b) it is irrational of S not to consent to the violation of a moral rule involved in A's doing X for S's good,
(c) one could universally allow the violation of the rule in such cases as that in which A,S find themselves.

Dworkin's notion is somewhat similar in that he conceives of justified paternalism as a sort of universal social insurance program to which rational persons would consent to protect themselves against episodes of irrationality to which they expect to be subject (pg. 32, source 4). Actually, the two conceptions are more similar than they seem, since Gert and Culver make hypothetical universal agreement by rational person a condition of the truth of (c) above. (pg. 44, source 5)

Now of course one thing that is wrong with Gert and Culver's account is that it is designed to rebut a presumption of wrong that may not even exist. Contrary to their definition of "paternalism" we have seen that no violation of a moral rule need be involved in a paternalistic act. But beyond this, both Gert and Culver's and Dworkin's accounts suffer from two important defects: (1) agreements that would be or would have been made under certain circumstances but which are not made in fact have no force what so ever. They neither confer rights nor limit them. This is a point which Dworkin himself has elsewhere argued. And (2) both the judgment that the objecting beneficiary of paternalism is being irrational and the judgment that all rational agents would agree to something or other require a fairly strong theory of rationality. But anyone familiar with the relevant literature knows that this area of investigation is at least as full of disagreement and controversy as any other in ethics. More specifically, what both Gert and Culver's and Dworkin's accounts presuppose is a theory of what prudence is along with some account of its authority (if any). In both the analysis of prudence (or self-interest) and the question of its authority are hotbeds of endless controversy. Both these difficulties, in my view, are fatal to accounts of justification relying on hypothetical consent (e.g. the notion that the beneficiary *would* consent, were he rational).

Komrad (Source 8) sees the problem quite differently, and seeks to give what appears to be intended as a small-blanket justification of specifically medical paternalism. Perhaps because professional practice involves a lot of rule-breaking, he accepts an earlier published version of Gert and Culver's defintion (D4, without clause (5)) but his story as to what justifies paternalism is quite different. Perhaps sensitive to the rise of criticism of the "doctor knows best," authoritarian style of medicine, Komrad sees his task as one of defending medical paternalism against the charge that it is practiced at the expense of the patient's autonomy.

His defense does not appeal to any real or imaginative act that doctor does, indeed, know best, but rather to pecularities of the state of mind which, he says, are inherent in "the sick role". "The object of both [i.e. paternalism and autonomy] is the good of the same moral agent," he tells us (pg. 57, source 8). Paternalism on the part of the medical establishment rushes in to fill a void when autonomy recedes. And autonomy always *does* recede on the side of the patient owing to the "fear, shame, self-concern, weakness, vulnerability, neediness and dependence" that are dealt into this sick role (pg. 60, source 8). This rather harrowing mental state is what he thinks distinguishes the status of a patient vis-a-vis the doctor from that of the auto owner vis-a-vis the mechanic. Both have something "broke," so to speak, and they want it fixed. Both are ignorant of what is best. But the patient is in a state (as one says) while the auto owner is not. So someone has to decide things for the poor, wretched sickies while the auto owner could decide for himself if sufficient information were given (pg. 60). Furthermore, Komrad says, the very goal of paternalism is the restoration and maximization of the patient's (emotional) autonomy. So there.

The absurdity of this entire story overwhelms comment. It constantly amazes me, what manages to get into print. The portrait of the patient as a hysterical, bleating sheep, far to worked up to do anything sensible with information that might be provided him (as contrasted with the cool, cagy car owner) is so far from reality as to make one fear for the strange disturbing affect on the mental states of professionals of the doctor's role (if Komrad is a doctor). As for all that about "fear, shame," etc., my own impression is that the car owner is as vulnerable to such actions in the presence of the mechanic as a patient as in the presence of a doctor as neither is all *that* worked up (not every patient is in for cancer, after all).

But besides getting the story of the doctor–patient relationship descriptively wrong, Komrad's account can do no more than narrow the focus of our concern to those cases where the patient really is in a terrible state. Of those cases he has no more to say, really, than that *someone* has to decide *for* people in such states. This is true, of course. But it doesn't take us very far.

On the other hand, perhaps asking for a thorough-going full account of necessary and sufficient conditions for justification is asking too much. Perhaps that is just too great a task. At any rate, it seems that this may be Childress' idea. for, as I understand him, he provides us with a series of conditions, each of which is necessary for paternalism to be justified but which are not jointly sufficient (source 7).

The conditions Childress gives are as follows:

(1) the principle of encumbrance: there must be relevant, adequate "defects, encumbrances, and limitations of a person's decision-making in acting" (pg. 51, source 7).

(2) the principle of risk: there must be a "probability of harm to that person unless there is intervention" (pg. 51, source 7).

(3) the principle of proportionality: "the probable benefit of intervention should outweigh" (a) the probable harm of nonintervention and (b) the probable benefit of *other* modes of intervention, even when the weight of violation of morals rules is taken into account (pgs. 53, 54, source 7).

(4) "the least restrictive, humiliating, and insulting alternatives should be employed" (pg. 55).

Childress does not count rejection of treatment on religious grounds as satisfying the principle of encumbrance (pgs. 52, 53).

Conditions two through four are unobjectionable, indeed it is refreshing to see the intended benefit of paternalism play so essential a role. My quarrel is with his condition one and here are two points I wish to make.

First as the reader will recall Childress accepts one of the least restrictive of the definitions offered by our writers as he has it

D5. paternalism is nonacquiescence in a person's wishes and choices and actions for that person's benefit.

Allowing wishes in D5 to cover wishes the subject would have if he knew of the action of the paternalist, Situation 3, (the swimmers Peter and Paul) satisfies the definition. For Peter's withdrawal to be justified, is it *really* necessary that Paul's (potential) opposition be a consequence of some "encumbrance" to his decision making capacity? It seems to me that what has happened is that Childress has defined paternalism with sufficient breadth to cover non-professional instances (such as Situation 3) but then has gone on to consider its justification with the professional context uppermost in his mind. In that context, a claim that for crossing the will of the beneficiary to be justified, there must be something wrong with his decision-making, is much more plausible.

But this leads to my second point. Childress refuses to count odd beliefs that people entertain on religious grounds, which lead them to decide on medically unsound courses of action, as satisfying the requirement of encumbrance. While it is doubtless right not to count religious belief as clear evidence of medically unsound mind the result is that the principle would require us to hold certain paternalistic interventions as unjustifiable which most of us would in fact think right.

Situation 4: Abdul and Mohammed, brothers are soldiers in the Iatolah's army on the Iraq border. A captain asks for volunteers for a suicide mission, and a mulah assures all the troops that the men killed on the mission (expected to be all of them) will immediately be transported to Paradise. Mohammed, same as anyone, is afraid of death. But, a devout believer and devoted follower of Komani, he sees this as a rare chance to assure himself of a blissful eternity. He tells his brother Abdul that he is going to volunteer in the morning. Abdul, an aetheist educated in the west, bashes Mohammed on the head and imprisons him for three days, knowing full well that Mohammed will hate him for this, forever.

Personally my sympathies are entirely with Abdul. For me, this situation is much like the following:

Situation 5. Frank and Jessie, famous missouri train robbers, are camped outside St. Louis with their gang. Jessie, in love with Marabelle, wants to enter the town for a last meeting with her before her father sends her to a New York finishing school. Frank has learned that her father has pressured her into being the bait for a trap to capture Jessie, who will surely be hanged if caught. Frank places his evidence before Jessie, and, while it convinces everyone in the gang, it does not convince Jessie who sees it through the eyes of love. Jessie is about to depart for the town when Frank and the boys set upon him, tie him up, and hold him prisoner for two days, until Marabelle is known to have left for New York. Jessie's rage is all the greater for he knows that Frank and the boys do not know Marabelle personally at all and can be no judges of her character.

It seems to me that Frank and the boys didn't suppose that there is something wrong with Jessie's decision-making capacity. If there is anything wrong with him at all, it is with his beliefs; were his beliefs correct, his intended actions would be perfectly alright, and the same is true, I think, for Mohammed, and it is not essential that Jessie's beliefs be disturbed by some psychological phenomenon known to impede reasonable belief-formation (the theory of rational belief is at least as much of a mess as that of rational conduct). What is essential to Frank (or Abdul) is that he thinks Jessie (or Mohammed) is *wrong*, and that the error promises to cost him dearly.

Situation 6: Tom and Tim, left wing terrorists, are robbing a bank. Tom glances out the window and sees a right wing terrorist wiring a gun to the get away car, aimed at the driver. They leave the bank and run toward the car as police dash up the street towards them. Tim jumps into into the driver seat, and Tom shouts at him not to start the car—that a gun is wired to it that will kill him. Tim disbelieves this and is about to start the car when Tom pulls him out of it into the street. The police drag them toward a van and the rightwinger removes the gun, unnoticed by all but Tom. Tim is furious and will never believe that Tom saved his life.

There is nothing wrong with Tim's beliefs, except that one of them is false: the belief that no gun is wired to the car. Neither his decision-making capacity nor his style of belief acquisition displays any "encumbrance." But Tom, I think, has certainly done the right thing.

Childress, of course, gives a reason for thinking that religious beliefs are special. He says they belong to a class of beliefs that are unverifiable. Just what he means by this he does not make clear (philosophers have still different views); nor is it obvious that it should matter.

The fact is that our society's diffidence to religious belief can certainly be carried too far. None of us thinks that just anything anyone might want to do in God's name has to be protected by the law, and I see no special reason why in general, just anything has to be protected provided the believer proposes to do it only to himself. It may be that we have too much reason to care for him to allow such latitude. Of course, if the believers are right, then we will have cost them a great deal by our interference, which will have turned out to be well-intended meddling. Will it then have been wrong?

I will end with some general remarks on the justification of paternalism. As the reader will have gathered, I do not believe that paternalism requires case by case justification in the sense that types of action that are always necessarily suspect do. Nor do I believe that any blanket justification, large or small, is possible.

Every wrong act is of a suspect type but, such types differ in important regards. Suspect types of action, (e.g. homicide) such that, if an instance is wrong, it is wrong in virtue of being of that type and of being done in circumstances such as to preclude justification rather than being so merely in virtue of belonging to a broader type and being done under such circumstances as to preclude justification, are intrinsicly wrong. Suspect types not satisfying this condition are *parasitically* wrong, the suspicion (and the wrongness) being based on that pertaining to a broader type of which the parasitic type is a subclass. Instances of types of acts not suspect at all (e.g. acts done on a Tuesday) are, at most, extrinsically wrong in virtue of belonging to an intrinsically wrong type as well (and being done in such circumstances as to preclude justification). Gert and

Culver and Carter define paternalism in such a way as to make it parasitically wrong; the first in reference to the moral rules and the second in reference to a presumed right of non-interference. But as the reader knows, I think that paternalism is not even parasitically wrong.

In consequence, paternalistic acts are wrong, if at all, only extrinsically, as an act done on a Tuesday can be wrong in virtue of also being a wrongful homicide. Or rather, it will be wrong in the way that wrongful *attempts* done on a Tuesday are wrong (if at all), since paternalism is always a doing of such-and-such in an attempt to benefit someone. Since, presumably, it can never be wrong to benefit someone, if an act of paternalism is wrong, it is so because something suspect was done in the attempt and the resulting benefit (if any) failed to suffice to justify that suspect act.

This does not quite leave us where we began, but it leaves us rather close. Not quite, because it may be that in a particular paternalistic act nothing suspect is done, in which case the act is simply not wrong at all. Close, because the cases that interest us are just those in which something suspect is done in an attempt to benefit someone. About these, I feel that there is not much to be said beyond this: attempts are not wrong only if success would not be wrong. And if successful paternalistic action, though something suspect is done in the course of it, is not wrong this will be because the extent of the benefit realized is sufficient to outweight the moral weight of the suspect act done, and there is no clear rule about how such weights are to be worked out.

One more point before I close. The dilemma of the wars of religion in Europe left us with a society in which peace is preserved by a sort of universal forbearance in matters of religion, erected by our Founding Fathers into a constitutional principle. But this forbearance, born of frustration with endless warfare is no great virtue in the eyes of believers (sincere believers one another and all athesists to everlasting torment), nor in the eyes of aetheists (who view religion as deadly nonsense altogether poisionous to the social atmosphere). Liberals have, in various ways, tried to make a virtue of what strikes both believers and aetheists as the lesser evil of peace, declaiming on the value of pluralism and the ideal of tolerance. In this way they have sought to place beliefs regarding matters of religion in a different moral category from beliefs, say, regarding such mundane mattes as whether or not Jessie's girl friend really would betray him. But believers and aethesits alike treat their beliefs in matters of religion, so far as action goes, in the same way as any other sort of belief that might be relevant to action. From these differences in belief, different sorts of action flow, as from the differences between Frank and Jessie different actions seem best. Just as it would have seemed odd for both Jessie and Frank to treat beliefs about Jessie's girl friend as an special moral category, so that Frank was for that reason forbidden morally to interfere, so, too, neither the sincere believer nor the sincere aethesist can accept that, because their differences are about religion, neither can for that reason interfere with the other seems best.

The upshot is that in some cases of paternalism, whether or not an interference is morally right may depend entirely on the truth or falseity of beliefs pertaining to matters of religion. If Frank and the boys were wrong about Marabelle, then they deprived Jessie of a valued last night with his lover and did him no good at all. Their restraint of him, deprived of its justification, will be at best excusable because well-intended, but still wrong because deprived of the counterbalancing weight of the benefit which, though intended (and we may suppose itself sufficient in weight to *justify* in case of success) was not realized in fact. In a similar way, Abdul's restraint of Mohammed will be justified only if Mohammed's death would indeed lead merely to the altheist's nothing at all rather than the Moslem believer's Paradise.

All which is as much to say that the truth of religious beliefs leading to a rejection of treatment will suffice to insure that paternalistic treatment would be wrong; since, far from benefiting the patient, it will greatly harm him in his relationship with God and his faith in the hereafter. But the falsehood of these beliefs would mean that paternalistic interventions could lead to a real benefit sufficiently large to justify treatment against the patient's will.

This, of course, is not what either the medical profession or the legislature wants to hear, for it means that decisions about what to do in such cases, and decisions about what to legally sanction, so far as these are intended to reflect moral considerations, cannot come from a standpoint that is neutral on religious beliefs. Doubtless, however both courts and the medical profession will find some way to pragmatically resolve these cases by somehow appealing to the "specialness" of religious matters, and adopt a rule which, while being advertised as a sort of balming compromise intended to satisfy everyone a little, will necessarily enjoin or forbid courses of action that will in some cases be immoral supposing the believer is right, and in others be immoral supposing the aetheist is.

APPENDIX

H

Rules for the Analysis of Text Structure

The analysis of text structure was carried out in four phases. In the first phase, texts were divided into T-units.

In the second phase, this list of T-units was divided into rhetorical units linked by: (a) explicit connecting phrases such as conjunctions, comparatives, demonstratives, enumeratives, and various linking phrases; (b) anaphoric links or any transition from the indefinite to the definite article; (c) intended parallel structures; (d) some connecting punctuation; and (e) narrative schemata.

In the third phase, the structure of each rhetorical unit was diagrammed as a series of subordinations and coordinations in which each T-unit was attached to one of the rightmost nodes of the developing tree. T-units were coordinated if they served the same function, were in some standard relationship to one another, concerned the same superordinate T-unit, or elaborated upon a multi-T-unit entity rather than a single T-unit. They were subordinated if one was an elaboration of the other.

In the fourth phase, rhetorical units were joined together into an integrated tree.

I

CHRONOLOGICAL LISTING OF PARTICIPANTS' NARRATIVES

Transcript excerpts from participants' protocols in the following tables include punctuation to make them more readable. Material in quotation marks is being read from text.

TABLE I.1
Jeff's Narratives

Session	Narrative	Transcript
5a	Father	Father knows best what's good for his children.
6a	Father	Father lets kid make great mistakes 'cause he thinks that it's good for the kid to go out and try this stuff and make these mistakes. He's basically thinking, "I remember when I was young and foolish. He just needs to work himself out of it."
6b	God	Maybe I just got what's involved in in a picture of a guy as the father the big father, big daddy. From God's point of view this is your best interest.
6c	Daughter	A daughter is *prima facie* incompetent.
6d	Socrates	I wonder if Socrates was a paternalist. I mean, certainly his ideal . . . . I mean, the official story, he must . . . that he didn't know anything about what was in his best interests.
7a	Father	Ah . . . Thinking about fathers and sons. Fathers know more about the world. They know more about expected benefits and payoffs and courses of actions. They were sons themselves. That's important. Well that covers . . . that's a unique experience category.

(Continued)

TABLE I.1
(Continued)

Session	Narrative	Transcript
7b	Phil faculty	Teachers actually act paternalistically towards their pupils. Surely in philosophy departments they do. That is, the assumption is the faculty knows best what you should do, the problems you should worry about. They think they can tell better than you, student, what things to get wrapped up in and things to worry about, what things to read, what things to show confidence in, and that all has to do with your demonstrated lack of knowledge. If you're giving your consent to be trained by this person. Okay.
7c	Phil faculty	That's really philosophy faculty. That's the basis for their paternalistic attitude . . . is to make you an autonomous . . . make you, against your will almost, into an autonomous thinker.
7d	God	Maybe I ought to think about God too. That's why God gave us a free will.
7e	My father	Well, let's see. Let's think about fathers and sons. I guess my father wasn't too paternalistic a father. He kind of let me go.
7f	Beaver	Leave it to Beaver. Think about Beaver's dad. What does Beaver's dad think about Beaver's competence with regard to ah . . . knowing, deciding, ascertaining, whatever . . . what's in his . . . that is, Beaver's best interest. He think's Beaver's basically pretty much totally incompetent. In that regard, Beaver is. . . . Beaver goes out and does all those kind of silly shit. His father knows that. Some of the times, his father let's him go ahead and do it because he thinks that the consequences are minor enough that they won't . . . ah . . . cause any . . . ah . . . real damage to the Beav. But . . . ah . . . there will be some kind of important life lesson learned. So even though he knows that Beaver's about to do something in his own best interest . . . ah . . . against his own interest long-term interest. Let's see long-term long-term interest is going to be another problem . . . ah. Well, anyway, even though he knows what Beav's about to do, it's going to be against his best interest, he let's the Beav go ahead and do it. He coun . . . but he thinks conceptualizes it this way. He's allowing the Beaver to do it, take this blind path, walk down this wrong road because he's going to learn something. So the experience itself will be in his own best interest. So that's acting paternalistically. He's really refraining from doing something. He's refraining from warning off . . . the Beav . . . warning the Beav off some . . . ah . . . course of action. And the purpose . . . his explicit reasoning is that allowing the Beav to do this . . . to sell Christmas cards or whatever it is. To . . . collect bottles and all that kind of stuff will teach him some important lesson . . . about life. So you can not just interfere with someone's liberty or anything like that, but you can allow them to do things. You can refrain from warning them about things . . . refrain from giving them full knowledge of the situation . . . all based on your somehow implicit

(Continued)

TABLE I.1

(Continued)

Session	Narrative	Transcript
		right, claim to the right to interpret that person's best interest. You see and pretty soon Beav will grow up and take that claim to excel . . . He'll earn the right to be the best judge, the *prima facie* best judge, or the privileged judge of his own best interest.
7g	Rutherford	And usually with adults interacting with adults. . . . ah. Well, what's the difference when Beaver's dad thinks that um . . . that Mr. Rutherford guy is about to do something really stupid and let's him do it anyway. He's not really acting paternalistically because ah . . . he's not um . . . Or is he? . . . He's claiming a right. He sees himself as a better judge of Rutherford's interest than Rutherford does. But it doesn't matter to him.
7h	J. R.	Even, you know, J. R. Ewing knows what's in Cliff Barnes' best interest and allows him to walk down the garden path, tricks him. With [the] difference that he's not concerned with and pursues the best interest.
7i	Beaver	Fathers let their kids. . . . Beaver goes out and gets into wild scheme where he sells Christmas card. Where he consciously thinks, let the Beaver do this because he's, I don't know, growing up or something.
7j	Rutherford	Well, Ward knows. . . . Ward Beaver knows everything about people's best interests and he watches these other guys, his pals, at work. . . .
8a	Doctor	Doctors only have a short-term. . . . All those cases where doctors were interfering it was al . . . it was always to prevent some immediate harm. There's always some kind of relatively short-term goal. I mean, they really aren't concerned with what the person does after getting out. Patch him back together. That's the short-term benefit.

TABLE I.2

Roger's Narratives

Session	Narrative	Transcript
3a	Race	A withdraws from competition so that B will win. B wants A to stay in the competition.
3b	Race	Suppose A and B are competing for a prize. It's a foregone conclusion that A is going to win. A likes B. Decides to withdraw from the competition so that B will win. B, however, is offended and does not want A to withdraw. A withdraws.

(Continued)

TABLE I.2
(Continued)

Session	Narrative	Transcript
4a	Race	You recall the case of the two competitors, A and B where B doesn't want A to withdraw but A does want to withdraw for B's good. And now, at least on the face of it, it just isn't up to B to
6a	Race	A case where A and B are entered in a contest and A is withdrawing — the case I mentioned before — A withdraws so that B can win against B's will. Is that paternalism or not? I'm inclined to say no that it is not normally up to B whether A does or does not withdraw. Who is he to say?
6b	Lottery	A case where A enter B's name in a contest or buys him a lottery ticket or something in B's good against B's will. But these are cases where it would — it normally is up to B whether his name is entered into a contest or not.
6c	Lying	A crosses B's will by lying to B for B's own good. A crossing of wills occurs in that. We presume that B's desire is that he not be lied to. Suppose that's true. Now, the object with respect to which will is crossed is whether or not B is to be lied to. And that's something that's normally legitimately within B's control.
6d	Withholding Information	Suppose that the case is simple withholding for a condition, not lying. Just stalling against the will of B. Is that normally legitimately within B's control?
6e	Cornflakes	Nobody thinks it's necessary to provide justification — an account of when it is justified to have cornflakes for breakfast, excuse me, or cornflakes rather than Cheerios.
6f	Refusal	If you cross B's will but not for B's good, this does not suffice to show that something has to be justified. Suppose A and B are competing. A is a sure thing to win. B desires A to withdraw. A does not withdraw. B desires that A withdraw solely for B's good. A declines and crosses B's will but for A's good. Nobody supposes that A has to justify this.
9a	Race	Peter and Paul Jones are avid swimmers. A race is to be held at their junior high. Peter, the faster of the two, finds out that Paul has entered. Having won several previous races in which Paul was entered, Peter, not wishing to demoralize Paul any further, does not enter the race in the correct belief that this virtually ensures Paul's victory and that were Paul to know of his action, he would oppose it.
9b	Race	Suppose in Situation 3 that Peter tells Paul in advance that he will not compete.
9c	Lying	Any case where a patient is just lied to for his own good is a counter example to D1'.
9d	Race	Situation 3, Peter & Paul, should make that clear.
9e	Doctor	A doctor delays telling a patient the bad news for a few moments until he calms down and is able to handle it

TABLE I.3

Janet's Narratives

Session	Narrative	Transcript
2a	Small Child	"A small child cannot be said to be acting paternalistically toward his parents even when he satisfies all other conditions." Someone younger reading this thing would have different opinions.
3a	Drunk Parent	"It is plausible to hold that a child can act paternalistically to help a drunk parent without believing that he is generally qualified to act on behalf of the parent." Okay. So Childress says that a person CAN act paternalistically without believing that he is qualified. Example: young child, drunk parent.
5a	Drunk Parent	Can that young child help the drunk parent and act paternalistically? I don't see how that relates 'cause paternalistically is when you help somebody and they don't want you to help. A young child couldn't help a drunk parent unless the drunk parent let him.
5b	Drunk Parent	I don't think a that a child could do anything for a parent without the parent's consent. If child were to get help then he would be qualified to do so. Anyone who is qualified to dial a phone number is qualified to call for help.
5c	Helping	Someone is out to hurt someone you care for. You will stop that person from doing so if it's for the good of the other person. Oh. Um. React and you believe he'll want your consent.
5d	Blood Trans	If the doctor decides to give blood, he's acting paternalistically 'cause he's seeing a person, taking action that the patient . . .
5e	Blood trans	Giving blood to Mr. N when Mr. N said not to before is paternalistic because the doctor is doing what he believes is right against the will of the patient.
5f	Withholding	There's withholding of bad information
5g	Deception	There's also deception.
5h	Fluoride	I mean fluoride in water
5i	Commitment	Mr. K put into hospital for almost jumping off roof is a paternalistic act that takes away freedom.
5j	Pills 1	Husband removing pills from house so wife does not take them
5k	Son	Mother breaking son's arm so he would not go into the marines
5l	Accident	If you are at the scene of an accident and you don't help by being a witness, you are being immoral because um. . . . Well, not really . . . are you? I mean what's the definition of immoral? Are you being immoral by not acting? Um, well, in this case, it's the law. In other cases it's up to the person what action he or she thinks is the most moral.
5m	White Lies	Suppose I'm saying that if you tell a clack . . white lie that you're really not becoming immoral, are you? 'Cause I thought white lies . . . I thought white lies were like that?

(Continued)

300

TABLE I.3
(Continued)

Session	Narrative	Transcript
5n	Denial	On page 13 Dr. T talks to patient so she would be emotionally relieved later on. Although many people may think that he did wrong, it doesn't matter. It all depends on what the helper thought.
6	Small child	Says young child cannot act paternalistically towards parents 'cause he will probably know that he does not know better. This is not always the case. Might be a smart kid.
9a	Older child	People naturally want to interfere with other people and try to help them as a child. That's why, for example, a three-year-old child tries to help a one-year-old.
9b	Denial	Although it might not have helped her, it was a paternalistic act because the doctor thought he was helping her at the time.
11a	Vegetables	All paternalistic acts don't deceive or cheat. Forcing a child to eat vegetables
11b	Son	"Mother breaking son's arm so he will not go into the Marines." That's a little extreme.
11c	Pills 1	Throwing away somebody's pills. I can use that example. I like this one.
11d	Knock out	Knocking someone out before he robs
11e	Withholding	Withholding bad information
11f	Deception	Deception
11g	Pills 1	If a husband were to hide pills from an upset wife who threatened to take an overdose, he would be acting paternalistically toward her. He is taking the authority to interfere in order to prevent her from harming herself. He considers himself to be in a more rational state that she and therefore feels qualified to act.
12a	Pills 2	If a wife were to hide pills from an upset husband who threatened to take an overdose, she would be acting paternalistically toward him. She is taking authority to interfere in order to prevent him from harming himself. She considers herself to be in a more rational state than he and therefore feels qualified to act. When the wife mentioned previously hides her husband's pills, she is not acting completely morally because she is infringing on her husband's personal rights in depriving him of his opportunity to take the pills.
13a	Skiing	As a young girl, my father used to force me to try to improve my skiing ability so that I could be a good skier for the rest of my life. Although he was forcing me to practice against my will, he also hoped that he was giving me an invaluable experience that I would appreciate later in my life.
13b	Meal plan	Requiring a freshman to go on the fifteen or nineteen meal contract is a silly example.

(Continued)

TABLE I.3

(Continued)

Session	Narrative	Transcript
13c	Drunk Friend	A concerned friend might prevent a drunk person from driving home after a party. The paternalist in this case is the sober friend who takes responsibility to interfere with his friend's actions in order to prevent him from harm. He does this without the drunk person's permission but assumes that he will appreciate the interference at a later time.
15a	DWI	I like that example. Drunk driving. 'Cause that affects you. I mean it also affects the other person. So when I say making drunk driving an offense, is that paternalism? I'm not really sure. Well, my examples don't have to be perfect.
19a	Drunk Friend	Example: known rules among friends to take car keys away when drunk.
30a	Skiing	A father may force a daughter to practice skiing so that she could become good at it. Although he forces her to do something against her will, he hopes that she will appreciate the learned skill throughout her life.
30b	DWI	The law forbidding drunk driving to prevent drunkards from injuring themselves on the road as well as injuring others who they might happen to hit. This law is enforced for all drivers and therefore makes every person a second and third party at the same time. All drivers are restricted when they drink but are also protected when others drink and may not drive.
30c	Licensing	A doctor who is required to practice medicine only with a medical licence is protected from the law. The patients are also protected from people who claim they are doctors but aren't.
30d	Org crime	Laws prohibiting organized crime protect the general public from being harassed by criminals. The lawmakers are the paternalists. The criminals are the groups whose freedom is being restricted and the general public is the one who is being helped.
32a	Dorms	Many universities require noncommuting freshmen to live on campus so that they adjust well to college life.

TABLE I.4

Leslie's Narratives

Session	Narrative	Transcript
1a	Unknown J Wit	The guy's probably not going to save his life. "Mister N, a member of a religious sect that does not believe in blood transfusions, is involved in a serious automobile accident and loses a large amount of blood. On arriving at the hospital, he is unconscious and no one is aware of his religious beliefs. The doctor believes that if Mister N is not given a transfusion he will die. Thereupon, Mister N is

(Continued)

TABLE I.4
(Continued)

Session	Narrative	Transcript
		still unconscious. While Mister N was still unconscious, the doctor arranges and carries out the blood transfusion." Well, that's alright if you didn't know about his religious beliefs. But knowing b . . . still gave blood transfusion. . . . He first job is to save his life . . . hmmm. . . . I don't know if he's right to give blood.
1b	Dead J Wit	"Mister N, a member of a religious . . . Wait. "Case two b, nonexample of paternalism." On the second one here, "Mister N, a member of a religious sect that does not believe in blood transfusions, is involved in a serious automobile accident and loses a large amount of blood. On arriving at the hospital, he is still conscious and informs the doctor that he would rather die than undergo the blood transfusion." Shouldn't give him the blood transfusion at all. "Immediately thereafter he faints from loss of blood. The doctor believes that if Mister N is not given a transfusion, he will die. After agonizing about what to do, the doctor finally calls in a leader from Mister N's religious sect to administer final rites to Mister N before he dies." Well actually, that was about right.
1c	Christian Scientist	"Requiring a Christian Scientist to receive a blood transfusion." Hmm . . . I don't know. 'Cause if he says . . . if he signs a paper saying that he doesn't want to, then I don't think it should be done 'cause it's against what he wanted for himself. And, then again, it's hard on the family because they don't want to lose him or anything. But, anyhow, it's harder for their kids.
1d	Known J Wit	"On arriving at the hospital, he is still unconscious." Wait. "is still conscious and informs the doctor of his views on blood transfusion." Um. Did he write it down or anything?
1e	Interfered Grandfather	I think if a patient says. . . . Like sometimes when they have . . . um . . . patients who don't want to be on respirators and stuff like that, and you. . . . Some. . . . Like the family doesn't want them to be on. I mean, they wanta to have them alive as long as possible. But when my grandfather was in the hospital, he said. . . . Before. . . . When he got. . . . Before he got into the ambulance, he signed a paper that he wanted to be on a respirator, and still. . . . I mean, I guess it was my family and doctor decided to have him on one because we sorta decided that we wanted to know whether or not he, you know. . . . He could still. . . . It was. . . . They didn't know if he was brain dead or not, and we wanted to know for sure if he was or wasn't . And I . . . I. . . . Well I think people should know the truth about their own . . . , what's wrong with them. I think it's better all around that they know. But, I mean, if people request that they, that they just don't want to know, I think it's up to them because it's their own decisions. Okay.

(Continued)

TABLE I.4

(Continued)

Session	Narrative	Transcript
2a	Dead J Wit w/ Family	I'm not a doctor or anything. I . . . I really. . . . Sometimes I don't think that doctors should be able to . . . to decide either. . . . I think it's really up to the person . . . and if they say. . . . If a person decides what they want . . . like the guy with the blood transfusion. . . . If you say you didn't want it . . . he shouldn't be given it . . . because that only creates more problems for him and his family . . . and I don't think. . . . I think they should follow the orders of a person . . . who's um . . . I mean who is in need of medical help or whatever.
2b	Changed Mind	Sometimes . . . its like . . . you think well . . . maybe they had second thoughts . . . you know . . . and then sometimes you don't know if a person did have second thoughts . . . 'cause they might have died or something . . . and ah . . . I think that . . . well. . . . There was one place where it said. . . . There was one part in here it said that the guys . . . he told them not to do something to him and . . . that . . . if he changed his mind . . . they'd listen to him. . . . Boy that would have aggravated me. I would have been . . . "Wait. I really don't want you to do this to me." I mean . . . I just thought that was aggravating . . . because . . . he said . . . "Whatever I say . . . don't reverse my decision that I made."
3a	My Kid	If I ever get married and have kids. . . . If I. . . . I'd probably say, "Yeah." . . . I mean if something happened to them where they were ill . . . or something . . . happened to ah . . . I mean . . . what would I say if something happened to my mother or father . . . and. . . . But I'm not the oldest . . . and their parents . . . my father's parent . . . my . . . his mother would be too old to decide. . . . If what would happen. . . . If something happened . . . my mother . . . well my grandmother would probably have a nervous breakdown . . . because my grandfather just died . . . so . . . she wouldn't know what to do. . . . And my dad couldn't decide for my mother . . . because . . . I don't think they can stand each other . . . so. . . . It would just be terrible.
4a	Alive J Wit	If somebody gives specific orders . . . specific orders . . . like the lady on the. . . . What the heck it called . . . yeah. . . . She wanted . . . um . . . She didn't want blood transfusions . . . because of the religion she was in . . . and . . . she let the doctor know that before she fainted . . . and he still went ahead and did it . . . and. . . . I mean . . . now I wonder if the girl is happy that she was alive . . . or if . . . if she . . . you know. . . . I . . . they don't . . . they don't . . . I don't think they ever . . . they didn't ever say . . . how she felt about it . . . that he gave her the transfusion. . . . They just said . . . well he gave her the transfusion . . . and she's alive. . . . But I wonder how the . . . how the girl felt.

(Continued)

TABLE I.4

(Continued)

Session	Narrative	Transcript
5a	? Competent Person	If a person gives specific orders of what they want to be done . . . if they don't follow those . . . I don't think that's right . . . because . . . the person who gives it . . . well. . . . See they may talk about well if they weren't competent to make the decision . . . and . . . like why didn't you find that out before . . . you do it . . . you know. . . . You go ahead and do something against their wishes . . . [hmm-hmm] . . . You should find out whether or not they were competent before. . . . And then I wonder how they're going to find that out . . . you know . . . Who is supposed to decide whether somebody is competent or not . . . They just . . . they just . . . they just say about being competent is whether or not you're . . . um . . . um. . . . I don't know. . . . If you understood the situation . . . before. . . . Sometimes . . . they say if you have . . . a . . . you know . . . inability to understand something . . . so those people are incompetent. . . . But other . . . otherwise . . . not even sometimes they say somebody is incompetent and they had . . . inabil. . . . Maybe just at the time . . . they didn't have. . . . Wait. . . . They had the ability to understand . . . but they've just decided to do something else . . . and decided to do something else . . . for some reason unknown.
5b	Competent J Wit	The person that was . . . um . . . had the blood transfusion . . . I didn't see anything . . . or they didn't show anything in them . . . that showed that they were incompetent at the time . . . and they didn't know what was going on . . . or anything. . . . And I'm sure the person knew that if they weren't going to get the blood transfusion . . . they were going to die. . . . And . . . I think that the decision that they made . . . should have . . . should have been enforced . . . because it was their decision . . . and they were competent. . . . And I don't see how they justify . . . giving them a blood transfusion.
5c	Competent J Wit	The transfusion patient . . . his decision meant . . . if he didn't have a blood transfusion . . . he was going to die. . . . And . . . I feel that he understood that . . . because. . . . I don't remember . . . quite . . . you know exactly if the doctor said . . . "Well you're going to die if you don't get that." . . . But . . . I'm sure the person understood . . . you know . . . I can't have any blood transfusions. . . . And . . . you know . . . maybe he knew the possibility . . . that it was possible that he would die without it.

(Continued)

TABLE I.4
(Continued)

Session	Narrative	Transcript
6a	Known J Wit	I think that was wrong of the doctor. . . . I know he's there to save lives . . . and stuff . . . but I mean . . . the person of a religious sect . . . if they didn't want that blood transfusion. . . . If they are religious . . . If their religious . . . If their religion meant that much to them . . . they're willing to die for it . . . then . . . that was up to them. . . . I think it was . . . it was their . . . you know. . . . Whatever they wanted to do . . . that was . . . If they didn't want that blood transfusion . . . they should have never been given it. . . . I mean . . . it would have been . . . if they would have realized after they're dead. . . . I don't know what happens after you're dead. . . . But . . . they might have realized . . . that . . . "Well I would have rather have been alive" . . . but that would have been your own fault . . . 'cause you would have said . . . you know . . . "I don't want that blood transfusion . . . because I'm really into my religion here." . . . I just . . . I mean . . . I don't think the doctor should have gave it to them . . . 'cause . . . they . . . that was their wishes.
6b	Brain Dead Person	I think that's wrong is when . . . people that have um . . . heart attacks or something like that . . . or they have a stroke . . . and . . . there's cases where they go brain dead . . . and they have signed a paper . . . they . . . saying they don't want any . . . um . . . life-sustaining . . . ah . . . machines on them . . . and they do that. . . . I think . . . I think that's wrong because . . . to some people . . . they find that degrading . . . or . . . it's . . . it sorta of takes. . . . And I don't know. . . . They just don't want to be in that state. . . . I think that's wrong 'cause . . . if a person . . . has signed a sheet before . . . and the doctor knows this . . . I don't think he should go against the person's wishes.
6c	Informed Grandfather	My grandfather . . . he was a . . . doctor. . . . He . . . He knew that . . . He knew what happens to you and stuff. . . . And he knew he didn't want to be on life-sustaining things. . . . And the doctor still put him on it. . . . But . . . I mean . . . I realize . . . that my family . . . or my grand . . . my grandmother and my . . . my mother and her sisters . . . they all . . . they all wanted to know if he was . . . if he was really brain dead. . . . If they were positive that he couldn't be . . . um . . . you know . . . he couldn't understand anything or enjoy life anymore. . . . They really wanted to know . . . for sure. . . . But . . . in a way I think that was wrong. . . . And I realize they don't want to live him and everything. . . . But I think it was wrong . . . 'cause . . . my grandfather didn't want that . . . and they went against it. . . . And . . . to me . . . they sort of . . . degraded him . . . by putting him on those. . . . And I don't . . . I don't think it was right.

(Continued)

306

TABLE I.4

(Continued)

Session	Narrative	Transcript
7a	? Competent Grandfather	It really makes me mad . . . no not mad . . . furious . . . makes me . . . really makes me furious . . . is to think . . . that the doctor went . . . went against my grandfather's . . . grandfather's wishes. . . . I really think it makes me furious. . . . No. . . . No . . . I know I really think . . . it really . . . Leave that there. . . . It really makes me furious to think that . . . to know . . . that the doctor went against my grandfather's wishes . . . when he was totally competent of deciding . . . when he was totally competent. . . . He was a doctor . . . doctor . . . and knew what the cause and what . . . He knew what would happen to his body . . . body . . . if he. . . . Wait. . . . Compe . . . He was totally competent in deciding. . . . Wait. . . . He was totally in deciding . . . He was totally competent of deciding . . . He was a . . . He was a doctor . . . and knew what would happen to his body if he had. . . . Wait. . . . He had a stroke. . . . He had a stroke and . . . and . . . Okay wait. . . . He had a stroke and . . . I don't remember. . . . But I don't think he was very much affected. . . . I think it . . . one side of his body was paralyzed. . . . But I can't remember. . . . I was too immature at the time. . . . It doesn't really matter. . . . I mean it does . . . but it doesn't now. . . . Okay. . . . He was a doctor and knew what . . . knew what would happen to his body if he had . . . if he had another . . . another stroke . . . another stroke. Or he . . . he . . . Wait. . . . He knew what would happen if . . . Okay. . . . Shit. . . . He knew what was going to happen to . . . He knew the process and . . . He didn't know the process . . . but he knew what went on . . . what the effects were . . . of a stroke . . . how it worked . . . how the blood clots happened . . . and things like that. . . . He knew that . . . he understood it . . . and . . . I think he was totally . . . he was competent. . . . He said he didn't want any life-sustaining. . . . Okay. . . . Yeah. . . . Okay. . . . He was competent. . . . Okay. . . . I said that already. . . . He knew . . . He knew that . . . He knew that . . . Okay. . . . When he was totally competent . . . of deciding . . . he was a doctor and he knew what would happen to his body . . . and he knew . . . the process . . . process . . . not process . . . but effects. . . . What the hell did I say? . . . He knew the process . . . He knew the effect . . . effects a stroke could have on him. . . . He signed a paper saying he did not want to be on any life-sustaining machines . . . machines . . . machines. . . . I never thought of this . . . thought. . . . But what if . . . what if at the time he signed it . . . it . . . in the ambulance . . . at his house . . . at his house . . . he was not competent? . . . But I really . . . I do think . . . think he was competent. . . . Ah . . . Signed a paper saying he did not want to . . . want to have . . . be on any life-sustaining machine. . . . I never thought. . . . But . . . what at . . . what if at the time . . . he signed it . . . the ambulance at his house he was not incompe . . . he was not competent? . . . But I really think he was

(Continued)

TABLE I.4

(Continued)

Session	Narrative	Transcript
		competent. . . . I mean . . . he knew. . . . He knew he had high blood pressure . . . pressure . . . and he knew the effects it could have. . . . He knew the effects it could have. . . . I . . . I feel . . . Wait. . . . I think . . . I think my grandfather . . . grandfather . . . grandpa . . . my grandpa thought about this situation.
7b	Considerate Grandfather	I think my grandpa thought about this situation . . . before it happened. . . . And he only wanted to prevent . . . prevent having . . . my family . . . his family . . . his family to decide on whether to keep him on life . . . him on . . . wait . . . keep him on . . . keep him on life-sustaining . . . sustaining . . . sustain . . . life-sustaining machines. . . . Wait. . . . Okay. . . . Family whether to keep him on life-sustaining machines . . . after . . . after he possibly . . . he possibly went . . . went . . . w . . . e . . . n . . . t . . . went . . . after he possibly was brain dead. . . . He thought it was possible. . . . He thought of this possibility. . . . He thought of this possibility . . . t . . . Okay. . . . Okay he was brain dead. . . . I . . . It's really . . . a really hard . . . confusing . . . stressful. . . . It's really hard . . . confusing . . . stressful. . . . It's just a hell of a situation . . . hell of a situation . . . to be in . . . I realize. . . . His family . . . or my grandmother . . . aunts . . . and my mom . . . my grandmother . . . my grandma . . . I don't call her grandmother. . . . Wait. . . . Situation to be in. . . . I realize my grandmother . . . aunts and . . . my grandmother . . . aunts . . . and mother wanted . . . wanted to know . . . whether he could live . . . could live a life any more because they didn't . . . they didn't want to face losing him. . . . Also I think they had to know to have peace within themselves . . . to know they did everything possible to prevent his death.
7c	Angry Grandfather	I really want to know how . . . sorta. . . . I sort of really want to know how they justified . . . the doctor not following my grandfather's instructions. . . . And I . . . And reading this . . . it really didn't . . . it made me think about it more clearly but. . . . Well it didn't make me think about it more clearly. . . . It made me think about it more . . . and what . . . and what I think really should of been done . . . and . . . in this case. . . . But . . . I don't know. . . . It's really hard to . . . think . . . about . . . I don't know . . . like losing somebody. . . . And I real . . . I . . . I think I . . . I mean I think of . . . Well I think that . . . my grandfather he want . . . he didn't want to be on any life-sustaining things. . . . But . . . still at the time . . . I realize that . . . I realize that my family . . . my mom . . . my grandmother . . . didn't want him to die. . . . But . . . I . . . I know that . . . they prob . . . I know . . . I know these people believe me. . . . I know these women. . . . They would not have rested . . . knowing that . . . um . . . they didn't do everything to save him. . . . So I think it . . . I don't know . . . it's really hard when . . . I don't . . . It's really hard to explain. . . . It's

(Continued)

TABLE I.4
(Continued)

Session	Narrative	Transcript
		really hard for me to decide what was right about them trying . . . I mean. . . . I think if I had been in this situation . . . I would of tried everything to try and keep him alive. . . . Or to keep anybody . . . that would . . . you know like family member alive. . . . See but . . . I mean they thought about it . . . and . . . they thought about it a lot. . . . And they said well . . . he didn't want to be on these things. . . . And . . . don't you think he'd be upset with us? . . . Or he would . . . he'd be . . . you know he'd be mad about it if he knew that we did this.
8a	Me Brain Dead	If I was in an automobile accident and signed . . . no . . . and was somehow . . . was somehow . . . Okay. . . . If I went brain dead . . . I would want my . . . well I wouldn't want my parents to decide.
8b	Your Kid	How do you decide if you want your kid . . . See but . . . brain dead supposed to be where . . . all that's alive with your body. . . . You can't speak or talk . . . or you can't feel anything . . . so that . . . how do they know that you can't? . . . I mean . . . I know they can do all those tests and stuff. . . . But . . . how can they . . . I mean . . . They say that . . . he's brain dead . . . and um . . . he's . . . all that's there is his body. . . . And he can never be the same. . . . And he's just . . . you know . . . all it is . . . is his body. . . . But . . . I don't understand . . . how they can um . . . how can you expect somebody's parents to decide . . . if they want to take you off a respirator. . . . You can't do that . . . can you? . . . I don't think they can take you off a respirator . . . 'cause that's um . . . supposedly murder . . . I think. . . . But I'm not sure. . . . um . . . um . . . I don't . . . I mean it's probably really hard . . . if parents have to decide whether or not to take their . . . I don't think you can decide . . . whether or not to take somebody off the respirator . . . or . . . life-supporting . . . quote . . . unquote . . . life-supporting . . . system. . . . I don't think they can . . . 'cause that's supposedly murder.
8c	Me Brain Dead	If this was me . . . and I was brain dead . . . But . . . Let me think. . . . Well I know I'd better be brain dead . . . before . . . I don't know.
8d	His Kid	Can you really expect a parent to decide whether . . . I think . . . Well some parents probably could. . . . But . . . how can a parent decide whether or not . . . he's not killing his child? . . . But . . . sort of . . . suffering . . . sort of what their doing . . . 'cause . . . sort of in um . . . in limbo.
8e	Me Competent	I myself . . . feel that I'd be competent to decide . . . on about anything. . . . Then again . . . I'm pretty indecisive about things. . . . um . . . I feel that I could decide when something would happen to me. . . . I mean . . . Okay. . . . Let's see. . . . I'm nineteen. . . . When . . . I'm probably . . . I mean . . . I'd probably . . . Even

(Continued)

TABLE I.4
(Continued)

Session	Narrative	Transcript
		though I'm not no nineteen . . . I would . . . you know . . . minor . . . not a minor . . . I'd probably ask . . . ask my mother . . . you know. . . . I'd probably ask my mom . . . you know . . . of what she thought. . . . And she . . . I mean . . . I think it would be best to get . . . more than one doctor's opinion. . . . I think that it would be best to . . . ask you family for opinions . . . and see.
8f	They	In cases where you have time to decide . . . on what's going to happen to you . . . I think that um . . . they should be able . . . they should be told everything. . . . Like they shouldn't be kept from you. . . . And if it's something bad that they'd have to explain . . . they should know how to do it . . . you know . . . in not too bad of um . . . you know. . . . That seems to me like using on the patient. . . . But I think that the patient should be able to just . . . to decide for themselves . . . what's going to happen to them. . . . And . . . I think they should get . . . you know . . . like another doctor's opinion . . . and possibly ask for your spouse . . . or . . . a good friend for their opinion. . . . And I . . . If you really can't decide . . . you can't make a decision . . . then ask a doctor what he thinks. . . . But I don't think the doctor should say. . . . I really think you should do this. . . . I think you should . . . say. . . . You know what he thinks what would be the best solution . . . um . . . and I think that once you've made your decision . . . you shouldn't go back on it. . . . You should of made some type of a decision . . . like.
8g	Resigned J Wit	They said she could of died from it. . . . But . . . you shouldn't die. . . . You should of wound up with some other kind of side effect. . . . I think that um . . . you know . . . she should of been . . . she should of been responsible enough to . . . accept that that was her decision . . . and her religion meant that much to her. . . . But then . . . maybe again . . . she might of . . . just said . . . Well I mean . . . That's what whoever her God . . . to whoever . . . I mean . . . She might just say . . . "Well that's what he wanted from me." . . . And she might accept that.
8h	Angry J Wit	Another person . . . might get mad about it . . . 'cause . . . if they're having some kind of . . . defect or something was wrong with him after they didn't get the blood transfusion . . . and they were still alive . . . possibly. . . . I don't know how that would work. . . . But if they were still alive . . . I don't think . . . Answer the phone. . . . But I think that um . . . people should be responsible enough to . . . be able to decide for themselves . . . and to accept their decisions that they have made. . . . I mean . . . if people aren't responsible enough . . .

(Continued)

TABLE I.4

(Continued)

Session	Narrative	Transcript
8i	Competent Grandfather	He knew he had high blood pressure . . . so I'm sure he thought of it . . . [hmm-hmm] . . . He knew he didn't want to be in that situation. . . . And I just don't understand . . . how they can . . . Well . . . I don't know. . . . My . . . I mean . . . I mean . . . I think that he was competent. . . . And I mean . . . I'm sure he thought of it. . . . Because . . . I mean . . . 'cause he was a doctor . . . he knew what was going to happen to him . . . and what could possibly happen . . . and what . . . would be the effects of a stroke or . . . or if he was brain dead or something . . . like that. . . . I mean he was brain dead . . . but . . . I mean . . . he . . . he didn't want to be in that position. . . . And they put him there. . . . And I don't think that was right . . . [hmm-hmm] . . . 'cause he didn't want to be like that.
10a	Dead Person	Example of paternalism . . . Person who did [] . . . Person who did not act p . . . a . . . t . . . n . . . l . . . paternalistically . . . in his or her decision . . . decision. . . . Instead . . . instead . . . of giving . . . Instead of giving the person . . . the blood transfusion . . . the doctor . . . But the doctor . . . that would have . . . have saved the man's . . . the person's life . . . Okay. . . . Okay. . . . Instead of giving the person . . . the blood transfusion that would have saved his life . . . the doctor didn't . . . the doctor didn't . . . he . . . Wait. . . . The doctor did not . . . and the result was the person's death . . . death . . . death . . . death. . . . And the result was the person's death. . . . Okay.
11a	Alive J Wit	"An example given by Childress is the blood transfusion administered to a member of a religious sect. . . . Before the patient was administered the transfusion . . . he informed the doctor . . . that his religious . . . his religion forbid this action." . . . This type of action . . . This action . . . This action . . . "The doctor performed this act in order to save the man's life. . . . therefore . . . acting paternalistically." . . . Therefore . . . comma . . . his action was paternalistic. . . . His action was . . . was . . . his action was carried out . . . out . . . to save. . . . His action was carried out. . . . "The doctor performed this act in order to save the man's life." . . . The . . . Therefore . . . his action was carried . . . was . . . his action was . . . pater . . . paternalistic. . . . "Therefore his action was paternalistic."
11b	Regretful J Wit	When they gave that guy from a religious sect a blood transfusion . . . I didn't agree with that. . . . Because . . . I mean . . . if the guy . . . if it really didn't mean that much I mean . . . you might as well let him keep it. . . . [hmm-hmm . . . hmm-hmm] . . . I mean . . . let him find out what. . . . Well I don't know what happens after you die but . . . let him find out . . . you know. . . . "Well that was a mistake. . . . I shouldn't have been so into my religion."

(Continued)

TABLE I.4

(Continued)

Session	Narrative	Transcript
13a	Alive J Wit	"The doctor performed this act in order to save the man's life . . . therefore . . . his action was paternalistic." . . . He saved the man's life . . . and when doing so . . . wait . . . comma . . . and by doing this . . . this . . . he also disregarded the patient's . . . patient's . . . the patient's . . . the patient's . . . the patient's . . . um . . . same feature that's . . . the patient's wishes. . . . "Therefore his action was paternalistic."
18a	Grandfather	When my grandfather had a stroke . . . he . . . I mean . . . He's a doctor. . . . [hmm-hmm] . . . He was a podia. . . . He was a podiatrist. . . . But he knew. . . . He knew . . . like what happened to his body when he had a stroke . . . and everything like that. . . . And . . . I don't see any place where he was incompetent . . . of judging for himself. . . . But he didn't want to be on any life support systems. . . . [hmm-hmm] . . . And when he signed the paper in the ambulance . . . they didn't go by it . . . after he was in the hospital. . . . And I say it was mostly 'cause my mother and . . . her sis . . . and my grandmother on the other side . . . and my grandmother. . . . They . . . I mean . . . they didn't want to let go because . . . they were afraid. . . . Well what if he . . . well he . . . were brain dead . . . and was on life support system? . . . They . . . they wanted to know for sure . . . if he was . . . if he really couldn't understand . . . and if he wouldn't be able to live . . . you know . . . like . . . a so-called normal life. . . . And they wanted to know for sure and I guess they would have felt guilty if . . . if they wouldn't have done everything they . . . they could possibly do. . . . But I think in a way . . . it sorta . . . degraded him [hmm-hmm] because he was put on that life support system . . . and he didn't want to be. . . . Because maybe . . . he . . . he saw that . . . as a sign of . . . maybe not weakness . . . but . . . well . . . well . . . yeah . . . maybe weakness. . . . But . . . maybe he didn't want . . . you know . . . his family to see him like that [hmm-hmm]. . . . And I don't . . . And I don't think that that was right at all . . . 'cause I think he knew what he was doing.
24a	Family Member	Its sort of sad . . . how it can be very serious . . . sometimes. . . . And how . . . in a way it can affect you. . . . And it can affect people in your family . . . and that are close to you. . . . And how doctors can . . . make decisions for somebody who's a member of your family when . . . you know . . . yourself . . . that they're making a decision that's wrong. . . . 'Cause . . . the family member that they're making the decision for . . . Wait. . . . This is getting confusing. . . . That they're making the decision for . . . isn't what . . . what they wanted. . . . And they're going against their wishes and you know it's wrong and that's paternalistic right there. . . . And it's affecting you. . . . And it's affecting the patient. . . . And . . . it shouldn't . . . it shouldn't be that way. . . . If the person had . . . already given . . . not like . . . well it's like

(Continued)

TABLE I.4
(Continued)

Session	Narrative	Transcript
		a prior consent . . . he'd already given a prior consent . . . [hmm-hmm] . . . and the doctor went against it . . . and . . . I mean. . . . I wrote . . . I wrote a note in there. . . . I mean I realize there's times when people just don't want to let go . . . of family members. . . . But . . . there just . . . there has to come a point when you just have to. . . . You want to try everything . . . that you know. . . . You want to try everything to save that person. . . . But in a way . . . you know that you're going against their wishes. . . . But . . . you don't feel right . . . [hmm-hmm] not doing anything about it . . . not trying to see if you can . . . you know . . . do anything. . . . So it . . . sort of . . . It sort of relieves your guilt. . . . You know what I mean? . . . It . . . It makes you guilty to think that you know well . . . somebody didn't want to be on a life-preserving system . . . and they are. . . . That makes you guilty. . . . And I think that . . . mean . . . you know that you're going against somebody's wishes. . . . So . . . when they're on that life support system . . . you say to yourself . . . "Well . . . now that they're there . . . and there is . . . they're at this point . . . and we've already gone against their wishes . . . why not try everything" . . . [hmm-hmm] . . . to see . . . you know . . . to try to . . . get rid of the guilt by going against their wishes in the first place.
25a	Comatose Patient	"Paternalism can be a very serious matter with very serious effects especially serious when it is applied in a situation of life or death or in a situation of a comatose patient. Many times patients who are seriously ill or who are suffering from brain damage are subject to having their prior consent disregarded. People don't realize that everyday a doctor and a patient's family make paternalistic decisions thereby affecting a patient in a way he or she did not want to be affected. These disregarding decisions might not be what the patient wanted but is usually what the family member feels if for the patient's own good. Many times disregarding prior decisions by patient's is done in order to prolong a patient's life. The condition in which the patients have to live is a minor factor. The family just wants them to breathe air. Communication is often lost. Paternalism is an important issue because of the serious effects it can have on you and members of your family. Paternalistic decisions are on a scale of life to death. Often people aren't give a chance to choose their fate."

J

RULES FOR AGGREGATING CONVERSATIONAL INTERCHANGES

DIVISION OF INITIATED INTERCHANGES

1. Circle all initiations (questions, invitations, etc.) in the transcript.
2. If initiations are repeated within the same speaker's turn as rephrasings of each other, then consolidate them as a single initiation. Note that a rephrased question has to be syntactically related to the first question.
3. Make a division prior to the initiation either:
   - Immediately before it, or
   - If the previous T-units were used by the same speaker to introduce the initiation, then right before these introductory T-units. Note that an introduction has to be more than material on the same topic; it has to explicitly refer forward to the initiation or be related to it syntactically.
   - If a general introduction precedes a specific question, divide following the introduction.
4. Make a division following the initiation and label as follows:
   - If the initiation does not receive a response from a second speaker, divide after the initiation when silence is noted in the transcript.
   - Once a question is on the floor, it requires a response from another speaker unless it is a real rhetorical question. If no response is forthcoming, divide after the question.
   - If a question has within it evidence that the speaker is not looking for a response then it should be treated as a rhetorical question and consolidated as part of that speaker's turn.

- If a response is given by a second speaker and then commented on either by the first speaker or by other speakers, then divide after these comments. In general, all comments by speakers on previous speakers' turns should be included in the interchange. A comment is related material, but has to be related to what comes immediately before it.

- If a question is answered with a question, break between the questions.

- If a response is given by the second speaker and not commented on by any other speakers, then divide after the response. Responses can take more than one T-unit.

- If a speaker shifts focus from one audience to another, break the interchange.

- A tag question can end a monologue

DIVISION OF CONTIGUOUS INTERCHANGES

Return to the beginning of the transcript and locate interchanges that begin following the ones you just marked. Mark where these interchanges end as follows:

1. Mark before the beginning of the next marked interchange if no speaker changes occurs in between.

2. If a speaker change does occur, mark before the speaker change unless the speaker's T-units are related. If they are related, mark after the speaker change. If you are in doubt about the material's relationship, make a break. Note that overheads cannot, by definition, comment on the preceding material.

DIVISION OF THE REMAINING UNMARKED MATERIAL

1. Return to the beginning of the transcript and locate all speaker changes in remaining unmarked material. Put a ∞ around them.

2. Look at the T-units before the speaker change. If they are unrelated to what is immediately before them, then divide the interchange before the speaker change. If they are related, divide before the related units. Material must be clearly related to be related.

3. Look at the T-units following the speaker change. If they are related, divide after them. If they are unrelated, divide before them.

K

CODING THE WORLD OF DISCOURSE

RHETORICAL PROCESS

Code as rhetorical process (RP) any T-unit that refers to the worlds in which people make claims as authors. This includes referring to: (a) the texts, or parts of texts, in which claims are made: "the book," "the introduction"; (b) the authors of claims, including the students and teacher as makers of claims: "Childress," "I," "you"; (c) nominals that characterize actions taken by authors as claim makers: "question begging"; (d) descriptions of the interactions among authors as claim makers: "discussions," "disagreements"; (e) the requirements or directions for the assignment: "a paper in two sections"; (f) general categories of claims that can be made by authors: "a definition," "a justification," "a reason," "a question"; and/or (g) any consideration or product relevant to the generation of claims: "my notes."

DOMAIN CONTENT

Code as domain content (DC) any T-unit that refers to the world of truths about paternalism. These truths have an eternal flavor to them: They are said to be true independent of any claim. This will include T-units referring to: (a) philosophical concepts related to paternalism: "paternalism," "respect for persons"; (b) terms for the standard components of paternalism taken in an abstract way: "agent," "actions," "features," "case"; (c) relationships between these concepts or components: "connection"; and/or (d) characteristics, either positive or negative, of these concepts or components: "principle."

NARRATED CASE

Code as narrated case (NC) any T-unit that refers to particular worlds in which (paternalistic) narratives take place that are taken to exist independently of domain concepts. These will include: (a) specific people or actions that are taken to exist independently of the concepts in the domain but that may potentially be characterized with respect to these concepts; (b) general categories of people or actions that are taken to exist independently of the concepts in the domain but that may potentially be characterized with respect to these concepts; (c) characteristics of specific or general people or actions that are taken to exist independently of the concepts in the domain but that may potentially be characterized with respect to these concepts; and/or (d) "you" or "I" when cast in a role involving an action that is taken to exist independently of the concepts in the domain but that may potentially be characterized with respect to these concepts.

L

WEEK-BY-WEEK ANALYSIS
OF THE CLASS

WEEK 1

Tuesday's class was unusually focused on domain content for this period of summarizing. The teacher planned to teach rhetorical process and students did learn rhetorical process, but the teacher actually began with domain content—the mismatches with the criteria from which he generated process heuristics. In class, he found the students could not understand heuristics, and he had more success with examples of definitions. His criteria appear to be the bridge between process and content.

WEEK 2

Tuesday's class was almost exclusively about rhetorical process. The teacher prepared for it by doing the task himself because the papers seemed off base.

One student interviewed, who was in class on Tuesday, changed his conception of definition from domain content to rhetorical process. One student, who was absent, thought too much focus was being put on paternalism content.

WEEK 3

Tuesday's class was almost entirely devoted to presenting heuristics for evaluating by hierarchy, which both students who were interviewed picked up.

The one student interviewed was becoming concerned about the grading of a heuristic process.

WEEK 4

In Thursday's class, the teacher planned to introduce the concept of metaknowledge and use sample papers to talk about what they knew and did not know. Thursday's class was mostly rhetorical process, but with some domain content. After class, the teacher felt he had hit a chord.

The one student interviewed did not complete the assignment for Tuesday for lack of motivation. He reported having trouble with this way of thinking and being concerned about a professor who says he does not know how to do the task either.

For Thursday's class, the teacher planned to just go in and react to students' questions. He had no plans because he was confused about metaknowledge. In class, their questions were so off base that he spent the period telling them what a good definition was and laying out the assumptions of the authors. This was the first time that he had intervened to tell them something specific about domain content.

WEEK 5

In Week 5, the teacher tried to give the students more structure and to level the differences between graduates and undergraduates by giving them a framework, the British analytic tradition, in which to understand all the definitions. He felt that the undergrads lacked a framework and therefore could not understand basic concepts whereas some of the grad students have alternative frameworks that keep them from really coming to terms with the issues in the readings. In Tuesday's class the teacher went over these alternative frameworks and explained the British analytic tradition.

For Thursday's class, the teacher planned to review the difference between rules and principles and go over the multidimensional scaling heuristic as a way of deciding among competing definitions. He definitely felt by this time that Childress had the best definition and that the students needed to accept it in order to go on to justification. By this time, the teacher had also changed his mind about some of the framework he gave them on Tuesday so he wanted to clarify that. He reported becoming concerned about the instability of the course, about the negative impact of his continual activity of knowledge making in the area, and felt the students might feel better if he did not change his mind about things. But he also felt that this was the only way he could teach them this stuff.

No students were interviewed during this week, but a student was interviewed the following Monday. She did not find the metaknowledge assignment hard to do and liked the teacher's focus on rhetorical process rather than domain content. Her paper showed her appreciating the teacher's focus on strategies, but concerned about issues in ethical content. Two other students' responses to the metaknowledge assignment showed one student, an undergraduate, reflecting about the impact of his lack of sincerity on his ability to know what he knows and does not know. The second student, a graduate student, wrote a narrative of her analysis of the authors' positions on the role of consent in a definition of paternalism. Both showed the growing impact of rhetorical process concerns.

WEEK 6

In Week 6, the students turned in the results of the multidimensional scaling heuristic and the class as a whole moved on to justification. The teacher distinguished between the interpersonal and social framework and declared, on Tuesday, that they would be using the interpersonal rather than social framework for the rest of the class.

There was no class on Thursday. The teacher used the time to meet with students individually and to look in the library for more material related to paternalism. He began to realize that assumption digging and situating depend on having a cultural framework and that his limiting things to interpersonal frameworks was wrong.

Both student interviewed this week found the heuristic routine but also revealing of some things they did not know. Tuesday's class itself was heavily case-bound because the teacher read through the controversial cases.

WEEK 7

In Week 7, the class moved full force into the issue of justification and the task of assumption digging. The teacher has moved from constructing heuristics for class use to constructing a framework for class interpretation. On Monday, he has come up with a framework, based loosely on Childress, that arranges the possible constraints placed on the paternalist in levels and predicts the amount of paternalism a person would sanction depending on the level of constraints he or she is concerned with. The teacher presented this metaperspective in class and used it to classify Dworkin "On Justifying." He felt that the students were much more interactive than they had ever been, perhaps as a result of last week's individual interviews.

For the assignment, students were asked to analyze Dworkin's line of argument and then predict how he would decide on each of the controversial cases. The teacher expected to use this same assignment repeatedly through justification. Student 6 reported that he read the cases, read Dworkin carefully several times, and then wrote a case-by-case analysis. He said if he would do it over again, he would also summarize the author's argument first. He said he was feeling good about what he was learning in the class although he was not yet sure where he stood on the issue. His actual writing showed that he had picked out several features of justification from Dworkin's argument (consent and rationality) and used these to judge the cases.

After Thursday's class, the teacher became a bit concerned that the controversial cases would not clearly distinguish among the authors. He was also concerned about possible incoherences in his own metaperspective, especially with the way that he had characterized Dworkin. He felt he himself had to do more work on it.

WEEK 8

In Week 8, the teacher came head-to-head with the difficulties of constructing an interpretative framework on the fly. After last week's doubts about his "levels" perspective, he had done library research and made several decisions to move away from the specific texts and heuristics that he had thus far adopted. First, he decided that students should be dealing with the generalizability argument in its traditional form rather than the specialized form of the public advocacy argument that Gert and Culver had put forward. He did this on the grounds that the public advocacy argument was obviously too weak and the generalization argument strong. In making this decision, he moved away from a text-bound approach. He also decided that his six controversial cases were not going to do the job of distinguishing among authors and so he changed the task to one of constructing cases to highlight differences among the authors.

In making these two changes, the teacher also saw himself as changing the tactics he had adopted the week before. Instead of heading out on his own to construct a framework that he then comes into class with, he decided to take one author at a time and try to construct more solid links. He was happy with Tuesday's class in which he primarily lectured about the generalization argument, but in Thursday's class, things fall apart. He expected to have students tell him how Gert and Culver were different from Dworkin and then have himself argue the opposite and see what happened. He had in mind a dense/sparse distinction. In class, he saw himself as playing this distinction too early. Comments from one of the students showed him that he had not fully understood the generalization argument to his satisfaction. The class ended in conceptual disarray.

Both students were interviewed this week after Thursday's class. S28 was more or less satisfied with his progress in the course and reported that he had learned a lot about reading and argumentation. His reaction to Thursday's class was to conclude that it was very hard to distinguish between Gert and Culver and Dworkin. S2, interviewed the following Monday, seemed much more discontented. He admitted that he had learned a lot about close reading and argumentation, but he was sick of the topic of paternalism and he saw the class sessions as a lot of hot air without any real importance to his life.

WEEK 9

In Week 9, the teacher moved on to a discussion of Rosemary Carter, further clarified the generalization argument, explained assumption digging, and gave the final assignment. The students wrote the final short assignment for the course, an application of Carter's position to the six controversial cases.

After last week's difficulties with the generalization argument, the teacher had sought out a Kantian scholar for a discussion. Under his influence, the teacher had reconceptualized the purpose of general ethical principles not as helping one to decide in particularly sticky cases (as he had been asking students to do) but to express generalizations about intuitions one has about a whole range of cases. Thus when he gave the final assignment on Thursday, he also gave students a list of 30 potentially paternalistic acts and asked them to use those, and any others they can generate, to make some general statements about what was and was not paternalism, what was and was not justified.

The teacher had also changed his conception of the final assignment under the influence of my concern about the audience students will be asked to address. At first, he thought the audience should simply be him as the teacher. He and I had a long discussion about this and by the time he actually made the assignment on Thursday, he decided to ask them to write for a naive audience unfamiliar with the issue or the readings.

The teacher also had a renewed commitment to the importance of giving students a framework for interpretation. He distinguished between the expert, like himself, who was able to build an independent knowledge structure for an issue just by reading multiple articles and moving back and forth between making assumptions and checking the scholarship, and novices who were unable to generate this kind of structure for themselves and must be given it with some combination of lecturing and deft questioning. But he also employed a strategy on Thursday of deliberately not reading Carter closely himself so that he could use the students' input to help generate an interpretation of her that solved what he, on a superficial reading, had seen as a major paradox.

The students interviewed this week are two of the most outspoken of the graduate students. Both wrote articulate and long papers on Carter, although coming to opposite conclusions about whether Carter would justify Case 1. S25 provided a summary of the McIntyre case and some discussion of her own about the inadequacies of the entire set of articles. S1 simply summarized the principles in an outline analytic form and then went through the cases. Both thought the course was fun, but had slight reservations. S25 was concerned about the inconsistency between the theory of close reading she had learned in this course and the critical theories she had been exposed to in a graduate literature course. She had decided to treat them for now as different games, but did want to reconcile them at some point. S1, who had a strong background in philosophy, felt the reflective awareness of methodology was the most valuable aspect of the course for him and wished there had been more heuristics after the first one on summarizing.

WEEK 10

In Week 10, the first week back after spring break, the teacher had drafted the first chapter of his book on argumentation about paternalism and he used his insights in that draft to expand and clarify what he wanted the students to do in the final assignment. He gave them an expanded set of 50 cases to consider that attempted to go beyond the hierarchical realms of paternalism in law and medicine with which the readings have been concerned and moved them into nonhierarchical realism like families, friends, and peers—a more cultural view of paternalism, as the Kantian scholar had suggested. He also introduced what he calls the boundary conditions, the issues with which the students will have to contend and gave them a model essay on crime from *Atlantic Monthly*, which he invited them to follow section by section. He also briefly reviewed the application of Childress' principles and discussed Komrad briefly for the way he was dealing with nonhierachical relationships.

In his discussion with me about his structuring of the course, the teacher recalled the impact that a semester at the University of Chicago had on his own development as a writer. He realized by being there that there were politics behind texts and that authors had interests in the way things came out. He believed that such an understanding of a field was only possible to acquire by being at the best schools and that his students could not possibly acquire it bootstrapped by reading texts. So he had to give it to them.

By the end of Thursday's class, the teacher was once again dissatisfied with his own understanding of paternalism and said he realized that he still had a lot of structuring to do for the students.

Both students interviewed this week had been interviewed before. S25 felt that she had learned a lot from the class about the nature of language. S12 reported a lot of anxiety about the openness of the upcoming paper and frustration about the way her completion of the last paper (on Childress) had become too mechanical. She did appreciate the teacher's giving more structure to the final assignment.

WEEK 11

I was out of town at the beginning of Week 11, so only one interview took place, after Thursday's class. Both the teacher and the students reported that he talked more about the structure of the assignment (reducing the original six parts to four parts) and about the different kinds of definition (historical, linguistic, scientific, dialectic). The teacher was unsure about where the course would go from here because he had been unable to structure the final section of the paper (expanding analysis into the cultural realm) intellectually. He thus assumed that it might be based on personal experience. He wished he had found something in the literature on power in nonhierarchical relationships, but he had not.

The two students interviewed this week, one undergrad and one graduate, felt the course is going well. S22, a science major, felt that he had learned a lot about thinking in the course, less about writing. He reported that he was intimidated by the grad students at first, but after talking with the teacher privately started to speak up. S12 also felt the course was going well. At first, she was scared and frustrated because she thought she was supposed to come up with the right answer, but now enjoys coming to class, the arguments, the bright people.

Both students reported that the topic of conversation had shifted away from paternalism to how to do the paper although this shift did not become clear in the classroom transcripts until next week.

WEEK 12

In Week 12, the teacher moved into a workshop mode. On Tuesday, he planned to ask a student to talk about a way of sorting the cases he had mentioned and then take it from there. In Tuesday's class, he found himself quickly dissatisfied with the way the discussion was going because the students were not putting themselves into the issue. The teacher was being influenced by an article by Susan Brownmiller that has become his prototype for mixing personal experience and reflection with the scholarly literature. He had located this article in response to his concern last week about not knowing how the paper should end. He now knew and saw where students were off track. He now saw it as important to have students keep a log of personal reflection from the very beginning of the course. For Thursday's class, he took the same workshop approach and once again reacted to how dominated the students were by the literature. He tried to encourage them to explore their own positions even more.

The teacher was also as an author coming to have a fairly well-defined position on paternalism himself, distinguishing it from institutional power relationships and locating it squarely within the personal realm. In this realm, all hard paternalism was unjustified except in the case of incompetence and the justification of soft paternalism depended on the conditions of the act and the consequences of intervention.

The three students interviewed this week, one grad and two undergrads, all spoke of the need to situate themselves personally in the issue. S19 felt the course had an unexpected though beneficial emphasis on heuristics as self-teaching. S9, also an undergrad, felt the course had been too easy for her with too much emphasis on text summary at the expense of analysis. S18, a grad, expected to learn about academic writing and felt the recent work was more exciting than the middle assignments, which got bogged down.

WEEK 13

In Week 13, the teacher swung back to a more literature-based conception of the final paper. In preparing for Tuesday's class, I pointed out that by telling students not to deal with medical and legal paternalism and instead to deal with nonhierachical cultural paternalism, he was presupposing his own solution to the issue, which is that nonhierarchical paternalism was the only true paternalism that was not inextricably enmeshed in issues of power. I was concerned that this conception of the paper would simply encourage students to forget about the literature entirely and indulge themselves in opinion making. Tuesday's class suggested that I was wrong, that students were not being overly subjective, but were still erring on the other side of not having a personal perspective.

By Thursday's class, the teacher had changed his mind. He had read an early student draft that was not sufficiently anchored in the literature and recognized its inadequacies. In working out his own conception of the paper, he now had in mind that the paper should examine the tension between beneficence and respect for persons in the legal and medical domains with which the literature had dealt and then extend that analysis to the nonhierachical domains. The personal thing was no longer important. I suggested that the choice of a paradigm case with which to open the paper was essentially a subjective choice and thus resolved the dilemma of anchoring a subjective stance in the literature.

In an unscheduled interview, the teacher also reported that he now realized he had to tell students what kind of definition he wanted rather than let them pick among them.

The two students interviewed this week recognized the importance of developing a personal perspective and that they had to make choices in structuring the paper. S23 had a fairly well-defined idea of the sections of the paper. S30 thought he was writing for semieducated readers, and was using the literature to piece together his own ideas. They both wished they had learned more about writing in the course.

WEEK 14

In Week 14, the teacher continued with his workshop method, realizing that students were either not yet started on the paper or were too much in the middle of it to talk. He did not see any of them taking recognizable approaches and was worried that they were not making adequate use of the literature.

The three students interviewed this week all had different conceptions of the final assignment. S14 planned to focus on the issue of competence. S3 thought she was constructing her own definition of paternalism. S21 thought he was constructing an exposition of the scholarly issue rather than presenting his own opinion. All had some vague idea of what they were going to do but had not done it yet.

REFERENCES

Ackerman, J. (1991). Reading, writing, and knowing: The role of disciplinary knowledge in comprehending and composing. *Research in the Teaching of English, 25,* 133–178.

Adolph, R. (1968). *The Rise of the Modern Prose Style.* Cambridge, MA: MIT Press.

Afflerbach, P., & Johnston, P. (1984). On the use of verbal reports in reading research. *Journal of Reading Behavior, 16,* 307–322.

Akinnaso, F. N. (1982). The literate writes and the nonliterate chants: Written language and ritual communication in sociolinguistic perspective. In W. Frawley (Ed.), *Linguistics and literacy* (pp. 7–36). New York: Plenum.

Alvermann, D. E., & Hague, S. A. (1989). Comprehension of counter-intuitive science text: Effects of prior knowledge and text structure. *Journal of Educational Research, 82,* 197–202.

Alvermann, D. E., Smith, L. C., & Readence, J. E. (1985). Prior knowledge and comprehension of compatible and incompatible text. *Reading Research Quarterly, 20,* 420–436.

Anderson, J. A. (1983). *The architecture of cognition.* Cambridge, MA: Harvard University Press.

Apple, M. (1989). The political economy of text publishing. In S. de Castell, A. Luke, & C. Luke (Eds.), *Language, authority and criticism: Readings on the school textbook* (pp. 155–169). London: Falmer Press.

Applebee, A. N. (1981). *Writing in the secondary school: English and the content areas.* Urbana, IL: National Council of Teachers of English.

Applebee, A. N. (1984a). *Contexts for learning to write: Studies of secondary school instruction.* Norwood, NJ: Ablex.

Applebee, A. N. (1984b). Writing and reasoning. *Review of Educational Research, 54,* 577–596.

Armbruster, B. B. (1984). The problem of "inconsiderate text." In G. G. Duffy, L. Roehler, & J. Mason (Eds.), *Comprehension instruction: Perspectives and suggestions* (pp. 202–217). New York: Longman.

Arons, S. (1989). Lessons in law and conscience: Legal aspects of textbook adoption and censorship. In S. de Castell, A. Luke, & C. Luke (Eds.), *Language, authority and criticism: Readings on the school textbook* (pp. 203–219). London: Falmer Press.

Arrington, P. (1987). Tropes of the composing process. *College English, 48,* 325–338.

Atkinson, R. C., & Shiffrin, R. (1968). Human memory: A proposed system and its control processes. In K. Spence & J. Spence (Eds.), *The psychology of learning and motivation* (Vol. 2, pp. 575–589). New York: Academic.

Baker, C. B., & Freebody, P. (1989). Talk around text: Construction of textual and teacher authority in classroom discourse. In S. de Castell, A. Luke, & C. Luke (Eds.), *Language, authority and criticism: Readings on the school textbook* (pp. 263–283). London: Falmer Press.

Bartholomae, D. (1985). Inventing the university. In M. Rose (Ed.), *When a writer can't write: Studies in writer's block and other composing process problems* (pp. 134–165). New York: Guilford.

Bauman, Z. (1987). *Legislators and interpreters: On modernity, post-modernity and intellectuals.* Ithaca, NY: Cornell University Press.

Bazerman, C. (1980). A relationship between reading and writing: The conversational model. *College English, 41*, 656–661.

Bazerman, C. (1988). *Shaping written knowledge: The genre and activity of the experimental article in science.* Madison: University of Wisconsin Press.

Bazerman, C. (1991). How natural philosophers can cooperate: The literary technology of coordinated investigation in Joseph Priestley's *History and present state of electricity (1767).* In C. Bazerman & J. Paradis (Eds.), *Textual dynamics of the professions* (pp. 13–44). Madison: University of Wisconsin Press.

Bazerman, C., Bizzell, P., Connors, R. J., Faigley, L., Hillocks, G., Jr., Schriver, K. A., Geisler, C., & Jarratt, S. C. (1989). What are we doing as a research community? *Rhetoric Review, 7*, 223–93.

Bazerman, C., & Paradis, J. (1991). Introduction. In C. Bazerman & J. Paradis (Eds.), *Textual dynamics of the professions: Historical and contemporary studies of writing in professional communities* (pp. 3–10). Madison: University of Wisconsin Press.

Becker, A. L. (1979). The figure a sentence makes: An interpretation of a classical Malay sentence. In T. Givon (Ed.), *On understanding grammar* (pp. 243–259). New York: Academic.

Belenkey, M. F., Clinchy, B. M., Goldberger, N. R., & Tarule, J. M. (1986). *Women's ways of knowing: The development of self, voice, and mind.* New York: Basic.

Bender, T. (1984). The erosion of public culture: Cities, discourses, and professional disciplines. In T. L. Haskell (Ed.), *The authority of experts: Studies in history and theory* (pp. 84–106). Bloomington: Indiana University Press.

Bereiter, C., & Scardamalia, M. (1982). From conversation to composition: The role of instruction in a developmental process. In R. Glaser (Ed.), *Advances in instructional psychology* (Vol. 2, pp. 1–64). Hillsdale, NJ: Lawrence Erlbaum Associates.

Bereiter, C., & Scardamalia, M. (1987). *The psychology of written composition.* Hillsdale, NJ: Lawrence Erlbaum Associates.

Berkenkotter, C. (1983). Decisions and revisions: The planning strategies of a published writer. *College Composition and Communication, 34*, 156–172.

Berkenkotter, C. (1989). The legacy of positivism in empirical composition research. *Journal of Advanced Composition, 9*, 62–82.

Berkenkotter, C. (1991). Paradigm debates, turf wars, and the conduct of sociocognitive inquiry in composition. *College Composition and Communication, 42*, 151–169.

Berlin, J. (1987). Rhetoric and ideology in the writing class. *College English, 50*, 477–494.

Bernstein, R. J. (1983). *Beyond objectivism and relativism.* Philadelphia: University of Pennsylvania Press.

Berthoff, A. (1971). The problem of problem solving. *College Composition and Communication, 22*, 237–242.

Beuchamp, T. L., & Childress, J. F. (1979). *Principles of biomedical ethics.* New York: Oxford University Press.

Bitzer, L. (1978). Rhetoric and knowledge. In D. Burks (Ed.), *Rhetoric, philosophy, and literature: An exploration* (pp. 67–93). West Lafayette, IN: Purdue University Press.

Bizzell, P. (1982a). Cognition, convention, and certainty: What we need to know about writing. *Pre/Text, 3,* 213–243.

Bizzell, P. (1982b). College composition: Initiation into the academic discourse community. *Curriculum Inquiry, 12,* 191–207.

Black, J. B., & Bower, G. H. (1980). Story understanding as problem solving. *Poetics, 9,* 223–250.

Bourdieu, P., & Passeron, J. C. (1977). *Reproduction in education, society and culture.* London: Sage.

Bowles, S., & Gintis, H. (1976). *Schooling in capitalist America: Educational reform and the contradictions of economic life.* New York: Basic.

Brannon, L., & Knoblauch, C. H. (1982). On students' rights to their own texts: A model of teacher response. *College Composition and Communication, 33,* 157–166.

Britton, J., Burgess, T., Martin, N., McLeod, A., & Rosen, H. (1975). *The development of writing abilities (11–18).* London: Macmillan.

Brodkey, L. (1987a). *Academic writing as a social practice.* Philadelphia: Temple University Press.

Brodkey, L. (1987b). Writing ethnographic narratives. *Written Communication, 4,* 25–50.

Brooke, R. (1989). Control in writing: Flower, Derrida, and images of the writer. *College English, 51,* 405–417.

Brown, A. L., & Day, J. D. (1983). Macrorules for summarizing texts: The development of expertise. *Journal of Verbal Learning and Verbal Behavior, 22,* 1–14.

Brown, A. L., Day, J. D., & Jones, R. S. (1983). The development of plans for summarizing texts. *Child Development, 51,* 968–979.

Brown, J. S., Collins, A., & Dugid, P. (1989). Situated cognition and the culture of learning. *Educational Researcher, 18,* 32–42.

Bruffee, K. A. (1984). Collaborative learning and the "conversation of mankind." *College English, 46,* 635–52.

Bruner, J. (1983). *Child's talk: Learning to use language.* London: Oxford University Press.

Bruner, J. (1986). *Actual minds, possible worlds.* Cambridge, MA: Harvard University Press.

Bundy, A., & Byrd, L. (1983). Using the method of fibres in mecho to calculate radii of gyration. In D. Gentner & A. L. Stevens (Eds.), *Mental models* (pp. 254–265). Hillsdale, NJ: Lawrence Erlbaum Associates.

Campbell, J. A. (1987). Charles Darwin: Rhetorician of science. In J. S. Nelson, A. Megill, & D. N. McCloskey (Eds.), *The rhetoric of the human sciences: Language and argument in scholarship and public affairs* (pp. 69–86). Madison: University of Wisconsin Press.

Carter, M. (1990). The idea of expertise: An exploration of cognitive and social dimensions of writing. *College Composition and Communication, 41,* 265–286.

Carter, R. (1977). Justifying paternalism. *The Canadian Journal of Philosophy, 7,* 33–145.

Cazden, C. B. (1979). Foreword to H. Mehan, *Learning lessons: Social organization in the classroom* (pp. vii–xii). Cambridge, MA: Harvard University Press.

Cazden, C. B. (1989). The myth of autonomous text. In D. M. Topping, D. C. Crowell, & V. N. Kobayashi (Eds.), *Thinking across cultures: The third international conference on thinking* (pp. 109–122). Hillsdale, NJ: Lawrence Erlbaum Associates.

Chafe, W. (1980). *The pear stories: Cognitive, cultural, and linguistic aspects of narrative production.* Norwood, NJ: Ablex.

Chafe, W. (1982). Integration and involvement in speaking, writing, and oral literature. In D. Tannen (Ed.), *Spoken and written language: Exploring orality and literacy* (pp. 35–53). Norwood, NJ: Ablex.

Chafe, W. (1985). Linguistic differences produced by differences between speaking and writing. In D. R. Olson, A. Hildyard, & N. Torrance (Eds.), *Literacy, language, and learning: The nature and consequences of reading and writing* (pp. 105–123). London: Cambridge University Press.

Chafe, W., & Danielewicz, J. (1987). Properties of spoken and written language. In R. Horowitz & S. J. Samuels (Eds.), *Comprehending oral and written language* (pp. 83–113). New York: Academic.

Charney, D. (1993). A study in rhetorical reading: How evolutionists read "The Spandrels of San Marco." In J. Selzer (Ed.), *Understanding scientific prose* (pp. 203–231). Madison: University of Wisconsin Press.

Chatman, S. (1978). *Story and discourse.* New York: Cornell University Press.

Chi, M., Feltovich, P., & Glaser, R. (1981). Categorization and representation of physics problems by experts and novices. *Cognitive Science, 5,* 121–152.

Childress, J. (1982). *Who should decide?: Paternalism in health care.* New York: Oxford University Press.

Clancey, W. J. (1988). Acquiring, representating, and evaluating a competence model of diagnostic strategy. In M. T. H. Chi, R. Glaser, & M. Farr (Eds.), *The nature of expertise* (pp. 343–412). Hillsdale, NJ: Lawrence Erlbaum Associates.

Clement, J. (1983). A conceptual model discussed by Galileo and used intuitively by physics students. In D. Gentner & A. L. Stevens (Eds.), *Mental models* (pp. 325–340). Hillsdale, NJ: Lawrence Erlbaum Associates.

Clifford, J. (1983). [Review of *Cognitive processes in writing*], L. Gregg & E. Steinberg (Eds.). *College Composition and Communication, 34,* 99–101.

Cohen, J. (1960). A coefficient of agreement for nominal scales. *Educational and Psychological Measurement, 20,* 37–46.

Collins, H. (1985). *Changing order: Replication and induction in scientific practice.* Beverly Hills, CA: Sage.

Collins, R. (1979). *The credential society: An historical sociology of education and stratification.* New York: Academic.

Comaroff, J. (1975). Talking politics: Oratory and authority in a Tswana chiefdom. In M. Block (Ed.), *Political language and oratory in traditional society* (pp. 141–161). London: Academic.

Condit, C. M. (1987). Crafting virtue: The rhetorical construction of public morality. *Quarterly Journal of Speech, 73,* 79–97.

Connors, R. (1983). Composition studies and science. *College English, 45,* 1–20.

Cook-Gumperz, J. (1986). Literacy and schooling: An unchanging equation? In J. Cook-Gumperz (Ed.), *The social construction of literacy* (pp. 16–44). Cambridge, England: Cambridge University Press.

Cooper, M. (1986). The ecology of writing. *College English, 48,* 364–375.

Cooper, M., & Holzman, M. (1983). Talking about protocols. *College Composition and Communication, 34,* 284–293.

Cooper, M., & Holzman, M. (1985). Reply to Linda Flower and John R. Hayes. *College Composition and Communication, 36,* 97–100.

Copeland, K. A. (1985, November). *The effect of writing upon good and poor writers' learning from prose.* Paper presented at the annual meeting of the National Council of Teachers of English, Philadelphia. (Reproduced as ERIC Document Reproduction Service No. ED 276 993)

Crane, D. (1972). *Invisible colleges: Diffusion of knowledge in scientific communities.* Chicago: University of Chicago Press.

Crismore, A. (1989). *Talking with readers: Metadiscourse as a rhetorical act.* New York: Peter Lang.

Crismore, A., & Farnsworth, R. (1990). Metadiscourse in popular and professional science discourse. In W. Nash (Ed.), *The writing scholar: Studies in academic discourse* (pp. 118–136). Newbury Park, CA: Sage.

Davis, M. (1990). The ethics boom: A philosopher's history. *Centennial Review, 34,* 163–186.

deKleer, J. (1983). Assumptions and ambiguities in mechanistic mental models. In D. Gentner & A. L. Stevens (Eds.), *Mental models* (pp. 155–189). Hillsdale, NJ: Lawrence Erlbaum Associates.

DiPardo, A. (1990). Narrative knowers, expository knowledge: Discourse as a dialectic. *Written Communication, 7,* 59–95.

diSessa, A. A. (1983). Phenomenology and the evolution of intuition. In D. Gentner & A. L. Stevens (Eds.), *Mental models* (pp. 18–33). Hillsdale, NJ: Lawrence Erlbaum Associates.

Dobrin, D. (1986). Protocols once more. *College English, 48,* 713–725.

Dole, J. A., & Niederhauser, D. S. (1990). Students' level of commitment to their naive conceptions and their conceptual change learning from texts. In J. Zutwell & S. McCormick (Eds.), *Literacy theory and research: Analyses from multiple paradigms* (pp. 303–310). Chicago: National Reading Conference.

Dole, J. A., & Smith, E. L. (1989). Prior knowledge and learning from science text: An instructional study. In S. McCormick & J. Zutwell (Eds.), *Cognitive and social perspectives for literacy research and instruction* (pp. 345–352). Chicago: National Reading Conference.

Durst, R. K. (1987). Cognitive and linguistic demands of analytic writing. *Research in the Teaching of English, 21,* 347–376.

Dworkin, G. (1972). Paternalism. *The Monist, 56,* 64–84.

Dyson, A. H. (1988). Negotiating multiple worlds: The space/time dimensions of young children's composing. *Research in the Teaching of English, 22,* 355–390.

Edwards, A. D., & Furlong, V. J. (1978). *The language of teaching: Meaning in classroom interaction.* London: Heinemann.

Edwards, A. D., & Westgate, D. P. G. (1987). *Investigating classroom talk.* London: Falmer Press.

Edwards, D., & Mercer, N. (1987). *Common knowledge: The development of understanding in the classroom.* London: Methuen.

Elbow, P. (1991). Reflections on academic discourse: How it relates to freshmen and colleagues. *College English, 53,* 135–55.

Emig, J. (1971). *The composing process of twelfth graders.* Urbana, IL: National Council of Teachers of English.

Emig, J. (1977). Writing as a mode of learning. *College Composition and Communication, 28,* 122–127.

Emig, J. (1982). Inquiry paradigms and writing. *College Composition and Communication, 33,* 64–75.

Erickson, F., & Mohatt, G. (1982). Cultural organization of participant structures in two classrooms of Indian students. In G. Spindler (Ed.), *Doing the ethnography of schooling* (pp. 132–174). New York: Holt, Rinehart & Winston.

Ericsson, K. A., & Simon, H. A. (1980). Verbal reports as data. *Psychological Review, 87,* 215–251.

Ericsson, K. A., & Simon, H. A. (1984). *Protocol analysis: Verbal reports as data.* Cambridge, MA: MIT Press.

Etzioni-Halevy, E. (1985). *The knowledge elite and the failure of prophecy.* London: Allen & Unwin.

Fahnestock, J. (1986). Accommodating science: The rhetorical life of scientific facts. *Written Communication, 3,* 275–296.

Fahnestock, J., & Secor, M. (1991). The rhetoric of literary criticism. In C. Bazerman & J. Paradis (Eds.), *Textual dynamics of the professions: Historical and contemporary studies of writing in professional communities* (pp. 76–96). Madison: University of Wisconsin Press.

Faigley, L. (1986). Competing theories of process: A critique and a proposal. *College English, 48,* 527–542.

Faigley, L., & Witte, S. (1981). Analyzing revision. *College Composition and Communication, 32,* 400–414.

Farrell, T. B. (1976). Knowledge, consensus, and rhetorical theory. *The Quarterly Journal of Speech, 62,* 1–14.

Fisher, W. (1987). *Human communication as narration: Toward a philosophy of reason, value, and action.* Columbia: University of South Carolina Press.

Fitzgerald, J. (1987). Research on revision in writing. *Review of Educational Research, 57,* 481–506.

Flower, L. (1979). Writer-based prose: A cognitive basis for problems in writing. *College English, 41,* 13–18.

Flower, L. (1984). Response to Anthony Petrosky, review of Linda Flower, *Problem-solving strategies for writing. College Composition and Communication, 35,* 96–97.

Flower, L. (1988). The construction of purpose in reading and writing. *College English, 50,* 528–550.

Flower, L. (1989). Cognition, context and theory building. *College Composition and Communication, 40*, 282–311.

Flower, L., & Hayes, J. R. (1980a). The cognition of discovery: Defining a rhetorical problem. *College Composition and Communication, 31*, 21–32.

Flower, L., & Hayes, J. R. (1980b). The dynamics of composing: Making plans and juggling constraints. In L. Gregg & E. Steinberg (Eds.), *Cognitive processes in writing* (pp. 31–50). Hillsdale, NJ: Lawrence Erlbaum Associates.

Flower, L., & Hayes, J. R. (1981a). A cognitive process theory of writing. *College Composition and Communication, 32*, 365–387.

Flower, L., & Hayes, J. R. (1981b). Plans that guide the composing process. In C. H. Frederiksen & J. F. Dominic (Eds.), *Writing: The nature, development, and teaching of written communication* (pp. 39–58). Hillsdale, NJ: Lawrence Erlbaum Associates.

Flower, L., & Hayes, J. R. (1981c). The pregnant pause: An inquiry into the nature of planning. *Research in the Teaching of English, 15*, 229–243.

Flower, L., & Hayes, J. R. (1984). Images, plans, and prose: The representation of meaning in writing. *Written Communication, 1*, 120–160.

Flower, L., & Hayes, J. R. (1985). Response to Marilyn Cooper and Michael Holzman, "Talking about protocols." *College Composition and Communication, 36*, 94–99.

Flower, L., Hayes, J. R., Carey, L., Schriver, K., & Stratman, J. (1986). Detection, diagnosis, and strategies of revision. *College Composition and Communication, 37*, 16–55.

Flower, L. Stein, V., Ackerman, J., Kantz, M., McCormick, K., & Peck, W. (1990). *Reading to write: Exploring a cognitive and social process.* New York: Oxford University Press.

Fodor, J. A. (1983). *The modularity of mind.* Cambridge, MA: MIT Press.

Forbus, K. D. (1983). Qualitative reasoning about space and motion. In D. Gentner & A. L. Stevens (Eds.), *Mental models* (pp. 54–73). Hillsdale, NJ: Lawrence Erlbaum Associates.

Foucault, M. (1980). *Power/knowledge: Selected interviews and other writings, 1972–1977.* New York: Pantheon.

Foucault, M. (1983). The subject and power. Afterword to H. L. Dreyfus & P. Rabinow (Eds.), *Michel Foucault, beyond structuralism and hermeneutics* (pp. 208–226). Chicago: University of Chicago Press.

Frentz, T. S. (1985). Rhetorical conversation, time, and moral act. *Quarterly Journal of Speech, 71*, 1–18.

Friedson, E. (1984). Are professions necessary? In T. L. Haskell (Ed.), *The authority of experts: Studies in history and theory* (pp. 3–27). Bloomington: Indiana University Press.

Friedson, E. (1986). *Professional powers: A study of the institutionalization of formal knowledge.* Chicago: University of Chicago Press.

Galison, P. L. (1987). *How experiments end.* Chicago: University of Chicago Press.

Gardner, H. (1985). *The mind's new science: A history of the cognitive revolution.* New York: Basic.

Garfinkel, H., Lynch, M., & Livingston, E. (1981). The work of a discovering science construed with materials from the optically discovered pulsar. *Philosophy of the Social Sciences, 11*, 131–158.

Garfinkel, H., & Sacks, H. (1970). On formal structures of practical actions. In J. C. McKinney & E. A. Tiryakian (Eds.), *Theoretical sociology* (pp. 338–366). New York: Appleton-Century-Crofts.

Garner, R., Belcher, V., Winfield, E., & Smith T. (1985). Multiple measures of text proficiency: What can fifth-grade students do? *Research in the Teaching of English, 19*, 140–153.

Gebhardt, R. (1983). Writing process, revision, and rhetorical problems: A note on three recent studies. *College Composition and Communication, 34*, 294–296.

Geisler, C. (1990). Toward a sociocognitive model of literacy: Constructing mental models in a philosophical conversation. In C. Bazerman & J. Paradis (Eds.), *Textual dynamics of the professions* (pp. 171–190). Madison: University of Wisconsin Press.

Geisler, C. (1991). Reader, parent, coach: Defining the profession by our practice of response. *Reader, 25*, 17–33.

Geisler, C., & Kaufer, D. S. (1989). Making meaning in literate conversations: A teachable sequence for reflective writing. *Rhetoric Society Quarterly, 19*, 229–243.

Genette, G. (1980). *Narrative discourse: An essay on method.* Ithaca, NY: Cornell University Press.

Gentner, D., & Gentner, D. R. (1983). Flowing waters or teeming crows: Mental models of electricity. In D. Gentner & A. L. Stevens (Eds.), *Mental models* (pp. 99–129). Hillsdale, NJ: Lawrence Erlbaum Associates.

Gert, B., & Culver, C. (1976). Paternalistic behavior. *Philosophy and Public Affairs, 6*, 45–57.

Gert, B., & Culver, C. (1979). The justification of paternalism. *Ethics, 89*, 199–210.

Gilbert, G. N., & Mulkay, M. (1984). *Opening Pandora's box: A sociological analysis of scientific discourse.* Cambridge, England: Cambridge University Press.

Glaser, R. (1984). Education and thinking: The role of knowledge. *American Psychologist, 39*, 93–104.

Goetz, J. P., & LeCompte, M. D. (1984). *Ethnography and qualitative design in educational research.* Orlando, FL: Academic.

Goody, E. N. (1983). *From craft to industry.* New York: Cambridge University Press.

Goody, J., & Watt, I. (1963). The consequence of literacy. *Comparative Studies in Society and History, 5*, 304–326, 332–345.

Gouldner, A. W. (1979). *The future of intellectuals and the rise of the new class: A frame of reference, theses, conjectures, arguments, and an historical perspective on the role of intellectuals and intelligensia in the international class contest of the modern era.* New York: Continuum.

Gradwohl, J. M., & Schumacher, G. M. (1989). The relationship between content knowledge and topic choice in writing. *Written Communication, 6*, 181–195.

Graff, H. (1979). *The literacy myth: Literacy and social structure in a nineteenth century city.* New York: Academic.

Gragson, G., & Selzer, J. (1990). Fictionalizing the readers of scholarly articles in biology. *Written Communication, 7*, 25–58.

Greene, S. (1990). Toward a dialectical theory of composing. *Rhetoric Review, 9*, 149–172.

Greeno, J. G. (1983). Conceptual entities. In D. Gentner & A. L. Stevens (Eds.), *Mental models* (pp. 227–251). Hillsdale, NJ: Lawrence Erlbaum Associates.

Griffin, C. W. (1985). Programs for writing across the curriculum: A report. *College Composition and Communication, 36*, 398–413.

Haas, C. (1993, April). *Writing in three-dimensional space: Stretching our theories to include technologies of composing.* Paper presented at the annual meeting of the Conference of College Composition and Communication, San Diego.

Haas, C. (1994). Learning to read biology: One student's rhetorical development in college. *Written Communication, 11*, 43–84.

Haas, C., & Flower, L. (1988). Rhetorical reading strategies and the construction of meaning. *College Composition and Communication, 39*, 167–183.

Haas, C., & Flower, L. (1989). Reply to Ruth Ray and Ellen Barton. *College Composition and Communication, 40*, 482.

Hairston, M. (1982). The winds of change: Thomas Kuhn and the revolution in the teaching of writing. *College Composition and Communication, 33*, 78–86.

Hairston, M. (1986). Different products, different processes: A theory about writing. *College Composition and Communication, 37*, 442–452.

Hall, P. K. (1984). The social foundations of professional credibility: Linking the medical profession to higher education in Connecticut and Massachusetts, 1700–1830. In T. L. Haskell (Ed.), *The authority of experts: Studies in history and theory* (pp. 107–141). Bloomington: Indiana University Press.

Halloran, S. M. (1983). Rhetoric in the American college curriculum: The decline of public discourse. *Pre/Text, 3*, 245–269.

Haskell, T. L. (1977). *The emergence of professional social science: The American Social Science Association and the nineteenth-century crisis of authority.* Urbana: University of Illinois Press.

Haskell, T. L. (1984). Professionalism versus capitalism: R. H. Tawney, Emile Durkheim, and C. S. Peirce on the disinterestedness of professional communities. In T. L. Haskell (Ed.), *The authority of experts: Studies in history and theory* (pp. 180–225). Bloomington: Indiana University Press.

Havelock, E. (1963). *Preface to Plato.* Cambridge, MA: Harvard University Press.

Hayes, J. R., & Flower, L. (1980a). Identifying the organization of writing processes. In L. Gregg & E. Steinberg (Eds.), *Cognitive processes in writing* (pp. 3–30). Hillsdale, NJ: Lawrence Erlbaum Associates.

Hayes, J. R., & Flower, L. (1980b). Writing as problem solving. *Visible Language, 14,* 388–399.

Hayes, J. R., & Flower, L. (1983). Uncovering cognitive processes in writing: A introduction to protocol analysis. In P. Mosenthal, L. Tamor, & S. A. Walmsley (Eds.), *Research on writing: Principle and methods* (pp. 206–220). New York: Longman.

Hayes, J. R. Flower, L., Schriver, K. A., Stratman, J., & Carey, L. (1987). Cognitive processes in revision. In S. Rosenberg (Ed.), *Advances in psycholinguistics, Vol II: Reading, writing, and language processing* (pp. 176–240). Cambridge, England: Cambridge University Press.

Hayes-Roth, B., & Hayes-Roth, F. (1975). A cognitive model of planning. *Cognitive Science, 3,* 275–310.

Heap, J. (1985). Discourse in the production of classroom knowledge: Reading lessons. *Curriculum Inquiry, 15,* 245–279.

Heath, S. B. (1983). *Ways with words: Language, life, and work in communities and classrooms.* Cambridge, England: Cambridge University Press.

Heath, S. B. (1987). The literate essay: Using ethnography to explode myths. In J. Langer (Ed.), *Language, literacy, and culture: Issues of society and schooling* (pp. 89–107). Norwood, NJ: Ablex.

Heritage, J. (1984). *Garfinkel and ethnomethodology.* Cambridge, England: Polity Press.

Higham, J. (1979). The matrix of specialization. In A. Oleson & J. Voss (Eds.), *The organization of knowledge in modern America, 1860–1920* (pp. 3–18). Baltimore: Johns Hopkins University Press.

Hobart, M. (1975). Orators and patrons: Two types of political leader in Balinese village society. In M. Block (Ed.), *Political language and oratory in traditional society* (pp. 65–92). London: Academic.

Hollinger, D. A. (1984). Inquiry and uplift: Late nineteenth-century American academics and the moral efficacy of scientific practice. In T. L. Haskell (Ed), *The authority of experts: Studies in history and theory* (pp. 142–156). Bloomington: Indiana University Press.

Hopper, P. (1979). Aspect and foregrounding in discourse. In T. Givon (Ed.), *On understanding grammar* (pp. 213–241). New York: Academic.

Horvath, B. K. (1984). The components of written response: A practical synthesis of current views. *Rhetoric Review, 2,* 136–156.

Hounsell, D. (1984). Learning and essay-writing. In F. Marton, D. Hounsell, & N. Entwistle (Eds.), *The experience of learning* (pp. 103–123). Edinburgh: Scottish Academic.

Howard, V. (1982). *Artistry: The work of artists.* Indianapolis: Hackett.

Howell, W. S. (1956). *Logic and rhetoric in England, 1500–1700.* Princeton, NJ: Princeton University Press.

Howell, W. S. (1971). *Eighteenth-century British logic and rhetoric.* Princeton, NJ: Princeton University Press.

Humes, A. (1983). Research on the composing process. *Review of Educational Research, 53,* 201–216.

Hynd, C., & Alvermann, D. E. (1986). The role of refutation text in overcoming difficulty with science concepts. *Journal of Reading, 29,* 440–446.

Jackendoff, R. (1987). *Consciousness and the computational mind.* Cambridge, MA: MIT Press.

James, W. (1987). *Writings, 1902–1910* (B. Kuklick, Ed.). New York: Literary Classics of the United States.

James, W. (1992). Writings, *1878–1899* (G. Myers, Ed.). New York: Literary Classics of the United States.

Johnson, E. J. (1988). Expertise and decision under uncertainty: Performance and process. In M. T. H. Chi, R. Glaser, & M. J. Farr (Eds.), *The nature of expertise* (pp. 209–228). Hillsdale, NJ: Lawrence Erlbaum Associates.

Journet, D. (1990). Forms of discourse and the sciences of the mind: Luria, Sacks, and the role of narrative in neurological case histories. *Written Communication, 7,* 171–199.

Kahneman, D., & Tversky, A. (1973). On the psychology of prediction. *Pyschological Review, 80,* 237–251.

Kaufer, D. S. (1984). Corpus on paternalism. Carnegie Mellon University, Pittsburgh, PA: Unpublished manuscript.

Kaufer, D. S., & Carley, K. M. (1993). *Communication at a distance: The influence of print on socio-cultural organization and change.* Hillsdale, NJ: Lawrence Erlbaum Associates.

Kaufer, D. S., & Geisler, C. (1989). Novelty in academic writing. *Written Communication, 8,* 286–311.

Kaufer, D. S., Geisler, C., & Neuwirth, C. M. (1989). *Arguing from sources: Exploring issues through reading and writing.* San Diego: Harcourt Brace Jovanovich.

Kaufer, D., Hayes, J. R., & Flower, L. (1986). Composing written sentences. *Research in the Teaching of English, 20,* 121–140.

Keenan, E. (1975). A sliding sense of obligatoriness: The polystructure of Malagasy oratory. In M. Block (Ed.), *Political language and oratory in traditional society* (pp. 91–112). London: Academic.

Kennedy, G. A. (1963). *The art of persuasion in Greece.* Princeton, NJ: Princeton University Press.

Kennedy, G. A. (1972). *The art of rhetoric in the Roman world 300 B.C.-A.D. 300.* Princeton, NJ: Princeton University Press.

Kennedy, G. A. (1980). *Classical rhetoric and its Christian and secular tradition from ancient to modern times.* Chapel Hill: University of North Carolina Press.

Kevles, D. (1979). The physics, mathematics, and chemistry communities: A comparative analysis. In A. Oleson & J. Voss (Eds.), *The organization of knowledge in modern America, 1860–1920* (pp. 139–172). Baltimore: Johns Hopkins University Press.

Killingsworth, M. J., & Steffens, D. (1989). Effectiveness in the environmental impact statement: A study in public rhetoric. *Written Communication, 6,* 155–180.

Knoblauch, C. H., & Brannon, L. (1983). Writing as learning through the curriculum. *College English, 45,* 465–472.

Knorr-Certina, K. D. (1981). *The manufacture of knowledge: An essay on the constructivist and contextual nature of science.* Oxford, England: Pergamon.

Komrad, M. (1983). A defense of medical paternalism: Maximizing patients' autonomy. *Journal of Medical Ethics, 9,* 38–44.

Kuhn, T. S. (1962). *The structure of scientific revolutions.* Chicago: University of Chicago Press.

Kuklick, B. (1977). *The rise of American philosophy: Cambridge, Massachusetts, 1860–1930.* New Haven, CT: Yale University Press.

Labov, W. (1972). The transformation of experience in narrative syntax. In *Language in the inner city* (pp. 354–396). Philadelphia: University of Pennsylvania Press.

Lampert, M. (1990). When the problem is not the question and the solution is not the answer: Mathematical knowing and teaching. *American Educational Research Journal, 27,* 29–63.

Langer, J. A. (1984). The effects of available information on responses to school writing tasks. *Research in the Teaching of English, 18,* 27–44.

Langer, J. A. (1986). Learning through writing: Study skills in the content areas. *Journal of Reading, 29,* 400–406.

Langer, J. A., & Applebee, A. N. (1984). Language, learning, and interaction: A framework for improving the teaching of writing. In A. N. Applebee (Ed.), *Contexts for learning to write: Studies of secondary school instruction* (pp. 169–181). Norwood, NJ: Ablex.

Langer, J. A., & Applebee, A. N. (1987). *How writing shapes thinking: A study of teaching and learning.* Urbana, IL: National Council of Teachers of English.

Larkin, J. (1981). Enriching formal knowledge: A model for learning to solve textbook physics problems. In J. Anderson (Ed.), *Cognitive skills and their acquisition* (pp. 311–335). Hillsdale, NJ: Lawrence Erlbaum Associates.

Larkin, J. (1983). The role of problem representation in physics. In D. Gentner & A. L. Stevens (Eds.), *Mental models* (pp. 75–98). Hillsdale, NJ: Lawrence Erlbaum Associates.

Larkin, J., McDermott, J., Simon, D. P., & Simon, H. A. (1980). Expert and novice performance in solving physics problems. *Science, 208*, 1335–1342.

Larson, M. S. (1977). *The rise of professionalism: A sociological analysis.* Berkeley: The University of California Press.

Larson, M. S. (1984). The production of expertise and the constitution of expert power. In T. L. Haskell (Ed.), *The authority of experts: Studies in history and theory* (pp. 28–83). Bloomington: Indiana University Press.

Latour, B., & Woolgar, S. (1979). *Laboratory life: The social construction of scientific facts.* Beverly Hills, CA: Sage.

Lawrence, J. A. (1988). Expertise on the bench: Modelling magistrates' judicial decision-making. In M. T. H. Chi, R. Glaser, & M. J. Farr (Eds.), *The nature of expertise* (pp. 229–259). Hillsdale, NJ: Lawrence Erlbaum Associates.

Leont'ev, A. N. (1981). The problem of activity in psychology. In J. V. Wertsch (Ed.), *The concept of activity in Soviet psychology* (pp. 37–71). Armonk, NY: M. E. Sharpe.

Lesgold, A., Rubinson, H., Feltovich, P., Glaser, R., Klopfer, D., & Wang, Y. (1988). Expertise in a complex skill: Diagnosing X-ray pictures. In M. T. H. Chi, R. Glaser, & M. J. Farr (Eds.), *The nature of expertise* (pp. 311–342). Hillsdale, NJ: Lawrence Erlbaum Associates.

Lieberman, J. K. (1970). *The tyranny of the experts: How professions are closing the open society.* New York: Walker & Co.

Lipson, M. Y. (1982). Learning new information from text: The role of prior knowledge and reading ability. *Journal of Reading Behavior, 14*, 243–261.

Locke, J. (1982). *Essay concerning human understanding.* Sheffield, England: University of Sheffield Printing Unit. (Original work published 1690)

Luke, C., de Castell, S., & Luke, A. (1989). Beyond criticism: The authority of the school textbook. In S. de Castell, A. Luke, & C. Luke (Eds.), *Language, authority and criticism: Readings on the school textbook* (pp. 245–260). London: Falmer Press.

Lundeberg, M. A. (1987). Metacognitive aspects of reading comprehension: Studying understanding in legal case analysis. *Reading Research Quarterly, 22*, 407–432.

Luria, A. R. (1976). *Cognitive development: Its cultural and social foundations.* Cambridge, MA: Harvard University Press.

MacDonald, S. P. (1990). The literary argument and its discursive conventions. In W. Nash (Ed.), *The writing scholar: Studies in academic discourse* (pp. 31–62). Newbury Park, CA: Sage.

MacIntyre, A. (1981). *After virtue: A study in moral theory.* Notre Dame, IN: University of Notre Dame Press.

McCloskey, D. N. (1985). *The rhetoric of economics.* Madison: University of Wisconsin Press.

McCloskey, M. (1983). Naive theories of motion. In D. Gentner & A. L. Stevens (Eds.), *Mental models* (pp. 299–323). Hillsdale, NJ: Lawrence Erlbaum Associates.

McCutchen, D. (1986). Domain knowledge and linguistic knowledge in the development of writing ability. *Journal of Memory and Language, 25*, 431–444.

McGinley, W., & Tierney, R. J. (1989). Traversing the topical landscape: Reading and writing as ways of knowing. *Written Communication, 6*, 243–269.

McLeod, S. (1988). *Strengthening programs for writing across the curriculum.* San Francisco: Jossey-Bass.

Mehan, H. (1979). *Learning lessons: Social organization in the classroom.* Cambridge, MA: Harvard University Press.

Mill, J. S. (1909). *Autobiography, Essay on liberty* (pp. 203–325). New York: Collier.

Miller, G. A. (1956). The magical number seven, plus or minus two. *Psychological Review, 63*, 81–97.

Morris, H. (1981). A paternalistic theory of punishment. *American Philosophical Quarterly, 18*, 263–271.

Murray, D. M. (1983). Response of a laboratory rat—Or, being protocoled. *College Composition and Communication, 34*, 169–172.

Myers, G. (1985). The social construction of two biologists' proposals. *Written Communication, 2*, 219–245.

Myers, G. (1991). Stories and styles in two molecular biology review articles. In C. Bazerman & J. Paradis (Eds.), *Textual dynamics of the professions* (pp. 45–75). Madison: University of Wisconsin Press.

Myers, G. (1992). Notes on the texts. In G. Myers (Ed.), *William James: Writings 1878–1899* (pp. 1168–1177). New York: Literary Classics of the United States.

Nelson, J. (1990). This was an easy assignment: Examining how students interpret academic writing tasks. *Research in the Teaching of English, 24*, 362–396.

Nelson, J. S., & Megill, A. (1986). Rhetoric of inquiry: Projects and prospects. *Quarterly Journal of Speech, 72*, 20–37.

Nelson, J. S., Megill, A., & McCloskey, D. N. (1987). *The rhetoric of the human sciences: Language and argument in scholarship and public affairs.* Madison: University of Wisconsin Press.

Newell, A. (1980). Reasoning, problem solving, and decision processes: The problem space as a fundamental category. In R. S. Nickerson (Ed.), *Attention and performance VIII* (pp. 693–718). Hillsdale, NJ: Lawrence Erlbaum Associates.

Newell, A., & Simon, H. A. (1972). *Human problem solving.* Englewood Cliffs, NJ: Prentice-Hall.

Newell, G. (1984). Learning from writing in two content areas: A case study/protocol analysis. *Research in the Teaching of English, 18*, 265–287.

Nisbett, R. E., & Wilson, T. D. (1977). Telling more than we can know: Verbal reports on mental processes. *Psychological Review, 84*, 231–259.

North, S. (1987). The formalists. In *The making of knowledge in composition: Portrait of an emerging field* (pp. 238–271). Upper Montclair, NJ: Boynton/Cook.

Nystrand, M. (1982). The structure of textual space. In M. Nystrand (Ed.), *What writers know: The language, process, and structure of written discourse* (pp. 75–86). Orlando, FL: Academic.

Oleson, A., & Voss, J. (1979). Introduction. In A. Oleson & J. Voss (Eds.), *The organization of knowledge in modern America, 1860–1920* (pp. vii–xxi). Baltimore: Johns Hopkins University Press.

Olson, D. R. (1977). From utterance to text: The bias of language in speech and writing. *Harvard Educational Review, 47*, 257–281.

Olson, D. R. (1981). Writing: The divorce of the author from the text. In B. M. Kroll & R. Vann (Eds.), *Exploring speaking-writing connections and contrasts.* Urbana, IL: National Council of Teachers of English.

Olson, D. R. (1988, April). *Interpretation and the autonomy of written texts.* Paper presented at the annual meeting of the American Educational Research Association, San Francisco.

Ong, W. J. (1974). *Ramus, method, and the decay of dialogue.* New York: Farrar, Strauss & Giroux. (Original work published 1958)

Ong, W. J. (1982). *Orality and literacy: The technologizing of the word.* London: Methuen.

Onore, C. (1989). The student, the teacher, and the text: Negotiating meanings through response and revision. In C. M. Anson (Ed.), *Writing and response: Theory, practice, and research* (pp. 231–260). Urbana IL: National Council of Teachers of English.

Pearson, P. D. (1984). Twenty years of research in reading comprehension. In T. E. Raphael (Ed.), *The contexts of school-based literacy* (pp. 43–62). New York: Random House.

Penrose, A. M. (1992). To write or not to write: Effects of task and task interpretation on learning through writing. *Written Communication, 9*, 465–500.

Penrose, A. M., & Fennell, B. A. (1992, April). *Agency and proof in scientific prose: Tracing socialization via semantic feature analysis.* Paper presented at the annual meeting of the American Educational Research Association, San Francisco.

Perelman, C. (1980). *Justice, law, and argument: Essays on moral and legal reasoning.* Boston: D. Reidel.

Perelman, C., & Olbrechts-Tyteca, L. (1969). *The new rhetoric: A treatise on argumentation.* Notre Dame, IN: University of Notre Dame Press. (Original work published 1958)

Perfetti, C. A. (1987). Language, speech, and print: Some asymmetries in the acquisition of literacy. In R. Horowitz & S. J. Samels (Eds.), *Comprehending oral and written language* (pp. 355–369). San Diego: Academic.

Perkins, D. N. (1981). *The mind's best work.* Cambridge, MA: Harvard University Press.

Perl, S. (1979). The composing process of unskilled writers. *Research in the Teaching of English, 13,* 317–336.

Petrosky, A. R. (1983). Review of *Problem-solving strategies for writing* by Linda Flower. *College Composition and Communication, 34,* 233–235.

Phelps, L. W. (1988). *Composition as a human science.* New York: Oxford University Press.

Philips, S. (1972). Participant structures and communicative competence: Warm Springs children in community and classroom. In C. Cazden, V. John, & D. Hymes (Eds.), *Functions of language in the classroom* (pp. 370–394). New York: Teachers College Press.

Pianko, S. (1979). A description of the composing processes of college freshmen writers. *Research in the Teaching of English, 13,* 5–22.

Polanyi, L. (1979). "So what's the point?" *Semiotica, 25,* 207–241.

Polanyi, L. (1982). Linguistic and social constraints on storytelling. *Journal of Pragmatics, 6,* 509–524.

Polanyi, M. (1958). *Personal knowledge: Towards a post-critical philosophy.* Chicago: University of Chicago Press.

Pomerantz, A. (1984a). Agreeing and disagreeing with assessments: Some features of preferred/dispreferred turn shapes. In J. M. Atkinson & J. Heritage (Eds.), *Structures of social action: Studies in conversation analysis* (pp. 58–101). Cambridge, England: Cambridge University Press.

Pomerantz, A. (1984b). Pursuing a response. In J. M. Atkinson & J. Heritage (Eds.), *Structures of social action: Studies in conversation analysis* (pp. 152–163). Cambridge, England: Cambridge University Press.

Popper, K. (1979). *Objective knowledge: An evolutionary approach.* Oxford, England: Clarendon.

Prelli, L. J. (1989). *A rhetoric of science: Inventing scientific discourse.* Columbia: University of South Carolina Press.

Prince, G. (1973). *A grammar of stories.* The Hague, Netherlands: Mouton.

Radway, J. (1984). *Reading the romance: Women, patriarchy, and popular literature.* Chapel Hill: University of North Carolina Press.

Ray, R., & Barton, E. (1989). Response to Christina Haas and Linda Flower, "Rhetorical reading strategies and the construction of meaning." *College Composition and Communication, 40,* 480–481.

Reder, L., & Anderson, J. R. (1980). A comparison of texts and their summaries: Memorial consequences. *Journal of Verbal Learning and Verbal Behavior, 19,* 121–134.

Reither, J. (1985). Writing and knowing: Toward redefining the writing process. *College English, 47,* 620–628.

Resnick, D. P., & Resnick, L. B. (1977). The nature of literacy: An historical exploration. *Harvard Educational Review, 47,* 370–385.

Rimon-Keenan, S. (1983). *Narrative fiction: Comtemporary poetics.* New York: Methuen.

Rogoff, B. (1990). *Apprenticeship in thinking: Cognitive development in social context.* New York: Oxford University Press.

Rorty, R. (1979). *Philosophy and the mirror of nature.* Princeton, NJ: Princeton University Press.

Rose, M. (1985). Complexity, rigor, evolving method and the puzzle of writer's block: Thoughts on composing-process research. In M. Rose (Ed.), *When a writer can't write: Studies in writer's block and other composing process problems* (pp. 227–260). New York: Guilford.

Rubin, A. (1980). A theoretical taxonomy of the differences between oral and written language. In R. Spiro et al. (Eds.), *Theoretical issues in reading comprehension* (pp. 411–438). Hillsdale, NJ: Lawrence Erlbaum Associates.

Rumelhart, D. E., & Norman, D. A.(1982). Simulating a skilled typist: A study of skilled cognitive-motor performance. *Cognitive Science, 6,* 1–36.

Ruthrof, H. (1983). *The reader's construction of narrative.* London: Routledge & Kegan Paul.

Rymer, J. (1988). Scientific composing processes: How eminent scientists write journal articles. In D. A. Jolliffee (Ed.), *Advanced in writing research, Volume Two: Writing in academic disciplines* (pp. 211–250). Norwood, NJ: Ablex.

Sacks, H., Schegloff, E., & Jefferson, G. (1974). A simple systematics for the organization of turn taking for conversation. *Language, 50,* 696–735.

Salmond, A. (1975). Mana makes the man: A look at Maori oratory and politics. In M. Block (Ed.), *Political language and oratory in traditional society* (pp. 45–63). London: Academic.

Schön, D. (1983). *The reflective practitioner.* New York: Basic.

Schumacher, G. M., Gradwohl, J. M., Brezin, M., & Parker, E. G. (1986, December). *Children's in-depth knowledge and writing processes: Of legends on broomsticks and rudderless boats.* Paper presented at the National Reading Conference, Austin, TX.

Schumacher, G. M., Klare, G. R., Cronin, F.C., & Moses, J. R. (1984). Cognitive activities of beginning and advanced college writers: A pausal analysis. *Research in the Teaching of English, 18,* 169–187.

Schumacher, G. M., & Nash, J. G. (1991). Conceptualizing and measuring knowledge change due to writing. *Research in the Teaching of English, 25,* 67–96.

Schwegler, R. A., & Shamoon, L. (1982). The aims and process of the research paper. *College English, 44,* 85–93.

Scollon, R., & Scollon, S. B. K. (1981). *Narrative, literacy and face in interethnic communication.* Norwood, NJ: Ablex.

Scott, R. (1967). On viewing rhetoric as epistemic. *Central States Speech Journal, 28,* 258–266.

Scribner, S., & Cole, M. (1981). *The psychology of literacy.* Cambridge, MA: Harvard University Press.

Selfe, C. L. (1984). The predrafting processes of four high- and four low-apprehensive writers. *Research in the Teaching of English, 18,* 45–64.

Selzer, J. (1984). Exploring options in composing. *College Composition and Communication, 35,* 276–284.

Sherrard, C. (1986). Summary writing: A topographical study. *Written Communication, 3,* 324–343.

Shils, E. (1979). The order of learning in the United States: The ascendancy of the university. In A. Oleson & J. Voss (Eds.), *The organization of knowledge in modern America, 1860–1920* (pp. 19–47). Baltimore: Johns Hopkins University Press.

Siegel, M. E. A. (1982). Response to student writing from new composition faculty. *College Composition and Communication, 33,* 302–309.

Simon, H. A. (1973). The structure of ill-structured problems. *Artificial Intelligence, 4,* 181–202.

Simons, H. W. (1985). Chronicle and critique of a conference. *Quarterly Journal of Speech, 71,* 52–64.

Simons, H. W. (1989). Introduction. In H. W. Simons (Ed.), *Rhetoric in the human sciences* (pp. 1–9). London: Sage.

Smagorinsky, P. (1989). The reliability and validity of protocol analysis. *Written Communication, 6,* 463–479.

Smith, C. (1978). The syntax and interpretation of temporal expressions in English. *Linguistics and Philosophy, 2,* 43–100.

Smith, F. (1971). *Understanding reading: A psycholinguistic analysis of reading and learning to read.* New York: Holt, Rinehart & Winston.

Soltow, L., & Stevens, E. (1981). *The rise of literacy and the common school: A socioeconomic analysis to 1870.* Chicago: University of Chicago Press.

Sommers, N. (1979). Revision strategies of student writers and experienced adult writers. *College Composition and Communication, 31,* 378–388.

Sommers, N. (1982). Responding to student writing. *College Composition and Communication, 33,* 148–156.

Sperling, M., & Freedman, S. W. (1987). A good girl writes like a good girl: Written response and clues to the teaching/learning process. *Written Communication, 3,* 343–363.

Spivey, N. (1984). *Discourse synthesis: Constructing texts in reading and writing.* Newark, DE: International Reading Association.

Spivey, N. N. (1991). The shaping of meaning: Options in writing the comparison. *Research in the Teaching of English, 25,* 390–418.

Sprat, T. (1966). *The history of the institution, design, and progress of the Royal Society of London.* St. Louis, MO: Washington University Press. (Original work published 1667)

Steinberg, E. (1986). Protocols, retrospective reports, and the stream of consciousness. *College English, 48,* 697–712.

Stotsky, S. (1990). On planning and writing plans—Or beware of borrowed theories. *College Composition and Communication, 41,* 37–57.

Street, B. V. (1984). *Literacy in theory and practice.* Cambridge, England: Cambridge University Press.

Swain, E. B. (1983). Wilderness and the maintenance of freedom. *The Humanist, 43,* 26–28ff.

Swales, J., & Najjar, H. (1987). The writing of research article introductions. *Written Communication, 4,* 175–191.

Swartz, H., Flower, L., & Hayes, J. R. (1984). Designing protocol studies of the writing process: An introduction. In L. S. Bridwell & R. Beach (Eds.), *New directions in composition research* (pp. 53–71). New York: Guilford.

Tannen, D. (1985). Relative focus on involvement in oral and written discourse. In D. R. Olson, N. Torrance, & A. Hildyard (Eds.), *Literacy, language and learning: The nature and consequences of reading and writing* (pp. 124–147). Cambridge, England: Cambridge University Press.

Tannen, D. (1987). The orality of literature and the literacy of conversation. In J. A. Langer (Ed.), *Language, literacy, and culture* (pp. 67–88). Norwood, NJ: Ablex.

Tierney, R. J., & Shanahan, T. (1990). Research on the reading–writing relationship: Interactions, transactions, and outcomes. In R. Barr, P. B. Mosenthal, & P. D. Pearson (Eds.), *Handbook of reading research* (Vol. 2, pp. 246–280). New York: Longman.

Tomashevsky, B. (1965). Thematics. In L. T. Lemon & M. J. Reis (Eds.), *Russian formalist criticism, four essays* (pp. 61–95). Lincoln: University of Nebraska Press.

Tomlinson, B. (1984). Talking about the composing process: The limitations of retrospective accounts. *Written Communication, 1,* 429–445.

Tompkins, J. (1988). Me and my shadow. *New literary history, 19,* 169–178.

Toulmin, S. (1958). *The uses of argument.* Cambridge, England: Cambridge University Press.

Trabasso, T., Secco, T., & Van Den Broek, P. (1984). Causal cohesion and story coherence. In H. Mandl, N. Stein, & T. Trabasso (Eds.), *Learning and comprehension of text* (pp. 85–111). Hillsdale, NJ: Lawrence Erlbaum Associates.

Turner, V. (1980). Social dramas and stories about them. *Critical Inquiry, 7,* 141–168.

United Nations Educational, Scientific, & Cultural Organization. (1976). *Experimental world literacy programme: A critical assessment.* Paris: UNESCO Report.

Vande Kopple, W. J. (1985). Some exploratory discourse on metadiscourse. *College Composition and Communication, 36,* 82–93.

van Peer, W. (1989). The invisible textbook: Writing as a cultural practice. In S. de Castell, A. Luke, & C. Luke (Eds.), *Language, authority and criticism: Readings on the school textbook* (pp. 123–132). London: Falmer Press.

van Peer, W. (1990). Writing as institutional practice. In W. Nash (Ed.), *The writing scholar: Studies in academic discourse* (pp. 192–204). Newbury Park, CA: Sage.

Veysey, L. (1965). *The emergence of the American university.* Chicago: University of Chicago Press.

Veysey, L. (1979). The plural organized worlds of the humanities. In A. Oleson & J. Voss (Eds.), *The organization of knowledge in modern America, 1860–1920* (pp. 51–106). Baltimore: Johns Hopkins University Press.

Vipond, D., & Hunt, R. (1984). Point-driven understanding: Pragmatic and cognitive dimensions of literary reading. *Poetics, 13,* 261–277.

Voss, J. (1984). On learning and learning from text. In H. Mandl, N. Stein, & T. Trabasso (Eds.), *Learning and comprehension of text* (pp. 193–212). Hillsdale, NJ: Lawrence Erlbaum Associates.

Voss, J. F., Greene, T. R., Post, T. A., & Penner, B. C. (1983). Problem-solving skill in the social sciences. In G. H. Bower (Ed.), *The psychology of learning and motivation: Advances in research and theory* (Vol. 17, pp. 165–213). New York: Academic.

Voss, R. (1983). Janet Emig's *The composing process of twelfth graders:* A reassessment. *College Composition and Communication, 34,* 278–283.

Vygotsky, L. S. (1962). *Thought and language.* Cambridge, MA: MIT Press.

Walters, K., Daniell, B., & Trachsel, M. (1987). Formal and functional approaches to literacy. *Language Arts, 64,* 855–868.

Wells, G. (1986). *The meaning makers: Children learning language and using language to learn.* Portsmouth, NH: Heinemann.

Wertsch, J. V. (1981). The concept of activity in Soviet psychology: An introduction. In J. V. Wertsch (Ed.), *The concept of activity in Soviet psychhology* (pp. 3–36). Armonk, NY: M. E. Sharpe.

White, H. (1980). The value of narrativity in the representation of reality. *Critical Inquiry, 7,* 5–27.

Williams, M., Hollan, J. D., & Stevens, A. L. (1983). Human reasoning about a simple physical system. In D. Gentner & A. L. Stevens (Eds.), *Mental models* (pp. 131–153). Hillsdale, NJ: Lawrence Erlbaum Associates.

Wiser, M., & Carey, S. (1983). When heat and temperature were one. In D. Gentner & A. L. Stevens (Eds.), *Mental models* (pp. 267–297). Hillsdale, NJ: Lawrence Erlbaum Associates.

Witherell, C., & Noddings, N. (1991). Prologue: An invitation to our readers. In C. Witherell & N. Noddings (Eds.), *Stories lives tell: Narrative and dialogue in education* (pp. 1–12). New York: Teachers College Press.

Witte, S. (1987). Pre-text and composing. *College Composition and Communication, 38,* 397–425.

Wood, D., Bruner, J. S., & Ross, G. (1976). The role of tutoring in problem-solving. *Journal of Child Psychology and Psychiatry, 17,* 89–100.

Wyatt, D., El-Dinary, P. B., Pressley, M., Stein, S., Evans, P., & Brown, R. (1991, December). *Reading behaviors of domain experts processing professional articles that are personally important to them.* Paper presented at the National Reading Conference, Palm Springs.

Yearly, S. (1981). Textual persuasion: The role of social accounting in the construction of scientific arguments. *Philosophy of the Social Sciences, 11,* 409–435.

Young, R. (1980). Arts, crafts, gifts, and knacks: Some disharmonies in the New Rhetoric. In A. Freedman & I. Pringle (Eds.), *Reinventing the rhetorical tradition* (pp. 53–60). Ottawa: Canadian Council of Teachers of English.

Young, R. E., Becker, A. L., & Pike, K. L. (1970). *Rhetoric: Discovery and change.* New York: Harcourt Brace Jovanovich.

Young, R. M (1983). Surrogates and mappings: Two kinds of conceptual models for interactive devices. In D. Gentner & A. L. Stevens (Eds.), *Mental models* (pp. 35–52). Hillsdale, NJ: Lawrence Erlbaum Associates.

Zbrodoff, N. J. (1984). *Writing stories under time and length constraints.* Unpublished doctoral dissertation, University of Toronto, Toronto.

Ziv, N. D. (1984). The effects of teacher comments on the writing of four college freshmen. In R. Beach & L. S. Bridwell (Eds.), *New directions in composition research* (pp. 362–380). New York: Guilford.

Author Index

Subject Index

A

Abstract, *see* Representation, abstract
Academic literacy, *see* Expertise and
    academic literacy, Literacy practices
Accounting, 236–238, 246
    for error, 17, 237–238
Activity, 92, 95, 120–124, 138, 251
    consciousness of, 113
    distinct organization of, 114–115, 170–172,
        179, 203–204
    distinct products of, 114, 173–178
    episodic structure of, 113
    in composing the philosophic essay,
        170–172, 179
    recursiveness of, 119–120, 203
Alternative discourse forms, 139, 145–146, 246
Amateurs, 164, 253–255
American Social Science Association, *see*
    Professionalization and the American
    Social Science Association
Analysis of structure, 173–174, 295
Apprenticeship, 139, 214, 230–231, 254–255
Archives, textual, *see* Autonomous text, ideal
    of
Authorship, 87, 91, 172–181, 251
Autonomous text, ideal of, 4–10, 25–27,
    32–36, 50–52, 82, 86, 93–94,
    212–213, 230, 248, 251, 253
Autonomy

individual, *see* Paternalism
professional, *see* Professions, autonomy of

B

Beaver case, 192–193, 297, 298
Bee feeding, *see* Writing in the sciences about
    bee feeding
Bernstein, Richard, 145–156
Biologists, research, *see* Writing in the
    sciences by research biologists
Block diagram model, *see* Cognitive process
    model

C

Case-specific adaptation, 63–64, 65–66, 84
Cases, *see also* Narrative
    Beaver, *see* Beaver case
    Child, *see* Child case
    Daughter, *see* Daughter case
    Father, *see* Father case
    God, *see* God case
    Grandfather, *see* Grandfather case
    J. R. Ewing, *see* J. R. Ewing case
    My father, *see* My father case
    Philosophy faculty, *see* Philosophy faculty
        case
    Pills, *see* Pills case
    Socrates, *see* Socrates case